Art, Dialogue and Outrage

Essays on Literature and Culture

WOLE SOYINKA

Methuen

The Editor and the Publisher would like to express
their thanks to the following:

Cambridge University Press, for permission to
reprint the essay 'The Fourth Stage' previously
published by them as an appendix in *Myth, Literature
and the African World*, and Professor Dapo Ade-
lugba, Head of the Department of Theatre Arts,
University of Ibadan, who made available to us from
his considerable collection of papers, a cyclostyled
copy of '*The Lysistrata* of Aristophanes' for publication in this volume.

First published 1988 by New Horn Press Limited, PO Box 4138,
University Post Office, Ibadah, Nigeria
This revised and expanded paperback edition
first published in Great Britain 1993
by Methuen London
an imprint of Reed Consumer Books Ltd
Michelin House, 81 Fulham Road, London SW3 6RB
and Auckland, Melbourne, Singapore and Toronto

A CIP catalogue record for this book
is available at the British Library
ISBN 0 413 62580 X

Typeset by CentraCet, Cambridge
Printed in Great Britain
by Clays Ltd, St Ives

Contents

Foreword to the Second Edition

The problem which the midwives of the first edition of this collection had to confront was quite straightforward, though often intractable: the essays were never intended for compilation. They were in the main lectures or conference papers and, while I would occasionally agree to tidy up one or the other for publication in a journal, until the determined intrusion of Dr Biodun Jeyifo and Professor Abiola Irele, there had been only one real attempt to place them between covers, and that was short-lived. The major consequence of this of course was that I did not hesitate to cannibalize an essay which appeared, at the time, to have completed its tour of duty.

The agony of Biodun Jeyifo in particular, as editor, was therefore to decide which assemblage could claim to be the 'master text', disentangling several claims to original ownership among thematic relations, a chore that I found too tedious to collaborate in as closely as both editor and publisher would have wished. It was always much easier to veto the inclusion of a problematic hybrid, even where it drew wails of despair from the editor. Biodun Jeyifo's acknowledgment of my collaboration in the compilation of that first edition was, I thought, extremely generous.

This is therefore to acknowledge the initiative and labour of the NEW HORN publisher, Professor Irele, and Dr Jeyifo, editor of the collection, for embarking upon what must have been an infuriating and frustrating task. Also, to absolve them of errors of attribution of awkward marriages in that volume. It must have been a daunting task, additionally, in the face of my stubborn insistence on retaining what they considered disposable idiosyncracies of expression, including what one commentator has described as 'linguistic anomy'. A few of these, hopefully, have now been put to right, though not without twinges of regret.

To conclude, but for the industry of those two masochistic scholars this volume would, quite simply, not exist.

Editorial Note

The texts of the essays that appear in this volume are as definitive as they could be within the exceptional place of the essayistic mode in Soyinka's literary oeuvre. The dramatic works of the author share something of this exceptionalism in that they undergo a considerable degree of revision and re-writing – but *before* publication. In the case of the essays, however, the publication of a particular version of an essay has often not stopped our author from re-thinking or re-formulating his ideas and positions. Even some of the unpublished essays have different versions or fragments of versions which have had to be cross-matched with an approximate 'master-text'. Finally, *between* and *within* published essays, many issues and ideas overlap: in the essays as much as in the literary works, Soyinka's vision is essentially integral and holistic.

For the present volume, the sources of the various items are as follows:

1. 'Towards a True Theatre' previously published in *Nigeria Magazine*, 75 (December 1962), pp. 58–60; *Transition* (Kampala), 38 (1963), pp. 21–2; and Yemi Ogunbiyi (ed.), *Drama and Theatre in Nigeria: Critical Source Book*, Lagos: Nigeria Magazine (1981), pp. 457–61.
2. 'From a Common Blackcloth: A Reassessment of the African Literary Image' previously published in *The American Scholar*, 32:3 (Summer 1963), pp. 387–96; *AMSAC Newsletter*, 6:6 (February 1966), pp. 4–6.
3. 'The Writer in a Modern African State' previously published in *L'Afrique Actuelle*, 19 (June 1967), pp. 5–7; *Transition* (Kampala), 6:31 (June–July 1976), pp. 11–13; Martin Kilson and Wilfred Cartey (eds), *The African Reader*, New York: Vintage Press, 1970, pp. 135–42; John Agetua (ed.), *When the Man Died*, Benin: Bendel Newspapers Corporation, pp. 25–30; Per Wastberg (ed.), *The Writer in Modern Africa*, 1975, Upsala: Scandinavian Institute of African Studies, 1968, pp. 14–36.
4. 'The Fourth Stage' previously appeared in D. W. Jeffers (ed.), *The Morality of Art: Essays Presented to G. Wilson Knight*, London: Cambridge University Press, 1973, pp. 140–60.
5. 'The *Lysistrata* of Aristophanes' previously unpublished.
6. 'Between Self and System' previously unpublished.

INTRODUCTION

Wole Soyinka and
the Tropes of Disalienation

We know, too, that dead writers are presences, never out of date. The bravest, most hermetic writers can even go further. They can reject the pragmatic, rational idea of history as time for the aboriginal concept of history as fable and myth.

Derek Walcott

A people who free themselves from foreign domination will not be free unless, without underestimating the importance of positive contributions from the oppressors' culture and other cultures, they return to the upward paths of their own culture. The latter is nourished by the living reality of the environment and rejects harmful influences as much as any kind of subjection to foreign cultures. We see therefore that, if imperialist domination has the virtual need to practice cultural oppression, national liberation is necessarily an *act of culture*.

Amilcar Cabral

An incident pertaining to the reception of one of the essays in this volume on the occasion of its delivery as a lecture by Soyinka serves well to indicate the controversies which have surrounded this aspect of Soyinka's critical and theoretical essays on literature and culture in contemporary Africa. The essay in question is 'The Writer in a Modern African State', perhaps the best known, certainly the most widely discussed of Soyinka's essays. The occasion was the gathering of African and Scandinavian writers organised by the Swedish Institute in 1967.[1] After elaborating on what he regarded as 'the lack of vital relevance between the literary concerns of writers and the pattern of reality that has overwhelmed even the writers themselves in the majority of the modern African States', Soyinka went on to place an ironic, mildly deprecatory bracket on the largely ineffectual activism of those few writers who had tried to break out of this 'lack of vital relevance' to the political and social realities of the continent's nation-states. Among instances of this desperate activism Soyinka included 'poets (who) have lately taken to gun-running and writers (who) are heard of holding up radio stations', this last being an apparent reference to the famous incident of 1965 which involved Soyinka himself and for which he was subsequently tried and acquitted.[2] The superb self-irony of Soyinka's allusion to this episode was almost completely lost on the assembled company of fellow African writers. One after another, many of the African writers present at this gathering inveighed against Soyinka's casual deprecation of gun-running poets and writers holding up radio stations. The scene could have come right out of one of Soyinka's own mordant satirical comedies, say the episode of the disputations of the Reformed Aweri Fraternity in *Kongi's Harvest*. The choicest 'rebuttals' of Soyinka came, in my opinion, from Ngugi and Dennis Brutus. From Ngugi: 'So this I will say to Soyinka: There is nothing wrong in running guns and holding up radio stations.' And from Brutus: 'But there was also an observation from Soyinka himself when he pointed out that he was not therefore opposed to the gun-running and radio station-seizing poets.'[3]

The overlay of an unintended irony on an intentional, self-directed one in this famous encounter is indeed symptomatic of the way in which the defining spirit of most of Soyinka's essays has been received, even by other writers themselves. This is hardly surprising since, fundamentally, this involves a tendency to be highly controversial, to jolt complacencies and orthodoxies of thought and attitudes in a manner which so directly and intimately affects writers and writing. Thus, in the same essay, 'The Writer in a Modern African State', Soyinka gave a most timely, if indirect and subtle assault, on the then prevailing smugness and superciliousness of many West African writers and critics toward black South African writers for what was deemed a constricting fixation with 'protest literature' as a weapon against apartheid:

> My concern with this task is primarily with the non-South African writer and
> why before very long, he may begin to envy the South African writer the
> bleak immensity of his problems. For the South African still has the right to
> hope and this prospect of a future yet uncompromised by failure on his own
> part, in his own right, is something which has lately ceased to exist for other
> African writers.

It goes without saying that a writer who confronts other writers with observations on their failures and evasions is, deliberately or otherwise, putting himself at risk, a risk only barely mitigated by the kind of self-irony which Soyinka on occasion directs at himself. For the question is: by what warrant, what mandate, does one writer adopt a solicitude for the health and vitality of literary tradition against the misperceptions and even depredations of other writers and critics? Expressed concretely, the provocative nature of this issue is dramatised by the following neither atypical nor gratuitous assessment of some of his colleages by Soyinka: 'The average published writer in the first few years of the post-colonial era was the most celebrated skin of inconsequence to obscure the true flesh of the African dilemma.' But if it is true that Soyinka on occasion makes such astringent analyses and observations on fellow writers and critics, it is equally true, as many essays in this volume demonstrate, that he is not unstinting with generous, appreciative plaudits for others. It is thus only too appropriate that this volume bears the title – Soyinka's own choice – *Art, Dialogue and Outrage*.

Even a cursory glance at the contents and the chronological sequence of the essays in this volume would indicate that throughout the entire period of over two decades when these essays were written, Soyinka's grand subject remained the vitality and direction of the literary enterprise in contemporary Africa. His earliest published essay – not included in this volume – was appropriately and proleptically titled 'The Future of African Writing'. Nothing is perhaps more illustrative of his sustained interest in this basic subject – the vitality of literature in Africa – than the fact that, at periodic intervals, Soyinka has undertaken the most comprehensive review of writers and the entire literary scene that we may encounter in contemporary African literary discourse, viewed from the vantage point of one writer on other writers. Since many of the writers reviewed in the earliest essays are still very much visible, very prominent in the literary landscape, there seems to be a repetition of assessments within such essays as 'And After the Narcissist?',* 'From a Common Backcloth', 'Cross Currents: The "New African" After Cultural Encounters', and 'The External Encounter: Ambivalence in African Arts and Literature'. This impression is however qualified by the fact that the complement of Soyinka's periodic assessments progressively include younger writers and newer trends in the writing and this expands the purview beyond a mere repetitiveness of themes and issues. Consequently, these essays between them indeed provide a comprehensive and intimate profile of the progress, the course of development of modern African writing seen, as it were, from *within*, from the privileged standpoint of a seminal figure in the literature itself. As parallels, think of analyses and assessments by Jorge Louis Borges or Octavio Paz of contemporary Latin American literature. This point alone lends considerable interest to these essays, but as we shall see, there are other, perhaps greater sources of interest in the theoretical and critical essays of Soyinka.

One great source of interest in these essays, in my view, resides in the fact that they have singly and collectively derived from Soyinka's pursuit of distinctively *African* cultural, paradigmatic matrices for literature and a sense of history, for literature and freedom and dignity in an epoch of unfreedom and alienation for the vast majority of Africans and the rest of the human race. It goes without saying that this is an exacting, complex task, since in Africa, as in the rest of the Third World, there is no single, all-pervasive vision of the path to freedom and disalienation. The essays in this volume testify eloquently to this point. With the exception of a minority category of essays which take the form of deliberate, involved theoretical speculations on the nature, sources and environment of art in Africa and the modern world – essays like 'The Fourth Stage', 'Drama and the Idioms of Liberation', 'Shakespeare and the Living Dramatist' and 'Climates of Art' – all the other essays in the volume are either polemical

* Although Wole Soyinka decided at the last minute to remove this essay from the present volume, all references to this essay have been retained in Dr Jeyifo's introduction (Publisher's note).

ripostes by Soyinka to particular disputants and ideological and theoretical adversaries, or essayistic interventions in general debates over the fate of and direction of modern African literature and culture. Thus, between the more rarefied theoretical speculations, the vigorous, eloquent rebuttals and the ideologically motivated surveys and assessments, we have in Soyinka's essays a vast, uneven space of critical and theoretical discourse. What follows in the rest of this essay is an attempt to define the peculiar topography of substance and nuance in this discourse.

If the earliest essays of Soyinka like 'Towards a True Theatre', 'From a Common Backcloth', and 'And After the Narcissist?' all seem so dated, so bound up with the specific cultural realities and moods of the first half of a decade of political independence for most of the African nation-states, it must nonetheless be recognized that Soyinka's basic stance in these essays is imbued with an uncompromising historic vision. And it is precisely this sense of history which endows these 'early' essays with a relevance beyond the contextual political, social and cultural immediacies of the period. To instantiate this point, we may allude to the general feeling of euphoria, to the pervasive sense of the dawn of cultural renaissance in Africa after the long night of colonial subjugation and alienation, and to the excitement over a 'literature of rediscovery', all of which were sharply problematized by Soyinka in these essays, much in the same way that his first major play, *A Dance of the Forests*, had distanced itself from the uncritical romanticism of the past and of tradition during Nigeria's independence celebrations. The following observation from 'And After the Narcissist?' reveals this stance vividly:

> In any culture, the cycle of rediscovery – Negritude or Renaissance,
> Enlightenment or pre-Raphaelite – must, before the wonder palls, breed its
> own body of the literature of self-worship. African writing has suffered from
> an additional affliction; apart from his own discovery, the African writer has
> experienced rediscovery by the external eye. It is doubtful if the effect of this
> has any parallel in European literature.

The central formulation which acts as the springboard for Soyinka in this early phase of his critical and theoretical writings is what he called 'indifferent self-acceptance' by the African writer of the 'common backcloth' of modern African literature. We might define this 'backcloth' as proposed by Soyinka as the roots of African literary creativity and cultural sensibility in the peculiarities of traditions and modes of thought and feeling which characterize the 'African world' in its interaction and confrontation with modern, contemporary experience. In these essays, Soyinka advances the thesis of the indispensability of African cultural matrices for the literature, but he does so in a manner which not only paradoxically casts him in the role of the leading 'Anglophone' opponent and scourge of Negritude – so far the most influential literary movement for the assertion of the values of the African world – but also contrasts very sharply with positions he was later to take from about the mid-1970s onward. But meanwhile,

Soyinka launched a vigorous critique, an eloquent assault on Negritude. Indeed this critique of Negritude in Soyinka's early essays is one of the great *conjunctural* moments in modern African literary aesthetics and ideology. If only for this reason, a brief review of this engagement is crucial for our present discussion.

The great transgression of Negritude, according to Soyinka in these early essays, was to make of the African cultural heritage a racial label, a badge of authenticity and significance to be displayed by all manner of pretenders, narcissists and plain exoticists. Soyinka's famous quip on tigers and tigeritude or duickers and duickeritude, took its provenance from the formulation of 'indifferent self-acceptance' and a corresponding vigorous attack on the facile, aggressive racial self-romanticization of the poets and critical pundits of Negritude.

Negritude has of course wrought its ironic revenge on the later course of Soyinka's critical and theoretical battles. Stated differently, a more mature Soyinka, embattled by both acerbic leftist critique of his culture 'backcloth' and right-wing simplifications of African literary and cultural authenticity, would come to re-think the ferocious short-shrift which he had given Negritude in his early essays; consequently, he would, so to speak, settle the philosophical conscience of Negritude by coming to terms with it with regard to the 'essences' of the African world. But in those halcyon days of a brisk clearing of the decks to unburden the African writer of the 'magnitude of unfelt abstractions' and false concepts promoted by Negritude, the young Soyinka's reputation as the *enfant terrible* of African critical discourse was earned largely as the nemesis of Negritudist literary traducers of African traditions.

'From a Common Backcloth' and 'And After the Narcissist?' remain the gems of that period of critical exorcism of the 'primitivist' incubus foisted on the African writer by Negritude's fallacies and superficialities. Moreover, the foundations of Soyinka's mature mythopoeic aesthetics, so deeply rooted in Yoruba mythology and ritual archetypes, are to be found in those essays. Critics of Soyinka who have inflated his passionate anti-Negritudist stance in these essays into a form of cultural deracination, a denial of the relevance of African cultural resources as the creative roots of modern African literature, would do well to go back to these essays and subject them to more dispassionate analysis.

Soyinka's analyses of both Negritudist-inspired writings and the work of writers like Mongo Beti, Chinua Achebe, Alex La Guma, Peter Abrahams, Lewis Nkosi and William Conton in respect of the aesthetic and moral integrity (or in a few cases, lack of these) with which they relate to the identified 'backcloth' of modern African literature remain memorable in many ways. In the opinion of this writer, only in Fanon's fragmentary remarks, in *The Wretched of the Earth*, on the psycho-historical imperatives which drive the African writer nostalgically back to the past, to tradition and folklore,[4] do we have about the only other insights to match Soyinka's illumination of the first phase of contemporary African literature, the phase Soyinka himself calls 'narcissistic', the phase of euphoric self-discovery before disillusionment with the political and cultural realities of post-colonial Africa was to overwhelm many writers. Many of the specific assessments of fellow-writers that Soyinka made in these essays, at a time when none of them had become *canonical* figures in contemporary African literature, have proved rather prescient. However, the most important contribution of these early essays to the evolving literary aesthetics of Soyinka is the manner in which the values and criteria which informed his aesthetic and psycho-social analysis of the literature of the period were given considerable intellectual force and imaginative scope by Soyinka's use of traditional African mythic archetypes and ritual paradigms. In other words, failure of craft and technique, evasion of social responsibility and misdirection of artistic vision were all grounded in powerful constraints provided by mythological tropes, by allusion to what Soyinka proposed as the 'essences' of a truly African creative sensibility. In short, what Soyinka commenced in these essays is what he would later flesh out and expand in the more 'mature' essays: the search for subtleties and intricacies of theoretical and critical criteria based on the representations and figurations of experience and reality elicited from endogenous African epistemologies and cosmogonies, and away from the primacy of European sources.

It is necessary to observe that beyond the use of discrete mythic and ritual sources, beyond the forays into the Yoruba myths of deities and avatars like Ogun, Sango and Obatala, Soyinka's theoretical purview in these early essays involved the attempted incorporation of what he deems the entire world-view of pristine African religious and metaphysical systems. Again the essays of the 1970s would give more extensive exploration of these issues and patterns in Soyinka's literary aesthetics. But even the early essays had begun to base what Soyinka proffered as the *true* African creative sensibility in the unified vision of *animist* metaphysics.

> It is not . . . a question of the difference between 'I' and 'We' but a deeper
> subsumption of the self into vision and experience. And although this applies
> to all poetry, we must insist that this is the true African sensibility in which
> the animist knowledge of the objects of ritual is one with ritualism, in which
> the physical has not been split from the psychic, nor can the concept exist of
> the separation of action from poetry.

In the conception of most of the Negritudist poets and theoreticians, animism had of course functioned little more than it had with colonialist anthropology: intellectualized primitivism and the traits of a supposed 'prelogical mentality'. Aimé Césaire, himself on occasion a self-willed primitivist, has given one of the most trenchant critiques of this tradition in his monograph, *Discourse on Colonialism*.[5] It would seem that Soyinka's rehabilitation of animism from the primitivist encrustations on Negritudist pundits and anthropological quaintness mongers belongs in this Césairean orientation: the organic, totalist vision of all experience and phenomena, of the fusion of object with subject, is not frozen in time, is able to accommodate the realities and cultural desiderata of the modern world.

Those who consider the modern imagery of Amos Tutuola a sign of impurity represent the diminishing minority of African primevalists. And even the more accommodating ones find only charm and quaintness in Tutuola's shotgun image-weddings. Unfortunately, in attempting to interpret his symbolism little attention has been paid to his modern experience; after all Tutuola lives now, and he responds to change and phenomenon.

This point is made more forcefully by Soyinka in demonstrating a 'contemporary animist sensibility' in the work of the late South African novelist, Alex La Guma whose novels, unlike the 'ghost novels' of Tutuola most of which are set in a phenomenal, mostly symbolic and non-referential spirit world in the forests, are set entirely in the urban inferno of South African black townships. In La Guma's fiction, Soyinka saw a contemporary manifestation of the animist sensibility:

Language again, the sympathetic comradeship with the dregs of society, animate or inanimate, human and stray. The contemporary animist sensibility urges physical details into an assumption of ironical and separate, commemorative motions within a still movement of the physical eye.

Since Soyinka's construct of an intuitive, unified animist sensibility bears so much resemblance to the Negritudist afflatus of 'emotive, intuitive reason', especially as contrasted deliberately with the assumed inherently 'analytic logic' of European thought, it is important to stress Soyinka's structural and theoretical distance from Negritude, even within the identifiable similarities of *his* ideas of the 'African world' and those proposed by the theoreticians of Negritude. This is best done, in my view, by analogically assimilating this distance to that distinguishable between *structuralism* and *poststructuralism*. By this reckoning, Soyinka's postulates of the 'African world' would then constitute something of a 'post-Negritude' revisionary 'deconstruction' of the 'classical' concepts of original (Senghorian) Negritude. For just as poststructuralism came to rupture, fragment, problematize and deconstruct the more or less fixed and stable interpenetration of the binary system of the 'signifier' and the 'signified', or *'langue'* and *'parole'*, so did Soyinka's reformulation of Negritude's paradigmatic binary opposition of European and African thought and sensibilities fragment and dissociate the received stable, manichean unitary postulates. Expressed differently, Negritude had proposed itself, had proposed the 'African world' as the 'sum total or synthesis of all the values of Negro-African civilisation' (Senghor). Against this additive, non-conflictual synthesis – what German philosophical idealism proposes as *Konfliktlose* or conflictless synthesis – Soyinka proposed the 'African world' as a nexus of dynamically disparate and contradiction-ridden matrices, paradigms, tropes and significations. Of these latter, Ogun, Obatala and Sango, encountered in Soyinka's theoretical constructs as varying, even contradictory 'essences' of creativity and reality, are only the most notable. Even Soyinka's choice of Ogun as Muse and tutelary spirit goes to the heart of his 'post-Negritude' break with 'classical' Senghorian synthesis without conflict or contradiction, for Ogun is the very embodiment of paradox, conflict and contradiction. What, in short, is being urged here is a recognition of Soyinka's fundamental theoretical break with Negritude, even as some of the features of that literary and cultural philosophy continued to exercise a hold on Soyinka's reformations. Beyond this, I urge that recognition of this break is crucial to an understanding of Soyinka's own creative and theoretical writings, and also that it constitutes something of a conjunctural moment in modern African literary aesthetics. Definitely it serves as an enabling fillip to all of Soyinka's subsequent critical and theoretical discourse.

If, as one of the polemical essays in this volume, 'Who's Afraid of Elesin Oba?', asserts, it is probably fatuous to attach great importance to the chronology of particular writings within Soyinka's total corpus, it is nonetheless significant that the particular period or circumstance of the publication of single essays, or groups of essays, bears some portentousness for the particular essays in question. For Soyinka, as an artist and intellectual, is deeply responsive to the realities and moods of moments of collective experience, especially crisis moments, and if in his creative writings he is able to give artistic refraction to this responsiveness, the essays generally bear more direct, telling marks of their socio-historical and spiritual provenance. In two essays written towards the end of the 1960s – the first decade of political independence for most African states – namely, 'The Writer in a Modern African State' (1967), with which we began our discourse in this essay, and 'The Fourth Stage' (1969), Soyinka's evolving mythopoeic aesthetic assumed its decisive *tragic* character. And the tragic theory drew both from the historical realities of the period and more particularly from mythological sources.

An expression which has become something of a cliché in discussions of Soyinka's tragic aesthetic – 'the recurrent cycle of human stupidity' – appeared first in Soyinka's critical writings in 'The Writer in a Modern African State'. There is almost no other essay in all of Soyinka's non-fictional writings, save for a few passages in *The Man Died*, which plunges as much as this essay to the depths of pessimism concerning the realities of Africa and the rest of the world towards the end of the first decade of political independence in Africa. Even the vision of a possible universal holocaust which informs the considerable metaphorical richness of 'Climates of Art' (1985) does not begin to approach the despair of the earlier essay. Concerning the specific realities and moods in Soyinka's own country, Nigeria, which formed the immediate background to the surfeited gloom of 'The Writer in a Modern African State', Soyinka himself gives direct, literal testimony in the essay. It is indeed significant that the Nigerian civil war, and Soyinka's incarceration for virtually the entire duration of the war, followed hard on the heels of this essay.

Meanwhile, it is necessary to retrace our steps to the very first appearance of the formulation of the tragic sensibility, and a specific *kind* of tragic hero, in Soyinka's critical and theoretical writings. This is in 'And After the Narcissist?' where Soyinka positively contrasts what he regards as the true tragic expression of Alex La Guma in the novella, *A Walk in the Night*, to the sentimental pathos of Senghor in *Chaka*:

It is a long way from narcissism; it is a different kind of tragic hero here, a different kind of tragic sensibility that observes the hero, Michael Adonis, upset a bin of rubbish to help a stray cat get at a dinner of entrails. An instant which suggests a destructive weakness, for goodness in this situation is weakness; the formula for survival lies in the jungle tenet of fitness, not in thoughtless moments of goodness to stray cats battling dustbins. A grim, remorseless stare at reality.

The term 'tragic sensibility' is crucial in apprehending the significations intended in this reading of la Guma's novella, for only this gives more than mere preciousness or bathos to the affective sympathies which link Michael Adonis' desperate, embattled existence in the violent world of crime, alcohol and casual sadism with that of the stray cat battling for its survival in the physical jungle of filth, putrefaction and discarded trivia. What we have here is the first expression of what would come to be the phenomenological foundation of Soyinka's reality and experience which insists on the moral and ontological necessity of passage rites and spiritual transactions between different orders or levels of existence. Within this 'animist interfusion' of all being and sensing, Michael Adonis projects himself into the hermetic interiority of the stray cat's feline battle for survival, yet remains bound by the savage codes of inverted individuation demanded by the degraded world of the victims of apartheid. Beginning from this kernel of a theoretical construct, Soyinka has in innumerable passages and evocations in his prose essays and creative writings fleshed out the psychic drive, the force of will and volition which makes his tragic protagonists cross and re-cross the different areas of experience and reality in the anguished recognition of the paradox of separation and identity between all things and being.

In 'The Fourth Stage' Soyinka makes the first attempt in his essays to ground this concept of tragic action in the ritual dramas and myths associated with three principal deities in the Yoruba pantheon: Obatala, Ogun and Sango. As many commentators have observed, the language and critical idiom of this essay is considerably difficult and often obscure. This is something of a departure from the previous essays, for even where, as in 'And After the Narcissist?', Soyinka is deeply subjective and deploys involved, intricate symbolism, the analytic thrust acts as a kind of restraining leash for the periodic rush of metaphysical and cosmological speculations. In 'The Fourth Stage', however, there is as much of free, extensive irruptions of these rarefied speculations as there is of analysis and exegesis of cultural phenomena. And the matter is further compounded by the fact that Soyinka somewhat assumes, on the part of the reader, a familiarity with the ritual dramas and mythological traditions surrounding the deities he so liberally draws upon in the essay. Soyinka was later to rectify the needless obscurity which arises from this assumption by giving more commodious accounts of these ritual dramas before proceeding to elaborate his views and positions, this, in *Myth, Literature and the African World*. These problems notwithstanding, 'The Fourth Stage' remains probably the most important and the most richly suggestive of Soyinka's theoretical writings. The core of the theoretical thrust of the essay is an attempt to elaborate a theory of tragic art rooted in an African sensibility, in African paradigms and metaphorical representations of crucial areas of experience and reality. Moreover, the essay ranges beyond this 'return-to-the-source' rubric to an affirmation of the revolutionary impulse in culture and art over the contending and perennial tendency toward inertia and complacency. In the course of this excursus, the essay purveys a celebration of the ideals of purposiveness and humanism in a universe both contingent and man-made, so replete with the irrational, the anti-human. In the opinion of this writer, this essay is probably the finest document of modern African idealist philosophy.

It is important to remark the centrality, for Soyinka's heuristic constructs in this essay toward the construction of a mythopoeic tragic paradigm, of the so-called 'fourth stage' of transitional passage between human and divine, birth and death, being and non-being, and disparately apprehended time sequences like past, present and future, or the worlds of the ancestors, the living and the unborn. Analogically, Soyinka calls this 'fourth' area of depth experience by such terms as 'chthonic realm', the 'abyss of dark forces', the 'infernal gulf', the 'cosmic lair', etc. While accepting that this construct is over-stretched and somehwat ineluctable in the multiplicity and diversity of significations it is intended to yield, it is equally true that it serves a powerfully integrative function between abstruse philosophical speculations on our intimations of the finite and infinite aspects of being and more easily apprehended and explicable ideas drawn from collective mythic representations on the nature and sources of creativity. Ogun's plunge through this 'chthonic realm' is an analogue of the stress and challenge of creativity. The positive altruistic aspects of this plunge, as well as the destructive obverse of the manic will which sees the god through the chaos, are the two contradictory aspects of creativity which philosophers and pyschologists of art have always recognized.

It is also important that Soyinka emphasizes that the Yoruba conception of this 'chthonic realm' is different from its usual representation in European metaphysics as a mere 'fictive' or 'illusionary' scaffolding on which art builds or creates:

> In our journey to the heart of Yoruba tragic art which indeed belongs in the Mysteries of Ogun and the choric ecstasy of revellers, we do not find that the Yoruba, as the Greeks did, 'built for his chorus the scaffolding of a fictive chthonic realm and placed thereon fictive nature . . .' on which foundation, claims Nietzsche, Greek tragedy developed: in short, the principle of illusion. Yoruba tragedy plunges straight into the 'chthonic realm,' the seething cauldron of the dark world will and psyche, the transitional yet inchoate matrix of death and becoming. Into this universal womb once plunged and emerged Ogun, the first actor, disintegrating within the abyss. His spiritual reassemblage does not require a 'copying of actuality' in the ritual re-enactment of his devotees, any more than Obatala does in plastic representation in the art of Obatala. The actors in Ogun mysteries are the communicant chorus, containing within their collective being the essence of

that transitional abyss. But only as essence, held, contained and mystically expressed.

It has been necessary to quote at length here in order to underscore the importance which Soyinka attaches to this central construct of a 'chthonic realm', a 'fourth stage' which stretches the protagonist's will to its utmost. And what we have here deals with both the intellectual structure of the ritual enactment and its emotional impact. In other words, what is stated here is a conception of tragic art that is vigorously and irreducibly ritualist in its rejection of a narrowly realistic, mimetic copy of the psychic energies unleashed or released by the tragic protagonist's process of individuation through hubris; it is a ritualist paradigm which seeks to give maximum affective power and mystical, symbolic depth to the tragic performance.

Music is indubitably vital to such a conceptoin of tragic art and again, it is remarkable how Soyinka carefully distances himself from both Nietzsche in particular, and European philosophy in general, in their basic conception of music as a 'direct copy of the will'. In Soyinka's view, this is contestable. Moreover, it is equally doubtful whether the European 'intuitive grasp of the emotions of the will' and European concepts of music can be deemed to have universal applicability.

Language which, we are told, in religious rites 'reverts to its pristine existence, eschewing the sterile limits of particularization', is thus the aesthetic and affective equivalent and extension of music: 'sterile limits of particularization' (in words, in language), like notions of 'direct copy of the will', are incommensurate with a conception of tragic art that is rigorously anti-mimetic, anti-realistic and correspondingly, power-fully ritualistic and mythopoeic:

> Language in Yoruba tragic music therefore undergoes transformation
> through myth into a secret (masonic) correspondence with the symbolism of
> tragedy, a symbolic medium of spiritual emotions within the heart of the
> choric union. It transcends particularization (of meaning) to tap the tragic
> source whence spring the familiar weird disruptive melodies. This masonic
> union of sign and melody, the true tragic music, unearths cosmic
> uncertainties which pervade human existence, reveals the magnitude and
> power of creation, but above all creates a harrowing sense of omnidirectional
> vastness where the creative Intelligence resides and prompts the soul to futile
> exploration. The senses do not at such moments interpret myth in their
> particular concretions; we are left only with the emotional and spiritual
> values, the essential experience of cosmic reality.

The scale of values in this conception of tragic art transcends that which produces conventionally didactic or narrowly illusionistic art which always requires 'particulari-zation' or mimetic representation. It is within this scale of values that Soyinka adumbrates an anti-positivist, non-relativistic conception of ethics which advances the view that penance and retribution, as important aspects of the fate of tragic protagonists, are not punishments as such but 'an invocation of the principle of cosmic adjustment'. It is this notion of ethics which justifies the higher, more positive value placed on Ogun's tragic flaw than Sango's, for in the case of the former we are in the realm of 'cosmic adjustment', far beyond the hopelessly relativistic, opportunistic claims and counter-claims of socially contingent or historically conditioned principles and criteria.

> Tragic fate is the repetitive cycle of the taboo in nature, the karmic act of hubris witting or unwitting, into which the demonic will within man constantly compels him. Powerful tragic drama follows upon the act of hubris, *and myth exacts this attendant penalty from the hero where he has actually emerged victor of a conflict.* [My emphasis]

For me, one of the most intriguing conceptions in 'The Fourth Stage' is the idea of tragic myth as an artistic and cultural mnemonic, as a memory code in periods of social stress or disjunction, and as an antidote to moral complacency and spiritual stupor.

> It is no wonder therefore that the overt optimistic nature of the total culture is the quality attributed to the Yoruba himself, one which has begun to affect his accommodation towards the modern world, a spiritual complacency with which he encounters threats to his human and unique valuation. Alas, inspite of himself from time to time, the raw urgent question beats in the blood of his temples demanding, what is the will of Ogun? For the hammering of the Yoruba will was done at Ogun's forge, *and any threat of disjunction is, as with the gods, a memory code for the resurrection of the tragic myth.* [My emphasis]

It is this particular idea of tragic myth as a cultural code in a period of social stress that informs the peculiar vision of 'The Writer in a Modern African State': surfeit of gloom, but invocation of the will to action, the will to resistance from the depths of the individual and collective psyche. Brecht had an enigmatic but powerful slogan for this structure: Pessimism of the Intellect, Optimism of the Will! And the great Marxist student of mythopoesis, Harry Slochower, has clarified the theoretical basis of this covergence of myth and history:

> On the historic level, each mythopoeic work is viewed as the centre which unifies the multiple cultural forms of its era, organizing its arts, psychology, religion and social currents. Intertwined with the historic level is a universal pattern. The Ariadne thread which runs through all mythopoesis is a structural unity that consists of analogous stages in the development of mythopoeic heroes from Job to Thomas Mann's Joseph and Sartre's Orestes.[6]

It may be a purely adventitious fact that Soyinka's essays of the 1970s and 1980s no longer deal with African writers and writing in the 'rediscovery' phase. Definitely the essays of the early seventies collected in *Myth, Literature and the African World*, have a different general subject than the pitfalls of euphoric narcissism and the contrived themes and concepts of 'culture conflict' literature. As explicitly announced by Soyinka in the preface to the book, these essays are devoted to elucidating what, for Soyinka, had clearly become a major preoccupation of African writers beyond 'rediscovery': the depiction of a replete 'African world' which derives its deepest truths and resources endogenously, not in exclusivist, racial-chauvinist terms but all the same as a distinctive presence in the world on its own terms.

It is perhaps inevitable that such a critical project would take over some of the issues and theoretical constructs of Soyinka's early essays on African cultural matrices of creativity and artistic sensibility, refurbish them and thus establish a continuity in Soyinka's critical and theoretical purview. This notwithstanding, a clear shift of critical tone and discursive stance is now discernible. At the most visible level, Soyinka's concern about the African writer's 'indifferent self-acceptance' is gone. At another level, the objects of Soyinka's most negative assessments now are not so much writers, though a few are included, but 'ideologues' and critics either hostile to, or dismissive of the identified project of racial and cultural 'self-retrieval'. And perhaps most important of all, Soyinka's analyses and specific judgements are now more solidly and sympathetically imbricated in the ideological currents of the period as a theoretical and critical partisan, whereas in the early essays his stand had been somewhat over-generalized and stand-offish with regard to the claims and counter-claims of ideology in the new nation-states of Africa.

Though this issue need not be belaboured, it is important to briefly expatiate on its significance for the development of Soyinka's critical and theoretical writings, if only because the point has been deliberately distorted by some of Soyinka's critics, both on the left and on the right. As for the early over-generalized stance, this is best illustrated by Soyinka's insistence in 'The Writer in a Modern African State' that:

> the situation in Africa today is the same the world over; it is not one of the tragedies that come of isolated human failures, but the very collapse of humanity.

It is significant that in the discussions which followed the delivery of this lecture to which we have already alluded, Ngugi took great exception to Soyinka's application of equal, undifferentiated oppobrium to Hastings Kamuzu Banda and Kwame Nkrumah.[7] But within the essay in question, this point finds contextual force in Soyinka's critical disapproval of how the claims of nationalism and the need to pool collective resources and energies in the new nations had subverted the *individual* integrity and vision of the writer. And in 'From a Common Backcloth', in condemning the insidious effects of the paternalism of foreign critics on African literature, Soyinka speaks dismissively of the 'restrictive ideology of regional art', stressing instead the universal complementarities in all artistic endeavours which made 'the African . . . one of the inspirations of modern art today'.

In gross distortions of the issues, these mere velleities of tone, attitude and nuance in essays which otherwise argue forcefully for a literature rooted in African cultural sensibilities, have been blown up into an explicit denial of artistic commitment and an abstract-universalist rubric of the African writer as exclusively a *writer* and only incidentally or indifferently African.[8] These distortions perhaps derive from the ambiguous consequences for Soyinka's literary aesthetics and critical theory of the fact that a large part of his essays arise from or themselves constitute polemical and critical interventions in the on-going discourse on culture and literature in Africa. For, if the heat of ideological and theoretical battles has fired such distortions of Soyinka's true positions, it cannot be said that Soyinka himself has not made short, sometimes inaccurate, work of the arguments and analyses of his opponents. What we perhaps have here is one of those ambiguities and paradoxes so much beloved of Soyinka by which the 'loss' in precision and accuracy that polemical theorizing has given Soyinka's essays is also the 'gain' of both making Soyinka rethink the more abstract, over-generalized and recondite critical and theoretical constructs of the 'early' and 'middle' essays and imbricating his ideological stance in objective realities and forces in a manner almost totally absent in the early essays. Definitely, Soyinka's defence of his positions against leftist critiques and the consequent considerable elaboration of his recourse to mythology and animist metaphysics in such essays as 'Who's Afraid of Elesin Oba?' and 'The Critic and Society: Barthes, Leftocracy and Other Mythologies' have clarified considerably the obscurer theoretical points of 'The Fourth Stage' and 'Drama and the Idioms of Liberation'. And when, in such essays as 'The "New African" After Cultural Encounters' and 'Theatre in Traditional African Culture: Survival Patterns', Soyinka draws considerably on objective historical and socio-economic factors shaping cultural production, the same sensibility, the same deep and intimate knowledge of the arts of Africa are deployed as in the early essays, but we are in a different terrain of intellectual and ideological discourse from these early essays. In a real sense, this may partly derive from the fact that of all the major, seminal figures of African literature, apart from Ngugi, it is Soyinka who has confronted more than anyone else, albeit reservedly, the increasing pervasiveness of a *class* approach to literature and culture. This is shown explicitly in the following observations from 'The "New African" After Cultural Encounters':

> . . . the most vexed aspect of the theme under discussion is easily the debate
> over the relevance or non-relevance of a cultural identity to the contemporary
> arts in Africa. The extreme approach is that the authentic sources which
> provide the individual in society with what we express as a 'cultural identity'
> are in reality non-authentic, since they have been transmitted largely through
> the selective machinery of the prevailing class at any given moment of a

people's history. This ideological line obtrudes far deeper into African
writing – fiction and essays – than is commonly imagined.

At the end of this essay Soyinka frankly acknowledges the 'complexities, paradoxes
and pragmatic challenges posed by black scholars and revolutionary leaders such as
Frantz Fanon, Agostinho Neto, Amilcar Cabral and others' with regard to the question
of cultural autonomy in Africa as a prerequisite of social revolution or reconstruction.
The essay also identifies the dilemmas and discontinuities of cultural expression and
socialization in Africa, pointing out the crucial absence in Africa, to a degree almost
unequalled in any other part of the modern world, of a constituted body of the 'classics'
of the culture which could serve as the foundation of aesthetic and cultural education.
Though these sights differ substantially from those of Soyinka's earliest essays, there is
a structural affinity between them, for in each case Soyinka's purview takes in the whole
continent and is deeply responsive to the fundamental issues of the historical moment.
It goes without saying that in the same manner that the essays of writers like Ralph
Waldo Emmerson, T. S. Eliot, Vladimir Nabokov, Jorge Louis Borges, André Brink,
Chinua Achebe and Ngugi wa Thiong'o provide a comprehensive intellectual framework for reading their creative works, so do the essays of Soyinka collected here provide
a kind of meta-commentary, a second-order critical and theoretical discourse on his
works. How can we fail to see the illuminating link between Soyinka's highly
idiosyncratic and original reading of Shakespeare and Aristophanes in, respectively,
'Shakespeare and the Living Dramatist' and 'The *Lysistrata* of Aristophanes' and his
thematic and formalist-ritualist explorations of death and the 'numinous' realms of
existence in such works as *The Road*, *The Bacchae of Euripides*, *Death and the King's
Horseman* and, in a more comic spirit, *Requiem for a Futurologist?* Drawing extensively on
some of the essays in this volume which have already seen publication, two critical
book-length studies and one brilliant critical essay have indeed thrown considerable
light on Soyinka's creative works: Stephen Larsen, *A Writer and his Gods*,[9] Ketu H.
Katrak, *Wole Soyinka and Modern Tragedy*,[10] and Ann B. Davis, 'Dramatic Theory of
Wole Soyinka'.[11] It is thus not merely fortuitous that an essay in this volume previously
published with the title 'Drama and the Revolutionary Ideal' now appears here with the
title 'Drama and the Idioms of Liberation'. For Soyinka in his creative works has been
as much concerned with the themes and subject matter of the negotiations of and
resistance to tyranny, brutalization and alienation as with finding the *idioms*, the forms,
and the rhetorical tropes to consummate the quest for disalienation, dignity and
freedom. The 'art', 'dialogue' and 'outrage' in the title of this volume relate suggestively
to this factor. I suggest that the prefaces to Soyinka's works, if read carefully, would
provide a kind of bridgehead between the 'meta-commentary' of the essays gathered
here and the intra-textual experimentation, within Soyinka's literary works, with the
expressive, representational means by which he explores and renders his themes and
subject matter.
It is also the case that Soyinka intends, as he himself does in several essays in this

volume, that the corpus of modern African literature be read in the light of his elaboration of the specific cultural sensibilities, the specific modes of thought and feeling which, in Soyinka's view, characterize the 'African world' and are best apprehended in the vast storehouse of paradigms and figurations of creativity, reality and social responsibility discoverable in the mythology, plastic arts, music and idioms of ritual performance of African peoples. This is definitely a more contentious realm of critical and theoretical discourse than the correspondence between Soyinka's essayistic meta-commentary and his own creative works. In some instances, Soyinka's recourse to this replete storehouse of tropes and analogues constitutes a veritable, memorable enrichment of discourse. Some instances come readily to mind: the evoked contrastive paradigms of two African sculptural masks in the opening paragraphs of 'The External Encounter', or the heuristic use in 'Climates of Art' of the 'abiku' motif of Yoruba mystical beliefs to represent the barren, destructive, nihilistic side of birth, being and creativity. This is enlightening, exhilarating 'tropophilia', and Ropo Sekoni's strictures against political and ideological readings of Soyinka's literary aesthetics which 'under-semioitize' or 'de-metaphorize' Soyinka's works is of especial relevance here.[12] But it remains true that Soyinka's paradigms and matrices pertain more to the anti-mimetic, anti-realist artistic modes (and their underlying epistemologies). Thus, Soyinka does tend to be a little short of critical sympathy for the great realists and anti-mythic iconoclasts of African writing, principally Chinua Achebe. We may even wonder whether Soyinka's pregnant silence on Ngugi's writings is not located precisely in this juncture.

The point of course is that for all his vigorous self-identification and self-justification as a *mythopoeist* in such essays as 'Drama and the Idioms of Liberation', 'Who's Afraid of Elesin Oba?', 'The Austistic Hunt' and 'Barthes, Leftocracy and Other Mythologies', Soyinka himself is also something of a *mythoclast*, a debunker or parodist of myths and mythologies. Obviously misperceiving this, the American theorist and scholar Henry Louis Gates included 'Barthes, Leftocracy and Other Mythologies' in his excellent book, *Black Literature and Literary Theory*[13] in the first, 'theoretical' part of the book sub-titled 'Theory: on structuralism and post-structuralism'; Soyinka's essay in fact deploys an elaborately irreverent assault on the hermetic interiority of the 'mythologies' of post-structuralist and other forms of self-enclosed, reified theoretical discourse. This *mythoclastic* impulse is often recognized in Soyinka's creative works where mythological or ritualist motifs and idioms are often juxtaposed or counterposed with their parodies. *The Road*, *The Bacchae of Euripides* and *Death and the King's Horseman* are particularly illustrative of this point, but one scholar, Philip Brochbank, has written a fine essay which demonstrates the wide distribution of this principle in Soyinka's dramatic works.[14] The most discernible thread of this principle in Soyinka's essays is his almost perpetual insistence that the literary, creative use of myth and ritual does not necessarily or inherently involve epistemologies which are static, ahistorical, retrogressive. More pointedly, Soyinka even makes the point in 'Drama and the Idioms of Liberation' that the ritual matrix is *inherently* an idiom of change and revolution. Thus when, in 'The

Writer in a Modern African State', we encounter the sentence 'A concern with culture strengthens society, but not a concern with mythology,' we know that it *seems* atypical of Soyinka only to the degree that we ignore or fail to recognize the existence in Soyinka's essays of the attempt at a dialectical 'mythoclastic' inversion of his basic mythopoeic aesthetics. This inversion, in theoretical terms, almost amounts to *aporia*, the emphasis being on the word 'almost'.

A word of clarification: in formal logic and in philosophy in general, an aporia consists of the virtual impossibility of establishing the truth or verifiability of a proposition for which evidence can be presented both to prove and refute it. Axiomatically and concretely, a discourse characterized by aporia presents considerable problems for precise, exact interpretation on account of the endless, limitless play for mutually self-cancelling, self-negating propositions. In my opinion, one of the sources of great interest, not to say the conundrum, of the extensive theoretical and philosophical speculation on literary epistemology in Soyinka's essays lies in the aporetic nature of some of his established positions. A brief examination of a few of these would, I think, suffice.

In many of his essays, but most particularly and rather magnificently in essays like 'Who's Afraid of Elesin Oba?' and 'Barthes, Leftocracy and Other Mythologies', Soyinka seizes on myth and ritual as the perfect paradigms for the artistic exploration of that which in human experience and natural phenomena is perennial, recurrent, unchanging, timeless, ineffable, imponderable and ultimately resistant to domination and control by man. This necessarily involves a bracketting or suspension of history, and Soyinka's retort is: why not? In the ultimate reaches of this line of reasoning even history itself, and not just myth, is de-historicized by Soyinka as shown by the following deliberately contumacious attack on historical relativism in 'Who's Afraid of Elesin Oba?': 'Historical material is permanently, irretrievably and irrevocably incomplete (Dedicated materialists of the ideological paradise – take note!).' Concretely, Soyinka in some of these essays adduces phenomena like *death* and *power* as analogues of this ultimate, ineffable incompletion and he asserts that art which aspires to explore and capture the reality of such phenomena should itself contain aspects of their inherent transhistorical, metaphysical nature. And music, of all the artistic idioms available to us, is, for Soyinka the greatest analogue of this structure:

> . . . the paradox of it is that it exploits the incompletion of *langue* to transmit a language. It is truly a form 'in solution'; even at its most replete, even when the main theme and sub-themes and variations have been explored and brought home with an overwhelming sense of release, the effect of music is that of a linguistic proposition which is still striving towards *total* resolution – hence the failure of criticism to find an appropriate vocabulary, even to narrate the musical experience . . . Because the obsessed materialists are defeated by the complications of this self-constitutive art which does not pretend to express *everything* but insists that there is *everything* to be expressed, comprehended, embraced and ravaged . . . they can only take their

revenge on the conceptual essentialization of objective reality in other forms, these being – like the literary – linguistically 'open'. ['Barthes, Leftocracy and Other Mythologies']

At this level, we are close to the inscrutable 'aura' and mystique which Walter Benjamin advanced as the principal means by which for centuries the 'ritual values' of art were made to hold sway over all other values.[15] And yet within Soyinka's essays there are parallel propositions of art as artefact or commodity even; there are propositions on the relations of artistic production and reception as objective, historically and sociologically variable and determinate structures. Indeed without such propositions it would have been hardly possible for Soyinka to insist so vigorously and unceasingly on the necessity and obligation of art to intervene in the historical process. This notion of objective process comes across quite clearly in the following observations from 'Climates of Art' which appears as nothing short of an aporetic contestation of other assertions in Soyinka's essays which promote the 'hermetic ritualism' of art:

> We do know that the effect of the artistic product is not always one which is limited to and is fulfilled exclusively by the composition of the artistic object itself. Sometimes the work of art commences its function and extends its objective properties through experiences outside the artistic object – other encounters, forms and properties of other spaces of imagination – Reality.

It is indeed possible, in my opinion, to read such essays as 'Towards a True Theatre', 'The Writer in a Modern African State', 'Language as Boundary', 'Cross Currents: The "New African" After Cultural Encounters' and 'Theatre in African Traditional Culture: Survival Patterns' as aporetic engagements of essays like 'The Fourth Stage', 'Drama and the Idioms of Liberation', 'Who's Afraid of Elesin Oba?', 'The Autistic Hunt' and 'Barthes, Leftocracy and Other Mythologies'.

The aporia in Soyinka's theoretical discourse achieves its most important aspect in the question of the place of *essentialist* thinking or a signification in his literary epistemology. This is of course not unconnected with the issue discussed in the immediate preceding section of this essay but it is a distinct matter in its own right. For if it is the case that Soyinka's mythopoesis makes him seek out, ritualize and hermeticize the recurrent, timeless, transhistorical phenomena and realities of existence and experience, it follows logically that this would involve the *essentialization* of life and its basic parameters beyond the non-recurrent, the fortuitous, variable or remediable aspects. And Soyinka not only insists on this as a chosen approach to art and reality, he even proffers it as fundamentally characteristic of the 'African world', most particularly in the animist totalization and unification of all experience and phenomena that we encounter again and again in Soyinka's essays.

But then there arises a counter to this point in Soyinka's own theoretical constructs. For if essentialization implies unchanging identity and singularity, what are all the assertions of paradox, contradiction and ambiguity doing in Soyinka's speculation? Furthermore, if essence requires totalization and unitary integration, why does Soyinka also advance views and techniques of artistic dissociation, fragmentation, ellipsis and disjuncture? This, it seems to me, is the very heart of the aporia which characterizes Soyinka's theoretical discourse.

An exhaustive discussion of these questions is of course impossible in the present context. Let us merely observe that Soyinka is only too aware of this aporia and the antinomies which it generates.[16] Let us also remark that what we have here is the powerful tension between literature and ideology and the effects that this has on a discourse on literary epistemology. If for Soyinka the traditional African world-view is fundamentally essentialist in its thought and sensibilities and this *ought* to be affirmed and defended, consider what Soyinka's response would be to this powerful negative historical comment on African traditional essentialist and ritualist beliefs by Denis Williams in his authoritative, momumental book on traditional African art, *Icon and Image*:

> The ritualising of iron is perhaps best explained within the structure of belief
> by means of which its strange techniques and processes were understood.
> For the Yoruba, iron was apprehended within an *orisa* system which served to
> explain all phenomena, spiritual and natural, in terms of the operation of
> inherent power, the *Ase* . . . Power inherent in the unfamiliar and intractable
> metal is to be controlled not so much by means of analysing the process of its
> operation as by propitiation and prayer addressed to the *orisa*, or god, who
> has been able to tame such power. The empirical development of iron
> metallurgy in Asia and in Europe was not therefore open to the African
> craftsman, trained from apprenticeship to suspect unfamiliar phenomena and
> to regard deviation from accepted practice as potentially harmful; the
> processes of his craft, strictly spirit-controlled, remained unavailable to
> inquiry.[17]

It has been Soyinka's ideological and theoretical struggle in virtually all the essays to argue against this historical critique, to argue in effect that the 'African world', in its ideational systems and ideological superstructures, is both essentialist and non-essentialist: a willed aporia as much as a verifiable construct. And we might remark in passing that Soyinka's aporetic arguments find powerful theoretical supports in some of the most influential works on philosophy of culture in Africa, notably W. E. Abraham's *The Mind of Africa* and Paulin J. Hountondji's *African Philosophy: Myth and Reality*. When Abraham writes: 'Essentialist views have themselves changed from era to era. One may even say that it is they which place a *cachet* on their eras',[18] we recognize not only the same aporia of Soyinka's theoretical discourse but also the very source of this factor – a theoretical anxiety to affirm archaic, autochtonous insights and yet be at one with the march of human thought and progress. In this respect aporia may well be the master trope for society, like contemporary Africa, wracked by profound antipodal impulses and rapid, vertiginious transformations. Paulin Hountondji's assertions on this point are even more clamant and recall very vividly the vigorous break which Soyinka has sought to establish with Negritude which we have earlier discussed in this essay:

> One of the most perverse myths invented by ethnology, whose effects in return contribute to the survival of ethnology itself, is the myth of primitive unanimity, the myth that non-western societies are 'simple' and homogenous at every level, including the level of ideology and belief. What we must recognise today is that pluralism does not come to any society from outside but is inherent in every society . . . The decisive encounter is not between Africa as a whole and Europe as a whole: it is the continuing encounter between Africa and itself. Pluralism in the true sense did not stem from the intrusion of Western civilization into our continent; it did not come from outside to a previously unanimous civilization. It is an internal pluralism, born of perpetual confrontations and occasional conflicts between Africans themselves.[19]

Perhaps the least intractable of the antinomies of Soyinka's theoretical constructs is that of the one and the many, of singularity and plurality, of an African uniqueness and presence in literature while recognizing and celebrating elective affinities with 'climates of art' elsewhere in the modern world. Surely, this is what is implied by the phrase 'wide cultural perspective' in his Nobel prize citation. Speaking only of myths, Soyinka not only delves deeply into the mythology of the Yoruba and other African peoples, he also ranges far into Asiatic and Judaeo-Christian traditions and sources. Where the specialists and pedants of ritual archetypes and mythological sources in literature distinguish between such distinct currents and usages as the 'euhemerist' school (myth as explanatory or aetiological fictions), the 'cognitionist' school (myth as storehouse of metaphor, analogical thought and symbolic logic) and the 'ritualist' school (the Cambridge-spawned theory of archaic rituals as the root of myth, art and culture), Soyinka's mythopoesis embraces all these currents. While this has long been recognized in his greatest plays, we can see that the last group of essays in this volume – 'Climates of Art', 'Shakespeare and the living Dramatist' and 'The External Encounter' – derive their great resonance, their polysemic significations from this factor, the unforgettable *abiku* trope of 'Climates of Art' being a particularly arresting concretion of Soyinka's love of, and obsession with, the 'numinous'. These essays between them show how Soyinka is able to range across different cultures and periods from the powerhouse and the plenitude of figurations and conceptualizations of experience drawn from the arts and cultures of Africa.

Can Soyinka's mythopoesis, since his art is endlessly experimental and modernist, his defence of tradition notwithstanding, be assimilated into the point Shklovsky and the Russian Formalists made that new art forms, new literatures are simply the canonization of 'inferior' (sub-literary) forms of folk sources and oral traditions? Put differently, is

Soyinka's artistic and theoretical immersion in myth and ritual a demonstration of what Max Lerner and Edwin Mims identify as the need of literature to constantly seek renewal in 're-barbarization'?[20] These questions are perhaps more reflective of the perspective of a one-sided Western bourgeois 'high culture' concept of literature than the motivations of an artist whose cultural and historical circumstance and whose artistic sensibility have not been burdened with such dichotomous concepts of the 'developed' and the 'barbaric'. (And let us recall Walter Benjamin's dictum that every document of civilization is also a document of barbarism). And nothing gives the lie to *this* reading of Soyinka's mythopoesis, Soyinka's elaborate deployment of tropes and figurations from the myths, ritual paradigms and cultural artefacts of Africa, than the fact that what we have in his essays is not one voice, one univocal point of view but many voices, many articulations, a plurivocal, polysemic and – why not? – often contradictory discourse. Variously traditionalist and modernist, pan-Africanist and liberal-humanist, individualistic and communalistic, gnostic and skeptical, unapologetically idealist and yet on occasion discreetly materialist, the essays between them not only faithfully record the passing moods and positions traversed by Soyinka in more than twenty years of a sustained, vigorous reflection on the being and *becoming* of modern African literature, they also demonstrate the complexities, tensions and ambiguities of modern African literature and the discourse(s) to which it has given rise. And for me, one of the greatest points of interest of these essays is that they very decisively refute what Hountondji has described as the 'artificial choice'[21] between 'Westernization' or 'Europeanization', the 'teleology' decreed by so many African and foreign critics of modern African literature, especially those written in the European languages, and its reactional, manichean product – a naïve, simplistic, romantic 'Africanization', 'Africanity', 'Negritude', '*authenticity*' or many of the appellations by which it is promoted as cultural nationalism. These are indeed the two ultimate alienated discourses on modern African literature and if there is any unity in Soyinka's essays gathered in this volume, it is the consistency with which he has either explicitly or implicitly assailed these two mutually self-reflecting, self-cancelling alienated discourses. It is this double refutation or disalienation which makes the theoretical accents and critical idioms of these essays simultaneously so very cosmopolitan, so very accessible beyond Africa and indeed applicable to literary discourse in many of the cultural spheres of the world, while rendering very powerfully and distinctly an African literary presence, even if this is dynamically and contradictorily apprehended. It is this quality which, above all others, places Soyinka's essays in the best writings of contemporary thinkers and essayists on society, culture and literature in modern Africa like Frantz Fanon, Amilcar Cabral, Agostinho Neto, Kwame Nkrumah, Ngugi wa Thiong'o, Marcien Towa, Cheikh Anta Diop and Paulin Hountondji.

Biodun Jeyifo
Ile-Ife
March, 1987.

NOTES

1. See Per Wastberg (ed.), *The Writer in Modern Africa*, Uppsala: The Scandinavian Institute of African Studies, 1968.
2. An account of this episode is given by Gerald Moore in *Wole Soyinka*, London: Evans Brothers, Ltd., 1978.
3. *The Writer in Modern Africa*, pp. 21–35.
4. Frantz Fanon, *The Wretched of the Earth*, New York: Grove Press, Inc., 1963, pp. 178–9.
5. Aimé Césaire, *Discourse on Colonialism*, New York and London: Monthly Review Press, 1972.
6. Harry Slochower, *Mythopoesis*, Detroit: Wayne State University Press, 1970, p. 22.
7. *The Writer in Modern Africa*, p. 26.
8. Needless to say, this point finds its greatest mullish advocacy in Chinweizu, in countless journalistic pieces, especially 'Decolonising the mind', in *South*, London, January 1983.
9. Stephen Larsen, *A Writer and His Gods*, University of Stockholm, Department of the History of Literature, 1983.
10. Ketu, H. Katrak, *Wole Soyinka and Modern Tragedy*, Westport, Connecticut: Greenwood Press, 1986.
11. Ann B. Davis, 'Dramatic Theory of Wole Soyinka' in James Gibbs (ed.), *Critical Perspectives on Wole Soyinka*, London: Heinemann, 1981, pp. 147–57.
12. In Biodun Jeyifo and Ropo Sekoni, 'Ideological and Semiotic Interpretations of *The Road*', University of Ife: Ife Monographs on Literature and Criticism, 3, 1984.
13. H. L. Gates (ed.), *Black Literature and Literary Theory*, New York and London: Methuen, 1984.
14. See Philip Brochbank, 'Blood and Wine: Tragic Ritual from Aeschylus to Soyinka', in *Shakespeare Survey*, 36 (1983) pp. 11–19.
15. In Walter Benjamin, *Illuminations* (edited by Hannah Arendt) New York, 1968, the essay 'The Work of Art in the Age of Mechanical Reproduction'.
16. See 'Introduction' to Wole Soyinka, *Six Plays*, London: Methuen, 1985.
17. Denis Williams, *Icon and Image*, London: Allen Lane, 1974, p. 87.
18. W. E. Abraham, *The Mind of Africa*, London: Weidenfeld and Nicolson, 1967.
19. Paulin Hountondji: *African Philosophy: Myth and Reality*, London, Hutchinson, 1982.
20. See Max Lerner's and Edwin Mims' entry 'Literature' in *Encyclopaedia of the Social Sciences*, IX (1933), pp. 523–43, and Abiola Irele, 'Tradition and the Yoruba Writer: D. O. Fagunwa, Amos Tutuola and Wole Soyinka' in James Gibbs (ed.), *Critical Perspectives on Wole Soyinka, op. cit.*, pp. 45–68.
21. Paulin Hountondji, *African Philosophy: Myth and Reality*.

PART ONE

Essays on Literature and Culture

I

Towards a True Theatre*

There were strange theatrical sights in Kampala. Two marvels essentially – a theatre (the structure), and a performance. That I elect to call attention to these two excruciating events is not because I wish to denigrate the efforts of an obviously prestige-conscious community, but to indicate the dangers of resigning the initial impetus for a creative institution to the death kiss of passionate amateurs. The building itself is an embodiment of the general misconception of the word 'theatre'. Theatre, and especially, a 'National Theatre', is never the lump of wood and mortar which architects splash on the landscape. We heard of the existence of a National Theatre and ran to it full of joy and anticipation. We discovered that there was no theatre, there was nothing beyond a precious, attractive building in the town centre. But even within that narrow definition of the word, we had expected an architectural adventurousness – Kampala is after all, a comsopolis – so we felt justified in expecting from the theatre, not only a sense of local, but of international developments in the theatrical field. What we found was a doll's house, twin-brother to our own National Museum. There were cushioned spring-back seats – I approved this, having nothing against comfort – but it was disconcerting to find a miniature replica of a British provincial theatre, fully closed in – another advantage this, extraneous noise at least was eliminated; there were vast corridors round the auditorium (for gin and the attendant small talk), the total corridor space was more than the auditorium; the toilets were sumptuous – there were good reasons for this we soon found, understanding for the first time the meaning of a wet performance. The stage? Well, no one could complain of the efficiency. And there were large rehearsal rooms located in the theatre whose constant utilization appeared to be classes in Ballroom Dancing, led by Indians in 22-inch bottom trousers.

There was one more sample of 'atmospherics'. Lining the walls of the foyer were posters (from *Look Back in Anger* and earlier) which made you think that the New

* First published in *Nigeria Magazine*, 75 (December 1962).

Shakespeare Theatre Company was touring East Africa. A closer look reveals however that these posters were three years older than the completed theatre. And photographs of Richardson, Olivier and others of the Old Brigade – tarnished slightly from a long stand in the agents' shop-windows of Piccadilly, provided the last word in imitativeness without the substance.

We were, however, fairly honest, and we soon fell to minding the beam in our own eyes. There is the Arts Theatre of our University College, Ibadan which possesses not even the outward deception of the Kampala structure, and cannot boast practicalities such as ventilation or sound-proofing. As if the original crime was not enough, a grant of some thousands of pounds was expended, as recently as a year ago (1961) on new curtains and a few symbols of theatrical 'arrival'. Interference from student radiograms and cross-balcony yells did not activate the financial imagination into worthier ways of spending this money. Motor-cars, indifferent to inadequate barriers, continue to punctuate the actor's lines with roars. It did not matter that audience enjoyment was, and still is, constantly punctured by arid saxophone blasts from a competing highlife ball. No, not all these considerations could persuade the controlling committee to spend the grant on erecting a barn somewhere beyond the depredations of college neighbour-liness, disembowelling the present bulk entirely and transferring the gadgets to the new, adaptable space where actor and audience may liberate their imagination.

For it still astonishes me that those who planned the University had the sense to isolate the chapels from the distractions of the ungodly, but not the foresight to place the theatre beyond the raucousness of student lungs.

And yet, there is the irony. There is a larger sense of theatre here, even of a National Theatre, than we found in Kampala. Of the two shows which we saw there, the less said the better. In Ibadan at least, the students, in spite of frequent misguidedness, have at last taken the theatre to the people. This has been due to the dedication of one or two staff members especially. Conscious, one hopes, of the static imposition of the Arts Theatre, they developed sufficient enthusiasm among the student dramatic team to undertake two highly successful tours of folk theatre. It is irrelevant that the plays from which the shows were adapted came from European theatre, the success of transfor-mation could be judged from each performance through Ilesha to Enugu and Port Harcourt. This was some compensation for the long tradition of formalism in university theatre.

Every event in the theatre, every genuine effort at creative communication, entertain-ment, escapism, is for me, entirely valid. It is very easy to sniff for instance at the efforts of the Operatic Groups. What one must regret is the atmosphere of sterility and truly pathetic preciosity that it seems to breed. For it must never be forgotten that the opera was written for a certain society; recreating that society in Ibadan, causing an 'opera expectation' in attitudes is sheer retardation. I am not of course trying to create a morality for theatrical selectiveness. *The Merry Widow* has its place even on the Nigerian scene as a piece of exoticism; the crime is that it is the forces of *The Merry Widow* which have upheld what we may call the Arts Theatre mentality. In the triumph of the Anouilh puff-ball tradition lies the perpetuation of the atrocity, lies the constriction of venturesome rarities like the musical *Lysistrata* – that show would, I contend, have been even more imaginative but for the symbolized tradition of the Arts Theatre. That medium of the arts proscribed true experiment – the result was a cheap English musical all over again, rescued however by genuine effort.

By all means, let us be accommodating – and I say this genuinely – there is room anywhere, and at any stage of development, for every sort of theatre. But when Anouilh and (for God's sake!) Christopher Fry – and Drew in true fusion of the Monolithic World – possess audience mentality and budding student talent in traps from which the British theatre is only slowly extricating itself, then it is probably time for a little intolerance against the octopine symbol of the Arts Theatre. If there appears to be some exaggeration in this, let me merely point out the theatrical age of the local critic, who, on seeing an example of simple space exploitation exclaims in disgust that it is very amateurish for actors to run in and out of the audience! This notice went on to say, '. . . admittedly the Museum grounds are not very suitable for a dramatic performance, in that case it would have been simpler for this group to find a hall in Lagos where their plays can be staged more conveniently'.

When the leading university proudly exhibits and reinforces the Perpendicular theatre, it is hardly surprising that the faithful twice-a-term weekend pilgrim will resent any invasion of his audience privacy!

There is the future, of course, which is what we are really talking about all the time. The only answer to the Perpendicularians was obvious to me from the start – construct an opposition plane. This has always proved more effective than bickering, and this of course still remains the only aim of tentative theatrical movements in the country. But it has become necessary to resort to words because, while the material facilities appear to elude the opposition, they practically beg to be abused at the hands of the in-breeders. One hears rumours of ambitious schemes for propagating – again that dirty word – culture! And the prestige symbol is again, as always, a 'National Theatre'. Since I saw the foundations, I have not dared to move near the completed theatre at Nsukka. Before the 'theatre' of the Nigerian College of Arts, Science and Technology was built, the designers pilgrimaged to the then University College Ibadan, to seek inspiration from Arts Theatre. In vain did a few harrowed producers plead with them to avoid repetition of existing crime – a replica was built and the 'Arts' was superseded in drabness and tawdry. J. K. Randle Hall now – the latest boil – would some imagination have cost it more? And these abortions will continue to rise all over the country, offensive to the eye and repressive of the imagination. It is surely because the structure controls, even manipulates the artist that it is more sensible to assist first of all the creative theatre, or at least – and since we are as in all other things, in a terrible rush and all steps must be taken together – at least look for architectural inspiration among countries with approximate traditions and a longer professional history – or simply use that common ordinary gift of sense and refrain from employing mud-mixers and carpenters to design media which must eventually control or influence the creative intellect.

This is no exaggeration. It has been proved for four years by an amateur group in Ibadan, *The Players of the Dawn*, who, in spite of the intelligence of the leaders, have consistently succumbed to the dictates of the British Council pre-historic structures and are incapable of seeing theatre as an activity which did not petrify with Galsworthy at the start of the century.

No one who is seriously interested in the theatre demands a playground for pushing buttons and operating gaily coloured panels. A university especially should refrain from such expensive pastimes. For this is not America where – to take one example, the Loeb Theatre in Cambridge, Massachusetts – a university theatre is built for five to six million dollars, a stupid amoral example of affluent patronage. Where, pray, is the university sense? But the tinny poor-cousins of this which, to judge from Kampala, Ibadan and Nsukka, will soon exert their calcifying influence over the continent should be stopped now, before Zaria and Ife, and even the National Five-Yearly Never-never Plans follow their example. For, as I have stressed from the beginning, we are not merely talking about the structure now, but of the dubious art to which it must give birth.

II

From a Common Backcloth:
A Reassessment of the African Literary Image*

Only when the political creature who persistently emerged from the common backcloth of an imposed identity – primitivism – began to display evidence of will, of individuality, of localized social and historical causation, only then did the European observer begin seriously to accept the validity of a creative imagination for the African outside folklore and ritual. Even so he still fights a rearguard action today. It has grown subtler. Accommodation is his new weapon, not dictation. The European critic, full of the burden of an alien tradition, appears to have brainwashed himself of existing standards. In some cases he has even undergone a deliberate mental retardation, a sort of: Takes a simpleton to understand a child.

In this, he has been confidently abetted by his subject, the African self-interpreter. He himself provides instances when European condescension is amply justified. Encountering Camara Laye's *Radiance of the King*, will the critic not say: Why has this man not stuck to the simple, straightforward narrative of his *Dark Child?* For presumably the Western critic knows his Kafka. The cultivated naïveté of *The Dark Child* charmed even the African reader. Even if it often grew precious, it carried an air of magic, of nostalgia, which worked through the transforming act of language. If the author was selective to the point of wish fulfillment, it was unimportant. That a reader could be so gracefully seduced into a village idyll is a tribute to the author.

But most intelligent readers like their Kafka straight, not geographically transposed. Even the character structure of Kafka's *Castle* has been most blatantly retained – Clarence for Mr K.; Kafka's Barnabas the Messenger becomes the Beggar Intermediary; Arthur and Jeremiah, the unpredictable assistants, are turned into Nagoa and Noaga. We are not even spared the role of the landlord – or innkeeper – take your choice! It is truly amazing that foreign critics have contented themselves with merely dropping an occasional 'Kafkaesque' – a feeble sop to integrity – since they cannot

* First published in *The American Scholar*, 32:3 (Summer 1963)

altogether ignore the more obvious imitativeness of Camara Laye's technique. (I think we can tell when the line of mere 'influence' has been crossed.) Even within the primeval pit of collective allegory-consciousness, it is self-delusive to imagine that the Progresses of these black and white pilgrims have sprung from independent creative stresses.

At the conference of African writers in Kampala, last June,* it was readily observed that the irreverence, the impatience that marked the critical sessions was the most memorable aspect of the entire conference. This attitude was natural. In order to condemn the European critic for his present patronage, for – at the other end – his rigid sensibility, for his unavoidable exclusion from the African imagination, there was an obligation toward total rejection of all substandards, of pastiche and stereotype. The sessions were truly ruthless, often wrongheaded.

It was the same at an Afro-cultural conference in Europe not long ago, where a young French-speaking intellectual gathered all his intolerance into one sentence, 'How can an African write like Kafka?' It was dishonest, he claimed. He pitted his sincerity against Camara Laye's. In the end, he conceded after much argument that Kafka was probably a South African black who escaped to Germany after the treason trials! As a principle therefore, his protest was untenable. It belongs in the same restrictive ideology of regional art. Forgetting that the African is one of the inspirations of modern European art today, the black or white Africanist turns his back on an abstract canvas, protesting that he came to view an exhibition of paintings by Africans. In many instances, this is justified; for the contemporary interpreters of African themes have not truly assimilated the new idioms. It is merely naïve to transpose the castle to the hut.

There are, in fact, two kinds of offerings directed at the moment to the European palate. One is for acceptance in the Western creative idiom. I have mentioned the example of *Radiance of the King*. There is William Conton's proper resolution in *The African* of a Durham-to-Jungle adventure by an outrageously imposed Christian forgiveness; and there are the new poets in Nigeria who regroup images of Ezra Pound around the oilbean and the nude spear. The prophets of negritude at least dared these and scorned them, substituting a forthright although strident reaffirmation of truly 'African' values, but breeding only the second offering, the burnt offering, image of the charred skin on a defiant platter. It is futile now to knock negritude; it is far more useful to view it as a historical phenomenon and to preserve the few truly creative pieces that somehow emerged in spite of its philosophical straitjacket.

But it is not so easy to ignore the facile exploiters of the fallacy, since they, even more than the muscular emblem-bearers of negritude, have been welcomed most readily into the bosom of the foreign critic. In a special issue of the *Times Literary Supplement*, a critic, reviewing a novel by a Nigerian writer, Nzekwu, says: '. . . but he cannot help presenting the traditional Ibo religion and culture in the more attractive light. It is this

---

* The reference is to the Conference of African Writers sponsored by the Congress for Cultural Freedom, and held at Makerere University, Kampala, June, 1962.

that will be the main attraction to the European reader: the masquerades, the prayers, the charms and the tribal social structure are described from within and with a luminous comprehension'. And, to substantiate his intercultural awareness? 'He is also old-fashioned enough to tell a straight story with a moral. This is the kind of story his people like.' Obviously, a book that has something both for the European and for the African reader cannot help but be successful! Even the fumbling first novel of this writer is described as 'very successful', and with two other Nigerian novelists the writer makes, 'an unbeatable Treble Choice'.

A very long time ago, the discerning African rejected the anthropological novel. Perhaps during the next twenty years his foreign counterpart will do the same. Since even now African writers work against a similar backcloth, it is on the level of interpretation that the individual artist, as in any other culture, must be judged. Over-effusiveness at obvious window dressing (loincloth only, preferably menstrual) has created a most unfortunate prejudice against truly imaginative writers like Amos Tutuola, and worse still dammed the man's true creative channels. Of all his novels, *The Palm-Wine Drinkard* remains the best, and the least impeachable. This book, apart from the work of D. O. Fagunwa who writes in Yoruba, is the earliest instance of the new Nigerian writer gathering multifarious experiences under, if you like, the two cultures, and exploiting them in one extravagant, confident whole. A study of his material, his imagery reveals this. But of course Tutuola has little in common with his African, even his Nigerian counterparts. The African writer-intellectual chooses often to dramatize his dilemma, and the hollowness of his anguish indicates only too clearly that he first of all created it. A society, an intrusion, an all too predictable conflict – this was the formula, compounded in near equal proportions. Some laughed, full of hysteria; others, full of the dignity of tragedy, invoked the entire catastrophe and died. From a distance, the cultural intruders felt themselves rebuked, sympathized with and praised.

This theme is not for Tutuola, but the legacy, the imaginative duality is. The deistic approach of the Yoruba is to absorb every new experience, departmentalize it and carry on with life. Thus *Sango* (Dispenser of Lightning) now chairmans the Electricity Corporation, *Ogun* (God of Iron) is the primal motor-mechanic. Those who consider the modern imagery of Amos Tutuola a sign of impurity represent the diminishing minority of the African primevalists. And even the more accommodating ones find only charm and quaintness in Tutuola's shotgun image-weddings. Unfortunately, in attempting to interpret his symbolism, little attention has been paid to his modern experience; after all Tutuola lives *now*, and he responds to change and phenomenon. Not, in fact, except for indefatigable American scholarship, that it serves any useful purpose to reduce a writer's symbols even to events of spiritual exploration (and I have read a thesis that turned three of Tutuola's Ghostesses into the three regions of Nigeria!), but it is a useful corrective to bear in mind the appreciative approach of a similar intuition to his – the poetic, that is.

'. . . a brief, thronged, grisly, and bewitching story . . . nothing is too prodigious or

too trivial to put down in this tall, devilish story'. This was by Dylan Thomas. Here now
is one of Tutuola's physical struggles with Nature at its most humanly thwarting:

> But as we were going on and when it was time that we wanted to branch to
> our left, to continue the journey inside another bush as usual, we were
> unable to branch or to stop, or to go back, we were only moving in the road
> towards the town. We tried all our best to stop ourselves but all were in vain.

Even if this did not come in the chapter, 'On Our Way to the Unreturnable – Heaven's
Town', the meaning would still, in the context, be obvious. But has Tutuola's inspiration
in this instance come from folklore? It is likely. Or else from the Sunday sermon? Death
or the Devil winds up the road behind the sinner and he cannot turn back. Again why
not? Should it matter? A minutiae essayist indignantly dismissed the Christian contribution of these two source materials and argued himself blind to a third immediate
possibility. The escalator. In today's African's ever-growing backcloth of symbols, the
escalator has a more vivid suggestiveness than the magical egg of plenty.

This is an important point, not in the immediate context of the Unreturnable-
Heaven's Town, but in assessing how individual writers make their creative emergence
from the true, not the wishful, untainted backcloth. We are now attuned to the loss of
Hamlet the histrionic. Hamlet of the grand gesture has been relegated for the Oedipal
prince. But the sex preoccupations of Western culture should not be allowed to intrude
to an extent detrimental to the enjoyment of what Amos Tutuola primarily is – a
storyteller in the best Yoruba tradition, pushing the bounds of credibility higher and
higher and sustaining it by sheer adroitness, by a juxtaposition of analogous experience
from the familiar. It is typical that even the last war should spill onto *The Palm-Wine
Drinkard*. The hyperbole of the bomb and the Complete Gentleman –

> ... and if bombers saw him in a town which was to be bombed, they would
> not throw bombs on his presence, and if they did throw it, the bomb itself
> would not explode until this gentleman would leave that town, because of his
> beauty

– is not a rupture in the even traditionalism of Amos Tutuola. It is only writers with
less confidence who scrupulously avoid such foreign bodies in their vision of the
traditional backcloth. The result in Tutuola is a largeness that comes from an acceptance
of life in all its manifestations; where other writers conceive of man's initiation only in
terms of photographic rites, Tutuola goes through it as a major fact of a concurrent life
cycle, as a progression from physical insufficiency, through the Quest into the very
psyche of Nature. *The Palm-Wine Drinkard*, as with Fagunwa's *Ogboju Ode* and universal
myth, is the epic of man's eternal restlessness, symbolized as always in a Search.
Between the author's own exorcism and the evidence of his immediate environment, we
may continue our own presumptuous search for meaning.

If, however, we elect to return, like Tutuola's hero, wise *only* from the stress of experience, it will not have been a totally valueless journey. For Tutuola involves us in a coordination of the spiritual and the physical, and this is the truth of his people's concept of life. The accessories of day-to-day existence only become drawn into this cosmic embrace; they do not invalidate it. Questioning at the end what Tutuola's reality is, we find only a tight web enmeshing the two levels of perception. In his other books, strain becomes evident, effect for the sake of effect; the involved storyteller has yielded to the temptations of the extraneously bizarre, a dictation of his early outsider admirers who thus diffused his unified sensibility. Tutuola is not a primitive writer. With this objection removed, it is possible that the audience for which Tutuola wrote primarily (not that he thought consciously at first of any audience) would come to recognize him for what his talents offer – the contemporary imagination in a storytelling tradition.

Chinua Achebe chose to bring out his backcloth in relief at the areas of tension. In a sense – not a pejorative one – he is a chronicler, content to follow creases and stress lines, not to impose his own rearrangement on them. That this can be a creative process is demonstrated by the inexorable fate that overtakes his hero, Okonkwo, in *Things Fall Apart*. The demand we make of an expressed way of life is, first and foremost, reality. The writer must impress an acceptance. Enactments of tribal peculiarities must emerge from characters in that society, not interfere with our recognition of basic humanity, not be just a concession to quaintness-mongers. Why, for instance, do we accept so easily and unreservedly the accident of the hero's exploded gun especially as a prelude to the final downfall of one of the village elite? Dissected coldly, events that are not part of the dramatic progression of character or other events are instantly suspect. But Achebe has established another pattern, a rhythm compounded not merely of motives but of understated mysteries – mysteries as much to the characters as to their remote observer – of psychical influences on daily routine, of a man's personal *chi*, of initiations, of guilt and purifications whose ethics are not those of a court of law but of the forces of Nature cycle, of the living and the dead. It is a subtle process, and its first principle, faithfully observed by the author, is the philosophy of acceptance. Not blind, slavish acceptance but a positive faith, an acceptance of forces that begin where the physical leaves off.

And within this, a difference of delimitations. For instance, where does a man leave events to his *chi*, to the communal *chi*, and where does he pursue them in defiance of apparent futility? We can respect and be overpowered by the tragedy of the man who destroys himself asserting the latter, but we cannot be anything other than impatient, as for instance in *No Longer at Ease*, with a modern driftwood, manipulated by events and making never a show of resistance. It is imperceptive to allege, as has been done, that the superiority of *Things Fall Apart* is the familiar delusion of exotic backsplash. That escape formula of most African poets and writers is there admittedly – status quo, intrusion and conflict – but Chinua Achebe has added the remaining dimension, individual depth in a credible hero. In a personal confrontation with values and implicit assertiveness that go beyond those of the society – and here is the point, society is not even – Okonkwo's oposition is one that has in fact dictated his actions and his distinct personality in that society. Where the society says: 'When a man blasphemes, what do we do? Do we go and stop his mouth? No. We put our fingers into our ears to stop us hearing,' Okonkwo retorts: 'If a man comes into my hut and defecates on the floor, what do I do? Do I shut my eyes? No! I take a stick and break his head.' The apostate Nwoye (through Okonkwo's eyes now), the nine ancestral spirits who administer justice in the land, even the lackey-agents of the new order are figures of this book's *moment* and contribute in their separate pressures toward the destruction of the man who became separated from his good *chi*. There is no good and no evil, however, only concepts of continuity – what works for society and what does not. And this knowledge, this magic is achieved from within society itself. The author, understanding this, has excluded all private imposition. He preserved the same integrity in *No Longer at Ease*. He preserved also, ineffectually, the evocative style imposed upon the former book by its framework of nostalgia, of a remote perspective, and total absence – let it be stressed – of sentimentality. Achebe required a stronger, more ruthless approach to create any lasting impression for such an effete character as the hero of his second book. Society emerges rather uncertainly even where it is felt as a corrupting agent. Language lends nobility to the life and downfall of Okonkwo; the same language in *No Longer at Ease* merely rebukes the author, as if he has taken his main character too seriously. It is doubtful if Achebe's forte lies in the ability to spit occasionally, or to laugh from the belly when the situation demands it, but he must learn at least to be less prodigal with his stance of a lofty equipoise. For this has bred the greatest objection to his work, this feeling of unrelieved competence, of a lack of the active spark, inspiration.

Compassion is the twin brother of Mongo Beti's grand iconoclasm (or perhaps what we are looking for is a word that combines the two). *Mission to Kala*, bawdy, riotous, bursting on every page with sheer animal vitality, reads like that rare piece of studied artistry, an unpremeditated novel. In the literary effort to establish the African as, first before all else, a human being, Mongo Beti with this novel has leapt to the fore as the archpriest of the African's humanity. Mongo Beti takes the backcloth as he finds it, asserting simply that tradition is upheld not by one-dimensional innocents, but by cunning old codgers on chieftaincy stools, polygamous elders, watching hawklike the approach of young blood around their harem, by the eternal troublemaking females who plunge innocents, unaware, into memorable odysseys. Hospitality is not, as we are constantly romantically informed that it is, nearly so spontaneous. There is a mercenary edge, and this, alas, is not always traceable to that alien corrupt civilization!

Peter Abrahams, Alan Paton, Onuora Nzekwu, William Conton – like the poetasters of the cultural dilemma – one after another they fall down and fail at the altar of humanity because they have not written of the African from the dignity and authority of self-acceptance. Peter Abrahams (*Wild Conquest, A Wreath for Udomo*) is especially something of a marvel in this respect – his black characters do not appear to talk, they use dialogue; they do not argue, they hold disputations. As for feeling, emotion, that is surely an invention of the English greens on Sunday. *Mine Boy* sustains its threat to be an exception until Abrahams's stagy exploration of the black-white relationship reduces his characters to cardboard. Alan Paton's *Cry, the Beloved Country* simply debases the gift of sympathy. Nzekwu shares with Conton the gift for fictitious heroes, waiting vainly for human metamorphosis at the magic application of a spurious denouement as dictated by 'Literature as a Higher Art'. And foreign critics conspire by suspending the meaning of tragedy. Writers like Chinua Achebe, Mongo Beti and lately the South African Alex la Guma are, however, making restoration to the human image of the African. Mongo Beti, unlike the others, has employed the medium of comedy, or as he himself puts it, 'my first, perhaps my only love: the absurdity of life'. It is a love that many Africans tend to spurn, for it flatly rejects inflation:

> Come and restore
> Again to us
> The dignity
> Of our ancestral past
> The charity of heart
> And benevolence of soul
> Regard for age . . .
> And readiness to use
> Our strength
> To animate the weak.

The lines of a Ghanaian poet. And pure fiction. The ancestral spirits surely enjoyed the irony, for only a few pages away in the same anthology the following stage directions appear in a play, *The Council of Abura*, also by a Ghanaian. 'A stalwart ruffian near-by readily obeys the command and strikes the poor blind face.' New dimensions in ancestral animation.

Mongo Beti has made tradition a thoroughly viable proposition. His Kala is the entire sweep of our now familiar backcloth, interpreted faithfully through a most suspiciously exact vein of wonder and participation. He has translated the slight alienation of his hero into village terms, with no condescension, no stances; the magnificent candour of the hero, Jean-Marie Medza, stranger to Kala, creates a vigorous clarity in characters, a precision of edges that Chinua Achebe, with no such uninhibited agent to hand, achieved in neither of his books. Sex is restored to its natural proportions, not a startling discovery made by the European every publishing day, nor a neo-Africanist venture sung by the apostles of negritude and sanctified in shrines to puberty. Beti makes sex an unquestioned attitude; the result is that he demonstrates a truly idyllic love dignified by humour, by pathos, and crucial to the novel as a major factor in the development of a young, sensitive personality.

So, it can be done. Biblical ponderosities in the mouth of black dignity prove, in the end, as unreal as gutterals in the mouth of Hollywood fantasia. And the bulk imitation of European *personal* idioms is simply so much schoolboy exercise. Only through the confidence of individual art, like the early Tutuola, through the hurtful realism of Alex la Guma, the sincerity of Chinua Achebe and the total defiant self-acceptance of Mongo Beti, can the African emerge as a creature of sensibilities. These are only a few examples. Idealization is a travesty of literary worth; worse still, it betrays only immature hankerings of the creative impulse.

III

The Writer in a Modern African State*

Does he exist at all, the writer in a contemporary Africa? If it were possible to suggest an oppposite background to the student of African literature or at least to create an entirely different background, would a stranger to the literary creations of African writers find any discrepancy between subject matter and environment or be any more deeply puzzled than he is today at the lack of vital relevance between the literary concerns of writers and the pattern of reality that has overwhelmed even the writers themselves in the majority of the modern African states? I do not concern myself now with the exceptions, which are in any case so few and without any impact. And I certainly exclude the South African situation for the moment, since I do not, alas, possess the superior complacency of a fellow writer from Africa who uttered sentiments more or less in the following words: 'One is tempted to ask,' he says, 'what is the South African writer doing for himself? A little less talking and protest and a bit more action, especially from the so-called exiles, might be more to the point . . .' etc. I regret very much that I have not the exact quotation here, for it is the kind of remark which proves very clearly that the easiest solution to any problem is to maintain complete ignorance of it.

One opposite temptation is to simplify the task by refusing to consider South Africa as an African state, and this certainly has some validity; for is the South African population not legitimately a white one in its entirety, since the black Africans within it have not the status of human beings? The situation in which the South African writer finds himself is quite simply out of this world, and many people who do not possess divine omniscience and do not contain in themselves a one-man verbal guerilla force, like the writer I have just quoted, are beginning to feel that the solutions are literally out of this world. The experience of the South African writer is approached by that of other Africans only remotely, that is to say, wholly inadequately.

---

* Address delivered at the Afro-Scandinavian Writers' Conference, Stockholm, in 1960, shortly before the Nigerian Civil War.

My concern in this talk is primarily with the non-South African writer and why, before very long, he may begin to envy the South African the bleak immensity of his problems. For the South African has still the right to hope, and this prospect of a future yet uncompromised by failure on his own part, in his own right, is something which has lately ceased to exist for other African writers.

While we may debate what constitutes an African writer and what does not, one breed of humanity which we cannot comfortably deny is that of the writer. In new societies which begin the seductive experiment in authoritarianism, it has become a familiar experience to watch society crush the writer under a load of guilt for his daring to express a sensibility and an outlook apart from, and independent of, the mass direction. The revolutionary mood in society is a particularly potent tyrant in this respect, and since the writer is, at the very least, sensitive to mood, he respects the demand of the moment and effaces his definition as a writer by an act of choice. And in the modern African state especially, the position of the writer has been such that he is in fact the very prop of the state machinery. Independence in every instance has meant an emergency pooling of every mental resource. The writer must, for the moment at least (he persuades himself), postpone that unique reflection on experience and events which is what makes a writer – and constitute himself into a part of that machinery that will actually shape events. Let this impulse be clearly understood and valued for itself; the African writer found that he could not deny his society; he could, however, temporarily at least, deny himself. He therefore took his place in the new state as a privileged person, placed personally above the effects of the narrowness of vision which usually accompanies the impatience of new nations, African, European or Asian. He, the special eye and ear, the special knowledge and response, lost even his re-creative consciousness, which might from time to time, left active and alert in uncreative work, have demanded a re-examination of his own position.

If he has not already arrived at this discovery, the writer from East and West African states is coming closer to the terrible understanding that it is not his South African comrade who is the object of compassion. Already he has begun to shrink from the bewildered stare of the South African, knowing that he, the supposedly free mind who once symbolized a loop-hole for the dead-end of the South African dilemma, has himself become the creature of despair. The change in circumstances is quite direct. The background starts at the united opposition by the colonized to the external tyrant. Victory, of sorts, came and the writer submitted his integrity to the monolithic stresses of the time. For this any manifesto seemed valid, any -ism could be embraced with a clear conscience. With few exceptions the writer directed his energies to enshrining victory, to re-affirming his identification with the aspirations of nationalism and the stabilization of society.

The third stage, the stage at which we find ourselves, is the stage of disillusionment, and it is this which prompts an honest examination of what has been the failure of the African writer, as a writer. And this is not to say that, if the African writer had truly responded to the political moment of his society, he would not still be faced with disillusionment. For the situation in Africa today is the same as in the rest of the world; it is not one of the tragedies which come of isolated human failures, but the very collapse of humanity. Nevertheless the African writer has done nothing to vindicate his existence, nothing to indicate that he is even aware that this awful collapse has taken place. For he has been generally without vision.

The distractions away from vision were, of course, enormous, the distractions away from a vision clarified in human terms and not in dogma. And they were such as gave full scope to the exploitation by demagogic opportunists of the new aggressive national consciousness. Reality, the ever-present fertile reality, was ignored by the writer and resigned to the new visionary – the politician. Since the phase of anti-colonialist tracts, poetry and general inspiration was clearly over and that purpose rendered redundant, a new distraction must be created for the aggressive demands of the writer's restless mind. And the publishers were at hand, waiting. Cultural definitions became a new source of literature – not so new, in fact, but they acquired a new significance in the context of political independence. The curiosity of the outside world far exceeded its critical faculties and publishers hovered like benevolent vultures over the still-born foetus of the African Muse. At a given signal they tore off bits and pieces, fanned up with powerful wings delusions of significance in commonness and banality. The average published writer in the first few years of the post-colonial era was the most celebrated skin of inconsequence to obscure the true flesh of the African dilemma.

This was the beginning of the abdication of the African writer, and the deception which he caused by fabricating a magnitude of unfelt abstractions. Isolated by his very position in society, he mistook his own personal and temporary cultural predicament for the predicament of his entire society and turned attention from what was really happening to that society. He even tried to give society something that the society had never lost – its identity. Now identity is a much-abused word, and perhaps the African writer is a much-abused person in this respect, for, poet, novelist or sculptor, the artist labours from an in-built, intuitive responsibility, not only to himself but to his roots. The test of the narrowness or the breadth of his vision, however, is whether it is his accidental situations which he tries to stretch to embrace his society and race or the fundamental truths of his community which inform his vision and enable him to acquire even a prophetic insight into the evolution of that society.

In the movement towards chaos in modern Africa, the writer did not anticipate. The understanding language of the outside world, 'birth pains', that near-fatal euphemism for death throes, absolved him from responsibility. He was content to turn his eye backwards in time and prospect in archaic fields for forgotten gems which would dazzle and distract the present. But never inwards, never truly into the present, never into the obvious symptoms of the niggling, warning, predictable present, from which alone lay the salvation of ideals.

I do not suggest that nothing of this literature was valid nor that there was not to be found in it genuine literary value. Only that the present philosophy, the present direction of modern Africa, was created by politicians, not writers. Is this not a contradiction in a society whose great declaration of uniqueness to the outside world is that of a superabundant humanism? In pre-colonial days there was no real collaboration between the creative mind and the political; there was hardly the practical, fruitful acknowledgement of the existence of the one by the other. The seeming exception of the French colonial territories had in fact the most disastrous effect of all, for there, more determinedly than in other examples, the articulate élite became in fact the ruling class – and here incidentally we may refute the literary historic sense of many observers who insist that African writing was in fact a product of political freedom. To take the obvious example, one may as well suggest that the *négritude* movement and its literature did not exist before Kwame Nkrumah set the precedent in independence for other African states. The French case was, only slightly more so than the British colonial, the crystallization of the writer's image in Africa in the character of the Establishment. When the writer woke from his opium dream of metaphysical abstractions, he found that the politician had used his absence from earth to consolidate his position; more often than not the writer, who in any case belonged to the same or a superior, intellectual class, rationalized the situation and refused to deny himself the rewards of joining the others in safety and comfort. He was in any case still blinded to the present by the resuscitated splendours of the past. When he is purged from the long deception and has begun to express new wisdoms, the gates of the preventive-detention fortress open up and close on him. He becomes an exile, impeccable in his dark suit in the offices of the UNO or UNESCO, or resorts to new weapons of violence. Poets have lately taken to gun-running and writers are heard of holding up radio stations. In several independent states the writer is part of some underground movement; one coup at least in Africa is reputed to have involved a novelist and a poet.

Perhaps it is time to move away from generalities and remark briefly on one situation with which I am at least very familiar and in whose details I have naturally been involved, since it happens to be in my own country. Details are, when we look at them, quite pointless, for I am certain that, whatever developments of the situation are as yet unechoed by other African states, will, before long, be duplicated in the same disheartening details and senselessness. I say this with the sense of obviousness with which I am able, for instance, to look at America today and understand very clearly that here is one society which is on the very edge of collapse. Now, Nigeria was at least one African state where, from the beginning, the writers made an effort to protect their own existence by remaining articulately watchful. At no stage was a level of suppression reached comparable to what existed in Ghana before Nkrumah's fall or exists now in Malawi, where a paranoid has successfully muzzled any hope of free expression. Yet, in spite of this, irrational events have so far deranged the course of basic human intercourse that it is impossible, physically impossible, at the moment for the writers of the country to even come together. And a pattern of this appears to me to be establishing itself over the continent. The African writer needs an urgent release from the fascination of the past. Of course, the past exists, the real African consciousness establishes this – the past exists now, this moment, it is co-existent in present awareness. It clarifies the present and explains the future, but it is not a fleshpot for escapist indulgence, and it is vitally dependent on the sensibility that recalls it. This is not to deny the dangers which attend the development of this *historic vision* – a convenient term for the total acceptance of the human heritage. A historic vision is of necessity universal and any pretence to it must first accept the demand for a total re-examination of the whole phenomenon of humanity. I regard it as dangerous, because to what else can it lead but to the destruction of the will to action? What we are observing in our own time is the total collapse of ideals, the collapse of humanity itself. Action therefore becomes meaningless, the writer is pushed deeper and deeper into self-insulation and withdrawal; his commitment accepts its own hopelessness from the very beginning.

The consideration which brings me, personally, down to earth is the thought of the Angolan or South African writer, either in exile or making his last feeble twitches before the inexorable maul of a desperate regime ends him. It is the exercise of trying to read his mind when he is confronted by the operation of the human factor in black states in which he had fixed his rights and which always represented, at the very least, a temporary haven. And he sees, and he understands for the first time that, given equal opportunity, the black tin god a few thousand miles north of him would degrade and dehumanize his victim as capably as Vorster or Governor Wallace. This fact has been ever-present, this knowledge is not new, and the only wonder is that the *romancier*, the intellectual myth-maker, has successfully deleted this black portion of a common human equation. And the intermittent European exercises in genocide have been duplicated on the African continent admittedly on a lower scale, but only because of the temporary lack of scientific organization. We, whose humanity the poets celebrated before the proof, whose lyric innocence was daily questioned by the very pages of the newspapers, are now being forced by disaster, not foresight, to a reconsideration of our relationship to the outer world. It seems to me that the time has now come when the African writer must have the courage to determine what alone can be salvaged from the recurrent cycle of human stupidity.

The myth of irrational nobility, of a racial essence that must come to the rescue of the white depravity, has run its full course. It never in fact existed, for this was not the problem but the camouflage. And it has become important to state this because the old camouflage has begun lately to take on a new camouflage of fresh understanding. The movement which began with the war-cry of cultural separatism, modified itself with an acknowledgement of historical expediency of the revolt – I refer, of course, to *négritude* – has found a latter-day succession in a call to be the bridge, to bring about the salvation of the world by a marriage of abstractions. It is a remarkable fact that the European writer, who had both the leisure and the long history of introspection to ascertain his spiritual needs, has not yet sent out a call to the black writer for rescue. Surely the game has become transparent by now; the writer's philosophy does not prescribe for his own society, his enlargement of commitment conveniently ignores his own inadequacies, overlooking the well-tried adage which cautions very simply, 'Physician heal thyself'.

This reconciliation of cultures, this leaven of black contribution to the metallic loaf of European culture, is only another evasion of the inward eye. The despair and anguish which is spreading a miasma over the continent must sooner or later engage the attention of the writer in his own society or else be boldly ignored. For both attitudes are equally valid; only let there be no pretence to a concern which fulfils itself in the undeclared, unproven privations of the European world. When the writer in his own society can no longer function as conscience, he must recognize that his choice lies between denying himself totally or withdrawing to the position of chronicler and postmortem surgeon. But there can be no further distractions with universal concerns whose balm is spread on abstract wounds, not on the gaping yaws of black inhumanity. A concern with culture strengthens society, but not a concern with mythology. The artist has always functioned in African society as the record of the mores and experience of his society *and* as the voice of vision in his own time. It is time for him to respond to this essence of himself.

IV

The *Lysistrata* of Aristophanes*

The sinister aspect of satire is easily overlooked – in exaggerating to a ludicrous degree it also poses a threat – suppose it really happens? Laughter, after all, is a two-sided affair: it expresses a superior attitude but it also covers up fear. The more effective satire teeters successfully on this knife-edge of laughter-superiority and self-centred fear; the posed thesis can be dismissed but its exposition has succeeded in arousing thoughts of possibilities. *Lysistrata* is one such work. Ironically, only half humanity is arraigned in its major trial, this is the male sex, the warring, superior, organizing sex. The female comes in only for tangential attention. The concern for decent values is all theirs while their menfolk are destroyers of those values. But Aristophanes is too objective an observer (and exponent) to gild the weaker sex in pure colours; from the beginning of the play we are introduced to a truly weak, vacillating half of humanity who are only barely held together by the iron will of an exceptional woman, Lysistrata. Once again, Aristophanes permits no mouthpiece of his, the dramatist's, values to appear unblemished, giving to them just that degree of credibility of human weaknesses which endear them (in this case) to the audience's own superior stance and takes the edge off the audience's resentment of the satirist's unstated claims to moral superiority. Aristophanes' army of rebellious women do not really meet with audience resistance since they tacitly encourage the audience in their protective and superior inclinations. 'Lewd to the least drop in the tiniest vein' laments Lysistrata. 'Our sex is fitly food for Tragic Poets'.

And the sinister level, the thought that just such a rebellion might indeed be feasible, becomes in turn an added thrill to audience enjoyment whether male or female – in different ways. For the female it is perfect wish-fulfilment. For the male it is a mild form of perversion, the latent craving for a reversed sex-domination which is allegedly present in every male (I am not absolutely sure that I agree with this, I will only go so far as to admit that sex-starvation, initiated by woman herself, may be enjoyably experienced

* Seminar Paper, University of Ibadan, 1964.

by man as a sort of prolonged prelminary sex-play.) What matters is that Aristophanes has woven his play around a well-observed psychological relationship of the sexes, in addition to the down-to-earth bawdiness and crude-to-witty phallic images. The humour therefore is of that visceral breed which goes beyond mere belly laughter. Aristophanes is the figure of Satyr bounding through the thickets of Athenian licentiousness and awakening the fearful pleasures that attend the rites of fertility, the prospects of abandon after religious discipline, the destruction of restraint and inhibition for the goal of a spiritual (ideological) rebirth. The idiom of Lysistrata is the idiom of fertility rites; it is no wonder that passages of lyricism vie with slapstick imagery and bawdy encounters.

It is this background of ritual that gives *Lysistrata* its rounded dimensions. The question is – Does it fit with the object of the playwright's attack? And the answer is – Yes. A conflict which centres around the question of war is clearly one between Life and the forces of death. *Lysistrata* is a pagan hymn to Life. The Life-deniers are cruelly punished when the armaments of Life are turned against them, punished and mocked by the denial of those processes on which Life is dependent. It is often difficult to recognize within comic forms that same Life impulse which governs tragedies. *The Bacchae* of Euripides is a glorification of the Life (Dionysiac) impulse which routs inimical efforts that threaten to dam its flow. What, after all, is the sin of Pentheus but this? The orgy and libertinism of the Bacchantes is merely the overt expression of the Life force itself. The crime of Pentheus was his refusal to acknowledge the validity of this force. The Athenian men, who place their destructive patriotism before the dues of Life, the purveyors of civil or martial puritanism are descendants from the tragic line of Pentheus. But we do not now talk of *hubris*, for our poet Aristophanes has elected the satiric vein; nevertheless, the mould is one and the same. Peace and harmony form the message of the son of Zagreus; the followers of Lysistrata are true inheritors of the mantle of Dionysos; they force their men to bear that phallus they have impudently neglected in a posture of humiliation.

A sustained mock of the heroic, a parody of ritual, a physical subversion of the principle of sanctuary – these are some of the ingredients of this Satyr's version of the fertility broth. Let us listen to the valorous hortations of the Old Men, preservers of Authority and the values of male ascendancy;

> By Demeter, they'll get no brag while I've a vein to beat
> Cleomenes himself was hurtled out in sore defeat
> His stiff-backed Spartan pride was bent.
> Out, stripped of all his arms, he went
> A pygmy cloak that would not stretch
> To hide his rump (the draggled wretch) . . .
> That was a siege! Our men were ranged in lines of seventeen deep
> Before the gates, and never left their posts there, even to sleep.
> Shall I not smite the rash presumption then of foes like these,
> Detested both of all the gods and of Euripides –
> Else, may the Marathon plain not boast my trophied victories.

The mock-heroic strain is clearly recognizable. The 'weaker' sex are to be assailed on a physical level at one with military siege, and in language of lyrical passion which equates the battle of Marathon. As usual, Aristophanes cannot resist a sideswipe at his *bête noire*, the tragedian. The same impatience with the 'divine afflatus' of tragedy has given *Lysistrata* great theatrical moments where ritual is parodied and a wine-skin 'slaughtered' to provide entrails for the solemn oath. The comic reduction of the code of valour is further enhanced by the use of the martial shield as a receptable for this blasphemous act, an interraction of visual images on a comic level:

> LYSISTRATA: First lay the shield, boss downward, on the floor
> And bring the victim's innards . . .
>
> What oath!
> In Aeschylus they take a slaughtered sheep
> And swear upon a buckler. Why not we?
> . . .
> First set a great dark bowl upon the ground
> And disembowel a skin of Thasian wine . . .
>
> Put down the bowl. Lay hands, all, on the victim
> Skiey Queen who givest the last word in arguments,
> And thee, O Bowl, dear comrade, we beseech:
> Accept our oblation, and be propitious to us . . .

And the pledges of bedroom strike that follow complete the rout of the solemn oath.

Aristophanes does no more than hint the reversal of positions in the relationship of the seekers of sanctuary and their persecutors, and yet this touch of Anarchy, approved or even legitimized by principles with which the dramatist has tried (at least) to identify with us gives to the play its element of intellectual strength. The women have taken over the Acropolis; under guise of going to offer sacrifice they have barricaded themselves in, but not as suppliants. They are here to dictate the terms. The Chorus of feeble Old Men may be no more than a dramatic device, yet this device does induce, dramatically, a certain observation. In times of crisis, there are only old men left to cope with it; an argument, we might say, which favours the women's stand. The Magistrate is not only a figure of fun but appears at the beginning at least to further the women's cause with arguments which should appeal to the men's self-interest. The Chorus of Men have just complained to him:

> O if you knew their full effrontery!
> All of the insults they've done, besides sousing us
> With water from their pots to our public disgrace
> For we stand here wringing our clothes as though we'd pissed on 'em.

But the Magistrate is not very sympathetic:

By Poseidon, justly done! For in part with us
The blame must lie for dissolute behaviour
. . .
We go into a shop and say, Here, goldsmith,
You remember the necklace that you wrought my wife;
Well, the other night in fervour of a dance
Her clasp broke open. Now I'm off for Salamis;
If you've the leisure, would you go tonight
And stick a bolt pin into her opened clasp.
Another goes to a cobbler, a soldierly fellow,
Always standing up erect, and says to him,
Cobbler, a sandal strap of my wife's pinches her,
Hurts her little toe in a place where she's sensitive.
Come at noon and see if you can stretch wider
This thing that troubles her, loosen its tightness.

The Magistrate is not merely a mouthpiece for these and many other Aristophanic double-entrendres, saucy, witty, and downright crude, but also serves the dramatist the purpose of steeping the play in that orgiastic mould – bent to the satyric purpose – that we have already noted:

Have the luxurious rites of the women glittered
Their libertine show, their drumming tapped out crowds,
The Sabazian Mysteries summoned their mob,
Adonis been wept to death on the terraces,
As I could hear the last day in the Assembly?
. . .
And there the woman, up to the ears in wine,
Was screaming. Weep for Adonis on the house top . . .

He is, of course, like the Chorus of Men, routed. His assault party cannot withstand the spartan allies of Lysistrata, handicapped presumably by the awkward lances they bear before them, a great impediment for in-fighting.

The scene of the torment of Cinesias by his wife Myrrhine is of course comedy on a high level. The comic image of this single encounter, focussed now for the first time both visually and dramatically, is generalized when both Spartans and Athenians are forced to meet and work out a peace. The puns, some of which are simply outrageous, come in fast and furious. The ailment which has been particularized with such comic ingenuity is now widened to embrace male humanity; the humour is not diffused but multiplied by the simple ploy of playing verbal variations on the same theme, and the other device of gathering the threads of the play together with the male assembly who are now on their knees in a compelled quest of the theme of the play – peace. Our physically handicapped combatants are faced with a situation which is of the making of their refractory natures. Is is possible that government can be the prerogative of such a vulnerable part of humanity?

Aristophanes does not neglect the direct critical assessment of the capability of such people for good judgement. Here is Lysistrata in one of her many indictments against her war-mongering compatriots:

> I am a woman, but I'm not a fool
> And what of natural intelligence I own
> Has been filled out with the remembered precepts
> My father and the city elders taught me
> First I reproach you both sides equally
> That when at Pylae and Olympia,
> At Pytho and the many other shrines
> That I could name, you sprinkle from one cup
> The altars common to all Hellenes, yet
> You wrack Hellenic cities, bloody Hellas
> With deaths of her own sons . . .

The argument is emotional, nevertheless it is truth, and it is an argument that borrows from patriotism, appealing at the same time to feelings which are more personal, more immediate than the patriotic code of valour. Lysistrata as the protagonist is indeed created as that blend of courage, idealism and earthy common sense which serves the practised satirist much better than the virtuous one-dimensional touchstone, a flat sanctimoniousness which soon bores the audience and loses it sympathy. Aristophanes' heroine is self-identifiable – quick, witty, sharp and uninhibited, she corresponds to that 'common-sense' aspiration of the audience which the satirist so often exploits for turning the tables on the self-esteem of the audience individual. Her recipe for a moral cleansing of society could easily prove long and precious, except that the character of Lysistrata, the bonhomie that she never quite discards despite her authoritative position among her women, and her down-to-earth saw-swapping responses to her challengers compel listening even by the bitterest opponents or victims of the satirist's thesis. Are domestic wisdoms any poorer than martial follies? This is the weighted question Aristophanes asks. Not forgetting political corruption:

> MAGISTRATE: So with these trivial tricks of the household,
> domestic analogies of thread, skeins, and spools,
> You think that you'll solve such a bitter complexity
> unwind such political problems, you fools!

> LYSISTRATA: Well, first as we wash dirty wool so's to cleanse it,
> so with a pitiless zeal we will scrub
> Through the whole city for all greasy fellows;
> burrs too, the parasites, off we will rub.
> That verminous plague of insensate place seekers

soon between thumb and forefinger we'll crack.
All who inside Athens' walls have their dwelling
into one great common basket we'll pack
Disenfranchised or citizens, allies or aliens,
pell-mell the lot of them in we will squeeze
Till they discover humanity's meaning . . .

'Till they discover humanity's meaning'. Tucked between domestic images, between thumb and forefinger that will crack 'the verminous plague of insensate place seekers' is found the dramatist's article of faith. Not that he is bound to have or to state one. It is enough that his pen delineates, distorts and denounces what to him constitute the negative or reprehensible principles. Aristophanes, however, reveals more than the satiric dramatist's basic iconoclasm. A passion for certain humane values pervades his work and I believe that in that phrase. 'Till they discover humanity's meaning', may be found his most clearly stated sense of mission, the impulse behind his irreverence, his gaily uncompromising stance against intellectual cant, hypocrisy and cruelty. The format of a sommersaulted world in which the women take over by wielding the basic weapon of sex is in itself a kind of poetic justice over that humanity which so wastefully works against itself. Common sense has been overthrown (the humane common sense which places creativity above destructiveness.) So what is more natural than that other norms should be accordingly overturned:

When as the swallows flocking in one place from the hoophoes
Deny their legs love's gambols any more,
All woes shall then have ending and great Zeus the Thunderer
Shall put above what was below before.

This is the pronouncement of Zeus as fabricated in all likelihood by Lysistrata. It is more than a prophecy on orthodox sexual positions; on its slightly more menacing level it is a warning that the abdication of humane values may go with abdication of human rights. The women, in this case, are custodians of the final weapons of implementation.

V

The Fourth Stage: Through the Mysteries of Ogun[1] to the Origin of Yoruba Tragedy*

The persistent search for the meaning of tragedy, for a re-definition in terms of cultural or private experience is, at the least, man's recognition of certain areas of depth-experience which are not satisfactorily explained by general aesthetic theories; and, of all the subjective unease that is aroused by man's creative insights, that wrench within the human psyche which we vaguely define as 'tragedy' is the most insistent voice that bids us return to our own sources. There, illusively, hovers the key to the human paradox, to man's experience of being and non-being, his dubiousness as essence and matter, intimations of transience and eternity, and the harrowing drives between uniqueness and Oneness.

Our course to the heart of the Yoruba Mysteries leads by its own ironic truths through the light of Nietzsche[2] and the Phrygian deity; but there are the inevitable, key departures. 'Blessed Greeks!' sings our mad votary in his recessional rapture, 'how great must be your Dionysos, if the Delic god thinks such enchantments necessary to cure you of your Dithyrambic madness'. Such is Apollo's resemblance to the serene art of Obatala[3] the pure unsullied one, to the 'essence' idiom of his rituals, that it is tempting to place him at the end of a creative axis with Ogun, in a parallel evolutionary relationship to Nietzsche's Dionysos-Apollo brotherhood. But Obatala the sculptural god is not the artist of Apollonian illusion but of inner essence. The idealist bronze and terra-cotta of Ife which may tempt the comparision implicit in 'Apollonian' died at some now forgotten period, evidence only of the universal surface culture of courts, never again resurrected. It is alien to the Obatala spirit of Yoruba 'essential' art. Obatala finds expression, not in Nietzsche's Apollonian 'mirror of enchantment' but as a statement of world resolution. The mutual tempering of illusion and will, necessary to an under-standing of the Hellenic spirit, may mislead us, when we are faced with Yoruba art, for much of it has a similarity in its aesthetic serenity to the plastic arts of the Hellenic.

* First published in *The Morality of Art: Essays Presented to G. Wilson Knight* (1973).

Yoruba traditional art is not ideational however, but 'essential'. It is not the idea (in religious arts) that is transmitted into wood or interpreted in music or movement, but a quintessence of inner being, a symbolic interaction of the many aspects of revelations (within a universal context) with their moral apprehension.

Ogun, for his part, is best understood in Hellenic values as a totality of the Dionysian, Apollonian and Promethean virtues. Nor is that all. Transcending even today, the distorted myths of his terrorist reputation, traditional poetry records him as 'protector of orphans', 'roof over the homeless', 'terrible guardian of the sacred oath'; Ogun stands for a transcendental, humane but rigidly restorative justice. (Unlike Sango, who is primarily retributive.) The first artist and technician of the forge, he evokes like Nietzsche's Apollonian spirit, a 'massive impact of image, concept, ethical doctrine and sympathy'. Obatala is the placid essence of creation; Ogun the creative urge and instinct, the essence of creativity.

> Rich-laden is his home, yet decked in palm fronds
> He ventures forth, refuge of the down-trodden,
> To rescue slaves he unleashed the judgment of war
> Because of the blind, plunged into forests
> Of curative herbs, Bountiful One
> Who stands bulwark to offsprings of the dead of heaven
> Salutations, O lone being, who swims in rivers of blood.

Such virtues place Ogun apart from the distorted dances to which Nietzsche's Dionysiac frenzy led him in his search for a selective 'Aryan' soul, yet do not detract from Ogun's revolutionary grandeur. Ironically, it is the depth-illumination of Nietzsche's intuition into basic universal impulses which negates his race exclusivist conclusions on the nature of art and tragedy. In our journey to the heart of Yoruba tragic art which indeed belongs in the Mysteries of Ogun and the choric ecstasy of revellers, we do not find that the Yoruba, as the Greek did, 'built for his chorus the scaffolding of a fictive chthonic realm and placed thereon fictive nature spirits . . .' on which foundation, claims Nietzsche, Greek tragedy developed: in short, the principle of illusion.

Yoruba tragedy plunges straight into the 'chthonic realm', the seething cauldron of the dark world will and psyche, the transitional yet inchoate matrix of death and becoming. Into this universal womb once plunged and emerged Ogun, the first actor, disintegrating within the abyss. His spiritual re-assemblage does not require a 'copying of actuality' in the ritual re-enactment of his devotees, any more than Obatala does in plastic representation, in the art of Obatala. The actors in Ogun Mysteries are the communicant chorus, containing within their collective being the essence of that transitional abyss. But only as essence, held, contained and mystically expressed. Within the mystic summons of the chasm the protagonist actor (and every god-suffused choric individual) resists, like Ogun before him, the final step toward complete annihilation.

From this alone steps forward the eternal actor of the tragic rites, first as the unresisting mouthpiece of the god, uttering visions symbolic of the transitional gulf, interpreting the dread power within whose essence he is immersed as agent of the choric will. Only later, in the evenness of release from the tragic climax, does the serene self-awareness of Obatala reassert its creative control. He, the actor, emerges still as the mediant voice of the god, but stands now as it were beside himself, observant, understanding, creating. At this stage is known to him the sublime *aesthetic* joy, not within Nietzsche's heart of original oneness but in the distanced celebration of the cosmic struggle. This resolved aesthetic serenity is the link between Ogun's tragic art and Obatala's plastic beauty. The unblemished god, Obatala, is the serene womb of chthonic reflections (or memory), a passive strength awaiting and celebrating each act of vicarious restoration of his primordial being. (We shall come later to the story of that first severance.) His beauty is enigmatic, expressive only of the resolution of plastic healing through the wisdom of acceptance. Obatala's patient suffering is the well-known aesthetics of the saint.

For the Yoruba, the gods are the final measure of eternity, as humans are of earthly transience. To think, because of this, that the Yoruba mind reaches intuitively toward absorption in godlike essence is to misunderstand the principle of religious rites, and to misread, as many have done, the significance of religious possession. Past, present and future being so pertinently conceived and woven into the Yoruba world view, the element of eternity which is the god's prerogative does not have the same quality of remoteness or exclusiveness which it has in Christian or Buddhist culture. The belief of the Yoruba in the contemporaneous existence within his daily experience of these aspects of time has long been recognized but again misinterpreted. It is no abstraction. The Yoruba is not, like European man, concerned with the purely conceptual aspects of time; they are too concretely realized in his own life, religion, sensitivity, to be mere tags for explaining the metaphysical order of his world. If we may put the same thing in fleshed-out cognitions, life, present life, contains within it manifestations of the ancestral, the living and the unborn. All are vitally within the intimations and affectiveness of life, beyond mere abstract conceptualization.

And yet the Yoruba does not for that reason fail to distinguish between himself and the deities, between himself and the ancestors, between the unborn and his reality, or discard his awareness of the essential gulf that lies between one area of existence and another. This gulf is what must be constantly diminished by the sacrifices, the rituals, the ceremonies of appeasement to those cosmic powers which lie guardian to the gulf. Spiritually, the primordial disquiet of the Yoruba psyche may be expressed as the existence in collective memory of a primal severance in transitional ether,[4] whose first effective defiance is symbolized in the myth of the gods' descent to earth and the battle with immense chaotic growth which had sealed off reunion with man. For they were coming down, not simply to be acknowledged but to be re-united with human essence, to reassume that portion of re-creative transient awareness which the first deity Orisa-nla possessed and expressed through his continuous activation of man images – brief reflections of divine facets – just as man is grieved by a consciousness of the loss of the eternal essence of his being and must indulge in symbolic transactions to recover his totality of being.

Tragedy, in Yoruba traditional drama, is the anguish of this severance, the fragmentation of essence from self. Its music is the stricken cry of man's blind soul as he flounders in the void and crashes through a deep abyss of aspirituality and cosmic rejection. Tragic music is an echo from that void; the celebrant speaks, sings and dances in authentic archetypal images from within the abyss. All understand and respond, for it is the language of the world.

It is necessary to emphasize that the gods were coming down to be reunited with man, for this tragedy could not be, the anguish of severance would not attain such tragic proportions, if the gods' position on earth (i.e. in man's conception) was to be one of divine remoteness. This is again testified to by the form of worship, which is marked by camaraderie and irreverence just as departure to ancestorhood is marked by bawdiness in the midst of grief. The anthropomorphic origin of uncountable deities is one more leveller of divine class-consciousness but, finally, it is the innate humanity of the gods themselves, their bond with man through a common animist relation with nature and phenomena. Continuity for the Yoruba operates both through the cyclic concept of time and the animist interfusion of all matter and consciousness.

The first actor – for he led the others – was Ogun, first suffering deity, first creative energy, the first challenger, and conqueror of transition. And his, the first art, was tragic art, for the complementary drama of the syncretic successor to Orisa-nla, Obatala's 'Passion' play, is only the plastic resolution of Ogun's tragic engagement. The Yoruba metaphysics of accommodation and resolution could only come *after* the passage of the gods through the transitional gulf, after the demonic test of the self-will of Ogun the explorer-god in the creative cauldron of cosmic powers. Only after such testing could the harmonious Yoruba world be born, a harmonious will which accommodates every alien material or abstract phenomenon within its infinitely stressed spirituality. The artefact of Ogun's conquest of separation, the 'fetish', was iron ore, symbol of earth's womb-energies, cleaver and welder of life. Ogun, through his redemptive action became the first symbol of the alliance of disparities when, from earth itself, he extracted elements for the subjugation of chthonic chaos. In tragic consciousness the votary's psyche reaches out beyond the realm of nothingness (or spiritual chaos) which is potentially destructive of human awareness, through areas of terror and blind energies, into a ritual empathy with the gods, the eternal presence, who once preceded him in parallel awareness of their own incompletion. Ritual anguish is therefore experienced as that primal transmission of the god's despair – vast, numinous, always incomprehensible. In vain we seek to capture it in words; there is only for the protagonist the certainty of the experience of this abyss – the tragic victim plunges into it in spite of ritualistic earthing and is redeemed only by action. Without acting, and yet in spite of it, he is forever lost in the maul of tragic tyranny.

Acting is therefore a contradiction of the tragic spirit, yet it is also its natural complement. To act, the Promethean instinct of rebellion, channels anguish into a creative purpose which releases man from a totally destructive despair, releasing from within him the most energetic, deeply combative inventions which, without usurping the territory of the infernal gulf, bridges it with visionary hopes. Only the battle of the will is thus primally creative; from its spiritual stress springs the soul's despairing cry which proves its own solace, which alone reverberating within the cosmic vaults, usurps (at least, and however briefly) the power of the abyss. At the charged climactic moments of the tragic rites we understand how music came to be the sole art form which can contain tragic reality. The votary is led by no other guide into the pristine heart of tragedy. Music as the embodiment of the tragic spirit has been more than perceptively exhausted in the philosophy of Europe; there is little to add, much to qualify. And the function and nature of music in Yoruba tragedy is peculiarly revealing of the shortcomings of long accepted conclusions of European intuition.

The European concept of music does not fully illuminate the relationship of music to ritual and drama among the Yoruba. We are inhibited even by recognition of a universality of concepts in the European intuitive grasp of the emotions of the will. First, it is 'unmusical' to separate Yoruba musical form from myth and poetry. The nature of Yoruba music is intensively the nature of its language and poetry, highly charged, symbolic, myth-embryonic. We acknowledge quite readily the technical lip-service paid to the correspondence of African music to the tonal patterns (meaning and allusion) of the language, but the aesthetic and emotional significance of this relationship has not been truly absorbed, one which springs from the primal simultaneity of art-forms in a culture of total awareness and phenomenal involvement. Language therefore is not a barrier to the profound universality of music but a cohesive dimension and clarification of that wilfully independent art-form which we label music. Language reverts in religious rites to its pristine existence, eschewing the sterile limits of particularization. In cult funerals, the circle of initiate mourners, an ageless swaying grove of dark pines, raises a chant around a mortar of fire, and words are taken back to their roots, to their original poetic sources when fusion was total and the movement of words was the very passage of music and the dance of images. Language is still the embryo of thought and music where myth is daily companion, for there language is constantly mythopoeic.

Language in Yoruba tragic music therefore undergoes transformation through myth into a secret (masonic) correspondence with the symbolism of tragedy, a symbolic medium of spiritual emotions within the heart of the choric union. It transcends particularization (of meaning) to tap the tragic source whence spring the familiar weird disruptive melodies. This masonic union of sign and melody, the true tragic music, unearths cosmic uncertainties which pervade human existence, reveals the magnitude and power of creation, but above all creates a harrowing sense of omni-directional vastness where the creative Intelligence resides and prompts the soul to futile exploration. The senses do not at such moments interpret myth in their particular concretions; we are left only with the emotional and spiritual values, the essential experience of cosmic reality. The forms of music are not correspondences at such moments to the physcial world, not at this nor at any other moment. The singer is a mouthpiece of the chthonic forces of the matrix and his somnabulist 'improvisations' – a simultaneity of musical and poetic forms – are not representations of the ancestor, recognitions of the living or unborn, but of the no man's land of transition between and around these temporal definitions of experience. The past is the ancestors', the present belongs to the living, and the future to the unborn. The deities stand in the same situation to the living as do the ancestors and the unborn, obeying the same laws, suffering the same agonies and uncertainties, employing the same masonic intelligence of rituals for the perilous plunge into the fourth area of experience, the immeasurable gulf of transition. Its dialogue is liturgy, its music takes form from man's uncomprehending immersion in this area of existence, buried wholly from rational recognition. The source of the possessed lyricist, chanting hitherto unknown mythopoeic strains whose antiphonal refrain is, however, instantly caught and thrust with all its terror and awesomeness into the night by swaying votaries, this source is residual in the numinous area of transition.

This is the fourth stage, the vortex of archetypes and home of the tragic spirit.

It is necessary to recall again that the past is not a mystery and that although the future (the unborn) is yet unknown, it is not a mystery to the Yoruba but co-existent in present consciousness. Tragic terror exists therefore neither in the evocation of the past nor of the future. The stage of transition is, however, the metaphysical abyss both of god and man, and if we agree that, in the European sense, music is the 'direct copy or the direct expression of the will', it is only because nothing rescues man (ancestral, living or unborn) from loss of self within this abyss but a titanic resolution of the will whose ritual summons, response, and expression is the strange alien sound to which we give the name of music. On the arena of the living, when man is stripped of excrescences, when disasters and conflicts (the material of drama) have crushed and robbed him of self-consciousness and pretensions, he stands in present reality at the spiritual edge of this gulf, he has nothing left in physical existence which successfully impresses upon his spiritual or psychic perception. It is at such moments that transitional memory takes over and intimations rack him of that intense parallel of his progress through the gulf of transition, of the dissolution of his self and his struggle and triumph over subsumation through the agency of will. It is this experience that the modern tragic dramatist recreates through the medium of physical contemporary action, reflecting emotions of the first active battle of the will through the abyss of dissolution.[5] Ogun is the first actor in that battle, and Yoruba tragic drama is the re-enactment of the cosmic conflict.

To recognize why Ogun was elected for his role (and the penalty of horror which he had to pay for his challenge) is to penetrate the symbolism of Ogun both as essence of anguish and as combative will within the cosmic embrace of the transitional gulf. We have said that nothing but the will (for that alone is left untouched) rescues being from annihilation within the abyss. Ogun is embodiment of Will, and the Will is the paradoxical truth of destructiveness and creativeness in acting man. Only one who has himself undergone the experience of disintegration, whose spirit has been tested and whose psychic resources laid under stress by the forces most inimical to individual assertion, only he can understand and be the force of fusion between the two contradictions. The resulting sensibility is also the sensibility of the artist, and he is a profound artist only to the degree to which he comprehends and expresses this principle of destruction and re-creation.

We must not lose sight of the fact that Ogun is the artistic spirit, and not in the sentimental sense in which rhapsodists of negritude would have us conceive the negro as pure artistic intuition. The significant creative truth of Ogun is affirmation of the re-creative intelligence; this is irreconcilable with naïve intuition. The symbolic artefact of his victory is metallic ore, at once a technical medium as it is symbolic of deep earth energies, a fusion of elemental energies, a binding force between disparate bodies and properties. Thus Ogan, tragic actor, primordial voice of creative man is also, without a contradiction of essences, the forerunner and ancestor of palaeotechnic man. The principle of creativity when limited to pastoral idyllism, as negritude has attempted to limit it, shuts us off from the deeper, fundamental resolutions of experience and cognition. The tragic actor for the future age (already the present for Europe) is that neo-technic ancestor Sango,[6] god of electricity, whose tragedy stems similarly from the principle of a preliminary self-destruction, represented (as in a later penalty of Ogun) in the blind ignorant destruction of his own flesh and blood. What, for Ogun, was a destructive penalty leading to a secondary drama of 'Passion' was in Sango the very core of his tragedy. The historic process of dilution in tragic challenge is manifested in the relationship of these two myths. Sango is an anthropomorphic deity; his history revolved around petty tyranny; his self-destruction was the violent, central explosion from ego-inflation. Where Ogun's human alienation was the postscript error, an exaction for his basic victory over the transitional guardians of the gulf, Sango's was 'in character', a wild vengeful slaughter upon menials who had dared to defy his authority. But the 'terror and pity' of Sango is undeniable, only it is the 'terror and pity' of human disavowal for that new disciple standing on the edge of the sublimating abyss already subdued by Ogun. We will not find the roots of tragedy in the Mysteries of Sango.

Yoruba myth is a recurrent exercise in the experience of disintegration, and this is significant for the seeming distancing of will among a people whose mores, culture and metaphysics are based on apparent resignation and acceptance but which are, experienced in depth, a statement of man's penetrating insight into the final resolution of things and the constant evidence of harmony. What moral values do we encounter in the drama of Obatala, representative though it also is of the first disintegration experienced by godhead? We are further back in Origin, not now engaged in the transitional battle of Ogun, but in the fragmentation of Orisa-nla, the primal deity, from whom the entire Yoruba pantheon was born. Myth informs us that a jealous slave rolled a stone down the back of the first and only deity and shattered him in a thousand and one fragments. From this first act of revolution was born the Yoruba pantheon.

The drama which stems from this is not the drama of acting man but that of suffering spirit, the drama of Obatala. Yoruba myth syncretizes Obatala, god of purity, god also of creation (but not of creativity!), with the first deity Orisa-nla. And the ritual of Obatala is a play of form, a moving celebration whose nearest equivalent in the European idioms is the Passion play. The drama is all essence: captivity, suffering and redemption. Obatala is symbolically captured, confined and ransomed. At every stage he is the embodiment of the suffering spirit of man, uncomplaining, agonized, full of the redemptive qualities of endurance and martyrdom. The music that accompanies the rites of Obatala is all clear tone and winnowed lyric, of order and harmony, stately and saintly. Significantly, the motif is white for transparency of heart and mind; there is a rejection of mystery; tones of vesture and music combine to banish mystery and terror; the poetry of the song is litanic, the dramatic idiom is the processional or ceremonial. It is a drama in which the values of conflict or the revolutionary spirit are excluded, attesting in their place the adequacy and certainty of a harmomious resolution which belongs in time and human faith. It is antithetical to the tragic challenge of Ogun in man.

Proportion in tragedy is governed by an element of the unknown in the forces of opposition or by a miscalculation by the tragic victim of such powers. The drama of Obatala dispenses with the effect of the unknown, and his agony is an evocation of the loneliness of the first deity, for this drama is, as we have stated, all pathos. And the essence is the emotional prelude to the creation of man, the limited, serene aesthetics of moulding man, not to be compared to the cosmic eruption within consciousness brought about by the re-creation of the self. The sympathetic need to be redeemed by evidence of love and human contact, by extension of the self into recognizable entities and other units of potential consciousness – this is the province of Obatala, the delicate shell of the original fullness. The profounder aspect of self-re-creation, the anguish of the Will, is the portion of original restoration which has been left to the peculiar talents of Ogun, and the statement of Yoruba tragic rites is the complement of his Will to the essence of anguish. The latter by itself is crystallized in the Passion play. The drama of Obatala is prelude, suffering and aftermath. It symbolizes firstly the god's unbearable loneliness and next, the memory of his incompleteness, the missing essence. And so it is also with the other gods who did not avail themselves, as did Ogun, of the chance for a redemptive combat where each might re-create each by submission to a disintegrating process within the matrix of cosmic creativity, whence the Will performs the final reassemblage. The weightiest burden of severance is that of each from self, not of godhead from mankind, and the most perilous aspect of the god's journey is that in which the deity must truly undergo the experience of transition. It is a look into the very heart of phenomena. To fashion a bridge across it was not only Ogun's task but his very nature, and he had first to experience it, to surrender his individuation once again (the first time, as a part of the original Orisa-nla Oneness) to the fragmenting process; to be reabsorbed within universal Oneness, the Unconscious, the deep black whirlpool of mythopoeic forces, to immerse himself thoroughly within it, understand its nature and yet by the combative value of the will to rescue and re-assemble himself and emerge wiser, powerful from the draught of cosmic secrets, organizing the mystic and the technical forces of earth and cosmos to forge a bridge for his companions to follow.

It is true that to understand, to understand profoundly, is to be unnerved, deprived of the will to act. For is not human reality dwarfed by the awe and wonder, the inevitability of this cosmic gulf? It must be remembered that within this abyss are the activities of birth, death and resorption in phenomena (for the abyss is the transition between the various stages of existence). Life, the paltry reflection of the forces of the matrix, becomes suddenly inadequate, patronizing and undignified when the source of creative and destructive energies is glimpsed. Suffering cancels the opaque pleasure of human existence; suffering, the truly overwhelming suffering of Sango, of Lear, of Oedipus, this suffering hones the psyche to a finely self-annihilating perceptiveness and renders further action futile and, above all, lacking in dignity. And what has the struggle of the tragic hero been, after all, but an effort to maintain that innate concept of dignity which impels to action only to that degree in which the hero possesses a true nobility of spirit? At such moments he is close to the acceptance and wisdom of Obatala in which faith is rested, not on the self, but on a universal selfhood to which individual contributions are fundamentally meaningless. It is the faith of 'knowing', the enigmatic wisdom of spiritual serenity. It is this which is often narrowly interpreted as the philosophy of the African. But philosophies are the result of primal growth and formative experience; the oracular wisdom of a race based on and continually acted upon by the collective experience of the past, present and unborn (prognostic) realities, complements the intuitive glimpse and memory of the heart of transitional being.

Yoruba 'classical' art is mostly an expression of the Obatala resolution and human beneficence, utterly devoid, on the surface, of conflict and irruption. The masks alone occasionally suggest a correspondence to the chthonic realm and hint at the archetypes of transition, yet even the majority of them flee the full power of cosmic vision, take refuge in deliberately grotesque and comic attitudes. Such distortions are easily recognized as the technique of evasion from the fullness of numinous powers. Terror is both contained by art in tragic form and released by art through comic presentation and sexual ambience. The tragic mask, however, also functions from the same source as its music – from the archetypal essences whose language derives not from the plane of physical reality or ancestral memory (the ancestor is no more than agent or medium), but from the numinous territory of transition into which the artist obtains fleeting glimpses by ritual, sacrifice and a patient submission of rational awareness to the moment when fingers and voice relate the symbolic language of the cosmos. The deft, luminous peace of Yoruba religious art blinds us therefore to the darker powers of the tragic art into which only the participant can truly enter. The grotesquerie of the terror cults misleads the unwary into equating fabricated fears with the exploration of the Yoruba mind into the mystery of his individual will and the intimations of divine suffering to which artistic man is prone. Ifa's cycle of masonic poetry – curative, prognostic, aesthetic and omniscient – expresses a philosophy of optimism in its oracular adaptiveness and unassailable resolution of all phenomena; the gods are accommodating and embrace within their eternal presences manifestations which are seemingly foreign or contradictory. It is no wonder therefore that the overt optimistic nature of the total culture is the quality attributed to the Yoruba himself, one which has begun to affect his accommodation toward the modern world, a spiritual complacency with which he encounters threats to his human and unique validation. Alas, in spite of himself, from time to time, the raw urgent question beats in the blood of his temples demanding, what is the will of Ogun? For the hammering of the Yoruba will was done at Ogun's forge, and any threat of disjunction is, as with the gods, a memory code for the resurrection of the tragic myth.

Yoruba morality has also contributed to the mistaken exclusion of tragic myth from present consciousness; for, as always, the placid surface of the process of healing for spiritual or social rupture is mistaken for the absence of the principles of psychic experience that went into the restoration. Morality for the Yoruba is that which creates harmony in the cosmos, and reparation for disjunction within the individual psyche cannot be seen as compensation for the individual accident to that personality. Thus good and evil are not measured in terms of offences against the individual or even the physical community, for there is knowledge from within the corpus of Ifa oracular wisdoms that a rupture is often simply one aspect of the destructive-creative unity, that offences even against nature may be part of the exaction by deeper nature from humanity of acts which alone can open up the deeper springs of man and bring about a constant rejuvenation of the human spirit. Nature in turn benefits by such broken taboos, just as the cosmos does by demands made upon its will by man's cosmic affronts. Such acts of hubris compel the cosmos to delve deeper into its essence to meet the human challenge. Penance and retribution are not therefore aspects of punishment for crime but the first acts of a resumed awareness, an invocation of the principle of cosmic adjustment. Tragic fate is the repetitive cycle of the taboo in nature, the karmic act of hubris witting or unwitting, into which the demonic will within man constantly compels him. Powerful tragic drama follows upon the act of hubris, and myth exacts this attendant penalty from the hero where he has actually emerged victor of a conflict. Sango's taboo is based on an elementary form of hubris. Over-reaching even beyond the generous toleration due to a monarch, he fell victim to a compulsion for petty intriguing which finally led to his downfall. A final, desperate invocation of unnatural strength gave him temporary ascendancy and he routed his disloyal men. Then came the desecration of nature in which he spilt the blood of his kin. Ogun not only dared to look into transitional essence but triumphantly bridged it with knowledge, with art, with vision and the mystic creativity of science – a total and profound hubristic assertiveness that is beyond any parallel in Yoruba experience. The penalty came later when, as a reward and acknowledgement of his leadership of the divinities, gods and humans joined to offer him a crown. At first he declined but later he consented to the throne of Ire. At the first battle the same demonic energies were aroused but this was no world womb, no chthonic lair, no playground of cosmic monsters, nor could the divisions between man and man, between I and you, friend and foe, be perceived by the erstwhile hero of the transitional abyss. Enemy and subjects fell alike until Ogun alone was left, sole survivor of the narrowness of human separation. The battle is symbolic of tragic hindsight common alike to god and man. In the Ogun Mysteries this drama is a 'Passion' of a different kind, released into quietist wisdom, a ritual exorcism of demonic energies. There is no elation, not even at the end of purgation, nothing like the beatified elation of Obatala after his redemption, only a world-weariness on the rock-shelf of Promethean shoulders, a profound sorrow in the chanting of the god's recessional.[7]

Once we recognize, to revert to his Hellenic equation, the Dionysian-Apollonian-Promethean essence of Ogun, the element of hubris is seen as innate to his tragic being, requiring definition in Yoruba terms, taking it to its cyclic resolution of man's metaphysical situation. Of the profound anguish of Dionysos, the mythic disintegration of his origin is the now familiar cause, and the process of the will, no less, is what rescues the ecstatic god from being, literally, scattered to the cosmic winds. The will of Zeus is as conceptually identifiable with that of Dionysos as the elemental fragmentation of Orisa-nla can be recognized as the recurrent consciousness within Ogun (and other gods) of this kernel of terror of a previous rendering. Ripped in pieces at the hands of the titans for the (by him) unwilled acts of hubris, a divine birth, Dionysos-Zagreus commences divine existence by this experience of the destruction of the self, the transitional horror. For it is an act of hubris not only to dare the gulf of transition but to mingle essences for extra measure. We approach, it seems, the ultimate pessimism of existence as pronounced by Nietzsche's sage Silenus: it is an act of hubris to be born. It is a challenge to the jealous chthonic powers, to *be*. The answer of the Yoruba to this is just as clear: it is no less an act of hubris to *die*. And the whirlpool of transition requires both hubristic complements as catalyst to its continuous regeneration. This is the serene wisdom and essential art of Obatala. All acts are subordinate to these ultimates of the human condition and recreative will. To dare transition is the ultimate test of the human spirit, and Ogun is the first protagonist of the abyss.

The Phrygian god and his twin Ogun exercise irresistible fascination. Dionysos' thyrsus is physically and functionally paralleled by the *opa Ogun* borne by the male devotees of Ogun. But the thyrsus of Dionysos is brighter; it is all light and running wine, Ogun's stave is more symbolic of his labour through the night of transition. A long willowy pole, it is topped by a frond-bound lump of ore which strains the pole in wilful curves and keeps it vibrant. The bearers, who can only be men, are compelled to move about among the revellers as the effort to keep the ore-head from toppling over keeps them perpetually on the move. Through town and village, up the mountain to the grove of Ogun this dance of the straining phallus-heads pocks the air above men and women revellers who are decked in palm fronds and bear palm branches in their hands. A dog is slaughtered in sacrifice, and the mock-struggle of the head priest and his acolytes for the carcass, during which it is literally torn limb from limb, inevitably brings to mind the dismemberment of Zagreus, son of Zeus. Most significant of all is the brotherhood of the palm and the ivy. The mystery of the wine of palm, bled straight from the tree and potent without further ministration, is a miracle of nature acquiring symbolic significance in the Mysteries of Ogun. For it was instrumental in the tragic error of the god and his sequent Passion. Like Obatala also, the gods commit their error after an excess of the potent draught. Ogun was full of wine before his battle at the head of the Ire army. After his dark deed, the wine fog slowly lifted and he was left with nothing but dread truth. Obatala, moulder of men, fell also to the fumes of wine; his craftsman's fingers lost their control and he moulded cripples, albinos, the blind and other deformed. Obatala the eternal penitent therefore forbids wine to his worshippers in or out of his seasonal rites while Ogun, in proud acceptance of the need to create a challenge for the constant exercise of will and control, enjoins the liberal joy of wine. The palm fronds are a symbol of his wilful, ecstatic being.

And how else may the inhibiting bonds of man be dissolved when he goes to meet his god, how else may he quickly enter into the god's creative being, or his inner ear and eye respond to the fleeting presences which guard the abode of gods, how else partake in the psychic revelry of the world when it celebrates a crossing of the abyss of non-being? The sculpted rites of the worship of Obatala are rapturous also, but lacking in ecstasy. His is a dance of amelioration to tyrannic powers, not a celebration of the infinite will of the Promethean spirit. The one is withdrawal, the other an explosion of the forces of darkness and joy, explosion of the sun's kernel, an eruption of fire which is the wombfruit of pristine mountains, for no less, no different were the energies within Ogun whose ordering and control through the will brought him safely through the tragic gulf. Even through the medium of this ecstasy, a glimpse is obtained of the vastness of the abyss; the true devotee knows, understands and penetrates the god's anguish. In the centre of the swaying, milling, ecstatic horde where his individuation is routed and he submits to a union of joy, the inner being encounters the precipice. Poised on the heights of the physcial mountain-home of Ogun he experiences a yawning gulf within him, a menacing maul of chthonic strength yawning ever wider to annihilate his being; he is saved only by channelling the dark torrent into the plastic light of poetry and dance; not, however, as a reflection or illusion of reality, but as the celebrative aspects of the resolved crisis of his god.

NOTES

1. Ogun: God of creativity, guardian of the road, god of metallic lore and artistry, Explorer, hunter, god of war, Custodian of the sacred oath.
2. Nietzsche, *The Birth of Tragedy*.
3. Obatala: God of creation (by syncretist tradition with Orisa-nla), essence of the serene arts. Obatala moulds the forms but the breath of life is administered by Edumare the Supreme deity. The art of Obatala is thus essentially plastic and formal.
4. I would render this more cogently today in terms of race origination, uprooting, wandering and settling. This group experience is less remote, and parallels the mythology of primordial chaos, as well as the rites of transition (birth, death etc.).
5. Or again the collective memory of dispersion and re-assemblage in racial coming-in-being. All these, and of

course the recurring experience of birth and death, are psycho-historic motifs for the tragic experience: the essence of transition.

6. Sango: God of lightning and electricity. A tyrant of Oyo, he was forced to commit suicide by factions, through his own over-reaching. His followers thereupon deified him and he assumed the agency of lightning.

7. In contemporary (public) festivals of Ogun the usual intermingling of idioms has occurred – the ritual dismembering of a surrogate dog, enactment of the massacre at Ire, the dispute between Sango and Ogun, Ogun's battle triumphs, etc. The note is summatively festive.

VI

Between Self and System:
The Artist in Search of Liberation

If I do not exercise great caution, I know that I may end up with no persuasive defence against some kind of declaration by a nettled European critic or artist that, 'in the early seventies, a certain notorious African playwright underwent a crisis of racism'. Certainly I am aware that my pronouncements on Euramerican society and culture have become more abrasive, less compromising, while recourse to the contrast provided by mine has tended, even by the very fact of comparison, to magnify its virtues. I hope I may yet withdraw from the brink – close to which I of course deny ever being. Culture is, however, a rather assertive environment in which one exists, willy-nilly, at all times and in all places. If there were any escape from it, it could be ignored. If culture meant what certain approaches occasionally suggest – heritage – one would visit the theatre or cinema as one would a life-size model of the Pilgrim Fathers landing on the shores of America. But if even the American people themselves have recognized the incalculable harm being done to their society by a culture of violence and materialism, it can hardly be surprising that I, who have never – in my formative years or for prolonged periods afterwards – been subjected to anything approaching such devaluations of humane sensibilities and values, will be struck by or moved to comment on a trend which percolates beyond its frontiers even as the originating society tries to reverse its trends. Well, notice it, I do say 'the society' when really I ought to say one section of society. This in itself is a clue to my faith in the redemptive potential of any society, including this.

But while that redemptive process is slowly lumbering under way, and while the counter-motions are discernible in every field and, most depressing and dangerous of all, in institutionalized intellectualism and in the creative arts, while the powerful, self-reproducing technology of transmission has become in itself an ogre that is allied to the interests of business and exploitation and grows more powerful and globally penetrating thereby, I may be forgiven for continuing to be critically absorbed by the phenomenon. Let me give an example: would anyone here dispute for instance that public exposure has already, in America, become an autonomous territory of values and ethos, meaning, in practical terms, that a very clamant culture of the 'public figure' has lately developed which is not subject to the canons of moral judgement which you and I understand? (I say 'you and I' rather hopefully, you see.) What you were doing, and how, has come to be of more relevance than: should you be doing it at all? – as long as the doing of it earns you admission into the autonomous community of the 'publicly mediated'. How else – forgive my parochialism – does an African cope with the phenomenon of Linda Lovelace, exponent of the ultimate in the pornographic decadance of capitalist society; how does she merit the attention given her in some 'serious' journals, including attempts to cast her in the same 'revolutionary' mould as the Betty Friedans or Germaine Greers (not that the latter doesn't ask for it!) of the Female Liberation Movement.

I wish to isolate one cause for this confusion of the metaphors of social engagement in the Western world, one which has begun to tyrannize over its artistic existence and increasingly poisons not only the values of the larger society but the tools of the creative individuals. It is, very simply, the novelty syndrome, allied to which is the 'with-it' hunger, the deep-seated craving for conformity in spite of loud creative claims to its contrary – individualism. To us, non-Europeans, it has become bewilderingly clear that the Western world thrives on the change of artistic fashions which are as rapid as our change of governments. In spite of the exaltation of the individuality of genius, the European artist feels safe within dictated fashion, however temporary. (The actual process of this imposition is of course outside my scope; I am more concerned with the effects.) I am well aware, needless to say, of artists of enormous integrity and talent who withstand the mainsteam hysteria and persist in 'doing their own thing'. But since critics and entrepreneurs themselves thrive on the novelty syndrome, and art has become a big business venture in America especially, we need not look further into the reasons why, between one promotion dynamo and another, the novelty gains papal authority for its allotted span of time and all theses outside it are effectively excommunicated. What is worse – as I shall illustrate as we go along – works which are outside the moment's trend but hold either the possibilities of making money, because of the author's 'name' perhaps, or provide a vehicle for an intermediary – say, the producer – are taken and distorted beyond recognition of its creator.

Perhaps, basically, the artist is an insecure being. Even when he says, 'This work is not open to dispute. I have brought it into being and it obeys no laws but those which are contained in its very process of being,' he is drawing, quite consciously, on the plausible though hotly disputed vocabulary of a special artistic community. And because, despite the legend he encourages, he is an innately regulated being, his sense of controlled individuality is enhanced by the setting up of laws which, while in some cases appearing to be of little relevance to the operations of the immediate society, are nevertheless laws. They are posed within the supposed inner truths of the universal world (i.e. transcending the immediate society) and therefore strengthen his sense of a unique status as a member of a special community. Could this be – I am trying now to assume that there is a profound cause for the ailment I have identified earlier in the

European artistic community – could it be a compelling need to renew his status, faced by the imagined rebelliousness (hostility, cynicism, contempt or indifference) of the immediate society, by revealing to that narrower world constantly novel aspects of the inner (and 'larger') world? In short, before society has time to assimilate, and therefore become contemptuously familiar with the new revelations about its own existence, to reject them as spurious or at best inconsequential, society's minority group, its 'sub-cultured', instinctively formulates new modalities of world-perception and rides, for a while, on the crest of bewilderment or brow-beaten acceptance.

If this is the truthful genesis for a cultural reality that more than baffles outsiders to Euramerican society, the explanation must lie in the contrast between such a society and others, between a society where art has lost its moorings to a humanistic shore and creates for itself an autonomous existence. It survives thereafter by creating an artifical hunger, an appetite for ephemeral reassurances which feeds on itself and is aroused from its lethargy just long enough to yawn, like Diaghilev, 'Amaze me!' To us, it seems that the modern Euramerican community has created its own Frankenstein in its own flesh, constantly demanding to be 'turned on'.

You will have gathered by now that I find that the system which threatens genuine creativity in American society especially today is not that of the supposedly phillistinic world which suffocates its genius but a novelty system of the artist's own creation to which he is now commercially and addictively enslaved. And what those who come into it from the outside, briefly or for prolonged periods, have to contend with is that tyranny of demand within the artist-critic conspiracy. Now this in itself would only be mildly irritating but for one curious fact: the Euramerican artist, even more so than the critic, expects a state of eternal stasis from the non-European artist. We will not even bother to go into the falsity of the image which our Western counterpart holds of the nature of experience in this alien artist, an image which affects him – the Euramerican animal – be it as a theatre director called upon to direct a play from – let us say – Bombay, or as a gallery owner mounting an exhibition of paintings and sculpture from the heart of the African continent. What is truly striking is his subconscious self-defence against innovatory forms from those areas of the world, he is conditioned to believe, have neither the will nor the capacity to vary those representational modes employed by their great ancestors who once whiled away their leisure by painting on cave walls, or treading out the mimetic dance around an animal fallen in the hunt.

There also, we are faced with the motives of self-interest. These areas we speak of constitute reservoirs of the esoteric which the Euramerican artist can draw upon to assuage his insatiable thirst for novelties. What would the British percussionist Ginger Baker do if the talking drums of the Yoruba were no longer the core of the musicality of the people of Western Nigeria? Or the Beatles without the Indian raga, determined to stay at the top of the commerical froth of European popular consumption? Or, right here in America, where would the American music racket be without the stubborn dark underground stream of black musicality which is plumbed again and again to irrigate the arid flesh of this continent's pop culture? With the same sacrilegious gall, we find the Tantric Art of the Orient debased to fill a slot in the commercial programming of the American artistic revelation. Stripped of history, spirituality, denuded of the totalistic vision of the self-renewing nature of the world that gave it beauty and meaning, Tantric art came into America's artistic menu in the early seventies to be gobbled up with drugs and strobe lighting for a brief self-gratification. In the meantime, societies from which these treasures were rifled are expected to remain within the same static creative mould, for millennia. 'But surely for your stage setting you will need bamboo and palm leaves,' or else 'Oh come on, the true African native doesn't conceptualize in that way.' Anyone would think Claude Lévi-Strauss had never written one word nor Levy-Bruhl undergone, after a lifetime of slander against the so-called primitive mind, a death-bed conversion. But let's get back to the artists.

When the Euramerican artist has made his pile from this passive benefactor, he expects to be able to make a well publicized pilgrimage to the fount itself and be photographed against the primitive exponents of his source material. Thus, with this new visible accreditation, having stolen a march over his rivals, he returns to squeeze the last mileage out of the now authenticated fad before it is superseded by another. As contrasted with the Beatles' pop raga, it would be interesting to know how many records the truly explorative American Indo-Jazz group have sold. Perhaps a hundred or two. But then they were not dealing with the superficial in either Indian or negro-jazz culture, nor did they take the precaution of going to meditate, in full view of cine-cameras, in the cave of a Yogi under the Himalayas. That the implications of this phenomenon are not to be sidetracked by any distinction between pop and non-popular culture is, I hope, sufficiently stressed by existing sensitive alliances (or misalliances, some may prefer) such as the Indo-Jazz group. Purists of jazz or the European classics may quarrel with the transposition of Bach into the jazz mode by the French 'Play Bach' group, but they cannot dispute the seriousness of intention and the continuing commitment to a process of discovery and re-discovery by those artists. Louis Armstrong and the London Philharmonic can get together for a moving and memorable rendition of 'St Louis Blues' and depart on their different courses without a vestige of corruption attaching to their art forms. But let no one tell me that anything of a revelation valid, moral or edifying can or even did emerge from the Beatles humping a sitar at the microphone to some syruppy, predictable lyric, tune and beat because they have eaten Indian curry for some six weeks even with the maestro Ravi Shankar, or with a half-naked guru in a Himalayan cave.

What are the implications for the alien artist who finds himself occasionally compelled to work in this milieu? Here, I draw on personal experience, concentrating on the medium in which I usually work – the theatre. And for this particular exercise I shall employ as example the production of an adaptation of *The Bacchae* of Euripides which I did for the National Theatre of Britain.

But first, a little digression. One of the tribulations of an eclectic approach to creativity – which I consider the only reliable antidote to the ever-changing establishment monomania of the artistic world – is that genuine eclecticism manifests itself more in awareness than in application. By that I mean, the eclectic mind employs for its own regulation a constant matrix of possible idioms of expression for a particular reality – be these idioms of history, politics, contemporary environment, design, social change, eating, building or sexual habits. From these various choices, it selects, evolves or recreates an apposite metaphor. But there is also a magpie eclecticism such as I have, to some extent, implied at the beginning in my tirade against the depredatory habits of the Euramerican artistic world.

The idiom of liberation (or revolution) will serve us as an example; it leads most conveniently into certain subjective experiences I shall discuss. Revolution is, I hope you agree, not what you will call an idiom indigenous to contemporary Europe and America. It never was to America (or to the majority of African states for that matter) however much the forcible extraction of independence is confused in most minds with the organic revolution of a society. Nor to the majority of European nations where the reformative, or evolutionary psyche is objectively prevalent. I will excuse myself from going deeply into such complicated questions as to when one can say a revolutionary psyche has developed in a society, how long it takes, how quickly the consolidation of a triumphant revolution can supplant it with a bureaucratic or conformist psyche, etc., etc. Where I ascribe a revolutionary psyche to any people, I speak of this moment, this decade and make no reference to its history at the time of the Magna Carta or the triumph of the Bolsheviks. Thus, it is possible to think of the revolutionary psyche of the contemporary Chinese. Or the Cuban, thanks to the slave beginnings of its nation existence, reinforced by the disseminated hagiography of the Maceos and the Che Guevaras: pick up the national newspaper *Gramma* any day and you will find a revolutionary hero or event whose anniversary it is, plus a detailed revivification of the historic moments. In Europe, France appears to qualify, and this not merely because of May 1968, whose memory still haunts the capitalist world of Europe. One can hardly think of that event, that romantic fervour and barricade intoxication occuring in England. Japan still nurses the hara-kiri complex, and the exploits of its 'Red Army', in spite of the rhetoric, are more easily classified as a mixture of that 'Hara-Kiri' syndrome and Western neurosis than as a reflection of a national revolutionary character.

And so when, in Europe, revolution as a metaphor of society is brought into the theatre, it is often an exotic animal upon which the audience is invited to gaze. It is yet another borrowed (or historically distanced) tradition which sells sweat-shirts and posters, a mould into which, when straightforward dramatic pieces are forced, bursts at the seams and exposes an unhappy scarecrow. There are of course always exceptions, although the immediate one that comes to mind took place in France which we have already conceded. Ariadne Mouschkine's *1789*, staged in the huge barn spatiality of the Cartoucherie in Vincennes, just outside of Paris, was one such memorable exception. There of course the theme itself *was* revolution, and the creator of that spectacle was a genius. Brecht created a theatre metaphor for revolutionary didacticism but not a metaphor of revolution. His genius also was undoubted and his commitment to a radical but humanistic ideology is amply demonstrated, but in none of Brecht's plays or dramatic theories are we confronted with the metaphor of revolution organic to theatre. One need only contrast his most 'revolutionary' works to Mouschkine's *1789* where the events of that moment of French history are fused, in their very progress, with the sensibility and trivia of life's reality. Revolution is made one with the activities of baking, kneading, courting, eating, copulating, death and fiesta. What happened therefore, the central event which marked this represented period as in some way distinctive from the decade that preceded it, was remarked dramatically as a heightened, even accelerated yet organic process of the human process of meaningful existence. If there was a break in history as experienced by the citizens of Paris in this event, it was essentially one of tempi: a moment's arrest of time, then an onward precipitation through the natural process of social renewal. This was the idiom of dramatic realization, and it stayed pertinent to any self-submissive audience.

But when the average European theatre seeks to re-interpret, shall we say, Shakespeare's *Othello* – an exercise I witnessed a year ago in London – through the idiom of revolutionary consciousness in Venetian mercantile prosperity, the result creaks disastrously and breaks apart. It becomes rather similar to the experience of that commerically calculating, or simply disingenuous mentality which seeks to liberate the evolutionary wisdom of the East in the strident accents of pop cultures.

Revolution, as idiom *of* the theatre and explication of Nature itself is, in my opinion, at the heart of *The Bacchae* of Euripides. The nearest effort by any contemporary dramatist I can think of is Max Frisch's *Count Oederland* which, however, poses, in its summation, certain questions on the theme of political legitimacy and responsibility which, in Euripides, are merely peripheral to the central examination of the visceral nature of human liberation. Where Euripides equates the liberation of the human pysche with a harmonious resolution in nature, thereby side-stepping, or at least subjecting the importance of a seeming situation of anarchy to the larger man-nature-community inter-related renewal, Max Frisch subjects his play to excitation via the modern malaise of meaningless violence and the diminution of human life, celebrating that cult of ego superreality which became memorable in modern times with the 'thrill' killings of the famous Darrow case in the United States and grew to fiendish proportions with the Manson so-called ritual murders. The language of Manson to his victims was, we may recall, a pastiche of the very rhetoric of social revolution that is shorn of the motivating essence of communal renewal. But it was faddish, and it still has its adherents. The idiom of revolution in modern European theatre is very much the language of Manson. You will understand therefore why, when I hear that outrageously simplistic cry of 'Culture is a gun', I feel like reaching for my culture.

But to return to Max Frisch. I would like to clarify the distinction and eliminate any suggestion that, in contrasting *Count Oederland* with the primeval ritual of revolution contained in *The Bacchae*, I thereby belittle the modern play. The basic understanding of theatre's ritual of liberation is quite clearly present in Frisch's play. A public prosecutor confronts a man who has committed what appears to be a motiveless murder. He is a bank teller. All his life he has done nothing but count other people's money, clock in, clock out, go home and plan his vacation. The routine has congealed into a deadness in his soul over the years. One day, he calls on the janitor of his bank, suddenly he recognizes that he too is a kindred non-soul, and sinks an axe into his head. Killing two birds with one stone so to speak – or redeeming two deaths with one soulful axe.

Everyone, his own defending counsel included, is puzzled at the meaningless act. The accused admits his guilt, pleads no extenuating circumstances. When the prosecutor confronts him alone in his cell however, the upholder of the law realizes too that he also is a kindred spirit. They recognize each other. Alone in his study, the Prosecutor thinks it over, looks over his papers and becomes aware that he has done a parallel thing every night for as long as he could remember. An ambiguous housemaid comes in to light his fire, begins to speak of the myth figure Count Oederland, a symbol of human freedom who descends on the social agencies of restraint and bureaucracy with an axe in hand. She persuades the Count to burn his papers. He does so, and the next time we encounter him, he is reincarnated, through the belief and longing of a forester's daughter into Count Oederland. Three policemen who ask for his papers a short while later are axed to death. The cult spreads. Axes flourish and are freely used. Finally the Count finds himself at the head of a revolution. In the last scene he is confronted with the choice of taking over the reins of government and restoring the order of papers, forms, legislation and bureaucracy, or being executed as a common criminal. The curtain closes without our knowledge of his choice. Or the dramatist's.

It is, as you will observe, an imaginative exploration of the human revolt against deathness, stagnation, the lack of renewal which runs contrary to man's viceral identity with the nature around him; an exploration which is taken to the ultimate extremism of the expression of the Life Force through a superman arrogation of the right to existence of – the other. Max Frisch is of course a moralist, and his unanswered dilemma at the end is his own moral signature on the entire escapade. What he ignores, and why his play is ultimately subversive in the deepest human sense, is that those – the non-creative, non-reflective members of the human community – who respond to the urges of self-renewal in this manner are fundamentally indifferent to the question he poses at the end. They respond at the most superficial, ego-gratifying level. They neither foresee nor desire the closing of the dialectic circle around them. Charles Manson provided the ultimate debasement of this grafitication in modern times.

I must return to *The Bacchae*. The excursion into Nowhere-land of Count Oederland was merely to emphasize the secular universality of this ritual, an idiom of liberation and renewal which has been appropriated in several bastardized forms in what one easily ecstastic critic in America has termed 'The Decade of Dionysos'. Well, perhaps that is only to be expected from the evangels of triteness who see in *Jesus Christ Superstar* or *Godspell* the ultimate in christian spiritual liberation. Being only a non-christian artist, I do not. And perhaps it is because of the recognition of Dionysos as, on one level, a universal paradigm for the artist – the dramatic artist that is, as illusionist, conjurer, agent of release and control, a medium of primordial chaos, yet midwife of beginnings – that a celebration of Dionysos becomes, truthfully, a celebration of theatre: theatre as community, as idiom of liberation and renewal. (This of course, is hardly applicable to *Count Oederland*.) *The Bacchae* is in many ways unique in dramatic literature, for here is the case of the shrine celebrating not only its origin but its very essence. And perhaps now is the moment where I should introduce that elder god Ogun who is in this context synonymous with Dionysos and who, conceptually, I have to confess I use interchangably with Dionysos as symbol of the destructive-creative unity of Nature. And now perhaps it is already becoming apparent why I find Europe totally alien to a true conception of the essence of Dionysos who, it is often forgotten, was never a European deity.

So now we come to the sad but predictable experience, a paradox which finds its roots in the deep malaise of Euramerican theatre where it is not possible any longer for theatre to celebrate its roots because the idiom of that celebration has been appropriated and trivialized by the activities of faddism. Because theatre was indeed the medium of that mono-thematic consciousness called 'The Decade of Dionysos', it proved ironically impossible to achieve the tiniest shred of ecstatic liberation on a subject that had supposedly provided the idiom for the theme of the decade. Here is where the tyranny of expectation comes literally into play. But even while clarifying what I set out to achieve in my adaptation, I must caution that this is not an attempt to extricate my own role – a full year later – from responsibility for that trauma inflicted on performers and audience alike. I have to emphasize this because, with one or two exceptions, the critics in justly consigning that production to perdition did not, with a handful of exceptions, distinguish between the script and the visual event, and even half of those who did only made the effort in order to demolish the entire undertaking even more effectively. There were the few exceptions – I recall the critic of the journal *New Society* especially with some measure of consolation – but it is quite likely that even when the text is published,* the reactions of the critic would still be the same. That really is not my concern; I am definitely dionysiac in ecstasy with merely visualizing my own version! The actual drama which surrounds the unlucky play happens to be however the best illustration I have yet of the System – as creation of the Artist Sub-culture – becoming its own instrument of suffocation and a censor of interpretative metaphors of the theatre, a syndrome which I can only liken to an incestuous masochism. It is also a testimony of one instance of the separation of a cultural milieu – for which directors and actors may act, in their failures, as litmus paper – from the interpretative medium in question.

The 'adaptor's note' which I prepared both for the guidance of the director and for the performance programme more than summarized my own attitude to the idiom of organic revolution in theatre and its expression on the stage as a ritual communion of society, The last paragraph, in view of what later developed, is particularly significant:

---

* The text was published under the title *The Bacchae of Euripides: A Communion Rite*, London, 1973, Methuen. (Editor's note)

I see *The Bacchae*, finally, as a prodigious, barbaric banquet, an insightful manifestation of the universal need of man to match himself against Nature. The more than hinted-at cannibalism corresponds to the periodic needs of humans to swill, gorge, and copulate on a scale as huge as Nature's on her monstrous cycle of regeneration. The ritual, sublimated or expressive, is both social therapy and reaffirmation of group solidarity, a hankering back to the origins and formation of guilds and phratries. Man re-affirms his indebtedness to earth, dedicates himself anew to the demands of continuity and evokes the energies of productivity. Re-absorbed within the communal psyche he provokes the resources of Nature; he is in turn replenished for the cyclic drain in his fragile individual potency.

After the production itself, and as a result of the experience of that production, I have since added, in the text prepared for pulication:

This version of *The Bacchae* has been conceived as a communal feast, a tumultuous celebration of life. It must be staged as such.

In order to fully understand some of the exchanges and anecdotes that follow, I need only add that in the preface I had also taken the trouble to indicate, very strongly, certain fundamental affinities between the already mentioned Yoruba deity Ogun, and the Phrygian god Dionysos.

Well then, to the event, some flavour of which may still be recaptured by quoting some anguished cries from the periodic notes which I felt compelled to send to the director as the production reached its latter stages – which was the time, by mutual agreement, when I first observed the rehearsals. But first, something from the early stages, just after I discovered that rehearsals had actually begun and, after a rigorous search, succeeded in obtaining a complete script of the director's adaptation of my adaptation. A meeting was held and the following is a follow-up note both to the director of the piece and to Peter Hall, the Artistic Director of the National Theatre who had, from the beginning, involved himself in the project:

Let me recall to you something I have already stated about my response to *The Bacchae*. I regard the play as an 'extravagent banquet', an expression of the periodic human need to 'swill, gorge and copulate on the same gargantual scale as Nature herself'. It seems to me that there is a reluctance to accept this definition. My emphasis is on the human; you keep putting things back into the lap of gods, game-playing gods at that. Divine enlargement of the human condition should be viewed dramatically, through man. The mode for this is Ritual. The medium is Man. Ritual equates the divine (superhuman) dimension with the communal will, fusing the social with the spiritual. The social liberation strands in the play are not therefore arbitrary but intrinsic. The progression from Eleusis to Kithairon (and vice versa, historically) is as much part of the dynamics of social change – even priesthood opportunism is part of the story – as it is a continuous human search to relate more integrally to Nature. The aspects of this exposition which Ken* for instance finds 'corny' are more acceptable to me than the reactionary god-ism which I have done my best to pare down as far as it is compatible with the spirit and genesis of the original.

I sense basic timidity in Roland's script. I am distressed that the production should not, from the beginning, give itself a chance to confront an important divergence from the original, whatever later changes are made. I don't accept the argument, put forward at the Monday meeting, that it was necessary to have a script which sets out from the start to . . . I no longer even remember what the point was. It seems to me that Roland is crippled by a narrow appreciation of the 'classic' mould – all this continuous reversion to the re-appearance of Dionysos and some form of literary summation! As if Euripides was not himself the greatest anti-classicist of them all. This is not to suggest that I am insisting on re-hashing for its own sake. (Sooner the gospels – and authorised Version to boot – than Jesus Christ Superstar: God help us!) But Roland's ability to accept, on the one hand, that the social (slave) reality of Greek society can be suggested in production without my iterative bias while on the other, insisting on his doubly iterative message of the Dionysian a-moral truths at the end, when this is more than symbolically realized in my version, seems, to me, a contradiction which can only be explained by an enslavement to the original. So why did you ask me, a playwright, in on the job in the first place? I was about to add that it has become fashionable in European theatre to relegate the dramatist's conception to some take-off pad for the director (or Artistic Management!) when I recalled that it is not my original work anyway.

Which brings me back to a realistic approach to a clearly irreconcilable position. Also the frank admission that, when I direct, I cannot stand the playwright; I always lock him out of the theatre. But I do this only after we are agreed on the central concept of the play; I don't run off a widely opposing version and start rehearsing the cast on that! I want my attitude to this to be quite clear – I consider commencing rehearsals with this version an outrage! But to the realistic approach which I promised – a reading should be held of the two versions. After the readings, you can take your own decision.

Enclosed, my immediate reactions to some of the more exclamatory revisions.

The 'exclamatory revisions' turned out to be a mild foretaste of what was to come. After atending a few rehearsals and holding a few discussions with the director, we came to a mutual agreement that, for the health of all concerned, I would stay off

---

* Kenneth Tynan, a maverick and inspired critic for the *Observer*, who was also Literary Adviser to the National Theatre.

rehearsals until the master-plan in the director's mind had had time to be made manifest. For over a month – the total rehearsal time was eight weeks – I kept clear of Acquinas Street and did not see the team at work until its 'active' phase and full entry into ensemble work. And this is what I saw in 1973 when Ogun/Dionysos committed the great impertinence of attempting to board the English stage. The scar is still fresh, so you must excuse the occasional expression of strong feelings.

One of the bastardized brothers of Dionysos, wearing the shape of Tantra, had already preceded him and was making the rounds of the artistic fleshpots of Great Britain. There was a bastardized sister too named Nudism, a deodorated teenage coquette who spent her time impersonating Eroticism. No one was fooled. Poetry of course, the flesh and blood of Dionysos, had been banished and his place taken by Motion and Business. The extent to which this travesty descended can be summed up in two examples: One, because I had expressed my subjective and intellectual obsession with the twinship of Ogun and Dionysos, the director felt obliged to introduce something from the culture from which I came; I had thought that the liturgy of Ogun which I had integrated into the hymns of Dionysos was quite sufficient. You may recall that I mentioned earlier, in passing, the debt which the percussionist Ginger Baker owes to the Yoruba talking drum. (It is incidentally a debt which the Yoruba would prefer to consider in every sense a bad debt.) During the two or three rehearsal sessions I attended, I did observe a Yoruba talking drum sitting among the usual debris of stage props. I thought nothing of it at the time, though it did occur to me that the Director might have been employing it in order to give the basically arhythmic British actors a dose of exotic rhythms. It was nothing that subtle. On the day of a run-through, who should enter upon the long *Kabubi* (!) causeway but the attendant to Pentheus, beating a two-tone rhythm to announce the entry of the King? A Yoruba talking-drum in the heart of Thebes, a two-tone march from an octave-plus capacity instrument which is actually designed to imitate the complex nuances of Yoruba speech. And that, by the way, was the one and only appearance of that alien intruder, the Yoruba talking drum.

The second point had to do again with the music, which again was intimately related to the overall conception. I should, I suppose, have guessed what was going on when I ran into a very depressed member of the cast in the bar who replied to my salutation 'How is it going?' with one word 'Tantric'. I pressed him for an answer less laconic and he added 'Tantrums'. After some persuasion he expanded the whole situation for me by swearing, 'Bloody tantric tantrums!' Well, it turned out that for nearly half the rehearsal time, the cast had done nothing but receive lectures from the director on Tantric Art. British actors, you know, are generally practical people, they knew there was only one more month to performance and they wanted to know where they would stand on the stage and when they would commence learning a definite script.

Shortly after this, I negotiated another rehearsal attendance. After all that cram course in Tantric art, it turned out that the only aspect of production to benefit from it was not even the set designing or movement, but the music. And a dubious benefit it was! Where I had called for some kind of recognizably Aegean music, specifying some compositions by Theodorakis as example, the composer had given the production a mélange of Indian and Japanese music. Hare Krishna silver bells, operated by an admittedly nubile nude, tinkled like demented fairies, drowning every spurt by the actors towards audibility. Bamboo percussions and cymbals seemed to promise the eruption of the fierce ghost of a sumarai from beneath that causeway which ran the whole length of the theatre – another oriental pseudism. But the bias came down decidedly on the side of India. Our Dionysos introduced himself onto the stage with the sign of the namaste and the lotus posture; the gestures which accompanied the recitation of his rout of Pentheus was a mixture of the dance of Shiva and Lord Krishna narrating the battle of Arjuna. Plus a touch of Kung Fu. I took one look at this peck-feast of Asian culture and said to me: Well, this is one eclectic mind that beats your own.

I have not finished with the subject of tyranny, both the conscious variety and the subconscious submission. I must refer you once again to the palpable existence of a community of pressures which takes its cues from whatever happens to be vaguely related to the artist's needs for full liberation but which, in their turn, create an orthodoxy that is in every way as reprehensible as the inhibitory society that they are meant to counter. In America, of course, you do not actually have a national theatre but you do have one or two institutions which you would say correspond to national institutions, and influence – in the more prestigious sections of the theatre – taste, usage, intellectual standards, etc. Well, the National Theatre in England almost single-handedly occupies that sort of position, and this is why it is legitimate to take note of the attitudes of those who operate it. The phenomenon I shall next describe is a very familiar one here; indeed, I believe it all started here and the States still remains its greatest champion.

We held a war-council over the disaster of the run-through we had just witnessed – Ronald, director of the play, Kenneth Tynan, literary adviser to the National Theatre, Peter Hall, the Director-Designate of the establishment and I. Those middle two are, I assure you, theatrical giants both in the fields of theatre criticism and directing. The question came up – I raised it I think – about the unappetising nudity of the Bacchantes. By unappetising, I am not referring to their natural endowments or lack thereof but to the obvious self-consciousness of the majority of them and the fact that this inhibited their movements and gestures in performance. The director responded by heaving a weary, long-suffering sigh, narrated the history of his efforts to get the girls to strip – which one of them would only strip as far as the waist, which one took it all off before she was asked, which one would only expose one breast but not both, and how Corinna or was it Josephine had been finally persuaded that there was something trendisophically wrong with her since she flatly refused to strip at all, or had agreed that she might strip on the actual night of performance, but not at rehearsals . . .!

I listened to this narrative in amazement and to the responses to it. There were these two arbiters of taste in the British theatrical establishment and their remarks were general variations of: 'What? Do you mean that in this day and age there are still actresses who think something of stripping?' and 'But really, and with a play like *The*

Bacchae? What do they think the play is all about?' and 'It's amazing how far behind the British actress . . .', etc., etc. When one of them asked, 'Can anything be done about it?' I had visions of stage-hands being employed to leap on the stage and rip the clothes off some poor shivering actress. I pleaded that (1) what would be unnatural was if *every* single one of the Bacchantes came on stage stark naked; (2) that a more convincing performance would be obtained if the actresses were permitted clothing or non-clothing in which they felt comfortable; (3) that Euripides in any case only *described* scenes in which the possessed women were naked. There was nothing in the play to suggest that the followers of Dionysos who had travelled all the way from the Afgans to Thebes had done this barefoot and completely naked. I mean, the play actually speaks of looms, so these primitives did weave clothes and presumably wore them!

The artist had become victim of his own orthodoxy, as narrow and inflexible, even unintelligently so, as the repressive situation which he set out to combat in defence of the full flowering of human expression. To berate the Puritanic principles of society, then legislate an inverse censorship that leads to expressive unease in an artistic interpretation, seems perverse and fundamentally anti-liberating. The part has begun to dictate to the whole with the result that the originator of a concept has that concept submerged under the prevailing thesis of the day. It could be comical of course, as for instance when Bernard Miles of the Mermaid Theatre in England insisted that his Desdemona must play the strangulation scene in *Othello* in the nude. The reason which he announced was that no one wore pyjamas in Elizabethan times when Shakespeare conceived the play. There are at least a dozen direct lies contained in that statement alone, not the least of which has to do with the fact that female roles were played by boys and, one wonders how a realistic performance could be obtained nude in such circumstances. I said it was quite comic but in fact it was not funny. An actress lost that acting job because she found the idea preposterous. Harold Piner was compelled only recently to take legal action against an Italian director who, for reasons of his own, decided to present characters in Pinter's play in the nude. I think I am familar with all of Harold Pinter's plays and do not *see* what role nudity has to play in them. I mean, why distract from the man's theatrical ideas by this deliberate physical titillation. It is a pity that the South African play *Sizwe Banzi* is not coming here after all. It would have been instructive to ask the audience their reaction when an actor takes his penis out from where it belonged and shakes it at the audience. I don't know, perhaps it was an over literal attempt to prick the audience's conscience. The truth is, it was superfluous, and I suspect that this piece of exhibitionism was not part of the performance in its original form in the South African setting. I had looked forward to questioning the troupe here – because when I watched the play in London, I was quite convinced that it was a concession to the atmosphere of 'total physical exposure equals totally liberated theatre' which at the moment distorts essential themes on the Euramerican stage.

To get back to *The Bacchae*, it remains a puzzle to me till today how, considering the insistence on several realisms, an opportunity should have been missed to convey one key realism, crucial to the Dionysos theme. It was strangely ironic. I shall quote from my final letter to the theatre, after I had permitted the entry into the fray of the new director of the National Theatre to raise hopes for an eleventh-hour salvage operation. That is, instead of sensibly fleeing the scene at that stage, I not only threw my energies into the last two days but was foolish enough to attend one of the first week's performances.

> Paint, viscous paint flowed from Pentheus' head on Tuesday! Roland promised after the run-through that he would get some wine. Instead we get obvious, viscous paint. Is this a school production? We get realistic, grisly innards and a mangled head but not a convincing wine fluid. Aren't the actors supposed to *drink* the stuff? Why invite the audience to burst into titters when that mixture flows out after the line, 'It's wine?'

> On the subject of the head, I think the head should now go back to what my script called for, which is a not-so-realistic head, shrouded in ribbons. I sat in the fourt or fifth row on Tuesday and it was only then that I realized that the wand which preceded Agave was knotted in the victim's guts. I have no objection to that level of bloodiness, but I did require a ribbon-wreathed head for one simple reason: it aids, visually and psychologically, the audience's acceptance of the flow of wine.

I must not permit the problems of wine and nudity to drown out the other corrupted idioms mentioned earlier. Nudity, Tantra, uni-sex, Brechtian alienation, tactilism (at present sweeping America in the so-called Liquid Theatre) – all these are theatrical idioms which the theatre artist's other face, that which seeks security by operating in a current 'tradition', constantly reduces to a state of sterility by over-exploitation and misapplication, operating within a consensus whose only criterion of acceptability is the range of extremism along that single road. In company with all this is the idiom of revolution, which was the central theme that finally wrecked, in company with many other theatre productions, *The Bacchae* of Euripides. The director of this play did an interview with a British theatre magazine – I think it was *Plays and Players* – in which he attempted to present his own vision of the play by paralleling the late President Kennedy and his prosecution of the war in Vietnam with the conduct of King Pentheus. It was, I must confess, a relevance which eluded me when he first brought it up during our preparatory discussions on the play. I put it down at the time as yet another come-on which is part of the armoury of the younger generation British artist-liberal. It was not a question of whether J. F. Kennedy was more or less villainous or reactionary than Pentheus. It was simply that, quite frankly, I could not see the relevance and felt that, like Tantra, it was merely yet another catch in the blind-man's bluff played in a maze of idioms. I was relieved to find that another journal, *Time Out*, shared the same feeling of irrelevance and dismissed the claim as pure pseudism. It was however part of the general buckshot application of the metaphor of radicalism which happens to be *de rigueur* at the moment in progressive theatre. So there we were with the Bacchantes waving the banner of revolution at the world in a manner calculated to put the world off the very idea of change for ever. To such an extent was simplification taken that (1) all the principal actors among the slaves and the followers of Dionysos were black – which, observe, is something of a feat in British theatre: the leading Bacchante was black, and the two who shared the principal role of Slave Leader were black, a reduction along racial lines which neither Euripides nor I his adapter ever indicated; (2) the sense of visceral liberation implicit in the poetry was made literal and agitprop, so that the audience were actually treated to a scene where the Slaves, in one orchestrated gesture, took off their chains and flung them into the wings. The build-up towards this had been evident in a ponderously metallic stage-set, the clanking of chains which drowned all speeches – it was a wonder that the metal grids and ramps and scaffolding did not themselves fly up into the wings to confirm the final liberation of the soil of Thebes.

I began by saying that certain theatre idioms are alien to some traditions of society. When such idioms are forcibly acquired, the result is predictably repulsive faddism and travesty. When ten such alien idioms are crammed into one production as was the case with this particular play the result is sheer bedlam. Again, we encounter the Janus duality of the artist's personality; one which, on the one hand constantly seeks to liberate his medium further, the other which dreads excommunication from the Community worse than a Spanish Catholic or an orthodox communist, is mortally afraid of not keeping up with the latest internal edict or worse, transposes the act of extending the frontiers of creative discovery to the commitment of excesses along the current route, often one that has been marked out by commercial success. The only private talisman I know of, as I have already admitted, against the limitations which this reality imposes on the artist is partly indicated by an eclectic awareness, that is, awareness of a universal catalogue of metaphors of art and the recognition that very rarely is one play accessible to more than one idiom of realization. Not every play of Shakespeare, for instance, no matter what anyone says, profits by the modern-clothes idiom of presentation. You may have a ball doing it, but no illumination needs come from that fact. An eclectic assurance enables one to take a stance of lofty indifference to the latest craze, no matter how heavily backed by the most authoritative critics, some of whom are in any case professional compromisers, scared to be considered square or purist in their profession. A study of the sociology of the theatre is probably what is desperately needed today to explore how these petty adventures in theatre metaphors came to acquire such authoritative stranglehold for intermittent reigns, what valuable works they have elbowed out of sight for lack of conformity, how many despairing playwrights have turned Count Oederlands and chased their producers with an axe, indeed, just how theatre, even at the most strident heights of its call for a total liberation of the medium, ensures the establishment of a closed Community whose tastes while they last, are monolithic and canonical.

What thoughts accompany the integrated African craftsman when he sets out to make a drum? He first of all recognizes the tree trunk as an organic member of his universe.

He celebrates this awareness in various forms, the commonest of which is the ritual of appeasement. And he celebrates this awareness in the animal also whose skin is going to provide the membrane. So when the drum is completed, when he launches the new entity into its new existence, into its new function in the affective consciousness of society, he celebrates through a poetic evocation the transformed existence of these objective manifestations of Nature. To sum up, his attitude towards these objects, even as he turns them to his use, is one of reverernce. This constitutes the holistic impulse of the African, an organic sense of unit-and-totality in consciousness which, as artist, teacher, sociologist or technologist is a constant necessity for the avoidance of alienation from the world of reality, and its selected vehicles of representation.

The human body, no less than the wood or the animal skin, is an essential piece of the integrated reality of a functioning universe of ethics and mores, and of human consciousness itself. For the creative mind from which an organic totalism is never absent, it must therefore not be abused, cheapened or exploited, not even for a self-claimed transcendental purpose.

This is very different from the superstitious attitude of Islamic religion – which by the way, whatever my black brothers on this continent believe, is *not* an African religion. The rationale behind the Islamic taboo on the figurative representation of the human body is not based on any respect for the human body or fears for his soul but is simply part and parcel of the religious mystification process – the quasi-divine attributes which the human form represents mandates in such religions a precautionary measure against the ultimate step in a logical progression – sacrilege, the appropriation of the divine form itself through its representation. This fear is a characteristic of 'received' religions in contrast to organic religions such as the animist faiths of the African peoples. But we must not get into the subject of religions, except insofar as they are a reflection of cultural attitudes. My comments about the human body I wish to restrict to its role of communication and representation, and to cultural mores which rebel against the debasement even in the service of the so-called art for its own sake and for revolution's sake.

Among the sessions which I attended yesterday were the multi-media presentation on the Aspen Academy of Martial Arts and the film from Argentina – *Alliance for Progress*. I was relieved to find a statement in the brochure of the earlier slide-show contradicted later by one of the exponents of the programme. I refer to the portion on the last page which declared that 'the philosophical and traditional approaches to martial arts in these cultures' – China, Korea, and Japan, that is – 'had been greatly responsible for the present day high level of interest (in the US)'. I had to laugh at that. The philosophical etc. approaches! However, the speaker I refer to supplied a corrective view by declaring emphatically that all one encounters in this part of the world is the commercialized and sensationalist approaches to the martial arts. Even more to the point however was the interpretation of the art of Aikido in the brochure: 'all body movements must agree with the Laws of nature; nothing that contradicts those laws is permissible'. The occasionally over-literal interpretation of this philosophy of Aikido paid visual, imagic homage to this principle. And for that reason, in spite of the reservations brought about by a moderately intimate knowledge of the contemporary American penchant for violence which finds nourishment in every culture, I could not fault the idea of this Academy. Indeed in Aikido I recognised certain principles which are kin to the African attitude towards man and Nature, a principle of harmony even in the exigency of physical violence.

Sadly, I cannot make the same claims for the Argentinian contribution. Let us begin by taking a look at the blurb which introduces this work. There would be no need for further comment if it were not clear that the makers of the film have made some false claims about the techniques of the film. This is typical of revolutionary pseudism whose favourite strategy is mystification through recourse to tried principles of art and their notable exponents – in this instance, Brecht.

> *Alliance for Progress* has the rather unique distinction of being offensive to the complete spectrum of political sensibilities. The film is banned by the right-wing government of Argentina on political grounds because it is clearly anti-capitalist and anti-imperialist and on moral grounds because of its explicit sexual scenes. The political left objects on the basis that on the one hand the revolutionary process depicted excludes the working class (in a marxist context, the makers of the revolution), and on the other because it plays primarily to the 'prurient interest' of the bourgeoisie by using sex as the vehicle for political explication. A further criticism which can be made is that it uses women, particularly their sexuality, as if it were a concrete metaphor for corruptibility. Although the film is subject to many valid criticisms of this sort, it is nevertheless a highly unique example of a reformulation of cinematic technique and mechanics in the context of making a political film.

> *Alliance* starts by replacing the psychology of the characters with the pattern of their interest . . . The characters of *Alliance* are symbols. Thus, actors must be at a distance from their parts, in order to skirt the danger of Naturalist reduction, to be able to reproduce the situation of the characters in their own social being, with objective aim of making it clear. Thus, the audience grasps the meaning of their actions, and instead of being thrilled by them compares, evaluates them. That is to say – *the audience judges*, Luduena.

And now to supplement the task of righteous demolition of the pretensions of this film from my own culturally secure premises. My essential objection to the metaphors employed in this film was in a sense stated yesterday after the McCullin picture-slide presentation on the Vietnam war, when Susan Sontag protested at the intrusion of the man behind the camera – his personal biograph so to speak – into a sequence of images whose independent statement was thereby compromised. I shared her reaction. In a moment I hope to make it clear that I was in fundamental disagreement with her and John Berger on the larger issues. I did not witness the presentation, but I thought I recognized, as she spoke, certain basic analysis which I found myself making – even as I watched the Argentinian film – about the man whose conception it all was. I found myself compelled to commence building up a *psychological* identikit of the director. That this should take place in a work which utilizes an idiom of graphic expression is not a trivial thing. And this is not to say that a similar process never takes place in works to which the viewer gives his warmest approval. It is not unusual for the mind to veer away momentarily from a work of manifest genius and say – what a brilliant mind is at work here! But the figure remains anonymous; nothing is formulated for the directing hand beyond admiration for some distant, impersonal genius. The distinction here is that, in the case of the Argentinian film, I dipped into a cultural and psychological box to fashion out a rough identikit of the director, in order to explain to myself – for I very definitely demanded explanation – why, in a film of supposed revolutionary import, the director should concern himself with such graphic images of sexual indulgence and perversion; why he should linger over them in such vicarious detail; why he should apply them in such an obviously contrived, arbitrary, gratuitous manner, so that they failed to render concrete or allegorize the state of social depravity which we assume he was trying to present; and if, finally, he was conscious of the fact that commercially pornographic films, the staple diet of that affluent predatory society which he set out to repudiate, employ precisely the same format – a transparent subterfuge of a story line for the more serious business of erotic titillation, and that with such efforts as his such a genre simply obtains a pseudo-radical badge of daring. Buried beneath it all is the sheerest skeleton of the manifesto for political awareness and social change.

This comes in the context of a holistic awareness in art or a lack of it; and holism precedes the revolutionary awareness and includes it. The debasement to which the human body, the human personality – physical and psychological – has been subjected by the exploitative decadance of the capitalist world is, I hope, something that never infiltrates the African sensibility. For the moment, I believe we are safe. There are at least a dozen excellent and a dozen mediocre films which have been made on the African revolutionary struggle by Africans, but I assure you, nowhere will you find one example which tried to promote the revolutionary consciousness of the people by accommodating the imagic debasement of the human body. I have sat on the jury of two or three film festivals in Africa and a few more of African films in Europe and, however much I may have squirmed at the amateurishness of the majority, I have never yet had cause to question the essential humane commitment of the film-makers. The Argentinian film is by contrast reactionary and decadent but its greatest crime is its pseudo-revolutionary language.

I must guard against any possible misunderstanding. I am not here speaking of the very controversial question of the acceptable boundaries of the explicit and the tacit in stage or cinematic presentation. There were for instance scenes of buggery in *El Topo*, plus scenes of lesbianism, with hermaphroditic sexual encounters thrown in for good measure. But, except perhaps as an artist in a constant search for expanding horizons of images, I was not seriously involved; *El Topo* made no claims on my judgement beyond an irritation with its occasional ponderousness and my admiration of its truly cool photography and rifled mythology. But even in *El Topo*, with its catalogue of violence and depravity, I did not observe anything like the lascivious fidelity of the camera in moments of intensely simulated sexual excitation. The buggery scenes in *El Topo* had the grace to arouse commiseration with the violated individuals – and this, let us remember, is the crux of the matter – that we are concerned here not only with the actual act of sexual depravity but with a human reaction to the violation of the humanity. *Alliance for Progress* sets out to condition us towards its acceptance – in the name of art and revolution! The commerically made film *Deliverance*, like *El Topo*, also presented us with a scene of homosexual rape, yet, without any claims of profundity, posed the degrading experience without facile de-contextualization, without attempting to inhibit a humane response. In the Argentinian film however, the very structure of the film rejected any moral considerations towards violation. The technique of Brechtian conscious role-playing was supposedly adopted, the audience given regulated reminders of this ploy throughout the film. It is necessary to assert however that whatever chance the film had of getting the audience to accept the idiom of role-playing was destroyed each time the camera lovingly played over the up-ended buttocks of both women during the lesbian scene, not to mention the meticulous detail with which the camera followed the progression of this erotic momentum to the point where the cuntkissing began. The buggery scene of the tortured insensible man aroused nothing but disgust, but wait – it was not disgust at the supposed villains of the piece, but a disgust displaced from the objective cause and transferred to the pretensions of the director who would seriously have us believe that the path to revolutionary *satori* is to be found in the forcible arse-hole of the revolutionary. I do not recognize what the orgasmic twitches on the face of a bugger-torturer in this film – and the realistic abuse of the immobilized body of the victim – had to do with alerting the audience to the capitalist menace of the establishment. As a sentient member of this public, I refuse to accept the private erotic fantasies of a film director as a testament for revolutionary action.

On a lighter note – I was in England last year when, in spite of public protests, the now toppled Prime Minister of Portugal, Caetano, paid a state visit to Britain. I must admit that, temperamentally, I find it difficult to participate in demonstrations or protest marches. I prefer other methods of involvement. On the occasion of this visit however, overcoming my sense of futility, I marched behind a banner of an African group with whose political ideas I identified, consoling myself with the thought that some physical discomfiture for the Portuguese Premier might be lurking just around the corner. When I attempted to look round the corner however, what I found blocking my view was not the banner I had started with but another which read – BRITISH GAY LIBERATION MOVEMENT SUPPORT OUR REVOLUTIONARY BROTHERS IN AFRICA. I could not quite believe my eyes. But the banner was real enough. The Homosexual League of Great Britain was voicing its support for their revolutionary 'brothers' in Africa. Heaven knows for how long I had marched defiantly beside that banner but that alliance ended pretty quickly.

Let me assure you – or if you refuse to be assured I will make my statement anyway – I am quite content that the adult homosexual, male or female, should be free to do his/her own thing, that as a group they form their own association, etc., and demolish whatever laws still act to restrict their freedom of taste. But that conscious intellectual mendacity which tries to equate the historic condition of, let us say, the oppressed peoples of the world, with a group of a minority sexual tastes whose practitioners range from blue-blood aristocracy to blue-blood Mafia – this attempt constitutes for me straightforward revolutionary subversion. This attempt to blur the lines of social motivation is of course only too fashionable in Europe and America. I shared Bobby Seale's feelings completely about the Hippie-Yippie 'revolutionary' presumptuousness – Drop out or drop dead, but don't confuse your stasis with the sweat and agony of those who are nailed body and soul to the cross of revolution! Come to think of it, wasn't it here that regligious priest declared Jesus Christ to have been a homosexual because – now watch the argument – as a revolutionary he always identified himself with oppressed social minority. Homosexuals have always been a repressed minority: therefore Jesus Christ was a homosexual! You can see where the argument will eventually take us – to be a revolutionary you must now be a homosexual. Well, maybe not exactly, but it helps.

Let me now try and restore a sense of proportion to these statements. I hope no one considers for a moment that I accuse films such as *Alliance for Progress* of being solely responsible for this phenomenon of the gradual emptying of revolutionary engagement. But it is symptomatic of an attitude of double standards so prevalent among so-called radical intellectuals. When a pharmaceutical company markets a drug such as thalido-mide and, through inadequate preliminary testing, deforms unborn foetuses, the guilty company is hauled up before representatives of us, the people, castigated and made to pay compensation to the surviving victims. Yet a so-called member of the intellectual community is able to preach the wholesale 'liberating' use of an untested drug such as LSD and be proclaimed a guru of contemporary transcendentalism. On the credentials of this 'revolutionary' commitment, which has left in its trail hundreds of minds that have literally been blown out of this rational world, he is able to find refuge in Algeria in company with Eldridge Cleaver and other refugees from racism, colonialism, etc. not to mention seriously engaged political movements. May I therefore sum up my reactions by suggesting very simply that *Alliance for Progress* is the sort of film a Timothy Leary might have made. Except of course that instead of buggery, sex and sadism, we would have psychedelic images of the Seventh or Eleventh Level of Awareness with a glamourised drug hero spattering his brains down the Empire State Building as a symbol of contempt for capitalist real-estate. Corrupt and depraved in its application, the villains would remain indistinguishable from the spokesmen of positive ideals.

The framework of my commentaries has not, I hope, been lost – the inevitable distortion of representation which is not informed constantly by the totalist awareness – man, nature, technology, etc. And it is within this framework that I find myself out of sympathy with the comments made by Susan Sontag and John Berger yesterday morning on the exhibition of Donald McCullin's war slides. I did not, I regret, witness the programme, but certain general principles which formed the body of their objections make it possible to comment on these objections. The employment of the visual image as a self-defeating overkill of communications is of course a hazard of the modern society in which we live. I cannot say if McCullin's programme achieved that negative effect, but I can say that a greater crime of social subversion, of the enervation of the active, redressive will is consistently committed through the very medium of words, especially as employed by the intelligentsia – radical or reactionary – of every community. This distancing of a demanding reality by analytical frameworks constructed by a self-enclosing community of demographers, ethnologists, sociologists, political analysts, etc., etc. has become a huge conspiracy guaranteed, by their very prestige within that community, to perpetuate the bloodless abstraction of those societal problems of critical urgency. The negative potential of a photographic essay such as McCullin's is surely infinitesimal beside the daily separation of analysis from actuality as practised today even in the so-called serious journals. I find myself taking a very opposite view to John Berger – the charitable instinct which, he claims, is the only one which could possibly be aroused by the level of vicarious experience of the photograph is precisely what is exercised today by the properties of sociological analysis from academia. The historic sense, the lack of which is complained of by both the participants in this dialogue, is the very tool by which the intellectual verbalizer of human anguish achieves the objective distance both in himself and in his audience, placing him beyond empathy, nullifying the potential for remedial action for human anguish. Political action, the commitment to political action, does not depend – and should not – on the particularization of place and time in an essay designed simply to transmit specific areas of universal experience: tragic, wicked, careless or catastrophic. To accuse a photographer of such events, of projecting a negativist outlook, is probably valid. We have a right to suspect such an outlook since it implies an acceptance of impotence in our remedial will. But to suggest that *he* offer a solution is equivalent to demanding of every member of the audience and of society that *they* offer a solution. I must repeat that I am in no position to comment on the specific objections to the method of presentation but can insist that, while the psychology of a man who returns again and again into areas of cruelty, in order to extract a personal testament for transmission, may be a subject of interest, the testaments themselves cannot, even through satiation, be considered wholly negative.

I should add that I find it rather ironic to find myself taking this position. It is not so long ago that, watching films of actual combat from Vietnam in which some journalists featured very prominently, I did find myself pondering over the real motivations of those photographers. Finding no satisfactory answer but empathizing desperately with the combatants I experienced the feeling that if I ever found myself in a fox-hole or its equivalent, engaged in a life-and-death struggle, and found some photographer so calmly pointing his objective, uninvolved camera in my direction, I would probably shoot him out of sheer annoyance at what, after all, is a grossly superior stance. It is, I concede, a rather ambiguous subject altogether, and there can be no last word on the subject.

Aspen, Colorado,
June 1974.
Symposium of Artists, Sociologists, Critics etc. on the theme 'Between Self and System'.

VII

Who's Afraid of Elesin Oba?*

Let me, from the outset, place the originals themselves in the foreground. Their sociology – often conveniently ignored – is most instructive. Innovators and creative thinkers all, Marx, Engels, Lenin, Trotsky avoided the constrictive thinking that came later with the enthronement of dogma. Their pronouncements were consequently (especially the first two) tentative, exploratory, contradictory and even – a fact so eagerly seized upon by enemies and 'hard-liners' equally – compromising. The *irrational* dynamics of great art did not therefore inhibit or frighten them; they tried to explain it, tried to *reason* the phenomenon of subjective response even to 'socially threatening' – ideologically speaking – forms of art. Their intellectual honesty led to a lot of floundering, particularly in the case of Marx and Engels, which, as we have said, has been crudely exploited by all shades of the ideological spectrum. The *total* process, however, rather than the conclusions – which are pretty inconclusive – is what should inform genuine Marxist criticism today, especially when faced with material based on social dynamics to which the ancients of Marxism were no more than uncommitted, theoretical acquaintances. Here we do not speak only of geographical, but also of historico-temporal estrangement, the *total* factors, from the unrecorded, lost and forgotten episodes and social accidents that led to the formulation of certain social patterns, to 'dialectical leap' even within scientifically obedient tempi of history; the phenomenon of 'acceptance', 'acquiescence', 'consolidation' which flout the contemporary revolutionary time-sense of followers locked within systems whose very *tidiness* is no different in quality and affective thinking than the *tidiness* of the medieval world architecture, or the pagan Renaissance that came in its wake. Historical 'data' is permanently, irretrievably and irrevocably, incomplete. (Dedicated materialists of the ideological paradise – take note!) Which is why the creative (or re-creative) imagination has any function in the world. 'Systems' may be elicited from the incomplete data,

* Paper delivered at the Literary Conference on 'Radical Alternatives', University of Ibadan, 1978.

naturally at the expense of regarding the missing, the distorted, the incomplete as non-existent or irrelevant. Not so, says the creative originator – poet or ideologue, for whom not only anterior, but potential human history remains – to his eternal frustration – 'permanently, irretrievably, irrevocably' incomplete. The only inhibition suffered by the creative originator is therefore only one of investigative humility – an equipment which appears to be foreign to the armory of the Marxystemist (the follower). A thoroughgoing reading of Marx's approach to art *and its functions* reveals the tentative, rather than the canonical approach. We shall extract some important lessons from this fact later on. There is yet another piece of sociological data which also belongs to the foreground of this paper; I shall introduce it at this point.

Of Chronologues and Ideologues

The author of *Death and the King's Horseman* first encountered Marx (apart from name) through Dr Arnold Kettle, an avowed communist who taught the novel at the University of Leeds. The year was 1955. In response to a remark in which I called his attention to the threats posed to individual freedom by any form of totalitarian state – Dr Kettle quietly reminded me of the far more devastating encroachments on individual self-fulfilment by the private exploiter of others' labour. The relevation was that simple, and total. Extensive reading followed naturally, but I doubt if I ever again experienced that sense of total illumination of the hideous anomaly of social relations in a world which I had, until then, taken so much for granted. Of course, even then I considered myself socialist rather than capitalist – my consciousness of the rich and the poor had long formulated definite attitudes about that, and the new affluent politicians with their exhibitionist vulgarity put a seal on it. It however took that remark of Arnold Kettle to make me begin to conceive society in such fundamental terms as a community founded on human labour. The effect was irreversible. I began to take an interest in Dr Kettle's circle of communists and sat in on their 'rap' sessions from time to time. I battled with an ever-growing reading list, succeeding perhaps in making sense of half. Stalinism, which then ruled the communist world, did not make communism a faith to be blindly embraced. This fact probably contributed to my immediate ambivalence. Thus, when the late Prime Minister Tafawa Balewa announced to the world that Mrs Funmilayo Ransome-Kuti had been prevented from going to a conference in Peking because 'personally, I find that communism is an evil thing', I seized the opportunity of his next visit to Europe to beard him in his hotel in Paris and demand of him just what he knew about communism to make such a ridiculous pronouncement.[1] On the other hand, I was just as certain that I was *not* a communist nor about to become one, and I soon returned the politics of my mind to its obsession with South Africa. A play resulted, such a bad one that, although it went through about four editions – on the copy-typist's machine, eating up all my precious pocket-money in clean-typing bills. I finally had to destroy it. *The Invention*, a satire on apartheid, ending cataclysmically, was little better. It went through an evening of experimental theatre at the Royal Court Theatre in 1959, together with a parcel of poems, mostly political. That same year, I participated at the

Royal Court in a collectively worked piece titled *Eleven Men Dead at Hola*, a reconstruction of the British colonial barbarity that led to the beating to death of eleven Mau Mau suspect detainees in Hola Camp, Kenya. *During that same period*, in a time sequence that cannot be guaranteed exact because I do not distinguish between gestation (the first idea, its mental formulation, amendments, re-adjustments, etc.) and final easy-birth or agonizing emergence onto the white sheets of paper, I 'wrote' and directed in London, for the Sunday Times Students' Drama Festival, the basically apolitical piece – not, however, without its socio-economic infrastructure – titled *The Swamp Dwellers*. A critic, Ulli Beier, unaware that my totally apolitical, mythological poem 'Abiku' pre-dated two sociological type poems – 'The Two Immigrants' – wrote something to the effect that Soyinka's vision had moved from the satirical to the tragic. He was unaware that both 'Abiku' and 'The Two Immigrants' pieces were written within and around and simultaneously and concurrently and harmoniously and bilaterally independently occupying the same creative period. (Oh wearisome thesisists, please note!) He remained unaware that both thematic effusions in the name of poetry happened together, on the same programme, on the Royal Court stage, to the accompaniment severally and jointly of trumpet and saxophone and African drums by Ambrose Campbell and Fela (then) Ransome-Kuti. So, even by 1960, the pattern was set. The critic had established a 'development schema' for the author which depended on when he, the critic, encountered the work in print or performance. The earlier, briefer version of *The Lion and the Jewel* happened about the same period as the 'sombre' *The Swamp Dwellers*. *A Dance of the Forests*, my first historical commentary in dramatic form, commenced gestation during that same (59/60) period, for although it was completed for the Independence Celebrations of Oct. '60, it had begun to make demands long before, as witness the composition and use of some of the lyrical choruses in the play during the poetry drama evening at the Royal Court Theatre a year before. And so on, and on, and on ... But the hidebound chronologues of criticism, in order presumably to make a point of their own, would have us believe that a writer's creative universe is some straight linear route trodden by only one idea at a time. Molara Ogundipe-Leslie throws prudence and critical sense to the winds in order to fall in line. In her commentary on *Ogun Abibiman*,[2] Ms Leslie exceeds all her previous affectation by a singularly offensive effort to sound patronizing: 'Soyinka's writing has become doubly interesting *since the writer became ideological*. His becoming 'properly' political is a welcome event for some of his watchers who have always regretted that the incandenscence of mind, word and artistic construct characteristic of the writer was not cohered by a total appreciation of society which conveyed adequately but through art, in non-physical and non-metaphysical terms how we came to this fastness in our historic journey. *We watched the expense of spirit in a waste of rage against the Kongis, the Calibans, and the Oguazors* who were but victims or products of a larger but undepicted drama which is political, historical and international in character.' (My emphasis.)

This lady would have her readers believe that a satirical interest in the Oguazors and other university social pestilences is 'frittering away' time and talent, that this is not 'properly political'. We will return later to this and similar critical bêtises, pointing out for now that misplaced pompousness is no substitute for industry in criticism. Critics to whom chronological development means so much had better understand that in dealing with literature as such, they must investigate all publishing media – journals, 'little publications', theatre, the radio and television. And finally, be a little more modest and self-retiring when it comes to offering the writer an opinion about what constitutes his 'proper' province.

1960. Back to Nigeria, to be confronted by the Marxist jargonizing of corrupt trade union leaders who sold out their followers at every opportunity. I recall only two dedicated Marxist theorists during this time – Bankole Akpata and Eskor Toyo. Gogo Nzeribe was marginal. He knew his Marx, but was no Marxist. I recall losing my temper with Eskor Toyo during the Morgan Commission Strike (1964). I felt certain that all the forces were right for the overthrow of the civilian government by a workers' revolution. He thought differently. My assessment at the time was that he was text-bound, incapable of making the 'quantitative leap' across the missing conditions for a text-book revolution. I cannot be certain today that I was right. Returned to Ibadan where we formed the 'June Committee' to raise funds, publish pamphlets and prosecute the strike. (An interesting member of this committee – simply as a footnote on historical ironies – was Tayo Akpata!) There are others who have similarly gone 'the way of all flesh'. After we discovered that one loudmouthed Marxist-Leninist, Marxist-Stalinist, Maoist-Leninist-Stalinist, etc. Trade Union leader who commanded a powerful following, a strategically located office at Mushin with printing facilities donated by East European countries, had locked up the offices and rushed out of the country to junket in the Republic of China until things cooled down, I began to develop rashes whenever I heard those hyphenated isms. E. I., one of the most active organisers in Ibadan even went slightly mad, I think. Naturally, we had not been without police attention, especially from our good friends of the 'E' Branch. Emerging from his house at Onireke one evening, he saw a police van cruising past. E. I. simply drew out his revolver, fired a shot at it and fled. Later, when I met him in hiding, I asked him why. Frustration, he said. He had felt so badly betrayed by the Lagos Marx-spouting leaders.

Back to academia – finding myself in charge of a Department in Ibadan with a mandate to create a full degree syllabus more or less from scratch, I was able to introduce what I had grown to regard as a crucial dimension in the teaching of literature in universities – Marxist criticism. I suspect it was the first time such a course ever appeared on the programme of a Nigerian university. However, it could not be taught at the time. By accident or design, the East German Professor whom I invited to come and begin the course, was never given a visa. I have since invited him here again – this time to Ife, with luck Dr Fiebach should join us in the department next year.* So much for the 'practical politics' of ideology.

---

* Professor Joachim Fiebach was Visiting Professor of Drama at the University of Ife during the academic year 1984–5.

That thumbnail sketch will do, I think, to correct a lot of ignorant assumptions. I sincerely hope that its uncharacteristic – for me – inclusion will not be misunderstood. This is, however, a largely Nigerian gathering and I have observed that in the haste to identify with progressive minds outside their own immediate polity, our intellectuals tend to construct a false or adumbrated reality of their own social milieu. The more 'historical' their claims the less factually history-conscious their analysis: I also serve warning of the end of my patience with would-be Dowagers of chic radicalism who ignore evidence of a permanent dimension of a writer's life and art in order to sound suitably and fashionably political. Since I am not a Marxist, I do not *spout* Marxist rhetoric. And when I say I am not a Marxist I mean that I dispute any form of thinking which insists on conceptualizing the *entirety* of experience through a Marxist framework. I find it childish. I have, however, had a long, questioning relationship with Marxism – in theory and practice. It is only in recent years indeed that it has become possible to hold, in this country, any intelligent dialogue with self-declared Marxists – I would say, only within the last seven years to a decade – at the most. For the former crop of 'Marxists' were – with the few exceptions – a bunch of self-serving opportunistic phonies who milked Russia, China, and the East European countries of millions of roubles and created false hopes, stoked up the fires of different ideological furnaces for the entertainment of the Nigerian reading public, leading that public to imagine that they were dangerous revolutionaries rooting in the rotten foundations of a corrupt society. Those who dared offer cynical, dissenting views were reactionary, naïve, apolitical, even CIA agents. Lawyers, university academics, trade union leaders, a handful of politicians all joined in the sordid game, fooling their Russian and Chinese backers into believing that the hour of revolution was nigh, and that more money and equipment should be poured into the struggle to ensure the triumph of their particular 'lines'. That phase, I believe, is now over. The vocal Marxists, or Marxians are mostly sincere, penetrating analysts and dedicated would-be transformers of society. Perhaps when an old grizzled politician like Chief Awolowo goes to Cape Coast University, Ghana to deliver a Marxian treatise on the basis and prospects of society, publicized in full in Nigerian newspapers, one should also exercise caution and examine seriously whether this is a sincere, thoroughgoing conversion or an effort to woo a growing generation of convinced socialists. Right now, however, our concern is with Marxist critical practice, and my particular concern is to caution against its degeneration into what Marxists themselves call 'vulgar marxism'. I actually prefer the title 'superstitious marxism'. The use of the latter expression should become clear in the course of the following remarks.

Folklory for the Avant-garde

I had proposed to ignore Rugyendo[3] entirely as being too confused and immature a theorist to merit attention. However, a recent notice on the review pages of *West Africa* indicates that he is not, as I thought, a first-year student, but a member of the Drama Faculty of the University of Tanzania. Also that he takes himself far more seriously than would be warranted by his theoretical writings – this being said without prejudice to his stature as a playwright. I shall therefore briefly indicate some typical elementary misconceptions and contradictions under which this critic labours in his efforts to evolve a theory of African drama. Rugyendo will also serve as our example of the inhibition against factual research and/or creative thinking suffered by those who choose to believe that art can be conveniently reduced to formulae. Thus, the tiresome regurgitation of the principle of partial causes for complex operations.

> While all societies had their performers and spectators, the forms of the performances were those which had historically developed as organic components of the *prevailing* socio-economic set-up, and the subjects of the performances were derived from or very relevant to the same set-up. (Emphasis mine.)

The subsequent pages naturally exhibit all the symptoms of undigested, therefore unreconcilable data. We are informed that:

> The subject of the performance might also be a popular hero, a dramatization of the adventures of a fateful heroine, a re-enaction of what had happened on a hunting expedition or the like. . .

only to encounter, in the next paragraph:

> In this context, it would seem, theatrical performances could be looked at as the forms of art most expressive of everyday human practice. And at this level too, they would not be portrayals of the whims and frustrations of individuals in society but of the practice of a collective and expressing the spirit of the same collective.

This level of uninformative padding, of imprecise projections into *facts* of the past characterize a singularly juvenile paper. And to that critical category of groping amateurism one would be content to leave Rugyendo were it not for the assertive, confident and persistent liberality with which he strews ignorance on the pages of paper. Commenting, for example, on the baneful influence of Western theatre on the development of African theatre, Rugyendo protests:

> Theatre in this respect came to us as Shakespeare, the elaborate theatre building in the heart of the town or city, the proscenium-arch stage, the well-made play and other things . . .

If Rugyendo were at all familiar with his subject he would never suggest that the theatre of Shakespeare was proscenium-arch, nor that Shakespeare's theatre could be accused of inflicting the 'non-participation' inhibition on the spectator. If Rugyendo went back to school (seriously) he might begin to understand something of the forces of concrete historic events and socio-economic changes which commenced the process of contracting the 'Shakespearean' stage to the proscenium, *after* the Age of Shakespeare. In short, it was not the Shakespearean stage which 'malformed' – during a particular period – the African colonial theatrical venturousness, but the Victorian. As a decidedly anti-proscenium stage artist, I hope to see fewer and fewer of those mind-constrictors left in the world. Yet only a singularly limited theatrical imagination dare suggest that the proscenium stage is never the perfect platform for certain forms of theatre. (Rugyendo should seek a better than nodding acquaintance with Brecht on the very point.) And incidentally, Rugyendo's glib conclusion that most African plays are written for, or controlled in the writing by a proscenium-arch mentality should serve as a warning to critics who move beyond text to 'theatre' yet ignore the theatrical genesis and progress of the plays themselves. Having directed a number of the cited plays myself both in the ramshackle space of the old MBARI theatre, in the Museum courtyard of Lagos (literally in-the-round), Ori-Olokun Theatre (Oshogbo), also in-the-round as frequently (if not oftener, by choice) as I have staged them in the Arts Theatre, Ibadan, Glover Hall, J. K. Randle Hall, Lagos – the latter groups being proscenium-arch, I am of course severely limited in my conclusions by actual experience, as opposed to the freedom of airy 'radical' speculations. In Rugyendo we have yet again another example – which I had hoped was limited to foreign critics – of the 'smart' habit of beginning with a conclusion and pronouncing facts to fit it. The actual genesis of J. P. Clark's *Ozidi* recorded *in situ* over several days both on tape and film is superfluous knowledge; the text on the printed page is apparent to any but the most untutored in the art of theatre as belonging to a genre which by no stretch of the imagination can be considered part of the 'Western' tradition. This is said without prejudice to other areas of criticism which one may level against J. P. Clark's own rendition of the play.

Lest he be accused of preaching naïve, undialectical art-form, Rugyendo pays the token lip-service of stylistic development:

> A lot of course depends on the people's tendency through time to regard such a form as the hard and fast rule for the formal structure of dramas, which must not be tampered with, as if they do not know that forms also change with changed socio-economic and socio-cultural reality.

We'll ignore the hyphenated formulae – they are presumably the only causes of changes in artistic form. Let's concentrate instead on the self-contradictions. Rugyendo would, for instance, have fully approved of J. P. Clark's *Ozidi* but,

> the main problem is that, even here, *story-telling* is not used as the base of drama. (Emphasis mine.)

While Wole Soyinka in *Kongi's Harvest*

failed to come down completely to wallowing in true African theatrical tradition . . . what we would otherwise expect is a drama whose *total form* is based on the traditional forms and with all the incidents in the drama existing within the confines of that form.

Why, I do not know, but Rugyendo conjures up for me the image of a blindman lost in night who, even when the morning sun shines suddenly on his face, clutches at a compass for direction.

A re-training programme is in order for Mr Rugyendo. Since he writes like a fledging student, a class assignment seems called for. I have selected the subject from his own obsession with the proscenium-arch. Since, however, he writes of Brecht with the warmest approval I now invite him to write a 5,000 word essay on the following theme:

The proscenium-arch is the dialectical child of Brecht's 'epic threatre'.

This is a serious exercise proposed not only for Mr Rugyendo, but for all would-be dabblers in the dangerous admixture of formalism, imagination, and ideology. All resulting effusions should be sent to Molara Ogundipe-Leslie for grading.

Myth is Dead; Long Live Metaphor?

For Femi Osofisan, my quotation with which he prefaces his 'Ritual and the Revolutionary Ethos' will do to sum up, to *reiterate* an unwavering position with regard to the meaning of ritual even in contemporary life:

In the symbolic disintegration and *retrieval* of the protagonist ego is reflected the destiny of being. ('The Fourth Stage')

Praise be, at least Femi Osofisan, unlike other over-anxious seekers of the individual-collective polarity themes, does not suggest that even this expression of the role of the 'protagonist ego' is a contradition of the collective activity. An essay, whose authorship eludes me for now, performed the incredible feat of ignoring passages in the same essay which elaborate the communal agency role of the protagonist ego. Typical of such elaborations:

The actors in Ogun Mysteries are the communicant chorus, containing within their collective being the essence of that transitional abyss. Within the mystic summons of the chasm, the protagonist actor (and every god-suffused choric individual) resists, like Ogun before him, the final step towards annihilation. From this alone steps forward the eternal actor . . . interpreting the dread essence in which he is immersed as an agent of the choric will. (And so on.)

The avoidance of that common vulgar polarism conceded to Osofisan, a terrible confusion is still apparent in his understanding of the place of ritual in *any* socio-political reality. It is a particular surprising failure, as Osofisan is additionally a poet and playwright, also one who significantly ends his essay by proposing a new mythic personage, 'not as deity now, but as metaphor', for resolving the tension between past, present and future – Orunmila. The acknowledgement of the viability of mythic metaphor for the contemporary writer – if he so wishes – is at least a beginning. Osofisan's failure to see Ogun also as a metaphor is extremely puzzling.

Now let me take the inhabitants of textual history on a short, bowlderized trip into the realistic hinterland of the poet's imagination. If, for just one moment, you can shed your clutter of pre-concepts, turn to the figure of one man in the swamps of some remote island, the lone survivor of a desperate insurrection, surrounded by the bodies of comrades and facing the stark realization of defeat. A leader. An attempted revolution. He alone the survivor. Finish. That figure was of course, Fidel Castro and the island is Cuba. That was the story of his first assault on the corrupt regime of Batista. In 1962, I actually walked the causeway which had been built over the swampy path taken by that group of brave men. I looked into the swamps which hold for ever the remains of the first martyrs of that revolution. I stood where Fidel Castro probably stood while the reel of his existence raced through his mind in one violent flashback. I stood, in other words, on a terrain that was severally and simultaneously tragic poetry and revolutionary will. That I happened to be there physically merely heightened the experience; it is by no means necessary and it contributes nothing (except maybe some realistic colour) into any work that would emerge from that if I made it my business to bring that experience into imaginative literature. Now read that passage again from 'The Fourth Stage':

> In the symbolic disintegration and retrieval of the protagonist ego is reflected the destiny of being.

That, of course, was not written as a result of any consideration of the specific person of Castro as the archetypal figure of our contemporary revolutionary times. But the moment of a mouthful of the ashes of defeat has been repeated millions of times in every corner of the world. It often ends, in real life, at the point of disintegration. My social temperament does not permit me to accept this curtailment of the process, hence my adoption of Ogun, and the reason why I point out the continuing cycle of this human experience, using contemporary figures like Castro. Is literary criticism presumptuous enough to deny that moment of total disintegration which may or may not be the prelude to social resurgence? Those who seek easy (optimistic) answers from literature are trapping themselves within the same cul-de-sac where extremist schools of European criticism of 'commitment' have stubbornly confronted opaque walls for over a century. How could Osofisan write, so simplistically, of Samson and his colleagues in *The Road*, and the Mendicants in *Madmen and Specialists*:

Their vision, romantic (sic) and mythopoeic, weakens their resources so that
instead of, for instance, organising their followers into a fighting group, for
active combat against their poverty and determination. . .

Efficient fighting forces on the pages of drama? The ultimate illusion! The ultimate
panacea for the frustrated revolutionary – by which I do not mean this critic specifically,
but refer to a disease that is fast spreading in the academic circles of chic radicalism.

I used the expression earlier: 'social temperament'. A deliberately subjective term
which, of course, would highly embarrass those who consider their social attitudes
formed only by objective considerations and scientific analysis of their socio-historic
conditions. Well, let us give those proponents their due – we will not go into the
precedence of chicken and egg – I shall save time by conceding that my so-called 'social
temperament' is not without its complementary objective study of the society we live in
and the societies we do not live in, but which do impinge on our own immediate society.
But that very study it is which enables me to repudiate *in toto* the alarmist dimensions,
the gross exaggerations and hysterical claims of subversive effects credited to the
ritualization of experience in my or any other works. Outside the confines of the
incestuous thought-reprocessing that goes on in academia, these claims have no
material foundation! Biodun Jeyifo, Femi Osofisan, Chris Wanjala (E. Africa) and
others of this school run the serious risk of beginning to believe their purely theoretical
propositions. They see it as the way it *should* be, given their phase of theoretical
conditioning – they ignore or deny the actual stage of socio-political evolution of their
audiences and/or readers of these dramas. Do I deny the *possibility* of reactionary
effects on one, two, three, maybe twenty audience readers? Of course not. That is
always a possibility. But Marxism and Maoism are no more guilty of mindless, anarchic
and counter-revolutionary violence by extreme 'Leftists' than *Death and the King's
Horseman* may be held accountable for a handful of backsliders. The revolution is well
off without these.

Ritual is a metaphor for the perennial and the perennial is not located in any one
such and such event. Birth is a perennial event, so is death. So are courage, cowardice,
fear, motion, rain, drought, storm . . . Ritual is the irreducible formal agent for event-
disparate and time-separated actions of human beings in human society. To suggest, as
Biodun Jeyifo does, that Ritual is a 'literary idealization', an 'easy victory', 'illusory', etc.
is to state a plausible direction of Ritual yet describe the entirety fictitiously. In objecting
to the 'reification' of Ogun, complaining that this leads eventually to 'the rout . . . of
true revolutionary potential' we have to point out that Biodun Jeyifo has stated a position
which we know is not borne out by the historic role of the mythopoet in society. Such
categorical distortions exist only in the 'reified realm' of literary propositions. I suggest
here that the phenomenon we have to deal with today is the divorced, hermetic existence
of literary theorists from the world of reality. In short, materialization, reification of a
choice of deductive alternatives. Certainly the deification of plausibles.

It is not a new or unique situation; the energy which is going into this phase of critical growth in our academic circles does, however, make it worthy of attention. Especially as false societies are being proposed in order to accommodate the 'danger' which is largely artificial. Femi Osofisan writes:

> The humanist asserts that a subliminal mythopoeic intuition identifies all humanity, that in every society at whatever age of growth or decadence, that progressive humane impulse – that is, *the human urge to come to terms with history* or even to transcend mundane imbecilities, resolves itself ultimately and dynamically into a continual drive to invoke the ancient communal psyche, *through a dance* – even transient – backwards into the womb of primeval chaos, into what Soyinka calls the 'chthonic realm'. Then the archetypal myths are again resuscitated, the symbols renewed, the community is again *reconciled with history*. (All emphases mine.)

Which society is this? Mine? What is this reconciliation with history? Not even *Death and the King's Horseman*, that purposefully 'unmediated' piece can be proposed as representing a society 'reconciled with history'. As for that society from whom the Ogun attributes are borrowed for my own mythology, here is what 'The Fourth Stage', where the expression 'chthonic realm' apepars, has to say about it:

> Yoruba myth is a *recurrent* exercise in the experience of disintegration, and this is significant for the *seeming* distancing of will among a people whose mores, culture and metaphysics are based on *apparent* resignation and acceptance but which are, experienced in depth, a statement of man's penetrating insight into the final resolution of things and the constant evidence of harmony . . . It is no wonder therefore that the *overt* optimistic nature of the total culture is the quality attributed to the Yoruba himself, one which has begun to effect his accommodation towards the modern world, a spiritual complacency with which he encounters threats to his human and unique validation. Alas, in spite of himself, from time to time, the raw urgent question beats in the blood of his temples demanding, what is the will of Ogun?

And what does the essay have to say of Ogun?

> The significant creative truth of Ogun is affirmation of the re-creative intelligence; this is irreconcilable with naïve intuition. Ogun not only dared to look into transitional essence but triumphantly bridged it with knowledge, with art, with vision and the mystic creativity of science – a total and profound hubristic assertiveness that is beyond any parallel in Yoruba experience.

And a final quote, in which the expressed contradictions in the various myths (of Ogun, Obatala, Sango, etc.) are affirmatively resolved:

We approach, it seems, the ultimate pessimism of existence as pronounced by Nietzsche's sage, Silenus: it is an act of *hubris* to be borne . . . The answer of the Yoruba to this is just as clear: it is no less an act of hubris to die.

It could be, of course, that it is the symbolic structure of this essay that is the problem – that would be another matter. What will always be intolerable is any attempt to suggest that the explication of social history and attitudes may not be expressed symbolically. That would be an unforgivable arrogation of functions by a minority cult of letters. But the thrust of 'The Fourth Stage' is clear enough: this society manifests the familiar Hegelian tension – that much is conveniently apposite. There is the apparent stasis as symbolized in Obatala's serenity, contradicted and acted upon when events demand by the revolutionary agent Ogun. The action is cyclic, yes, but is it claimed anywhere that society returns precisely to its original phase? Only a literalist reading would presume to equate the period of 'apparent resignation and acceptance' with preaching reconciling with history. If that is true, then the Marxist prelude phases of consolidation leading to social transformation must be read not only as preaching historical reconciliation, but as actively propagating capitalist ethics! We go further: 'Evidence of constant harmony'. Again, I suspect a problem of literalism. Unless, of course, only a declared 'scientific-socialist' vision is permitted the right to spell out evidence of constant harmony. I insist that the ideal community is possible, which is different from the declared end-goal of a communist state by dedicated Marxists. In short, the strength of any community to pursue its goals is, I propose, directly proportionate to the evidence it accumulates in the present for the assured attainment of those goals. To see the seeds of the future in present society is of a parallel analytical quality of optimism as the vision of communism.

Some attempt to claim that scientific socialism is contrary to the 'traditional' world-view of African society. We state instead that this is a very limited reading; that all socio-political systems believe in the 'final resolution of things' and that *many facets of experience in the process of catalyzing the status quo* into a new level of society are understandable and explicable through a recourse to myth. Naturally, this is not easy for some to swallow, for it says that there are other paths to exposition than 'scientific' procedures which are permanently embarrassed when confronted with formidable exceptions, or indigestable material data. 'Can the necessary culmination in Obatala harmony and serenity vitalize society or sharpen its awareness?' With what has gone on before, Femi Osofisan should now re-phrase that question and shed further uncalled-for self-anguish. 'Continutiy . . . of the past?' demands Osofisan. Answer: continuity of human society – which, as we have stated, is the battleground of change. The selective pessimism of Osofisan is very strange and certainly uncalled for in the essay under reference. Or is he saying society will only be satisfied if the death of Sango spelt out socio-economic improvements for society? If so, society has a very long wait ahead of it. 'What element, in the particular moral order of the society, is auto-dynamic, capable by itself, to provoke revolution. This is the heart of the problem for us.' Not for me, I'm afraid. Nor will I seek that answer in the play *Oba Koso* since the play nowhere provokes the question.

I return to Femi Osofisan's society whose conception appears to trigger off his fears:

> Because the animist world accomodates and sublimates disaster within the
> matrix of ritual, the Red Indian world collapsed, and so did ours, perhaps
> with slower speed.

This analysis does not match the facts of history. The Red Indian and our world collapsed because of technological deficiency. Let us not play ellision games with history. The conquest of the Incas by the Spanish is our classic example of one elaborately structured superstition confronted by another. Cortes won by a mixture of superior armoury and wily politics – formulating alliance with traditional enemies of the Incas on a terrain that was clearly disadvantageous to him. Superstition, within which I, at any rate, group 'animism', 'buddhism', 'roman catholicism', 'islam', 'protestantism', etc. etc., has never yet prevented the rise to technological heights of any society. Other factors must be sought. A little more gunpowder and not only the natives of South America, but their brothers in the North would have wiped out the white invaders. When Femi Osofisan claims, *à propos* of these false premises therefore, that the 'art that stubbornly weaves around the old mythologies, *unmediated*, prolongs the enfeebled past and is anti-progress', the question has to be asked: prolongs the past for whom? Whose revolutionary commitment does it sap exactly? Whose enfeebled *present* is it that is so threatened that it cannot take a poetic excursion, once in a while, to an *unmediated*, hermeticized moment of history, as lived, thought, experienced, and debated by the personae *of that moment?* Is it by any chance this present in which atomic scientists still go regularly to Roman Catholic Mass? Is it some special dispensation in the theory of unmediated-past, anti-progress equation which concentrates, among the adherents of one of the most unliberalized religions in the world – the Judaic – such as unfair proportion of scientific geniuses in the world? I am surprised to see that *Death and the King's Horseman*, staged at the University of Ife, has not prevented the basing of an Atomic Commission at Ife, any more than it has prevented the agricultural workers from jumping onto their tractors in Operation Feed-the-Nation.

I suspect that my impatience is beginning to show through, so let me 'mediate' this attitude by a declaration from my habitual projecting mind. In short, I claim that I already see the real danger of attraction of extreme alarmist positions which will be exploited (as has occurred in other socialist convulsions) at later stages in the revolutionary progress of our society by those to whom conformity – in every sphere of human activity – is a condition of power or the exercise of power. If that battle is to be joined later, let it begin now, while we are still far removed from the urgent, sweeping demands of revolutionary *acts*! We are already at a stage where rote is replacing perception and penetrating insights, where brilliant essays are being flawed by the contrived insertions of Pavlovian codes from elementary Marxist texts.

When art ceased to imitate life, it did not thereby aspire to imitate ideology: while criticism which fails to emulate life ends up as imitation of art.

In clarification of the above, 'emulate life' is used in the sense of making criticism subject to the interacting processes which we observe in life – in its totality, not hiding away from uncomfortable modes of realities or wishing them out of existence. In other words, not 'running away from life'. 'Imitate life' is of course the traditional objection to pallid reproductions, one-dimensional photographs. The danger is greater for criticism since Art confessedly elects its area of attention, its manageable scope for re-creation, while Criticism pretends to draw from the *entire* principles of life in order to penetrate the elective scope of Art. The most cursory reading of any of the schools of criticism, and most especially of Jeyifo's justly represented triad – Aristotle, Hegel, and Marx – confirms this.[4]

Criticism imitates art when it attempts to force all works of the imagination, including 'historic re-creation', into laws of its own hermeticization of the world. This may, of course, be a good or a bad thing – but let that fact first be recognized. The sociology of critics and/or criticism, therefore becomes doubly of interest and significance. As, for example, the original canons that form today's armoury of Marxist criticism, did they start out as part of the body of Party directives, becoming appropriated into 'objective' analyses of the relation of Art to society, losing, along the way, important reservations by the formulators themselves on the Nature of Art? Vatic certitude, absolutism and comprehensiveness, adopted for action at a particular moment in history, deliberately *suppress* uncomfortable deductions in over-all interest of a Cause. This we know as heavily documented historical fact. The questioning processes of the originals – Marx, Lenin, Engels and Trotsky – therefore offer greater illumination on the creative universe of the artist than the narrow schematism favoured by their followers. And this illumination comes, I find, not so much from the actual pronouncements, as from their 'history' or, to use my own prefered expression, the *process*, for this last brings the distanced intelligence into the formulative picture, not as a passive receiver, but as a reconstructing strategist of *his* world. Thus, for the narrow-schema approach, it is enough to evoke the authority of Marx in the familiar quotation:

> The ideas of the ruling class are in every epoch the ruling idea; i.e. the class
> which is the ruling material force of society, is at the same time its ruling
> intellectual force ... The ruling ideas are nothing more than the ideal
> expression of the dominant material relationships, the dominant relationships
> grasped as ideas ... (p. 15)

But suppose, in addition, we mediate this crucial analysis with the following (or a thousand equally valid examples):

According to the materialist conception of history, the determining element
in history is *ultimately* the production and reproduction in real life. More than
this neither Marx nor I have ever asserted. If, therefore, somebody twists this
into the statement that the economic element is the only determining one, he
transforms it into a meaningless, abstract and absurd phrase. (Engels in a
letter to Joseph Bloch, 1890)

The obvious mediation involves the critic in the *process*, which alone – not the literal
application of one or the other elicited principle from material reality – can lead to a
true understanding of the nature of Art and Ideas *in any given epoch*.

Concerning *Death and the King's Horseman*, the attempt to stretch its horizons beyond
the demonstrable intent of the author only contracts its universe into the schema of the
critic. The truly creative writer who is properly uninhibited by ideological winds, *chooses*
– and of course we can speculate on the sociological factors involved in this choice ad
infinitum – he *chooses* when to question accepted History – *A Dance of the Forests*; when
to appropriate Ritual for ideological statements – *The Bacchae of Euripides* and equally,
when to 'epochalize' History for its mythopoeic resourcefulness – *Death and the King's
Horseman*. In the last event, he deliberately eschews distractions from the mythopoeic
intent, especially such as happen to be fashionable, reserves its innate intellectual
muscularity for the deductive mechanism of the audience or else locates it legitimately
in the *dramatis personae* of the period and locality, in the 'probable' events of the period,
the 'probable' courses of those events and sometimes, even in the 'probable' resolutions.

Biodun Jeyifo's concern with the historical emendations of the play belong in the
same category of one of my professors at Leeds University who, on reading *The Swamp
Dwellers*, queried: But do your peasants think in such sophisticated terms? Jeyifo's
approach is, of course, the obverse: why do not your 'peasants' (substitute 'exploited
classes') speak, act, event-wise relate and generally conceptualize in a 'sophisticated'
ideological idiom (substitute framework)? My answer to the former was: Yes, they do
speak in such 'sophisticated' terms, they do conceptualize and give verbal expressions
to the resulting concepts, but – they engage in this routine exercise in their own
language. To the latter, I respond: No, they need not, for they already possess their own
organic language of experiential and history-summative understanding. Inadequate? Of
course, from the contemporary advance of human knowledge. But adequate at *their*
level of world and self-apprehending. The artist or the ideologue is quite free to
reconstruct History on the current ideological premises, and thereby prescribe for the
future through lessons thus provoked. But to insist that the *personae* of History
conceptualized experience anachronically is a presumption that offers no *exclusive*
orientation to the creative mind when it confronts an unarguably timeless phenomenon.
Such as Death. Valid or invalid though our reconstruct may be, it is of no consequence
to society *in its particular epoch* confronted with the problems of ameliorating an eternally
tyrannic negation of its will to being. The collective phenomenization of death is one
such ameliorating device. It is not only worthy of study or presentation within its own

terms; it confronts the arrogance of ideated systems with the authority of the irreducible. A study of society, even of contemporary society, reveals that Man resorts to the strangest devices for nullifying that unanswerable nullity of History, progress, materialist certitude, etc. *as experienced*, in the phenomenon of death. Now that is the ultimate, imponderable dialectic over which tragic poetry builds its symbolic edifice. It is better than nothing, and *nothing* is precisely what is offered even by the most radical and humanistic systems of world or self-apprehension, faced with this one definite human experience, and of its surrogate relations in the 'tragic' fortunes of the individual in socio-political contexts.

In other words, the desire 'to put off Death', 'to come to terms with Death', to 'communicalize' Death so as to make it more bearable for the individual, 'to humour Death' (a quasi-magical propitiation), these are all social and individual devices and of course they make for untidiness in 'scientific' systems, so they have to be wished away. Now the actual forms which such devices take can of course be translated in terms of property and productive relations, etc., the most direct expressions of which have been the slaughter of slaves and retainers, mummification, domestic animal cult, *egungun* and other court-originated cults, etc., etc. The poet, especially the mythopoet, is not entirely satisfied with that secondary level of forms of inventiveness or appropriation, however, and, while he deals in concrete manifestations, may choose not to further reduce the original primordial fear by new extra epochal analytical games. For that is to move away from the mythopoeic source – and for no discernible illuminating results from the specific poetic enterprise. Nobody, I hope, will tell us that the fear of – or at the very least, the *resentment of, sense of unpleasantness about*, etc. – death is simply due to the failure of the individual or society to as yet exist within an egalitarian environment. My suspicion is that this need to communually contain Death will always be there. Whether indeed the desperation with which this primary (human) hostility to death is sublimated under historico-materialist incantations is not in itself a superstitious device for evading the end of the material self is a question that can only be resolved by a deep probing of the critic's deeper subconscious. Certainly it leads easily to a tendency towards 'vulgar Marxist criticism' or, in this context, superstitious Marxism.

To substantiate the above, the paper by O. Onoge and C. G. Darah: *The Retrospective State: Reflections on the Mythopoeic Stage at Ibadan* should be contrasted to Jeyifo's essay. The comparison is most telling. The former is deeply conscious of a creative universe, however scant the lip-service the authors pay directly to it, while Jeyifo remains locked exclusively within a system where all properties of art that do not fit into it become evidence or reaction of bourgeois art. There is something very disqueting about the attempt to import wholesale the Stalinist-Zhdanovian line into Marxist criticism here, with all the sterile dogmatism of the hideous machinery of Proletkult! To return to the central axis of my historical emendations, around which Jeyifo's principal strictures are constructed, here is an alternative reading of history as material of creative presentation:

The District Officer has not been invented for the purposes of this reconstruction – that much of course is easily proved. His sociology therefore, insofar as it informs his attitudes to the colonized society, has not been invented. The District Officer and his world, in short, have *provoked* the argument of the drama. Furthermore, unless that District Officer is imbued by Jeyifo with a greater socio-political habit of analysis than *I* am prepared to credit him with, the motivating factor for his action, his interference is squarely and hermetically posed within the simple confrontation of 'civilized' values versus the 'barbaric'. Within those terms, the location of Olunde in wartime England, as opposed to Ghana (then the Gold Coast), is a legitimate device to equalize, *precisely within those terms and none other*, the claims of a 'civilization' which, historically speaking, has persistently incorporated no less barbaric usages into its social organization – the slave trade is one obvious, emotive example. My circumscription of the possible areas of 'argument', my rejection, for instance, of the option to make Olunde reject suicide because of 'overseas' enlightenment is a creative prerogative, logically exercised, since I have no wish to demonstrate that the colonial factor is ethically superior to the indigenous. Fastening onto the use of the concept 'honour' is an exaggeration which merely obscures the issue. The concept of 'honour' in that Oyo society is, for this dramatist, precisely on the same level of honour, mission, duty, as revealed in the imperialist ethic that brought Europe into Africa in the first place. Yet even here, the historic personae will – probably again – pose an unexceptional view:

> ELESIN: Even the honour of my people you have taken already; it is tied
> together with those papers of treachery which make you masters in
> this land.

When a mere word is used to do service for a number of differing concepts, acts, situations, etc. the exclusive attribution of one particular concept of it to the author is a fraudulent act by any critic. But does it merit such attention at all? A very possible reading is one of a portrayal of characters in a historical situation with differing and conflicting senses of 'honour', 'duty', etc. Perhaps such a reading is too prosaic since one side rhapsodizes 'honour', while the other (Pilkings and wife) merely castigate it in plain prose and action. A society whose usage, even in 1977, is to lyricize *guguru* in the streets of the city now creates ideological problems because, in a ritualistic encounter with Death, they reach into their deepest mythopoeic resources for an 'ultimate' experience. We must keep away from selective readings which lead to libellous assertions such as, 'the kind of *honour* which Soyinka deploys in *Death and the King's Horseman*', etc.

The actual language used in criticism is of course extremely revealing as a gauge of the critic's commitment to 'making a case' as opposed to objective commentary. 'It is illustrative of the gaps and dents in Soyinka's present ideological armour that he selected *this* particular metaphysical and philosophical order to symbolize African civilization, etc. etc.' *Selected* is of course not a chance word, any more than 'symbolize'. This slice of Oyo history has floated in and out of my creative consciousness since 1960. Once or twice I had been on the verge of writing it but other more pressing themes intervened. As Femi Osofisan pointed out in his own critical observations, a year's Fellowship at Churchill College, Cambridge, 72/73 finally provided some uninterrupted leisure. The actual triggering event was a bust of Churchill on the stairs in the college named after him. The history came back; the play was written. So much for *selection*. Now for *symbolize*. If a world has been deliberately re-created with little or no recourse to actual history, the author may indeed be held suspect; here, the 'symbolic intent' requires proof. Without it, the charge remains a wild presumption of intent. I find it particularly ironic when I recall that Ulli Beier actually suggested to me that history of Oyo as a usable theme for the Independence Celebrations Drama Competition in 1960. I preferred instead to write *A Dance* which, as fabricated history, may be more truthfully held to indicate any deliberate attempt to symbolize African civilization. Even without benefit of that knowledge, the existence of *A Dance* should have curbed this and other generalizations of dubious accuracy. At the moment I feel no particular anxiety about the possible corruption of the African will to egalitarianism through an 'unmediated' play such as *Death*. If any school of thought accepts the opposite, I suggest that this is because they are living almost wholly on the pages of books and are divorced from the *totalist* reality of African political consciousness within its active history, or underestimate the responsive intelligence of the general readership masses who are not locked within the reification realm of literature. For here we are once again back to that basic factor: the sociology of the critic.

Marx, Engels, Trotsky and Lenin were revolutionaries of the total society. I hope we do not need to spend any more time in libraries to have it accepted on all sides that, for every statement which can be used on behalf of the Stalinist-Shadnovian school of literacy culture, an equally weighty number can be adopted for the view that the critic owes serious obligations to the creative universe of the artist at work. The artist will continue to speak in his own voice; hopefully someday, the critic will learn to do the same.

Satire is Dead: Long Live Pedantry?

Thus at least Molara Ogundipe-Leslie would have it, who pronounces the satire of academic models of superficiality and false values a 'waste of rage' unless, of course, the satirist reveals, simultaneously, a consciousness that such targets are products of a 'much larger complex of history and economic forces'. Is this some form of anticipatory pleading on behalf of pedantic criticism? I must warn critics of this school that if they insist on laying themselves so pompously open, the puncturing needle of satire will be applied in all its corrosiveness without any dipping in the palliative broth of socio-economics. Any neophyte teacher of literature should know that, from Aristophanes and beyond to Baba Sala,* the art of the satirist does not entail a recognition of 'extenuating circumstances' – historic or socio-economic. It is possible of course that Ms Ogundipe-Leslie is pleading for a new definition of satire – that esoteric endeavour

---

* A popular Nigerian (Yoruba) comedian. (Ed.)

should be made clear and submissive artists programmed in the new art form. Until then, when Baba Sala chooses, as he has done recently, to treat with his iconoclastic eye the tragi-history of those same events of colonial Oyo, I propose to continue to enjoy the obverse face of my own tragic interpretation, without any regrets for the absence of prevailing or more fashionable 'extenuating circumstances' of history or socio-economics. And it is my conviction that the thousands of non-bourgeois pleasure-takers in this spectacle of wit and slapstick humour will find strictures on their unmediated, 'malicious pleasure' as boring, limiting and contrived as I do.

As with the motion towards absurd reduction, so with the opposite motion towards tragic elevation. Neither obeys any mono-chromatic or uniperspective law of post-facto analysis. If we sound warning here of literary warfare it is not merely because criticism – dealing with general principles and theories of creativity – has gone beyond its competence and dared to enlarge upon the 'legitimate' purlieu of imaginative projection, sealing off areas of uncomfortable (for the ideologue) verities – but because, being such a comprehensively *historic* consciousness, as opposed to the narrowly, conveniently selective and submissive ideophyte of history, I recognize the commencement of the destructive pattern which the first Socialist Revolution set in motion under the arch-paranoid Stalin, to the disgust and self-doubts of Lenin himself. If the REVOLUTION means the formulistic denunciation – as bourgeois, subversive, elitist, cloud-bound etc. etc. of works such as *Death and the King's Horseman*, then the Revolution cannot come too soon, for it has always remained my firm belief (from observation) that in *practice* revolution has to do with power, with the power-instinct in various shades and forms, with the *security* of power, and its exploitation. And it is not enough to say that there is no party yet; a Marxist commitment does not wait upon the formal structure; the party's coming-in-being gives expression to claims on its behalf, a fight for life extends to *all* fronts, anticipating and giving battle to autonomous thought-directions. In other words, when it is found that the *substance* of ideological conviction is equal on all essentials, theoretical cleavages emerge to narrow the pyramid of vocal identification, to contract an equilateral participation to the isosceles, until finally the apex sheds all dimension, is lost in ideological clouds, from where it rains and thunders down on the 'impurer' souls below.

Hysteria is, as we know, contagious. In the claustrophobic world of academia and Party intellectual caucuserie, ideological hysteria soon acquires the rage of an epidemic. The signs are already present and it is time to call to our aid the 'mediation' of the unglamorous 'sense of proportion' which resides in the world of reality, in a permanent awareness of society as total. If, in a moment of society – to return to our concrete example – even the legal superstructure makes of suicide (by pact, ritual, calculatedly provoked, etc.) a criminal offence, if beyond a few hidden, clandestine pockets of atavism, a society even considers suicide cowardly and ritual suicide an embarrassing recollection, the artist, encountering such material of the past, cannot feel he endangers society by exploring the synchronistic drama of such events. Nothing but tilting at the windmills of reaction can justify any sense of alarm at such a creative exhumation. My sense of this level of critical passion is that the real world does not yield enough ogres, and recourse must be made to inert historical scarecrows, suitably blown up to ideological dragons.

NOTES

1. This episode, with its many amusing asides, took place in Hotel Claridges on the Champs-Elysées and will appear in detail in some future narrative. For now it is sufficient to add that I did not discover until some months later that my encounter had been, not with Tafawa Balewa at all, but with the late Northern Premier, the Sarduana!
2. Molara Ogundipe-Leslie, 'Ogun Abibiman', *Opon Ifa*, Ibadan, 1976.
3. 'Towards A Truly African Theatre: A Study of the Use of Some Traditional Forms in Kigezi and Ankole in South-West Uganda', seminar paper by Mukotani Rugyendo, University of Tanzania.
4. Biodun Jeyifo: 'Tragedy, History and Ideology: Notes towards a Query on Tragic Epistemology,' Seminar Paper, University of Ife, now published in *The Truthful Lie*, London, 1985, New Beacon Books, pp. 23–45.

VIII

Language as Boundary*

I have chosen the above title for this paper largely because of recent events of a familiar pattern which have again occurred on this continent – I refer to the expulsion of Nigerians and other nationalities from countries in Central Africa. It is the same as the title of a paper I delivered in Dar es Salaam in 1971 and the contents overlap in some aspects. I feel it is time to go back to the subject – or more accurately – to this specific approach to the question of language because what happened in the Republic of Congo brings up once again the question of boundaries on this continent, and one of my contentions, any time that the problem of a continental belonging is raised directly or indirectly, and in any form whatsoever, is that of all of the forms of boundaries known to man, encountered by him as an act of Nature, created by him for reasons or unreasons of his own, or imposed upon him through the innate conditions of his own struggle for development and fulfilment, language as boundary is one of the most persistent, insidious and tragic. It is not through a wish to sound portentous that I ignore the comic and ludicrous effects of the linguistic boundary; it is simply that they are only good for belly-laughs and, once that is over, humanity finds itself face to face with the vengeful other side of that comic coin. In short, the need for a solution, for corrective strategies, never recedes.

Now, certain shades of ideological opinion prefer to insist that class as boundary is even far more dehumanizing and socially dangerous. I agree. Indeed it is impossible *not* to agree. But it seems to me that even in societies where boundaries in their class colouring have been erased near-totally, or at least blurred to indistinction, the separation syndrome crops up time and time again, and in increasingly bitter forms. Contemporary reality – and I am speaking here not in any time-slack sense but of *now*, today, this very moment – this contemporary reality, manifested in societies as ideologically apart as the United States and the Soviet Union, teaches us very simply

* Lecture delivered in Kaduna, 1978, at a conference on a National Language Policy.

that, for reasons which cannot be totally explained, man's linguistic self-affirmation and separation refuse to go away, re-surface even after the harshest repressions and must be confronted. Not so many years ago the greatest ambition of the Puerto Rican was to merge with his larger American society so thoroughly that he tried to speak American like John Wayne. Today, not only does he retain his Latin accent, he has compelled the state to broadcast radio and television programmes, regularly, in his native Spanish. Similarly, two or three years ago, the Bretons virtually went to war with France over their demands that their native language become the educational and official language of their region. You are quite familiar with the Welsh movement. You need only drive into Wales to see how fully the Welsh language has been thoroughly resuscitated and integrated into both the mundane and elevated activities of that society. What you may not recall is the amount of violent political activities that won it official recognition. Canada is on the brink of secession, thanks once again to the language issue. Of course, there are related factors. The class cleavage in that society appears to correspond more or less with the linguistic division, just as, in Northern Ireland, it corresponds for historic reasons, to the religious. Those crucial elaborations must be noted. Yet it needs to be equally asserted that linguistic solidarity in Quebec cuts across class stratifications; that it was a middle-class, more than affluent leadership which led the 'secessionist' Parti Québecois to victory; and that its very first major act on achieving power was to legislate that French become the official language of education. This in a country which carried the policy of bi-lingualism to such an extent that even notices in public utilities such as 'Please flush after use' are printed in French and English. The Québecois, a minority people among all of Canada, have put up determined barriers even as the central parliament had all but effectively removed them. Let me round up the rough survey with the case of Russia which, a few years ago, succumbed to pressures from the Ukraine, Georgia and one or two other Soviets whose names I forget, and granted them their own linguistic autonomy. Today, the business of those Soviets is conducted in their own languages; literature, the arts in general have, it was noted, flourished noticeably under the new dispensation. No slackening has been reported in the struggle for the triumph of socialism in the Union.

Back to our own continent, after barbaric usage from the bankrupt, 'dialogue' government of Busia, after the even more horrendous experience of Nigerian workers and other migrants at the hands of the black Count Dracula, Macias Nguema, after falling scapegoat to the unabashedly capitalist and corrupt government of Mobutu Sese Seko, after ... after ... after ... the Nigerian, in company of other unfortunates from other countries from West Africa, is bewildered to find himself once again at the receiving end, this time from a progressive, self-avowed socialist people's republic – The Congo! Now, let me avoid any possible misunderstanding. Whatever was the cause of this brutal expulsion of fellow Africans, it was *not* the probable inability of the expelled persons to speak French. It was not even the possible fact that they had failed in the meantime to speak the local languages. But I think we will all agree that those social handicaps, and the fact that, among themselves, they very likely speak their own languages, did mark them out as alien. Audibly at least. Visibly, they probably also looked different, especially if they had tribal marks on their faces. But verbal communication is the most penetrating means of identity within a community. A non-verbal man, except of course those very remarkable and exceptional individuals who, as we say, literally radiate the force of their personality by their very presence, a non-verbal man is equivalent, roughly, to a piece of inert utensil. I exaggerate of course but I'm certain you will concede some measure of truth in this. When it comes to those reacting attitudes within community large or small, it is largely what we hear that defines, that marks out and identifies the alien. 'Be seen, not heard' just about sums it up. To conclude: the degree of linguistic assimilation of any group within a community inversely affects the level of potential animosity which the community can evoke against itself for whatever reason: success in trade, monopoly of social positions, etc., and thereby lessens the probability of hostile action by the community.

Just one example to buttress my rating of this aural dimension. The Ibadan accent is, I know, to many Yoruba the butt of many linguistic jokes. It is certainly an accent and a dialect that you notice. In 1952 – I remember the details because I had gone to collect scholarship forms – I was at the Ibadan Secretariat when I heard a man speak to someone in the furthest-out Ibadan accent I had ever heard. I turned round involuntarily and was surprised to find no sign of the speaker. I continued along the corridor when the same voice resounded. I turned; again no one, yet the voice could have come from nowhere except from that corridor. As I stood pondering the strange phenomenon, the voice rang out a third time; only then did I notice the white man leaning over the balcony, giving orders to someone below. He was a full Caucasian, not even tanned. I found out his name and have never forgotten it – one Mr Kitto. I think he had lived in Ibadan for ten, twelve years – I forget that detail. Well, that is how effectively aural perception colours the visual – not surprisingly, since both forms of signal are interpreted by the same brain. And while no one would claim seriously that the policies of government are governed by the audio-visual sensors of officials, the truth is that the data which are fed into their basic statistical machines are gathered by human beings and coloured by their attitudes to 'aliens' which of course presuppose the process of group-identification. And, more pertinently, the executors of government decisions are the very members of the community whose subjective definition of aliens has been created by this very process. I sometimes encounter a Ghanaian who witnessed the summary expulsion of his or her neighbour Nigerians. Even when that Ghanaian has defended the policy of his government, he has been astonished and embarrassed at the gleeful participation of the local Ghanaians in the rounding up and expulsion of Nigerians of even a generation's next-door familiarity. Clearly, the triggering decision is not of one moment but of the entire length of their co-existence – the implantation, that is, of a mutual separate identity. At the very least, language is *one* of the key factors in embedding that separatist definition in social consciousness. The result, whenever the excuse is afforded from whatever direction, is the breakdown of the tenuous links of daily cohabitation, and the sudden resurrection of boundaries between linguistic groups.

We will not dwell on the lessons to be derived from our own internal experiences, only insist that it would be an extremely foolish or merely mischievous mind which fails to take our recent history into consideration in the mapping out of national linguistic strategies. Now, we must move from the realms of catastrophe and tragedy to some light relief – a very brief excursion into tragicomedy.

Five or six years ago, in the capital of a French-speaking West African country, a group of black statesmen-intellectuals gathered themselves together to confer on ways and means of preserving the purity of French language and culture. Black, African leaders of self-styled independent African countries. They came together with a representative of the French government and one or two members of the Académie Française. It is not clear what overriding fears, motives, ambitions or principle of self-denial created this urge to spring to the defence of an imperial tongue, especially one with a long history of cultural repression, one whose cultural vanity and linguistic superiority was already considered over-inflated even by her fellow European nations. That gathering met again recently, and on the same subject. I believe that one or two of those leaders did come to their senses in the meantime and dropped out. However, the question must be examined – what are their motivations? Could it be simply a fear of linguistic domination by yet another group of language-borrowers – the Anglophone Africans? I had begun to imagine that the message had become clear to all the world that the majority of English-speaking nations regard the language they speak as being nothing more than a tool of convenience, to be discarded whenever something more self-belonging was made viable. What was particularly ironic about the more recent conference was that the French visitors were at great pains to point out that the initiative for the Conference had come from the African leaders themselves. Maybe they were embarrassed at this persistent anachronism or merely wanted to put the French-Afros in their place. Maybe they were anxious to assure the world that, on their part, the French had given up on cultural imperialism. (By the way, they have not, as we shall come to see in a moment.) However, the conference did take place, has taken place twice in the last five years, and will probably recur once more in this decade. It only remains, I suppose, for the ex-Portuguese, the ex-English colonies, the ex-Spanish to appeal in retaliation to our former colonial masters to sponsor or attend 'rival' linguistic conferences on their own languages for the madness to become entire, making several *cordons sanitaires culturels* zig-zag their way across the continent. And now to melodrama.

That language is incorrigibly political in addition to anything else was very crudely illustrated by the recent election into the West African seat of the Security Council, our own Nigerian being one of the two contestants. I was in New York during the preceding week of feverish campaigning; I had business with a UN Agency there, so I am able to provide you a first-hand eye-witness ear-glued summation of the lines of division between the two factions: it was simply – language. Sure, from time to time the contest spilt over into ideological persuasions and power bloc alliances. But I can testify that the most frantic, feverish and unscrupulous campaigning was done by – I shan't name the specific embassies, we'll just call them – the champion of the French-speaking zones and the champion of the English-speaking zone. I was curious to know on which side Canada was. Now Canada was in a very interesting situation. As I have already admitted, there were other lines of division apart from the linguistic – there was for instance the French Community and the Commonwealth. Now Canada, with her split linguistic personality: which way would she fall? Well, before I left, I heard a representative from our own Embassy let out a howl of outrage at Canada's defection to the Froggies – as the French are called in diplomatic language. Maybe Canada was won back later for the English side, I never did find out. If you want the final details I shall simply add that the OAU was, as usual, hopelessly split.

The foregoing will do to remind us of *actualities*, to recall us to the fact that, theorize how we will, language is a *lived* phenomenon, acted upon by human beings and acting in turn upon human beings – individually and as community – in millions of ways from the most banal to the sublime; with a simplistic directness and with the uttermost complexity. And in looking critically at part of the complex nature of language, we come up against its boundary characteristic which, on an embattled continent like ours, cannot be allowed the same luxury of indulgence as those other societies we have pointed at – France, the United States, the Soviet Union, etc. I have already gone on record as advocating the adoption of Kiswahili as a continental language. What is constantly ignored, suppressed, or simply not understood is that I have just as fervently advocated the conservation and creative enrichment of all, repeat ALL existing African languages. Both commitments are complementary parts of a linguistic strategy of total liberation; they do not contradict each other.

Recent reports on the pages of *West Africa* and *New Nigerian* very conveniently afford me the opportunity of clarifying this strategy further. I read to my astonishment in *West Africa* a statement credited to Alhaji Akilu Aliyu that Hausa youths in Nigeria appear reluctant to speak Hausa. The Alhaji is supposed to have said further that this language is neglected by education policy planners. Now, as I said earlier, I find this claim astonishing. I appear to have been living with the exact opposite impression, that is, in Nigeria especially and certainly in most African countries of my knowledge, the indigenous languages receive massive encouragement by officialdom and are indeed the first choice of today's youths in daily communication. As for Hausa (same as for Yoruba, Efik, Igbo, etc.), I would have thought that the pattern was – where two or three Hausa are gathered, there would Hausa be spoken. And that includes all the new élite I regularly encounter. However, accurate or not as the Alhaji's claim might be, the formation of the Hausa Arts Writers Association is not only a welcome addition to the language-promotion societies and institutions in the country; it is a model which should be followed by all linguistic groups in the country. What is more, it should link up with similar associations in West Africa, thus playing its role in dissolving the artificial boundaries foisted on us by the colonial powers in so arbitrary and greed-oriented directions.

Not so positive however is my reaction to the other report, this time in *New Nigerian* (26 October 1977) which goes further and advocates Hausa as a national language. I must repeat here what I have said elsewhere. In the politics of this continent, I have no patience with any national strategy which in any way, overt or covert, solidifies the meaningless colonial boundaries which have created and are still creating such intense havoc on the continent among African nations and peoples. With C. L. R. James, the radical historian, author of *The Black Jacobins*, I believe that 'the nation state, as an ideal, belongs to the last century'. To consolidate untenable geographical boundaries with the linguistic is not merely stagnating in essence and effect; it is sterile and retrogressive. Obviously this is a standpoint from which my concepts of a linguistic strategy stem. There is no value in contesting related issues which take a contrary standpoint since this, to me, is basic.

A profound examination of the activity of liberation demands an uncompromising look into that phenomenon of man's condition which is rendered, to borrow an American expressive form as: 'where one is at'. I find this triggers off allied considerations such as 'where one is against' and uncovering, in the wake of squalor, inequality, exploitation, oppression, etc. – boundaries! As a language-user on more than the merely utilitarian level, it becomes intolerable that that favoured medium should constitute yet another boundary, on any level, between the peoples of a continent in search of a common identity. It is inevitable, confronted by retrogressive events such as earlier remarked, that we find ourselves asking questions which probe the very definition of boundary and its actualities: what it encloses, who it keeps apart, what it conceals and what it exposes. And ultimately: whether, specifically for us, language does not signify a wasteful extension of the boundary instinct.

In the process, it may be that we discover that boundaries – geographical, political, economic, cultural or linguistic – are walls of straw, that specifically in Africa, they were eaten long ago by the termites of black discontent, that they are held together only by the inheritors of white empires. Such an awareness makes instant demands on itself. Unfettered by past acceptances, it reaches down to the roots of society, rediscovers eternal causes for human association and proceeds to build new entities held together, not by artificial chalk-lines but by a recognizable identity of goals. It is a process of the mind which transcends the emotional content or separation of unification, and forges, in whatever field it can, the psychological, cultural and political tools for a healthy social entity.

One such weapon of entity restitution is of course, language. It is not as emotive or utopian as such a goal is often made out to be. We can argue that it is not a priority; but then we are compelled to ask whether or not any mass consciousness in a people which will go some way towards assaulting the acceptance and practice of social differentiation is not in itself a priority. And whether tools and activities which go some way towards creating that binding consciousness among peoples are not worthy of a prior place in social programming. Let me however anticipate some basic objections.

We should begin by moving away from, or at least re-examining, the traditional habits of accepted linguistic theories. Such an exercise is not designed to upset these, merely to use the pertinent data to clarify whatever decision which any community of peoples make for their own linguistic future. It is true for instance that language is itself the repository of a people's history and culture, but we cannot afford to agonize unnecessarily over the suspicion that the new African nations, because of the diversity of languages within their boundaries, may not actually possess a unified culture. (Amilcar Cabral was quite definite in denying the existence of one unified African Culture.) We shall waste as much time damning the artificiality of the existing national boundaries as bemoaning the fact that such boundaries have no cultural validation. These nuisances are more than compensated for by yet another fact – that neither history nor culture is static. It is possible therefore, given the necessary historic motivation, to create a new unifying culture from the uneasy amalgam of diversified ones. And where language is involved, we have at our disposal evidence of the revolutionary use to which the language of the oppressor has been used in oppressed societies: DuBois, Franz Fanon, Nelson Mandela, Agostinho Neto, Nkrumah, Malcolm X, Eldridge Cleaver, Angela Davies, Imamu Baraka, etc., etc. – an unending list through the history of colonial experience. This brutal reversal of the enslaving role of language – prophesied by that unusual Elizabethan, Shakespeare – tells us all we wish to know about the possibility of creating a synthetic revolutionary culture in place of the bastardized or eradicated indigenous culture of the colonized. The unaccustomed role which such a language is forced to play turns it indeed into a new medium of communication and simultaneously forges a new organic series of mores, social goals, relationships, universal awareness – all of which go into the creating of a new culture. Black people twisted the linguistic blade in the hands of the traditional cultural castrator and carved new concepts onto the flesh of white supremacy. The customary linguistic usage was rejected outright and a new, raw, urgent and revolutionary syntax was given to this medium which had become the greatest single repository of racist concepts.

The recognition of strategic options, through language, for African self-liberation has long preoccupied politicians, artists and intellectuals in the long history of colonialism. From Mahatma Gandhi to the modern colonial or ex-colonial poets and bureaucrats both on the mother continent and in the Diaspora, the same dismay has been voiced at the linguistic trap in which the colonial product finds himself. Each has sought his solution firstly in the conversion of the enslaving medium into an insurgent weapon; then in the search for a new medium of identity, indigenous, if not to him, then at least to others with whom he could claim a bond of kinship; often he has adopted both approaches simultaneously. David Diop wrote: 'If Africa were freed by compulsion, no (African) writer would even consider expressing his feelings and those of his people in anything other than his own, rediscovered, language.' And at the Second Congress of Negro Writers and Artists in Rome, 1959, this resolution was passed:

(i) that free and liberated black Africa should not adopt any European or
other language as a national tongue

(ii) that one African language should be chosen . . . that all Africans would
learn this national language besides their own regional language

(iii) that a team of linguists be instructed to enrich this language as rapidly as
possible, with the terminology for expression of modern philosophy,
science and technology

This resolution was taken at the same conference in which the Malagasy poet
Rabemanjara, in a mixture of self-disgust *and* triumph at the linguistic cleft in which
the colonial writer found himself, declared:

> Truly our conference is one of language thieves. This crime, at least, we have
> committed ourselves. We have stolen from our masters this treasure of
> identity, the vehicle of their thought, the golden key to their soul, the magic
> Sesame which opens wide the door of their secrets, the forbidden cave where
> they have hidden the loot taken from our fathers and for which we must
> demand a reckoning.

The ambivalent, even extreme reactions of the modern user of colonial language should
be seen therefore as a natural, even positive result of a realistic view of history. For we
must not underestimate the attitude of the original owner himself, one which understood
the fatal consequence of this acquisition of his own weapon of oppression, a fear, often
disguised under a veneer of the benevolent policy of separate development, lest the
oppressed peoples prove as skilled as the oppressor has been in the exploitation of the
now common medium. South Africa is the obvious example, and Paul Hazoume, an
ethnologist from Dahomey, (now Benin Republic) at the first Congress of Negro
Writers and Artists ripped the veil off such pretensions in the following words:

> Westerners seem today to regret having imposed the study of European
> languages. They are anxiously asking whether it would not be better to go
> back, as quickly as possible, on what they now take to have been an error on
> their part in the task which they had set themselves of educating the Africans,
> and to start teaching them their own languages. As an African, I cannot help
> wondering if the reasons used by westerners to justify their decision to teach
> Africans in their own language alone do not hide the real motives which they
> are ashamed to admit: motives of sordid, personal interest, prestige, fear of
> competition which they dare not allow to grow in face of the rapid
> development of the African elite, brought up until now without distrust of the
> same humanism as themselves. Some partisans of education in the vernacular
> have even suggested somewhat timidly, that their culture might produce
> social and even mental disturbances in Africans fed on it.

This accurately sums up the rationale of the South African Bantu education policy. And with this final concession to the argument for the principle of mastering whatever skills have contributed to the subjugation of millions, whether those skills be linguistic or technological, we turn now to give a little more attention to the alternative school of thought. Not alternative in the sense of being mutually exclusive, but simply as a proposition which, for multiple reasons – the least of which is not the reality of Africa's phenomenal self-advancement – demands that some attention be paid to the second phase of self-liberation: the creation of a continental language as an instrument of the continuing continental struggle.

We cannot – again it is necessary to approach this desirable goal realistically – we cannot immediately destroy the physical, colonial boundaries on the continent. That they will be destroyed is inevitable. That we need to destroy them is, I trust, equally unarguable, and not for any sentimental reasons. The need for their destruction arises from the simple fact that the work of rebuilding a new society, of the essential internal revolution which must follow the colonial liberation, this task is hampered by the physical existence of boundaries which have come to signify power separatist principles and reactionary bastions. What they mean to the masses is entirely separate from what they mean to their rulers. For the latter they are sacrosanct definitions of private ponds within which power can be made manifest. The principle of boundary for us at this moment is therefore allied to the principle of power and privilege, and its erosion becomes a long-term project whose realization can however be hastened by the erosion of symbolic and quasi-symbolic boundaries. By now I hope that we are in agreement that language belongs at the very least, in effect, among the quasi-symbolic boundaries.

A concern with language is fraught with many dangers. But none more serious than those which are posed by the *national* language alternative. Precisely because there is a predictable resistance to all forms of changes which threaten the sectarian and hegemonic mentality, the cry for a national language, where several already exist, is one which has been taken up in the most unlikely places. We have heard it in recent times from the mouths of the most abjectly worshipful colonial aristocrats on the coast of West Africa as stridently as from the genuine nationalist and even revolutionary idealists. When Nigeria was still split up in twelve states, one military governor decided unilaterally to impose on his state educational system the study of one of the Nigerian languages, this being one which he and a number of others believe is the obvious choice of a Nigerian national language. That it was, and still is a highly controversial choice, open even to dangerous political misinterpretation, counted for nothing. The national language debate erupts periodically in Nigerian newspapers with as much passion as in neighbouring countries such as Sierra Leone and, I believe, Ghana. True, some of those who espouse this cause are genuine believers. At the same time, experience teaches one to beware of the fomentors of chaos in society whose business it is to create diversions and divisions while they get on with the business of political manipulation. The harrowing lessons of other nations – India is one example – in their attempt to unify their peoples through the policy of a single language, are not lost upon them. The jealousies, the perennial fears of tribal domination, the possibilities even of civil conflict merely encourage their championing of the national chauvinist cause. The resulting internecine conflicts leave them unscathed, wealthier and more securely entrenched in the keypoints of control; for these social predators therefore the question of language is only one of many tactical weapons of discord. And one of the justifications for a sense of urgency on the linguistic question is very simple – to anticipate the situation of chaos which might ensue from the manoeuvering of such people. The attempt to impose a single language within the constrictions of petty nationalities, riven by internal dissensions, is a clearly explosive one and is ultimately negative.

Within the larger framework of a continental accord, however, the subjective resistance is diffused; the motivation is clearly presented as the attractive ideal of the coming together of a continent; the atavistic suspicions cannot be focussed on any single tribe within a politically claustrophobic, and therefore explosive social capsule. Quite simply, we defuse the linguistic bomb and take its control away from scheming little opportunists.

Once again, attention must be called again to the fact that our present national boundaries are colonial, that the cultural orientation is therefore still predominantly colonial, that the linguistic boundary is even more critical than the geographical because it is culturally divisive, but also that to replace such boundaries with several nation-linguistic boundaries is to enshrine for all time the principle of colonial fragmentation. Without actually waving the banner of the dream of the early Pan-Africanists who envisaged a United States of Africa 'without passing the middle-class chauvinistic nation phase' (Fanon) it is permissible, one hopes, to declare that the reverses which that dream has suffered so far do not validate the continuation of colonial boundaries, geographical or symbolic. This abstracted solace, even if it is all that is left of the dream, can be exploited to boost the present state of expedient compromise into the ultimate concrete direction of the original idea.

None of the foregoing precludes the continued use, development and enrichment of original languages in the fulfilment of their present functions, or the continued exploitation of colonial languages in order to, as Jean-Paul Sartre warned, 'shatter them, destroy their traditional associations and juxtapose them with violence'. Or even to use them routinely, as a tool of communication which is what language primarily is. The logical development of, or complementary phase to the revolutionary assault on the colonial language is however the creation of a new common medium of communication. The first stage of African liberation has been externally directed; it was the phase of liberation *from*. The conversionary use of the colonial language was logically related to this phase. The second stage, the positive, creative phase of liberation is the one in which we are, with the exception of Southern Africa, currently engaged upon; the phase of internal reconstruction. The place of language should relate to this phase in as logical a manner as the first, namely by the adoption of a language of symbolic and practical unity.

All languages are prime candidates for the continental choice. I can only re-affirm and put forward that of my own reasoned choice which also happens to be the choice of several groups and individuals, including the Union of Writers of the African Peoples. I may add that when the paper of this very title was first read in Dar es Salaam, it mentioned no specific language. On my own part, I already felt that Kiswahili provided the sanest choice; I was however still engaged in examining the candidature of other languages. If it is any consolation to that writer whose essay-review appears on the pages of the *New Nigerian* of 26 October 1977, I share with him all the enthusiasm which he expresses for Hausa. It is a graceful, lyrical language; it is also widely spoken in West Africa. In opposition to the European and Arabic authorities which he chooses to cite however, I hope he will concede that there are even more numerous European and Arabic scholars who advocate the suitability of Kiswahili as an *international* language. Of these I shall cite here only the earliest within my knowledge: R. W. Cuit who, in 1896, declared, in his study of African languages, that Kiswahili not only was one of the eight most important languages in the world but was destined to become recognized as the most suitable language for the African continent. I hope, with that, we can dispense with the authority of foreigners. What do African writers and scholars, teachers and all say on the subject? Pursuing the same goals as other gatherings of black writers, scholars and artists since the last two decades of the last century, the Accra meeting of African writers declared:

> This Union finds it regrettable that twenty years have been wasted since the
> Second Congress of African Writers in Rome recommended the adoption of
> one language for the African peoples. Resolved to end this state of inertia,
> hesitancy and defeatism, we have, after much serious consideration, and in
> the conviction that all technical problems can and will be overcome,
> *unanimously* adopted Kiswahili as the logical language for this purpose.

That meeting was by no means unanimous on the subject to begin with. Nor was the later Congress in Dakar which ratified that decision last year. What we are saying is that it is not something plucked out of some exotic hat with a wave of a magic wand or as in a lottery. Only a handful of Swahili speakers attended either Conference, but nearly all are familiar with the socio-history of most African languages, several were language experts and their analyses were objective in detail.

I shall cite as further example and authority the case of Professor Cheik Anta Diop, director of the IFAN research laboratory in the University of Dakar, who, to prove the adaptability of African languages, has written several learned scientific papers and a scientific text-book for schools in his native Wollof. This giant intellect is also an ethnologist, a linguist and historian; when it came to his choice of language for continental adoption he unreservedly chose Swahili. If arrangements proceed without any hitch, the country may be fortunate to listen to Professor Cheik Anta Diop this year or early next at the first full Congress of the Association of Researchers and Scientists of the Black World.* The promoter of partisan interests in the *New Nigerian* essay who equates objectivity with the trotting out of indifferent authorities who happened to have been civil servants of the colonial empire in Northern Nigeria will have the opportunity to exchange ideas – if he has any of his own – with Cheik Anta Diop. Only the worst type of colonial enslavement could lead anyone to use the 1975 MA Thesis of some putative scholar from an American University as *basis* for resolving the linguistic dilemma of the entire African continent! May I remark however – lest I be misunderstood (I shall be *deliberately* misunderstood anyway but no matter) – there will be as many favourites as there are languages, and every individual is at liberty to express and promote an opinion. We merely ask to be spared the kind of opportunism and slapstick 'reasoning' such as is exhibited in the article I have referred to. This is not a subject for partisanship or bonded interests, but of commitment and vision. I wish to end by referring to the linguistic experiences of Togo and the Cameroon. In the latter especially, during a mere half-century, its official language changed from English to French to German and French or English again – not necessarily in that order. The people of the Cameroons had no choice but to follow the whims of imperial fortune. Several other peoples on this continent have undergone degrees of the same experience. And so, from those who say, but why should we take the trouble to learn or promote another official language, we can only demand: why does the power of the gun so easily compel you to serve the interests of aliens, but never an act of political will the cause of your own self-interest?

There are no miracles involved. The All-Africa Teachers Union, meeting in Algiers in 1975, has also called for the adoption of one language for the whole of the African continent, and named Kiswahili one of their three first choices. They should know. On them falls the burden of implementing their own resolution. Even modest beginnings in the form of Swahili teaching in universities, as already practised by Ghana, Senegal and Gambia are actions of a positive nature. Most of East and Central Africa already speak and write this language. The real place to begin is the secondary school. Primary education, I believe, should *always* be given in the child's mother-tongue. On that principle, there should be no compromise. But the teaching of Swahili, just as a school subject, begun now, already promises a transformation of the linguascape of the continent within the next twelve years. The rest follows naturally, part of it even simultaneously – Swahili courses on national networks, the same as we now have for French, English, German etc. The mood throughout the continent today is to explore that continent and become acquainted with what the various modes of boundary have kept away from each of us – that mood was reflected in the government's directive to civil servants, urging them to spend their vacations on the continent. Sticking out of their pockets when they visit East Africa will be Swahili phrase-books. In twenty years, the phrase-books will not be needed. The Army of Liberation to the front-line states, what language will they communicate in? A babble of Ibo, Hausa, German, Wollof,

* It is sad to relate that Professor Cheikh Anta Diop died suddenly in June 1986 of a heart attack. (W. S.)

French, Ga, Yoruba, Portuguese Twi, English etc? Is it not more rational to move our minds where history is pointing and teach our mouths to form the language of that moment? We must not, in this phase of the continent's coming-in-being, contract our sights within boundaries of pettiness, insularity and narrow chauvinism.

IX

The Critic and Society:
Barthes, Leftocracy and Other Mythologies*

Alain Robbe-Grillet is not a familiar name to academia or the general reader in Nigeria. His recent death† occasioned the usual obituary notices, which appeared in the literary columns of European journals and brought back to mind instantly, in total recall, the picture of a plump, untidy don at Leeds University where I was a student. As he lectured, his plain academic gown fell constantly off his shoulders from wild Gallic gesticulations meant to propel forward certain ideas on fiction and reality. They were a drastic departure from our normal fare of fiction criticism. No, the figure was not that of the critic and novelist, doyen of the New Fiction, Robbe-Grillet himself – I never met him. The speaker was a visiting academic who had come to spread the gospel of the New Fiction from across the channel to conservative England. We were part bemused, part fascinated; here was the plain old novel being unnecessarily complicated, and words that were once simply words being turned into signs. A totally new langue of reality was introduced by this visitation, and the theories of Saussure and Barthes which were seminal influences on the New Fiction entered – at least peripherally – and with resentment – our intellectual baggage of fact and fiction.

Browsing in Dillon's bookshop (University of London) some days after the event of Robbe-Grillet's death, I was drawn nostalgically towards his writings but found myself arrested en route by some new volumes of essays by the major theorist of the movement, Roland Barthes. They were essays I had not encountered until then, being belated translations – some of them as recent as '77 – of his commentaries on the development of new mythologies, linguistic-semiological shorthands of the old which were created by the European (French) bourgeoisie. They involved, more importantly, a socially-

---

* First published in University of Ife Inaugural Lecture Series, No. 49 (1982).

† For this embarrassing gaffe, which is really too interesting to be corrected now, I have blamed in fact the original publisher of this volume with whom I had a conversation on the 'event'. He strenuously denies it. Alain Robbe-Grillet is still very much alive as I found out when I accused him of being dead at a meeting in Paris a year later. (W.S.)

directed investigation of the operations of myth on the daily sensibilities of social man – and of a particular class, the bourgeoisie. Increasingly engaged, I parted reluctantly with some precious pounds and took away the paperback. It did not take long for me to realize that I had stumbled on a perfect paradigm for the social reality of the radical shift in critical language in my own African community – and that is the genesis of the elaboration in the title of my paper.

I recalled also, as a student, providing my own private syntax for the semantic codes of the not new, but the then newly-introduced, Saussurean linguistics – a very simple one, in fact, created through my extremely rudimentary knowledge not even of the French language, but of a few French expressions. I shall occasionally draw on it for purposes of specifics, so I must explain it here. Such specialist terms as *langue* and *parole* will be very sparingly used; and when they are, the context will be so clear as to require no elaboration. I propose to stick to familiar semantic units and clusters such as language, meaning, vocabulary, syntax, and so forth in their most ordinary usage. But the word *language* can hardly ever be used in any ordinary sense; indeed, it obviously shed all ordinary sense since its first paradoxical employment as a description of its own system – that is, as a system of socially-agreed-upon significations. For language does not operate simply as communication but as matrices of discrete activities including those of articulation and meaning. And when we talk about the language of literature or criticism we assume multiple levels of internal operations of basic cognitives and their triggering social agencies, a matrix of latent and activated meanings which add to our problems of apprehension by acting in a self-constitutive way. To differentiate this particular activity, the socially constitutive activity, I recall that I found it useful to devise a simple phonetic pun on the French *langage*, that word being *l'engagé*[1]: the operation of social cogs within the code of meanings; the engagement of gears within a cluster of codes, shifting the actual intent of language from one matrix and coupling it to another in social operation. The French *langage* will continue to stand for the totality of options in a system; *l'engagé* indicates the selective operation within the *langue*, engaging the differential to deliver a socially active meaning – this last is the context of my basic interest and will be what is signified, unless otherwise stated, when the plain 'language' is used for convenience, in relation to what the critic or the creative artist actually does with the system. In short, *langage* is the cold topography before the linguist; *l'engagé* or language is the actual course being mapped by you and me.

And now to the critics, pausing only to state from the onset that their understanding of my work will not be avoided in this paper. After all, their preoccupations in recent times have tended to suggest that there are no other African authors left on the bookshelves or, if there are, that their study is incomplete without Mr W. S. being roped in somewhere. This is not an egotistical claim but a statistical fact. From an objective sense of proportion, it is necessary that this inert material return the compliment, manifesting its own critical voice just once in a while. No occasion could be more appropriate than this.

To my knowledge, very little has been attempted in studies of the critic as a socially-situated producer, and therefore as a creature of social conditioning, a conditioning which in fact offers no certitudes about the nature of his commitment to the subject which engages him, his motivations, or, indeed, about the very nature of his social existence. About the writer, on the other hand, we are traditionally overinformed – which is to say, ingenuously disinformed, since nothing but selective information, censored, even distorted to suit the critic's thesis, ever survives the pages in the direction of the reader. But at least the reader has some measure of fact, fiction, and speculations to engage his interest. But regarding the critic, none. And then, of course, what society? What is the critic's society? Is it, for instance, a society which we may describe as International Academia? Or is it Ipetumodu?* The distinction is crucial. There is a world of difference in the social situation of any critic – either as an exploiter of language for the weekly to twice-weekly seminars of the University of Nsukka, Ibadan, or Maiduguri; or as a critic who is profoundly angry that a writer has never even recognized the existence of the social anomalies within Ipetumodu, Abakaliki, or Koton Karfi in his writings.

We are familiar, probably even excrutiatingly bored, with the question: For whom does the writer write? Very rarely is the same degree of social angst encountered in the case of the critic. Indeed the question is very rarely posed: For whom does the critic write? For Mr Dele Bus-Stop of Idi-Oro? Or for the Appointments and Promotions Committee and the learned Journals International Syndicate of Berne, Harvard, Nairobi, Oxford, or Prague? Unquestionably there is an intellectual cop-out in the career of any critic who covers reams of paper with unceasing lament on the failure of this or that writer to write for the masses of the people, when he himself assiduously engages, with a remorseless exclusivity, only the incestuous productivity of his own academic – that is, bourgeois-situated – literature. It is a very convenient case of having one's cake and eating it, or feeding on it, yet damning the output of producers of literatures in one's community – often in the most scabrous, dismissive language – over and over again, treading the same grooves, looking for something new to say and never finding it, pouncing on the latest product of the same pariah writer like a famished voyager, building up CV's at the expense of the condemned productivity – the genuine productivity, not the parasitic kind which is the critic's – indeed, teaching it at all. 'Reactionary', 'elitist', 'privileged', 'a splurge of romantic decadence', 'articulator of the neo-colonial agent class' . . . well then, what is the critic doing?

But this is of course a very one-sided, partial view. It is true that the critics with whom we are here concerned do venture from time to time into the field of popular literature, popular theatre, popular music . . . in short, the so-called proletarian art. But we must ask: What *language*, what *langage* is deployed in this great, generous excursion into non-bourgeois art? When the 'committed' critic unwraps the poetry of the 'ewi' specialist Lanrewaju Adepoju,† the earthy Majority Music Club under Professor alias

---

* A village near Ife. (Ed.)
† Popular Nigerian music artistes.

Majority,* the exotic Dan Maraya*, whose *langage* does the critic speak and, therefore, to what society does he address himself? Is he speaking back to Dan Maraya or the 'Waka Queen,' Salawa*? Can they penetrate the critic's *parole* to commence a genuine engagement with *language*? Is this proletarian art returned to its producers, or is it merely refurbished in the *langage* of the assessors of the Appointments and Promotions Committee or of the Learned Journals? In short, is the excursion into Onitsha Market Literature or alias Majority music ever different from opportunism, an appropriation of proletarian production by a member of the bourgeoisie for its small, erudite coterie?

I experience in this, naturally, some embarrassment for, speaking of such society, I equally indict myself. An additional embarrassment, even inhibition, stems from the fact that one of the favourite fodders for the 'commitment machine' of these critics happens to be no other than me. However this is one debate which this paper must inaugurate; the situation of the African critic in *what* society? The stridency of recent criticism makes it inevitable, for criticism has lately outstripped creativity in quantity – at least in my country. I intend to introduce the discourse with an extreme example of the resultant language of alienation – not, however, from papers of the Department of Literature or Drama or Philosophy or African Languages and Literatures but from a popular journal. Indeed, the subject will not even be about literature but about a simple social phenomenon, violence. I propose wherever possible to employ the methodology of oblique references, just to widen the area of discourse and provide analogies involving related social concerns.

Let us begin with an obviously concerned social critic. He is *motivated* – shall we concede? – by the phenomenon of violence in society. The Journal in which the following passage appears in the Lagos *Sunday Times* of 20 July 1980,[2] and the immediate cause of the article is reported student violence at the University of Ibadan. Now nothing can be more proletarian than violence: violence, we know, is one of the few universal commodities; unlike rice, it cannot be placed under licence. Even so, I wish to stress that violence has to be *produced*. When offered, it is a product which has involved both risk and labour, and a level of commitment. In a sense, this act of criticism comes automatically into the same system of appropriation which I am about to engage. I mean, what is my purpose? What is the end of attempting to prove that one critic has appropriated the violence of a group of students, and converted it to neutral ends? If I were writing in support of, or in criticism of, the act of the students, I could claim that my motives were nobler; I would remain within the immediate, cause-and-consequence nexus of the originating event, possibly even initiate a movement towards redress. But here I am only concerned to buttress, by a slant of objectives, my contention that academic writers, when they move into the arena of proletarian production, adopt the conversion language of a particular class, the bourgeois intelligentsia. The commodity can be a piece of sculpture, a hunter's traditional chant, Ladi Kwale's pottery, Baba Sala's Comic Muse, a worker's strike, or student violence. And the language is indisputably the language of alienation, even deliberately so, as the following illustrates:

* Popular Nigerian music artistes.

> Some University of Ibadan students were some time ago reported as having physically affronted laboratory equipment. In the process the University and the entire Nigerian community lost invaluable science equipment.
>
> Predictably the reactions to the incident followed two lines. On the one hand, there were those who splotch [sic] the students as overfed, over-pampered and overpetted marginal adults who should be called to order . . . On the other hand there were those who glorified and lionized the students . . .

Beyond the queer semantic cluster 'physically affronted laboratory equipment', we are not yet irretrievably in the terrain of alienation. The field appears to be declared open, however clumsily (any intelligent member of society must know that there would be those two camps, so why tell us?), yet there is a promise here of something akin to motivation. Whatever the writer has done, he has succeeded in engaging us, within the matrix of contending forces, in the prospects of his own position, and the options are three: for, against or an arbitrating neutral between the two positions. Alas, and this is where we come to the crunch, there is a *fourth* position. What is *signified* turns out to be a confidence trick; the writer has no interest whatsoever in that physical confrontation, nor in its consequences on the rest of society. His sociology would help us, but we have no facts, only a name below the article; but the sign begins to come out strongly, barely three paragraphs later. We realize then that we are being moved from the field of 'physically affronted laboratory equipment' to the operational field of seminars at the University of Lagos or Maiduguri, into the structure of the seminar paper in which the subject only serves the linguistic ritual. Let us spend a little more time probing this intellectual tumor through all its tissues. I believe that the exercise is long overdue and may prove salutary.

> There are two equally tenable and plausible positions on one and the same issue. And philosophy, as a professional discipline, begins where two extreme but equally plausible propositions are asserted on one and the same event, topic or concept. This is true whether the concept in question, say 'violence' in this instance, is obviously philosophical or not. But things are made easy in this context because the term 'violence' happens to be a moral concept.
>
> Questions asking for explications and elucidations of the causes of violence and questions about the role of violence in a nation's consciousness and culture are legitimate and will be treated as cognates of the distinctively philosophical question: 'What is violence?'
>
> There are three ways by which it is possible to gain an insight into this question. The first is etymological, the second is definitional, and the third is distinctional. Concerning the etymology of the word 'violence' . . .

Need one go on? This is language which has not arrived at the edges of social topography, much less *l'engagé* of social signification. The contemporaneous *langage* is this: Heads are now being 'physically affronted', arrests are being made, detentions in police cells for students and workers . . . this is the indicative of the language-in-the-making of any projected resolution. And the obscured *langage* police slaughter of unarmed students (in Zaria, if you recall), the insolently corrupt findings of judicial enquiries, the police siege of campuses, loss of employment for staff, rustication of students, prohibition of unions, round-the-clock surveillance of suspected activists, seizure of passports, etc. This was the total language of violence out of which was carved the burning down of laboratory equipment in Ibadan as sign. But the essayist of the *Sunday Times* would have us believe that this event is best apprehended through the definitions of violence and opinions held by Professor Gaiver, Professor Robert Audi, 'whose article on violence earned him an award of the American Council for Philosophical Studies'; Heraclitus; Hegel; Machiavelli; Rousseau; Engels; Lenin (at least, their followers); Adolf Hitler; Henry von Trechschke, 'himself a brilliant Nazi theoretician' . . . I believe that exhausts the list. And so, a particular purposeful act – damn it or laud it – with its own finite, unambiguous, risk-committed clarity has been converted to the seminarist language with its infinite discursiveness – submerging, distorting, and finally appropriating the original commodity in its quotational garrulity. The annotations are bewildering. We understand why it is that this essayist needs to confer upon us the honour of listening to the opinions of Professor Robert Audi: thus the CV extract which narrates his credentials on the subject of violence – 'whose article on violence earned him an award of the American Council for Philosophical Studies'. Reader, the author thus informs you and me, you are in the presence of a man who knows what the subject is about! But by contrast, does it matter in the least in this context at what point of Greek philosophy, or indeed any school of philosophy, Heraclitus emerged? 'Heraclitus,' introduces Dr Momoh, 'a pre-Socratic philosopher . . .' Does it matter in the slightest if Heraclitus was a neo-Stoic sybarite or an Aeolian rhapsodist? The signification of that 'pre-Socratic' bunting is, of course, only an academic symbol, an iconic sign, à la Barthes. The matrix of Greek philosophy and history, the patina of antiquarian scrolls, have all been gratuitously introduced in order to distance the event of – at least – a contemporary gesture, act at best, a signification of urgent social import. To summarize: The author here is not speaking to the specific issue of one act of violence, not even to violence in general; he is not speaking to the issue of violence in his society; he is not even condescending to speak to his society, but is primarily, secondarily, and ultimately engaged in the act of appropriating a harsh reality to a *langage* of 'scholarship' – and one, incidentally, of the superficial catalogue variety. I have already stated that it is an extreme case. Nevertheless, anyone who believes that it is singularly atypical is recommended to make a sample study of seminar, conference, and Learned-Journal sociological papers on any one social problem from violence to pacific alcoholism.[3]

That task over, such a skeptic is perhaps more readily prepared to understand the mechanics of appropriation of direct products of intellectual labour, such as the artistic and literary. Just as violence is a value produced towards the attainment of a concrete expectation, a settlement to be concluded in social terms, so is a work of art – in whatever *language* – a value of labour, one which, curiously, without any self-criticism, the critic appropriates to ends other than the ends for which the work is produced and marketed. A mystique is created by the appropriator about the 'availability' of art, one which grants it special victim status and cannot question, in its turn, the status of the appropriator in the value scale of (1) the readership for whom the work is intended and (2) the production, intent and delimited goals of the commodity. No, the appropriator assumes and asserts ends, failure to attain which constitutes a crime against *his* calling.

Now Roland Barthes is a rare breed of academic worker who has tried to explore, in very concrete terms, the social situation of the critic/teacher in relation to the practice of his profession. I have described him as an academic worker because this is the very image which he appears to strive towards. It is part of the engaging honesty of Monsieur Barthes that he admits that, in the first and final analysis, he is not, and cannot become, a *worker* in the historical sense of the word. Roland Barthes is, I repeat, a rare exegetist in the world of the intellect because he does not merely debate; he acts out, almost by perverse example, the best and the worst of the paradox of the Leftist scholar, a would-be academic popularizer who, however, does not employ a 'popular' *langage*. Indeed, it is not so much what Barthes says, but his *l'engagé*, the social tension of his discourse, which makes him an obvious example for the radical, socially-committed critic of today's African intelligentsia.

Barthes is no friend of the bourgeoisie, and we can usefully begin by examining how this detestation manifests itself in his attempt to prune language of its bourgeois accretions, to expose the bourgeois mythology that lies beneath, sustains, and is indeed the very foundation of linguistic and imagic signifiers which society takes so much for granted. Like the group of academics who, we have suggested, occasionally attempt to enter proletarian art and relations, Barthes proves himself an obsessive leveller. What really lies beneath the *geste*? Within what code does a seemingly straightforward signifier transmit or trigger into public consciousness the real message, the signified, converting it into a neo-mythology, a semiograph if you prefer, establishing an autonomy of bourgeois values? To this end, Monsieur Barthes focuses his attention on what he appropriately labels the so-called mass-culture: professional wrestling, cinema stereo-types, the detective story, tourist guides, advertisements, soap powders and detergents, Charlie Chaplin, steak and chips, Greta Garbo, ornamental cookery, French toys, plastic technology, and so forth. Barthes, in his preface to the 1970 edition of *Mythologies*, reminds his society that the 'essential enemy' is still 'the bourgeois norm' and recalls that part of his hope with the collection of essays is that, 'by treating "collective representations" as sign-systems, one might . . . go further than the pious show of unmasking them and account in *detail* for the mystification which transforms petit-bourgeois culture into a universal culture'.[4] I suggest that special attention be paid to that last quote – the problem of the 'mystification which transforms petit-bourgeois culture into a universal culture'. Along the way we may have cause to suspect that the undiscriminating African critic has been trapped into transposing the petit-bourgeois signs and iconography of his mentor culture into a universal culture.

Barthes himself provides the very simple explanation for this transformation, one which we have already dealt with above, namely class appropriation. Petit-bourgeois criticism, even when it is very much of the Left, as it gropingly is these days in sections of our own academia, simply appropriates the object of criticism into the *langage* of its own class. Every essay in Barthes' collection *Mythologies* is an ironic repetition of the process, an unconscious act of linguistic vengefulness: even as language takes off the mask of petit-bourgeois mythology of objects and activities, it clothes them anew in the garb of bourgeois intellectualism. Roland Barthes, an honest intellectual, as I have already stated, is compelled to concede this much in *Image – Music – Text*. The final essay in that collection, titled 'Writers, Intellectuals, Teachers', is a must, I seriously suggest, for every single Leftocrat still left over if ever a genuine proletarian revolution is to overtake our universities. This overt act of grace does not, however, come remotely close in self-revelation of Monsieur Barthes' direct appropriation, in the socio-linguistic context, of the mass-culture, on behalf of the minority class to which he, Roland Barthes, belongs.

Fortunately television has been with us awhile, and *Wrestling from Chicago* is, I believe, still a staple diet to many addicts and even non-addicts of television in my country. It would be most instructive to find what such consumers make of the following passage from Mr Barthes' semiological analysis of these sweat-and-groan artists of muscular repulsion: 'In other words, wrestling is a sum of spectacles, of which no single one is a function: each moment imposes the total knowledge of a passion which rises erect and alone without ever extending to the crowning moment of a result' (*Mythologies*, p. 16). Or try this one: 'Each moment in wrestling is therefore like an algebra which instantaneously unveils the relationship between a cause and its represented effect' (*Mythologies*, p. 19). Just one final, irresistible quote:

> Armund Mazaud, a wrestler of an arrogant and ridiculous character (as one says that Harpagon is a character), always delights the audience by the mathematical rigour of his transcriptions, carrying the form of his gestures to the further reaches of their meaning, and giving to his manner of fighting the kind of vehemence and precision found in a great scholastic disputation, in which what is at stake is at once the triumph of pride and the formal concern with truth. (Ibid.)

I confess that I also have watched wrestling, both in the flesh and on the television screen. I have never seen more than two oversized, consciously theatrical monstrosities earning fair wages in return for sending a matinee audience hysterical with vicarious sadism. Nothing that I saw at any time recalled any scholastic disputation or brought regrets to my failings in school as an algebraic hope. Barthes' purpose is manifest: Wrestling is a mere input into the structuralist-semiotic computer programme which then emits a Barthes-specific *langage*. If I were an addictive econo-Leftocrat, I would, in accents of gravely committed proletariat empathy, accuse Monsieur Barthes of failure to relate the wrestling spectacle to the economic contradictions of his social situation and his performers' social situating. I would in fact demand that his treatment of wrestling should lead into the sort of socio-political coda he inserts in some of his other essays such as 'Wine and Milk', in which, after a totemistic exposition of wine in the life of the Frenchman, he concludes: 'There are thus very engaging myths which are however not innocent. And the characteristic of our current alienation is precisely that wine cannot be an unalloyedly blissful substance, except if we wrongfully forget that it is also the product of an expropriation' (*Mythologies*, p. 61). Thus is the radical conscience saved, by a double appropriation of the labour of the Algerian workers – first converting his labour into the language exchange of the intellectual class, then crediting his act with a basic political consciousness. Neither achieves anything concrete for the expropriated Algerian worker. The essay on wrestling is, in the end, more intellectually humble, for it pretends to nothing but the attempted transmission of the ontology of the game – in the language of the intellectual.

There is, however, more serious matter in that essay. The summary passage has a suspiciously essentialistic cast:

> In wrestling, nothing exists except in the absolute, there is no symbol, no allusion, everything is presented exhaustively. Leaving nothing in the shade, each action discards all parasitic meanings and ceremonially offers to the public a pure and full signification, rounded like Nature. This grandiloquence is nothing but the popular and age-old image of the perfect intelligibility of reality. What is portrayed by wrestling is therefore an ideal understanding of things; it is the euphoria of men raised for a while above the constitutive ambiguity of everyday situations and placed before the panoramic view of the univocal Nature, in which signs at last correspond to causes, without obstacle, without evasion, without contradiction. (*Mythologies*, pp. 24–5)

And yet I cannot pretend not to understand Monsieur Barthes or pretend that I have not endorsed in personal experience his re-creation of the physical moment in seemingly incongruous matrices – mathematical, musical, architectural, and of course linguistic. One need not go so far as Normal Mailer, whose floridly purple passages, especially those commissioned by *Life*, celebrated the first advent of man into space, a linguistic extravaganza which, in a rather impoverished way,[5] anticipated the time-out and spaced-out collaboration of the composer Richard Strauss, the philosopher Nietzsche, and the film maker Stanley Kubrik in the 'unfinished' space classic *2001: A Space Odyssey*. The film *Star Wars* and its follow-up *The Empire Strikes Back* are, in a comparative sense, the literal completion of the symbolic, mythological *2001: A Space Odyssey*. Constructed frankly on technological gadgetry and spectacle, these latter epics make no attempt at mystery and mythology and would therefore have provided, speculatively, more likely material for Roland Barthes than *2001*. The speculation, based on Barthes' own 'The World of Wrestling', is: Would the language of Barthes not have appropriated them into the 'bourgeois' linguistic field of *2001*, into that timeless mythological symbiosis of *Thus Spake Zarathustra*, Austrian nineteenth-century Romantic music, and the entire Wagnerian mythopoeic construct of Kubrick's film? We have seen that the critic, even at his most consciously Leftocratic, cannot escape his bourgeois linguistic situation. Remote and mysterious though Space appears, the cult of Space has been a mass one, resulting in the popular mythographic language of *Star Trek*. When Mailer undertook his mission to play tourist guide to the millions who could not be present at Cape Canaveral, he could have chosen the direct *langage* of the gladiatorial fanfare, the popular fiestas. Instead his choice was, predictably perhaps, a '60s bourgeois-literati *langage*. Barthes similarly succeeds in appropriating the modern gladiatorial arena of wrestling into a *langage* not of wrestling, but of *letters*. The linguistic rocket that launched the first spaceman into the galaxy is structurally identical with the Barthian semiotic transfiguration of two sweat-and-groan artists into a mystic paradox of Essence withdrawn and eternalized through unchanging Reality.

The writings of Roland Barthes constitute a paradox, which is perhaps the reason that he lends himself so readily to being conscripted into the role of critical paradigm of the new Left-leaning African, and especially the Nigerian, critic. And a basic divergence of one from the other is that this academic is not only conscious of, but takes great pains to particularize, his social situation. I have to insist that the majority of our critics do not. The traps into which they fall arise very simply from this fact, and their extremisms arise from this failure to understand that the language of criticism is very socially situated. The Leftocracy would deny it, but here is a typical failure, conveniently located in the realm of language. Writing on *Opera Wonyosi*, Yemi Ogunbiyi makes the following statement:

> In Soyinka's version of Macheath's opening piece, he refers to the Igbeti
> marble which led to the mysterious disappearance of enquiring citizens about
> the marble deposits. He however concludes in the cynically ironic tone which
> runs through the play that little can be done in the circumstances of Igbeti
> situation:
>
> > For it takes more than the darkness
> > To protect one beast of prey
> > When there's interest joined to interest
> > All we can do is pray.[6]

Translated back into the contextual language of the *dramatis personae*, that last, offending line would read, *Adura lo ku* (or *gba*). Any critic who succeeded in making that language leap, of situating himself and the action in the realistic environment of the *parole*, would recognize that this is a simple standard figure of speech, connoting by no stretch of the imagination a decision to leave everything in the hands of God. It is really necessary to particularize to this critic the fact that, when human throats were being meticulously cut during the Northern pogrom of 1966, the pious liturgy which was monotonously recited over the prone victim was '*Bisimillahi*' (with the name of God)? The question he should ask, in order to penetrate this specific *parole*, is: Do the characters in the play act with pious resignation? When, to a standard greeting of 'How are things?' an acquaintance responds '*Ambe'lorun* ('We are pleading with God') do you really conclude that he is just getting up from his knees? Ogunbiyi's reading of this line, and so many others, is a wholly alienated reading. Revolutionary aspirations, and the wish to see such aspirations clothed in a language of action, cannot eliminate the fact of the existence of tension within used, seemingly inert syntax.[7]

My experience in Nigeria alone, to go no further, is that in times of social confrontation, language is often used as a holding device, a massed coil before the release of the spring. But then the worker in language grasps both the sound of meaning and the meaning of sound within the mere gesture of articulation. What is even more strange is the fact that there are clues to this understanding to be followed by the willing critic. Ogunbiyi recognizes them but chooses to corral them into an alternative which is merely convenient for an a priori thesis: the thesis of ambiguity in Soyinka which is much favoured by Leftocratic criticism. Take the message of Anikura's song which follows almost immediately after the previously cited passage:

> But look one day you will find
> That pus-covered mask hides a mind
> And then – boom! Oga sah*
> What's that blur – oga sá?†
> With a red flame fanning his behind.

Ogunbiyi's footnote 12, commenting on the two verses quoted above, reads: 'The kind of ambiguity I refer to here relates to that statement or statements so fundamentally contradictory that they reveal a basic division or even contradiction in the author's mind.' Our critic resolves, in that last-quoted section, that the author of the play – to again use his own words – 'concludes [that] ... very little can be done in the circumstances of Igbeti situation'. This is a very large claim to the state of mind of the playwright, and one which is founded on a deliberate linguistic fragmentation. It removes the employment of a particular typology of *langue* from a real milieu and turns it *parole*-wise literal, leaving us a *signified* which has been plucked from a lingual matrix whose sole claim to compatibility is simplistically grammarian.

Ambiguity, levelled at the writer, is very often a cover for the critic's own social evasion. Ogunbiyi again finds that a problem of ambiguity has been raised because the playwright

---

* Yes Massa.
† Massa turn tail!

has satirized the buffoon figure of Emperor Bokassa, preening himself as a Marxist. He quotes from the play's monologue: 'Now a revolutionary dance must possess what we Marxists call social reality. So we are going to adapt this dance to the social reality of our progressive Centrafrique Social Experiment.' The socially-situated responsibility which Ogunbiyi evades here is that of information. He fails to inform his readers that the opportunistic ploy – which is the subject of satire here – notoriously adopted on this continent by nearly every reactionary ruler is this very one, adopting poses of radicalism, revolution, even Marxism. Idi Amin, Mobutu Sese Seko, Léopold Senghor, Bokassa, Macias Ngeuma, etc. – each one, at one time or the other, has presented himself on the podium of power as the heir of Marx and Lenin – with the significant, even deadly qualification. Ogunbiyi's stance towards the playwright therefore becomes charitable criticism – towards the fascist leaders, at the expense of the satirist.[8] It could be of course that the critic here considers the audiences of *Opera Wonyosi* to be in mortal peril of mistaking the barb for reality, but such criticism should be addressed to the sociology of the specific audience. Yet even that would require a thorough social situation of the critic, which is precisely what this brand of criticism lacks. There is yet further proof.

Footnote 7 deals with the danger of the ingredients of theatrical pleasure – melodies, costuming, dance, witty dialogue, etc. – becoming counter-productive to the aims of a work of social criticism. Drawing on an experience of the original production of Brecht's *Threepenny Opera*, on which *Opera Wonyosi* is based, Ogunbiyi recalls actress Lotte Lenya-Weill narrating how:

> Berlin was gripped by a *Threepenny Opera* fever. Everywhere, even in the streets, the tunes were whistled – a Threepenny Bar was opened where no other music was played . . . . Once when I was walking down the Tiergarten I passed a blind beggar. He called after me: 'Fräulein Lenya, you only have time for blind beggars on the stage eh?'

Now this of course is a very sobering piece of theatrical sociology, one which has always raised profound questions about the very activity of art and one which hankers back to what we have already described as the appropriation of the masses by the class of artists and intellectuals even down to their rags, their violence, and their misery. It is a subject which even radical ideologies evade, preferring to deal in platitudinous assertions such as those indulged in the essay in question: '. . . a committed work of art . . . must lay bare *unambiguously*, the causal historical and socio-economic network of society in such a way as to enable us to master reality and, in fact transform it . . .' The work of art that actually achieves this is very laudable, but the exhortation does not resolve the fundamental question of the appropriation of any human reality, and especially a cruel one, extracted and presented for the edification of a micro-society. We are speaking here of the very morphology of intellectual base material; of the social evasion that accompanies, deep down, the process of having 'done your bit' for the downtrodden masses, of the unreal nature of any presentation of reality, the psychology of its consumers, the medium of transmission which is at once limited, distortive, an act of fabrication which draws the most committed consumer into a conspiracy of evasion. When the critic says, 'enables us to master reality,' we must demand: Who are us? Precisely what class? What are their functions? Could this 'us' by any stretch of imagination be the proletariat?

And here is the clue: It is significant that in arriving at the alienation of the participants – the real, not theoretical, alienation of the players from the played – Ogunyibi's reader is privileged to know only the workings of the mind of the Berlin beggar, not of the ordinary member of the mixed working-class and bourgeois audiences who watched *Opera Wonyosi*. Instead, speculations abound, drawn from, then pushed back into, the background network of an essentially bourgeoisified theory of theatrical responses. But in this tangible, contemporary instance we did learn what effects *Opera Wonyosi* actually had on the audience. We have the concrete information of its effects on a Military Governor comfortably seated at the opening – to start with, that is. We know the reaction of a professor's wife, an effect freely admitted by her afterwards. We know of the effects on the parks and gardens workers and of other low-income workers such as Security Officers, who watched the show. We learned of the reverberations in Dodan Barracks, in military circles, in the National Security Organization. *Opera Wonyosi*, all set to appear in Lagos at the National Theatre, suffered a last-minute cancellation due to reasons which we also know. We – the critics, the producers, the commentators – know of the effect on those who participated in the production, not so famous as Lotte Lenya-Weill perhaps, but probably more articulate than the beggar along Berlin's Tiergarten.

Any theory of what theatre should or can do, what it can achieve, must be anchored in the sociology of what is actually written, done and experienced. What we are offered in the article under consideration, which I merely use as an example of the increasingly typical, is a criticism rooted in generalized theories of art or, more accurately, in a fragmentary ideology of art, for such an ideology must remain fragmentary unless it is amplified by the dialectics of equal partnership between accumulated theory and the concrete sociology of the artistic event itself. This is how the audience *ought* to feel – ambiguated, says the critic. We know our audiences did not. Well then, let the genuine dialectic begin!

The 'causal historical and socio-economic network of society' sought in every work of art by this particular school of criticism is, let it be understood clearly, only a further attempt to protect the hegemony of appropriation by the intellectual critic class *especially*, and this is especially true when such criticism chooses to ignore the *received* function as manifested in effect. Liberation is one of the functions of theatre, and liberation involves strategies of reduction to the status and stature of the power-wielding class in public consciousness, exposing and de-mystifying its machinery of oppression. Representing Hitler, just to theorize, as an imbecile dripping mucus on his iconographic moustache may not be the social answer to a horrendous aberration, but it is at least more honest and less presumptuous than wishing him away as a mere figment of the socio-economic imagination. The satirist operates with an implicit recognition of the social limitations of his art; his methodology is allied to the social strategy of preparation. The mastering of reality and its transformation requires the liberation of the mind from the superstition of power, which cripples the will, obscures self-apprehension, and facilitates surrender to the alienating processes ranged against every form of human productivity. DEFLATING THE BOGEY – this is also socially valid and progressive art. It becomes seriously flawed, a word carelessly employed by our critics, only when it attempts to pander to socio-historical causes, thereby explaining away oppressors in rational (including economic) terms. Bourgeois intellectualism actually prefers the latter, because it wishes people to leave the theatre having *understood*, and therefore remaining unchallenged by the need to destroy them. I know that such critical consumers will respond to this with yet more pages on how such-and-such a 'causated work clarifies and points the way to such destruction', but I must insist on the sociological truth of my observation that, for the critic, either (1) the work is totally deficient in such combative insights – which excuses his lackadaisical withdrawal – or (2) is filled with heavy insights, after which it serves only as a cause for intellectual satisfaction, settling neatly afterwards into the theoretical lumberyard of sociological inertia. Our Leftocracy has so far ignored the Bakalori massacre,* but the reason is simple: the playwright has not yet provided them with historico-socio-economic insights into what needs to be done! Art which identifies the enemy in a language which is instantly grasped – the language of satire, for instance, not available to yet another typewriter to be historically causated, pickled, and hung up to dry – may still *not* be a proletarian art; it is at least graphic *l'engagé* which escapes the bane of Leftocratic appropriation and addresses the proletariat *directly*.

Music, Essence, And Class
Consider now the following interjection by our guest scourge of bourgeois values; Roland Barthes is castigating here the degradation of real human beings, real trees, tunnels, mountains, and architecture to touristic *signs*, which are couched in the familiar trivializing language of the salesman as it appears in the French *Blue Guide*: 'We find again here this disease of thinking in essences, which is at the bottom of every bourgeois mythology of man . . .' (*Mythologies*, p. 75) Here is another: 'We find here again this bourgeois promoting of mountains, this old Alpine myth (since it dates back to the nineteenth century) which Gide rightly associated with Helvetico-Protestant morality and which has always functioned as a hybrid compound of the cult of nature and of

---

* The 2 a.m. massacre in 1980 of peasants at Bakalori village in Sokoto state by the armed Mobile Police Unit. These peasants had earlier occupied the offices of a dam construction firm, demanding compensation for their appropriated farms. A policeman was killed in the attempt to dislodge them. That night, a squad of the Mobile Unit was sent in. They descended on the sleeping village, firing into the thatched dwellings, indiscriminately, mowing down farmers, their wives, and children as they ran. A hundred and fifty were counted dead, by name. The President of Nigeria, in whose home state this atrocity took place, has yet to even set up an enquiry. The intellectuals, Left and Right, are content to let it pass.

puritanism . . .' (*Mythologies*, p. 74). As stated earlier, we must give Roland Barthes credit for knowing, for discovering and unmasking, his own social sensibilities in this direction. The question we now pose is as follows: Does the African critic, on encountering such categorizing claims, take the trouble to find out the sensibility of the Kilimanjaro goatherd towards his mountains, or does he simply ingest these claims into the language of his own class myths? Now some of us who constantly circle the globe – I am trying to avoid the prejudicial 'globe-trotter' – have had the opportunity of visiting these same Alpine natives – Italians, Bavarians, Yugoslavs – and encountered the peasant stock on its own territory, drunk and danced with them, and occasionally wondered whether one had been magically transported among the gorges and ranges of Nigeria's own plateau region. With such a background, one begins to critique the language of those quotes. It says too much, claims too much. It is rooted in a specific history, a peculiar intellectual development in which language has taken over reality as reaction to another form of productive aberration, the tourist industry, by a specific class at a specific time and in certain specific forms. On the literary field, there is of course the aesthesiogenic genre of Thomas Mann's *The Magic Mountain*, which would be an emetic even to a moderate hater of the bourgeoisie. Such literary malappropriation of Nature however, and a thousand like it – be these in music, dramatic or graphic forms – cannot contradict the truthful relations of those whose mountains were not appropriated by an elite group for the edification of a mini-society. They cannot be permitted to inhibit our own uncorrupted responses and creative exploitation of the many facets of Nature. When the Gikuyu locate their ancestry within the hidden heart of their local mountain, we do not think of Thomas Mann; if we must pick a European affinity, which we are not compelled to do, our 'soul-brother' would probably be a Russian composer Mussorgsky, one of the first composers to use folk music as a basic for orchestral work, of which one of the best-known is *A Night on the Bare Mountain*.

This is not to concede that any work or form of art does not lend itself sooner or later to appropriation by a different class from that responsible for the original production. When Rimsky-Korsakov returns to the same theme, collaborating with Mussorgsky for further refinement of the work, the new produce is already responding to the sensibilities of a developing class and moves closer to the bourgeois sensibilities of *The Magic Mountain*. That of course is another progression (or retrogression) well worth detailed analysis, but not here, for it belongs to the field of music criticism and sociology. It is relevant additionally here because Roland Barthes is at his most *embarrassed* when he has to evolve a language of music criticism, one which evades the clichés and baroque legacies of his society's *langage* of music criticism. He evolved a new music value, the 'grain', whose sum total of innovation appears to lie more in the transference of adjectives to this new value from the music itself. Mind you, he himself recognized the danger:

> Are we condemned to the adjective? Are we reduced to the dilemma of either
> the predictable or the ineffable? To ascertain whether there are (verbal)

means for talking about music without adjectives, it would be necessary to
look at more or less the whole of music criticism . . . This much, however,
can be said; it is not by struggling against the adjective (diverting the
adjective you find on the tip of your tongue towards some substantive or
verbal periphrasis) that one stands a chance of exorcising music commentary
and liberating it from the fatality of prediction . . . [9]

Roland Barthes' essay here is of course purely exploratory, but the methodology is
clear. We can see that he is struggling against the territory of the ineffable, against a
very stubborn product, one whose *langue* is highly arbitrary and less accessible to the
authoritarian language of Leftocratic criticism. Honesty struggles against music's willful
meta-langue ('. . . but isn't the truth of the voice to be hallucinated?'[10]) and compromises,
dissolving into clearly embarrassed contortions. At the conclusion of his comparison of
the singing of the German operatic singer Fischer-Diskau and the Russian Panzera, it
would appear that all that Roland Barthes had achieved in this laudable exercise has
been already summed up in the American black vocabulary – one has *soul*,[11] the other
does not.

Now *soul* is a language of one proletariat that we know, recognize, and identify as one
of many regional proletariats in need of socio-economic liberation. It is a community
that has a very distinct culture – very palpable, almost quantifiable in all its complex
structures and their social correlations. I will not sentimentalize this society, which is at
once violent and tender, at once cynical, acquisitive, and millenial; I will content myself
with asserting that it exists, that it is part of a much larger society whose capitalistic
philosophy it shares. This micro-society also has its own bourgeoisie which, to some
extent, also appropriates the language of black proletariat; nevertheless, the *signified* of
this *parole* – soul – is one which still firmly belongs within this proletariat, not only
within the large American continent but also in much of the Caribbean, especially
Jamaica. Soul has its own mythologies too, and it is highly marketable; nevertheless, it
is a summation of music to this very specific socio-polity, and it resists outright
appropriation, being woven tightly into the interstices of daily social interaction – in
short, into a vocabulary of a socially replete existence.

When Roland Barthes, in his own search for a winnowed value of music, settles on
'grain', he is responding to an apprehension of experience which, he implores, must be
rescued from the ineffable. This choice of words is significant, but more informative
still is the very explosion, the *cri de coeur* from the paradoxically unmelismatic throat of
the social critic. (Picture Lenin's dilemma, asked to explain why he would sit hour after
hour with his Inessa, requesting that she play the same composition over and over
again.) Would it really help if we built on Raymond Williams' typology and described
music as an analogue of subterranean structures of feeling?

For structures of feeling can be defined as social experiences in solution, as
distinct from other social semantic formations which have been *precipitated*

and are more evidently and more immediately available. Not all art, by any means, relates to a contemporary structure of feeling. The effective formations of most actual art relate to already manifest social formations dominant or residual, and it is primarily to emergent formations (though often in the form of modification or disturbance in older forms) that the structure of feeling, as *solution*, relates.[12]

Let us go back again. An analogue? Or perhaps an ellipsis? An ellipsis of subterranean structures of feelings? Music is a clue in the direction of our real battleground. As a language of man's aesthetic strivings, but one which reinforces, yet resists, the language of other forms of artistic production, it leads remorselessly to a value which 'radical' theories of art attempt to deny and even deride. The dictionary meaning of ellipsis is 'a figure of syntax by which a word or words are left out and implied'. I favour this expression because the paradox of music is that it exploits the incompletion of *langue* to transcend language. It is truly a form 'in solution', even at its most replete; even when the main theme and sub-themes and variations have been explored and brought home with an overwhelming sense of release, the effect of music is that of a linguistic proposition which quarries its way towards total resolution – hence the failure of criticism to find an appropriate vocabulary, even for a narrative of the musical experience. The creative vocabulary describes this escapist value, capable only of evocation, as essence. Sometimes, reification is a tool for its expression. Poetry also attempts in its own frustrated way to capture the essence of material objects, phenomena, human relationships, and feelings. Music, however, since it remains incomplete within man's socially linguistic upbringing, paradoxically projects the existence of this replete, structural reality. Because the obsessed materialists are defeated by the complications of this self-constitutive art which does not pretend to express *everything*, but insists that there is everything to be expressed, comprehended, embraced, and ravaged (Barthes employs the expression *jouissance*), there is left to them only the conceptual essentialization of objective reality in other art forms to be revenged upon – these being, like the literary, linguistically 'open'. Commencing by habit with a specific social development which gave birth contemporaneously both to those art concepts and to a new reactionary class, the bourgeoisie, the conscious language of that class struggle has been uncritically absorbed by critics in other societies in which the *language* of essentialization predated the birth of the bourgeoisie in other histories.

'Ori' among the Yoruba, is essential conceptualization; so is 'Ikenga' among the Ibo and 'Nommo' among the Dogon. We must return to this subject, and in a different language.

For now, we must pause to ask: Is this a purely academic problem? Alas, no. It is a serious social productivity problem. When the critics gather themselves together at the Annual Leftocratic Convention* in orgies of ideological puritanism, they seem unaware

---

* An Annual (Critics') Conference with 'Radical Perspectives', which has been running for about five years, usually held at the University of Ibadan and attended also by academics from outside the country. (W. S.)

of a process of attrition in the actual productivity of a potential generation of authors. Perhaps no literature is better than certain kinds of literature; that is quite possible. I only ask that they understand the negative, sterilizing effect which a misuse of critical notions, a misplacement of their own socio-critical situating now has both on the quality and actual quantity of output among students from their captive audiences in the lecture-room. For there is some mis-teaching involved in this also which fouls up the roots of the neophytes' resources and imprisons their imagination. It is my view that literary infanticide is being committed right now, and by a fanatic minority of Leftocrats.

It is one thing to plot the course of European bourgeois romantic or idealist literature and situate it in its socio-economic context; it is however a serious academic lapse to transfer the entirety of that language of criticism to any literature which, while undeniably cognizant of other world literatures, nevertheless consciously explores the world-view of its own societies. It is an irony that those very critics are the ones who decry the 'undialectical' nature of much of today's African writing, who resolutely refuse to accept the conceptual heritage or even material artifacts and their authentic significations (in history, origin and social intercourse, orature) as valid dialectical quantities for any received theory. On the streets of Havana and other cities of Socialist Cuba, the haunting fusion of magic and revolutionary history by Garcia Marquez is hawked daily. Throughout Latin America this unique evocation of timelessness even in the midst of revolutionary wars defies all calculations by remaining a favourite of the proletariat. In Nigeria the millipedes of a future literature are no sooner hatched than they are made to begin to count their feet. Naturally, they never walk.

The Fictogram as a Langue of Vacuum

It is possible, however, to sympathize with the extremist position of some of the Leftocrats when confronted by non-African interpreters of African literature who, to revert justly to some African terminology, 'carry their offering beyond the door of the mosque', or 'dye their cloth a deeper indigo than that of the bereaved'. For while the problem of African critics, blinkered by partial dialectics, appears to lie in areas of interpretation, certain European critics proceed from the abyss of ignorance on which they must erect a platform. They appear, superficially at least, to be good structuralists. I call the basic unit of their *bricolage* the fictogram. The critic Gerald Moore, a late developer currently knocking at the portals of the Nigerial Leftocracy, for instance, takes one look at the following lines –

I watch my dreams float vaguely through the streets, lie at the bulls' feet.

Like the guides of my race on the banks of Gambia or Saloum . . .

– and, from them, constructs this fictogram of an African world-view: 'Senghor, in any case, has expressed unforgettably *the classical African* view of the dead as the principal force *controlling* the living benevolent and watchful' (italics mine).[13] Biodun Jeyifo, in his monograph *Soyinka Demythologised*, efficiently strips away the excesses of such 'enthusiasts' even while – of course – refusing to compromise his own radical stance on my writings. Indeed, Jeyifo does not stint when making the mandatory declamations about the illusory, undialectical, bewitched nature of my myth-making and its 'vaporous zone of self-subsistence.' I wish to announce my intention to continue to re-create my own myths, unscrupulously, in images – consciously selective – of vapour and matter for my contemporary needs. But more on that theme in another place.

Gerald Moore's new book, I began to say, continues very much the old game of foisting typologies onto the works of authors while evading, in one or two remarkable cases, the ideological grounding which he announces in his preface. Professor Moore agrees, he announces, with 'basic Marxist proposition that a work of art is not and cannot ever be free from the conditioning imposed by history, and market conditions . . . We shall judge . . . [the artist] by what he makes of the conditions of his time and place in the continuum of history, but we shall not ignore those conditions.'[14] Only Gerald Moore can inform us where, in his chapter 'Assimilation or Negritude,' which deals with the life and work of Léopold Senghor, he carries out this vibrant declaration of radical intent. Obviously presidents and statesmen are entitled to a different level of criticism from others. It is necessary to point out only two more of Moore's canards to indicate just what level of illumination is to be obtained from his latest book. First, the canard against – who else? – Wole Soyinka:

> And yet Soyinka does not reject modern life in the manner of Yeats, Eliot or Pound. He believes that it can recover its meaning and its soul by a full-hearted espousal of African values or civilisations; an espousal of which Olunde's death is meant to serve as an image. The political, social, religious and even economic arrangements of Yorubaland offer a system which only needs reinterpretation to act as the blueprint for tomorrow.[15]

Against this it is necessary only to refer to my *Season of Anomy*, in which a tiny, atypical corner of Mooreland 'Yoruba' is deliberately quarried out to serve as an active agent in an endeavour to mobilize the rest of the country, it being nowhere suggested that this corner become a model, only that it is historically equipped for its agent role. Moore's claim is equivalent to saying that a Basque communist cell, seeking to revolutionize the entirety of Spain, is attempting to transform the Iberian Peninsula in the image of the entire Basque province because that cell has the support of the mayor of its host village and his council! This attempted cellular mobilization of the country, whose main targets are Workers' Communities, is transformed by Moore into a sign of the author's approval of the very structures the mobilization effort is trying to overthrow. Now what *sociology*, for that is at the heart of this enquiry, of a critic could have led him to attempt such a brazen reversal of literary evidence? Patently the sociology of a latecomer knocking at the portals of Nigerian Leftocracy, and clinging, as is evidenced in the body of much of his criticism, to the hem of the bush-jackets of Femi Osofisan, Jeyifo, Kole Omotoso, and others – indeed, pushing them ahead in order to attribute any proven gaffes to their proven record in recent critical thinking. Moore's *Against the Titans* can now be seen as his presentation of credentials in this bandwagon exercise, when read against the much earlier *Seven African Writers*, his first claim to African literary expertise.

Gerald Moore is, of course, too clever to ignore *Season of Anomy*. However, instead of positing his criticism on the arguable nature and strategy of the revolution which the novel places in action, Moore diverts his reader's sights towards a consecration of the earlier fiction: 'Soyinka manages to create the impression that there is something deeply and intrinsically Yoruba about the community's arrangements.'[16] The purpose here is to reinforce the earlier canard, one in which the novelist is conspiring to restore Yoruba Mooreland feudalistic structure to contemporary Nigeria. For a literary critic to ignore the deliberate distancing of a familiar physical terrain in which action is situated through the utilization of a myth from as remote a culture as Asia, which Moore does recognize, is to damn himself as either a singularly inept practitioner of his trade or as a critic with a hidden, quite unliterary motivation. The creation of a different *language*, an alien myth, interworking with the personages of the action on local ground is such an instant literary signification that only an expert would dare miss it. Perhaps Moore would prefer that the action be located in the 'neutral' Iboyoru of Ezekiel Mphahlele's *The Wanderers*. No reference is made here to other objectionable points in Moore's essay, for these might involve sustainable contentions, errors of judgement, or simply matters of opinion. The deliberate introduction of Yoruba acculturation, and specifically its negative baggage – feudalism, capitalistic economic arrangements, etc. – is a malicious invention of a Leftocratic achiever for which he fails to provide evidence – naturally, as there is none. Both the preface and essays in my *Myth, Literature and the African World* should have cured Professor Moore of the extravagant delusion that I believe in 'a full-hearted espousal of African values', but it is doubtful if Moore understands any longer the difference between a contestation of 'world-views' and a blanket endorsement of them. Moore's mendacity is only equalled, and to some extent surpassed, by that of Bernth Lindfors, Hagiographer Extraordinary, who 'recreates' my juvenalia, in the old University College of Ibadan; every page of his essay 'The Early Writings of Wole Soyinka' contains at least one inaccuracy of time and place and a series of absurd attributions.[17] The lucrative business of juvenile hagiography of everything that moves on two feet from pop stars to syndicated criminals is, of course, very much the life-style of American letters. It is to be hoped that it never becomes a way of life in Nigeria.

Others with more leisure and stomach for the task may catalogue the list of factual misrepresentations Gerald Moore has made in his attempt to deal with the nature of African society. I will refer here, finally, to just a typical sweeping generalization which again takes its root in the sociology of this critic, an egotistical emphasis which makes him compulsively imply greater knowledge of African societies than the knowledgeable African: 'This Africa of vast segregated modern cities, mine-dumps, skyscrapers and jazz clubs was as alien and remote to the Nigerian or Senegalese reader of that time as Dallas or Harlem might have been.'[18] 'That time' refers to the time of publication of

Ezekiel Mphahlele's *Down Second Avenue*, in 1971, and 'that Africa' to South Africa. I can only speak for the average Nigerian reader of 'that time', and indeed of at least ten to fifteen years before that time. Such a reader was weaned on *Drum* magazine, a South African black journal whose monthly, racy contents portrayed Ezekiel Mphahlele's country in just the images of Gerald Moore's description. But this is only another shutter on black Mooreland, where reality has yielded place to a fictographic memory.

Power, Essence, Ideal

We must take into account but reject the burden of bourgeois development of other societies, reject the framework of their bourgeois values and conceptualizations yet, in the process, ensure that concepts which are termed bourgeois in the societies of their origination also correspond to the values of bourgeois development of our own societies. For this, we do not even need to prove first the existence of a bourgeoisie or coerce social groups into identical class structures of other societies. Efforts in this direction – that is, attempts at direct correlations with classic European models, with their specific histories – have been regularly controverted. The existence of classes, however, is a universal reality: What remains permanently contestable is the *universality* of concepts and values attaching to each group. There is more than matter for suspicion when our Leftocrats, for instance, take on the mantle of abuse from European Leftist criticism as it automatically attaches itself to the sheerest idealist suggestiveness in any form of literature. My theory is that it is a guilty reflex, a defence mechanism. The Leftocracy feels it is on trial when it detects any trace of idealism in the arts and literature, precisely because the hard evidence of revolutionary history is that, while the motivating force of social transformation does exist within the realm of socio-economics, power, that manifestation of idealist craving, has proved a durable partner and an uncertain quantity within such transformations. This is a most embarrassing language, one which belongs to the 'mushy' world of psychology, an upsetting factor even within the internal history of revolutionized societies.

Power and music – these constitute two of the least addressed products and strivings of the human kind by radical criticism. Like music, power lacks completion, cannot be quantified or reduced to the language of historicism: it stands outside history. It reaches out constantly towards a new repletion, towards indeed an essentiality, a concept of the Ideal. This element of the idealist is therefore present in the fanatic radical critic, for he becomes a surrogate of authoritarianism for a system which is challenged by the one value that knows itself, like music, to be incomplete. What is manifested here, to situate it bluntly but succinctly, is a conflict of interests that straddles both the metaphysical and the political. Marxism has created for our Leftocracy a system that declares itself complete, controlled and controlling: an immanent reflection of every facet of human history, conduct, and striving, an end known in advance and only delayed by the explicable motions of economic production and development.

E. M. Barth identifies the system of thought to which Marxism belongs:

The absence of systematic constraints gets its full importance in combination with another feature of the system of thought we are concerned with here – perhaps with the exception of the works of Nietzsche. This is the *claim to systematic definitive complements in principle* in the matters dealt with, i.e. completeness as to what is of *fundamental* importance in [the structure of] *a philosophy of human life and affairs*. With the exception of Nietzsche, the authors of these systems are understood by friend and foe to make at *least* this claim (and are frequently understood to make even wider claims, concerning the inorganic sciences as well). They certainly do not refer to other thinkers for fundamental principles which they themselves do not formulate, except in order to refute them.

This claim to definitive completeness leaves no room for serious revision of any one principle and it leaves no room to the addition of one or more new basic principles. These systems are, as one often says, dogmatically closed.[19]

Adherents of the rigid pose of Marxism dare not – repeat, dare not – believe the evidence of their eyes when the 'mushy' essentiality of Power is made manifest – as was the case with Stalin, contemporaneously (such is the irony of history) with that of an obverse ideology, Nazism. The embrace of convenience of these two Colossi, Stalin and Hitler, was more than symbolic. It could not last, however, and it did not. The twists and turns of the interpreters of this monstrosity of a wedding do not concern us here; they need be balanced only by the opportunism of the reactionary world which sought, in this very complex aberration, to ring the death knell of socialist revolution. For my part, as a writer, myth-maker, and critic, I invoke such reminders on a metaphoric level to reinforce the unresolved question mark which hangs over the dialectics of power with any form of ideology – progressive or reactionary.

When radical criticism claims that idealism reinforces a static, historical, irremediable world-view, I recognize immediately that we have a problem of language. Music, whose nature lends itself to largely idealist striving, is not static; on the contrary, the interiority of its language provokes a constant dialectic with the world of reality, which is action, development, motion. The functioning of music in the language of art is parallel to the functioning of power in the realm of politics and economics. The latter is often vital and deadly, but that is no reason for evasion; certainly neither art nor literature evades it. Indeed literature attempts to *contain* it, and it is the very methodology of containment which arouses radical criticism to ire. Why, it demands, have you ignored *my langage*? One response is this: If the revolutionary socio-economist will at least share the burden of containing and controlling the forces and distribution of production, on behalf of the masses, art will try to contain and control power, metaphorically, again on behalf of the masses. Whether as Alfred Jarry's King Ubu, Rasputin, Shakespeare's Richard III, allegories of terrorizing monsters and captive communities, Achebe's Chief Nanga, Sembene's Colonial Factor, my Dr Bero, or even mythical constructs such as Ogun, the writer, being careful in most cases to give no utopian answers, structures into controllable entities these faces of Ideality, be they evasively disguised as State, Divinity, The Absolute, or History. The challenger is representative man, and this is the essence of a combative, even revolutionary humanism.

The above examples have not only been carefully chosen to reflect the expression of this particular genre, they also provide the consumer with other facets of reality, not excluding the socio-economic. The emphasis here is that, even where the ruled are not corporately manifested, power is neither so abstract nor so reified that it does not implicate, even in the very act of naming it, the disadvantaged existence of the ruled. This point must be made yet again for the benefit of those literal-minded critics for whom whatever is not physically portrayed is presumed to be denied, or not made manifest. But let us take yet another example of 'essentialist' relations.

I spoke earlier of a difficulty of language in confronting the materialist-essential bogey. It manifests itself in areas of seeming absurdity, but such as can probably be resolved by strategies of redefinition. For instance, I have come across a materialist claim which states that even love, as an emotion, is a product of the socio-economic relations in human society. Now it so happens that many Africans ridicule the concept of love; so here, at least, 'African' values do appear to correspond to a non-bourgeoisified view of human relationships. Such an African viewpoint, which I have heard expressed both by the articulate worker and the 'been-to' student, insists that 'love' is a luxury of welfare societies such as one finds in Europe – and this, of course, is quite possible. But is the African here utilizing the same language as his European counterpart? For one thing, the African worker was actually speaking of 'pairing' – by implication declining to forgo his polygamous privileges. The radical interlocutor from Europe is issuing, by contrast, a *critique* of the development of 'possessions' and, in that particular context, a debunking of the notion of an unchanging essence in human relations. There are immediate complications on both sides, complications of a nature which cannot be resolved in class typologies. 'Pairing' is still observed among animals, and no evidence has yet been offered on the relation of this to the level or their means of production. So has polygamy been observed among the animal species: doves, peacocks, and gamebirds have elaborate systems of courtship, and baboons have been known to fight to the death over any attempt to encroach on their harems. The expression which apply to these forms of attachment must transcend mere sexual terminology or the mere biological activities of hormones and the rounds of mating seasons. Some may see the baboon's polygamous herd as capitalistic accumulation; for for a rational observer it becomes necessary, on discovering similar conduct in human society, to accept the possibility of some other essence of a relationship which so demonstrably stands outside economic patterns. Since an analogue of this conduct or relationship exists ahistorically in the species which we have identified as peacock, dove, or ape, it is sheer perversity to deny that love, fondness, or some other emotion resulting in human attachment (or revulsion) has existed ahistorically in man. If love exists, then so too do hatred, meanness, generosity, perversity, strength, and weakness, variants of (perhaps psychologically rooted) instinctual conduct, undifferentiated by later class formations – including the power drive or instinct. The reification of such abstractions in the personae of deities is a device which serves purposes ranging from ethics to poetics. Such activity is, of course, open to social abuse, opportunism, social inertia born of superstition, and the like. But it also can, and has served society as a mechanism for combating every one of these very anti-humanistic malformations, including the abnormal development of the last-mentioned instinctual drive, the group's or individual's lust for power, by endowing the mythical figure with the collective force, with the negative or positive attributes of the total community. Concerning this aspect of social mechanics (which, let me emphasize again, is only *one* of the many functions to which myth has been put), when it is objected that such a method is not scientific, the provoked answer is that the so-called scientific systems of society have yet to find a scientific counter to the abnormal and unpredictable development of a personality cult around a strong leader with an unsuspected power drive who becomes the embodiment of the Ideal – infallible, supreme, an essence and apotheosis of the secret mythological yearning of the unsuspecting victim.

For the ramifications of the power drive throughout history – at all stages of socio-economic development; within and affecting the varied activities of man in public life and private; in magic and technology; in the arts, education, and civil service; across and within the class units of every form of society – any sentient being who refuses to accept the empirical deductions of his own environment may turn for a philosopher's view to Bertrand Russell's *Power*. Russell is not a fashionable philosopher among African intellectuals. He has neither a German nor a Russian name; moreover, his discourse is strangely lucid, easily comprehensible. And the work referred to here has hardly any footnotes. There are pitfalls in his exposition, especially his prescriptions, which border on political naïveté, but Russell's pursuit of the operations of power through the various levels of society down the ages yields enough matter for a true dialectic with other claimants to the motive force of history. We cannot rest upon any categories of ideas in which observable patterns within the societies which have produced those ideas have not been taken into full dialectical partnership. This would be to perpetuate the habit of excision which obscured the socio-economic reading of history in its time, enthroning the dictatorship of the mutant in the realm of human ideas. As a strategy of power seizure in a revolution or indeed outside a revolution or, as has been historically demonstrated, for the purpose of preventing a revolution, this might be pragmatically opportune. But begging the question in this way would permit the theory of power as a contributory motive force of history to have made its point.

In Conclusion

A sadist remains a sadist whether he is a fascist or a socialist. The former would rationalize his sadism under the arrangement of human beings into the superior, acceptable, and inferior or non-beings, and upon the last group he would permit any form of dehumanization, since you cannot really dehumanize a non-human, only reduce him to what he is. His fellow sadist, whose view of society is progressive, even radical, takes the battle to opponents of his conduct very simply by sneering at their 'bourgeois sentimentality'.

I am not involved here with ethical judgements in either case. What I wish to recall is that words do not lose their meanings, their significations because of any one ideology. Even if we spoke entirely in the language of manual signs, every gesture, curve, or slice of fingers, every conjunction of motions in wrists and palms would still signify a field of values, no matter the colouring through which the user were to subject such a signifier at its moment of application. When we use the expression *sadist*, therefore, we are not insisting on an irreducible condition of humanity even as we prove that such a quality cuts across class, ideology, or history. Specific cases of sadism can be accounted for by an individual's history or his social conditioning – perhaps some economic privation in the midst of others' luxurious existence which warped his humanity. Every explanation merely confirms that there is a certain conduct that is observable in human beings which cannot be termed exactly kindness, consideration, humaneness, or the like. On the contrary, the expression codifies one simple observation: some human beings actually enjoy inflicting pain. *Sadism*, then, is a linguistic convention which is used to signify that predilection of certain human beings to inflict horrid pains – mental, physical, economic, or psychological – on others.

A psychologist, a painter, a musician, a historian, a linguist, a teacher, a social worker, a dramatist, a novelist, a poet, or an architect may, therefore, each in his individual way, become preoccupied by this isolable human condition which clearly occupies a category of its own (and not merely in a linguistic sense), since it does not belong exclusively to any of the other categories we know – social, ideological, or class, or even human. Animal psychologists, even owners of domestic pets, recognize its existence in the animal kingdom. Like other values, which are signified by expressions such as anguish, ecstasy, euphoria, violence, or tenderness, sadism and its correlative, suffering, can be explored, though not exclusively exposed within the other categories in which it was first observed.

Picasso's *Guernica* provides one famous illustration of *correspondance*, in this case of graphic art to psychological values within human experience. Such three-dimensional art as Rodin's sculptures, African traditional masks, the works of Vincent Kofi of Ghana, or even some examples of Russian realist art like the works of the illustrator Vladmir Favosky, for instance, render the transmission of this essential value. It may be an unpleasant fact for the ultra-Marxist critic, but realist sculpture and expressionist wood-cuts, at their finest, exhibit the paradox of this same *essentialist* correspondence.

But I deliberately introduced Picasso's *Guernica*. The kind of ultra-revolutionary critic who has engaged our attention would, of course, damn Picasso's *Guernica* just as I damn his infamous daubing on the walls of the UNESCO foyer; it is called *Leisure*, and I consider it one of the most notorious con-tricks of art, an Emperor's Clothes delusion, no less. Where I part company with our imagined critic is (1) in his denial of the essential value of the correspondence of *Guernica* to the ahistorical, independent categories of terror, courage, fear, anguish, and so forth and (2) in what I am sure would be his rapid recourse to the examples of revolutionary art rendered in the works of Mexican muralists like Diego Rivera and Orozco, Russian and Chinese proletarian art, and the rest. The contestation, in short, would be this: Assuming that such categories of experience had been successfully isolated (which, he finds, is difficult to deny utterly) and rendered concretely, transmitted if you like, on the canvas, then it is the responsibility of the artist to point the way for the avoidance of, for the resistance to, and for the triumph of humanity over the mutilating agents of history. Picasso's *Guernica* would then stand condemned for daring to stand outside of history, or, at least, for laying itself open to essential interpretation. It would not matter that the event is located, by its very title, in a geographical place and is an outcry against fascism, against the sadism of a particular moment. Bourgeois art criticism has damned Picasso's *Guernica* by according it the title of masterpiece in a universal *l'engagé* which extends it beyond the class struggle, indeed places it outside the class struggle and mounts it on the podium of universal application. And since the painting is, irreversibly, a permanent abstraction of human anguish, it becomes an embarrassing testament of a historically provoked essentiality.

It is hardly surprising that Barthes' chapter 'Diderot, Brecht and Eisenstein' (in *Image – Music – Text*) is a marvel of analytical acrobatics. For how is Barthes to cope with the crafted essentialization of emotions in the meticulous, frame-by-frame compositions of the Russian cinema realist Eisenstein? Barthes' critical honesty cannot deny it; and were he to do so, he would simply render himself absurd to any reader acquainted with Eisenstein's expressionist techniques. Barthes' task is further complicated by the fact that he has elected to place Bertolt Brecht, a playwright and dramatic theorist whose stark techniques of presentation and emotional distancing are the very opposite of Eisenstein's, in tandem with the Russian. But he has problems even with Brecht's formalism, which wrings from him the unintended confession: '. . . it is pointless to criticize Eisenstein's [or Brecht's] arts for being "formalising" or "aesthetic": form, aesthetic, rhetoric can be socially responsible if they are handled with deliberation.' The prize passage, however, is to come. En route, Barthes concedes that the 'tableau', a favourite Brechtian device, is 'the presentation of an ideal meaning' – a great problem for a materialist, yet Brecht must not be damned. The stubborn paradoxes of Brecht and Eisenstein are absorbed through a jettisoning of rules, and the artists are provided with a formal absolution – one rule for Brecht, another for Eisenstein:

> . . . it is true that in Eisenstein . . . the actor does sometimes adopt
> expressions of the most pathetic quality, a pathos which can appear to be very
> little 'distanced', but distanciation is a properly Brechtian method, vital to
> Brecht because he represents a tableau for the spectator to criticise; in the
> other two, the actor does not have to distance: what he has to present is an
> ideal meaning . . .[20]

Truth will out, it seems.

The correlation of artistic forms and idioms with ideological precepts of any one persuasion is full of pitfalls which leave the agent or arbitrator dangerously exposed – and, ironically, the greater the agent's intellective faith, the worse his exposure. Despite all evasions and rationalizations, those penalties of willed adherence to compact systems of ideas, the language of art and creativity continues to pose problems beyond the merely linguistic or semiological. Why deny that a frame of the cinema picture, arrested in time, frozen, rendered ineffable, an extract from history yet an emotion or statement that stands outside of that sequential, *returns to reinforce the historic moment from which it is built with a force of that other level of truthfulness – recognition*? The viewer's own history completes the forms, the canvas, the sculpture, the ahistorical testimony of a poetic licence. That tableau is the myth; it may be progressive or reactionary, but it is *not* a bourgeois liberal-romantic convention. The actuality of the historical development of these *langues* of individual art forms spans the whole of human history, including the development of the bourgeoisie. Expressionism may have been appropriated by a dissatisfied group of middle-class artists in Germany, but its inspiration came from an ancient period in Africa whose carvers were not of the 'bourgeoisie'! The task of those who continue to find the myth-tableau unacceptable must be to find a relevant language – perjorative still. No one expects them to change their allegiances, only to make *meaning*. For my part, I shall endeavour to enshrine the essence of their negativity in appropriate mythologies.

They may, however, prefer to address an even more fundamental problem of their own situating, one which has already been engaged here and which Roland Barthes, our elected pointer, courageously faces even as he pours intellectual scorn on the bourgeoisie of his society. So far the Nigerian (and indeed most African) Leftocrats have shirked this responsibility in self-criticism. They have failed to discriminate even within their ranks the self-seekers, opportunists, the radical chic and the starkly ideological illiterate, for whom the company is all and for whom no social responsibility exists outside the social 'identifying-with' in repetitious seminars and coffee-rooms and staff clubs with their holiday resort facilities – beyond the public gesture of association with an equally unproductive Left. It is time to ask the rigorous question: *What are you really contributing to society while awaiting the revolution?*

Let our colleague from the ivory semiological towers of France have the last word. He is a teacher who has honestly critiqued his own situation, his relationship to his students even down to the lecturer's adoption of a physical stance among his students! Above all, however, as a demolition agent of bourgeois mythologies, he has paused to examine whether he, Roland Barthes, is not part of a new ideo-mythical *langage* which merely occludes the real possibility of an understanding and transmission of a proletarian culture:

> Then begins, however, for these procurators of proletarian meaning, a real
> headache of a problem since their class situation is not that of the proletariat:
> they are not producers, a negative situation they share with (student) youth –
> an equally unproductive class with whom they usually form an alliance of

language. It follows that the culture from which they have to disengage the proletarian meaning *brings them back round to themselves and not to the proletariat* (my italics). How is culture to be *evaluated*? According to its origin? Bourgeois. Its finality? Bourgeois again. According to dialectics? Although bourgeois, this does contain progressive elements; but what, *at this level of discourse*, distinguishes dialectics from compromise? And then again, with what instruments? Historicism, sociologism, positivism, formalism, psychoanalysis? Every one of them bourgeoisified. There are some who finally prefer to give up the problem, to dismiss all 'culture' – a course which entails the destruction of all discourse.[21]

NOTES

1. I am well aware that the French language purist will be greatly disturbed by this assault on French grammar. However, I am attempting here only to convey certain conceptual aids, thought process, or mnemonic cues, and not even the *Académie Française* can legislate against ungrammatical thinking.

2. Dr See Ess Momoh, 'The Two Faces of Violence', Lagos, Nigeria, *Sunday Times*, 20 July 1980, p. 8.

3. As a contrasting, harmless example of exchanges utilizing this language of appropriation, see T. Vidal, 'Of Rhythm and Metre in Yoruba Songs', Seminar Paper, Dept of Music, University of Ife, 20 Nov. 1980.

4. Roland Barthes, *Mythologies*, trans. Annette Lavers (London: Jonathan Cape, 1972), p. 9.

5. Norman Mailer, 'A Fire on the Moon', *Life*, 29 Aug, 1969, pp. 22–41; 'The Psychology of Astronauts', *Life*, 14 Nov. 1969. pp. 50–63.

6. Yemi Ogunbiyi, '*Opera Wonyosi*: A Study of Soyinka's *Opera Wonyosi*', *Nigeria Magazine*, Nos. 128–9 (1979) p. 5. (Note: *Opera Wonyosi* was performed for the Convocation Ceremonies, University of Ife, in December, 1978; the text is included in Wole Soyinka, *Six Plays*, Methuen, 1984.)

7. See the University of Ife Seminar Paper 'Sociology of Literature', uncredited (probably the Dept of Sociology or the Dept of Modern Languages). pp. 8–10, for cautionary words to the critic on the subject.

8. At the other end of the ideological spectrum, see Ali Mazrui's 'Chaka and Amin: The Warrior Tradition in African History'. Whereas Ogunyibi proposes a socio-economic understanding of an actively destroying social deformity, Mazrui blends it with myth-historic patterns. Both methods of distortion, unlike satire, plead a panacea of intellectual *understanding*, a soporific to the consumer, and a flattering of the type. Given the right socio-economic development and an eradication of the last vestiges of neo-colonialism, all forms of Aminism will vanish from the face of Africa. Empathy with those who experience the *actuality* is crude, unscientific response. I suggest that we ask the opinion of the vanishing breed of Ugandan intelligentsia, to see if they share this luxury of intellectual distancing!

9. *Image – Music – Text*, trans Stephen Heath (London: Fontana, 1977), p. 180.

10. *Ibid.*, p. 184.

11. Like all culture-originated metaphors, 'soul' is now employed to capture the 'ineffable' values of experiencing in other cultures, most significantly in music. Inevitably, categorization tends to be subjective. Mine includes, among others, the music of Amalia Roderiguez (Portugal – Fado), Russian folk music, a somewhat smaller proportion of Irish music, Fatima (Senegal), Brahms' German *Requiem* (unlike Verdi's or Faure's), Edith Piaf (France), Manitas de Plata (Spain – flamenco guitar), a vast number of Egba and Ekiti dirges, Nelly Uchendu (Nigeria – when she is not singing pop), and the majority of the blues greats, of whom Billie Holiday, Bessie Smith, and Ella Fitzgerald remain without equal. For all of these, I would also employ, interchangeably with 'soul', Barthes' most felicitous expression 'grain'.

12. Raymond Williams, *Marxism and Literature* (New York: Oxford Univ. Press, 1977) pp. 133–4.

13. Gerald Moore, *Twelve African Writers* (London: Hutchinson Univ. Library for Africa, 1980) p. 27.

14. *Ibid.*, p. 12.

15. *Ibid.*, p. 226.

16. *Ibid.*, p. 229.

17. In *Critical Perspectives on Wole Soyinka*, ed. James Gibbs (Washington, DC: Three Continents Press, 1980) pp. 19–44.
18. *Twelve African Writers*, p. 41.
19. *Perspectives on Analytic Philosophy* (Amsterdam, NY: North-Holland, 1979) pp. 41–2.
20. *Image – Music – Text*, p. 74.
21. *Ibid.*, pp. 210–11.

X

Cross Currents:
The 'New African' After Cultural Encounters*

Apologists and Rejectionists

There are any number of ways to describe or classify the attitude of African writers towards their experience of cultural encounters – which, for a start, is a euphemism. Many would prefer simply to call it a one-sided affair of cultural imperialism. Considering the major writers, some five or six categories immediately suggest themselves. But first, it is necessary to recall the identities of the 'alien' cultures, their properties and values as they affected – and still do – what we may describe as the authentic sensibilities of the various cultural groups which make up the black continent. Because of European domination of the principal techniques of dissemination, which means of course the control of education and information, it is often forgotten that there is more to cultural imperialism in Africa than what can be attributed to Christian Europe. Effectively sealing off all cultural contact with Asia, so that the major Asiatic cultures remain, even today, to the majority of African intelligentsia, only something that Coleridge or Hollywood occasionally dreams up, Europe still found it had not only to contend with, but often to collaborate in Africa with another powerful alien culture – the Arab-Islamic.

Taken together, therefore, the history of African people provides us with two principal enemies of their authentic traditions and their will to cultural identity. One is European imperialism, the other Arab-Islamic penetration and domination of significant areas of the continent. The creative methods of dealing with both provide a spectrum that reveals, sometimes in spite of the authors' conscious intent, the prior culture of the society which these foreign values have supplemented.

The first category includes cases where the author no longer queries, or indeed is hardly conscious of, the event of his ethno-cultural supplanting; his writing proceeds from a basis of self-negation, an 'ethnic submission' which need not be a matter of

---

* First published in *Writers in East-West Encounter: New Cultural Bearings* (1982).

conscious choice. The writer recognizes his being and his society in no other terms than what is easily proved historically alien. Cheikh Hamidou Kane, the Senegalese writer, is one illustration of the method of ethnic submission. His *Ambiguous Adventure (L'Aventure Ambiguë)* provides our first category of the various stances adopted by the African author towards his experience of cultural imperialsim. By placing the drama of cultural encounter squarely between two contending cultures, he appears to have taken an *a priori* position of dismissal of the earlier culture of his society. European philosophy and social pragmatism are launched against the sublimity of Islamic mysticism, the latter being made to stand for the authentic African society. What emerges of that prior society is only accidental, gleaned between the lines of drama and alien contentions.

Perhaps it was the phenomenon of ethnic submission, both in the society of the elite and their writings, which prompted the emergence of our second category – call it the 'Cartesian response' or more familiarly, 'Negritude', a phase of black affirmation by the great black francophone poets and dramatists – Leópold Sedar Senghor, Aimé Césaire, Léon Damas, David Diop, Birago Diop . . . even the Marxist stateman-poet Agostinho Neto, once upon the early days! To Descartes' 'I think, therefore, I am,' they responded on behalf of the black man: 'I feel, therefore I am.' Rationalism is essentially European, they claimed; the black man is emotive and intuitive. He is not a man of technology, but a man of the dance, of rhythm and song.

This simplified view of the black man's world did not pass without its challengers however, and even the early Negritudinists soon found themselves compelled to begin to modify their position.

Still, they did receive some unintentional bolstering from yet another category, the third in my list, best described as 'unmediated exposition' – of which Chinua Achebe, the Nigerian novelist, may be held as the finest practitioner. Dealing with his society's history at the moment of its encounter with the European, Chinua Achebe's *Things Fall Apart* is content to portray a tragic passage in history and leave it thus. This is how it was, neither more nor less. Achebe eschews judgement on the event itself, avoids exotic pleading on behalf of the threatened and soon-to-be-dominated culture, skirts tempting Negritudinist denigration of the imperial culture. The strengths and weaknesses of the prior society are faithfully rendered; the result – a poignant affirmation of a basically secure, traditional society whose socio-organic flaws any incoming cultures would probe until its structures succumb and its foundations teeter.

There is also a rather special category, a sub-category of the Negritude grouping, which appears to operate through 'stylistic bridges'. In effect, this was also a dialectical recognition within Negritude. First, black affirmation, next the synthesis of black leaven and white flour – humanism and technology – which would create a new, progressive brotherhood or being. Camara Laye's major work, *The Radiance of the King (Le Regard du Roi)*, comes closest to being the perfect symbol of this posture, ensuring however that the dominant partner is the black. It created heated controversy, resurrecting in a racial context the old question of form and content. Should an African writer apprentice his art to the construction of stylistic bridges, where the ethnic content is rarefied and therefore seductively universalised? Not now the strident chest-thumping of the proud black beast of Negritude, no! Black authenticity is elicited through a universal quest idiom, the pursuit as much of a 'holy grail' as of self-discovery. But in Laye now, also a baffling hunt for the key to a mysterious culture. The anti-hero, the questing white man, is finally brought to his knees. The cathartic climax suffuses a drama of black-value salvation with a suspiciously Christian 'mystic grace'. But what does it matter? The seeker for a change is the white man; he finds rest and fulfilment in the folds of the black king's divine cloak, purged, cleansed, accepted and absorbed into the radiant heart of the mystic king. Camara Laye's work is representative of the cultural osmosis that is a feature of receptive societies, and, in that sense, may be said to be non-partisan. Nevertheless, and despite the meticulous deployment of stylistic bridges, Laye's work is, in essence, an affirmation of prior cultural validation, of man's organic integration in traditional African society. He concedes little to the superior claims of the alien.

'Iconoclasm' as yet another category – the fifth major one in my list – was late in coming. Indeed, it did not surface at all – at least, not in its totally uncompromising form – until some ten years ago in the work of Yambo Ouologuem: *Bound to Violence (Le Devoir de Violence)*. Almost as if in conscious rebuttal of Hamidou Kane's *Ambiguous Adventure*, Ouologuem proceeds to demolish all claims by all cultures and religions to any value pre-eminence, or indeed, historic probity. Where Hamidou Kane had meshed Islamic thought so subtly in social hierarchical operations and domestic ambience that the reader accepts, unquestioning, his premise of an authentic black society in the Islamic, Yambo Ouologuem demolishes any such claims, repaints history in garish, clashing colours. The literary scene in Africa had of course boasted other rejectionists: Mongo Beti for instance (*The Poor Christ of Bomba, Mission to Kala*, etc.) had, by his irreverent, caustic humour, undermined the pretensions of the Christian church in Africa and its vanguard role in the European 'civilizing' mission. Yet even that very process ironically reveals such African terrain as communities which (like Hamidou Kane's through Islam) are regulated in essence, even pivotally, by a Christian culture and its subtle mechanisms.

Not until Yambo Ouologuem therefore, and Ayi Kwei Armah of Ghana in his last novel *Two Thousand Seasons*, do we encounter a fifth category, the uncompromising iconoclastic view, and the battle-cry, 'A Plague on both your Houses'. Indeed Oulougeum goes further than Armah with his cry, 'A Plague on *All* your Houses' – all pretensions of cultures, histories and civilizations – Judaeo-Christian, Arab-Islamic, Black-animist, European-imperialist, black-dynastic, explorer-European, *pax-universalis*, medieval-mystic etc. All cultures and civilizations are paraded in a violent course of collision. Ouologuem's view of history suggests that of a mind in daemonic possession, reducing the intellectual edifice of imperialist nations to rubble, battering the self-esteem of Negritude with a violent, self-destructive construct of Africa's 'true' history.

Armah groups Africa's historic models in two – the progressive and the reactionary.

In as much as he includes feudalism (or kingship) in the latter, he may be placed in the same camp as Ouloguem, though it is doubtful if Ouloguem is much bothered with such ideological divisions. Where Armah proves comparatively positive, that is, parts company totally with Ouloguem, is in his careful construction of mythical past as a potential model for the future. At the heart of Armah's desperate invectives against the European and Arab slaver, and Islamic and Christian mind-enslaver, we read the concepts of challenge to the new African – self-retrieval, self-identity, cultural recollection, cultural security etc., as prerequisites for social revolution. Armah's historic reconstruction is, however, filled with all the pitfalls of the simplistic, though this evocation of an authentic tradition in the cause of a society's 'coming-in-being' is of a far more ambitious order than, for example, Ousmane Sembene's evocation of an authentic tradition in the cause of society's transformation process.

Sembene's recipe for transitional society is more accessible because it selects its ingredients from contemporary reality. And although it deals with a colonial situation, the basis of conflict – exploited versus exploiters – remains nevertheless the true phase of the continent's birth-anguish today, with black heads grafted on the body of the colonial creed of alienation. Sembene's *God's Bits of Wood* is a literary irony: committed to a rejection of sentimentality in tradition, it nevertheless results in the triumph of the strengths of the positive in tradition. And since the question which haunts the culturally committed of African intelligentsia today is how to reconcile tradition with modernism and progress, it is a valuable example to offer to the extremist postures of total self-negation in the cause of radical values for society.

For we are referring now to 'tradition' as a lived thing, as a cohering mechanism of society, as a sum of beliefs, relationships, deployment of resources, control and exploitation of environment, attitudes to the imponderables of existence (birth and death) . . . in addition to the records, oral or written, of all these, their modes of representation in artistic form, and their strategies of mediation in the light of new experiences.

Towards Abolitionism?

With the above spectrum of attitudes in mind, we may consider that the most vexed aspect of the theme under discussion is easily the debate over the relevance or non-relevance of a cultural identity to the contemporary arts in Africa. The extreme approach is that the authentic sources which provide the individual in society with what we express as a 'cultural identity' are in reality non-authentic, since they have been transmitted largely through the prejudiced selective machinery of the prevailing class at any given moment of a people's history. This ideological line obtrudes far deeper into African writing – fiction and essays – than is commonly imagined. Viewed as an objective tool for dealing with identified 'enemy' superstitions, it has proved more than fashionably attractive to the black scholar and writer as he enters his self-conscious role as 'leader of thought' in society, and is resentful of the distractive role into which culture is manipulated by the new breed of black exploiters.

The theory of culture as the mere superstructure erected over the 'level of productive forces' by those who control the 'means of production' etc., surfaces with increasing frequency to disturb and confuse the practitioner within, or researcher into, cultural sources whose principal concern is to rediscover, express, re-interpret and otherwise creatively transform those elements which render a society unique in its own being, with a potential for its progressive transformation. The ethical confidence of the scholar and/or artist in the unique nature of his own society (and by nature we do mean *potential* nature also) becomes progressively undermined until he begins to question the usefulness of any sustained interest in his own cultural matrix, seeing that his discoveries can, in any case, be reduced to a universal formula which has all the compellingness of being not only 'scientific' in analysis but prescriptive for the progressive ambitions of society.

In contemporary creative writing, especially theatre, but also through essays and debates, the new, progressive face of ideological encounter appears to demand as price the dead-end of all claims to unique cultural definitions. The tendency is not of course without historical basis. The glamorization of the African past; the excesses of 'court literature' in its modern form of uncritical nationalist fervour; artistic chauvinism in all forms – an extreme historical reaction against the racist literature and sociology of European 'Africanists'; the shameless exploitation of racial pride by unscrupulous leaders and the distraction from contemporary realities which it poses – all this was bound to lead eventually to the contrary extreme. Thus the newly surfacing mood of negation, equally uncritical, but also self-defeating.

In the face of this mood, it is more than likely that genuine recourse to sources will be inhibited, that research becomes mediated even before the material is 'neutrally' exposed. The most immune area of such records would probably be the traditional scholars such as oral historians and art critics, the last-mentioned being an ill-recognized group even today, outfaced by the contemporary art critic. It may be therefore that the contemporary artist, seeking inspiration in the authentic material of his past, will opt for direct channels of communication with the traditional scholarship of his own society, not indeed for any purposes of reduplication, simply as alternative material which is comparatively unmediated by the competing interests of global ideologies. That this contact, or awareness, holds immeasurable prospects for the most progressive, committed writer today is more than demonstrated by the works of – to revert to our example – Ousmane Sembene, one of the most responsive minds to the contemporary imperatives of de-colonized societies *and* the intrinsic cultural properties of such societies. To move from Ousmane Sembene's cultural security southwards across the continent is to encounter a *plausible* demonstration of the effects of cultural insecurity (or vacuum) not only on illustrative characters, but on the quality of the artist's response to society and – on his very art! If we focus on the ultimate concerns of the artistic life of Africa in this particular context – that is, contemporary and future Africa – we can establish the humanistic definition of our own concern as the 'new

African'. Both Sembene and, by contrast, Peter Abrahams, are desperately concerned with the formulation of this new human entity.

Incidentally, it must be stressed from the outset that no suggestion is being made that the cultural security of the artist guarantees good art or necessarily provides progressive social prescriptions. William Conton's *The African* is one useful demonstration of the contrary. As concerned as Ousmane Sembene is, not only to create the new African, but to root him in his own culture, Conton's work ends up being not only artistically unsatisfactory but dramatically implausible. The value of Sembene lies indeed in the fact that his work enables us to demonstrate that it lies in the contemporary writer not only to deduce social strength from an organic traditional culture, but to demonstrate its weaknesses in an active context, and proceed to reveal how the workings of events promote the emergence of the new, unalienated African, a product of a culture-secured society.

South Africa is a logical example of the hideous effects of cultural negation. The urban sub-culture in which a typical hero is located, such as Xuma in *Mine Boy*, is shown to be no substitute for the deeper needs of the social animal, least of all in a situation of daily confrontation with oppressive forces. Peter Abrahams' injection of the hero's temporary escape into the bucolic idyll outside the mining town can be read as an expression of missing rootedness. Of course this injected interlude is unreal; it is ephemeral, and the author intends no less. Even the snippets of the obscured role of tribal culture – such as the dance gatherings – are no longer adequate for the crushing problems of survival in the superreality of the mine. Alex la Guma elicits the same problems of uprooting in *A Walk in the Night*; the hero's existential void is rendered palpable, his future foredoomed. The process of reformulating a sense of identity dominates crucial moments of struggle through Richard Rive, Lewis Nkosi, Dennis Brutus, Ezekiel Mphahlele, Bessie Head as deeply as the new generation of writers – poets, novelists and playwrights – Oswald Mitshali, Sipho Sepamla, Kereopetsile, KaNdlovu, etc. Faced with these examples of a *forced* cultural deprivation, and its reflection as a *human* negation in its most profound aspects, we may claim that a *prima facie* case is made for visibly securing the cultural basis of societies which have, at the very least, been directly threatened by the domineering claims of other cultures, and are indirectly weakened today by far more subtle methods – via superior technology, economic strength, ideological persuasiveness, etc. Indeed, it is hardly necessary to cross the Atlantic to the Americas to remind ourselves of the critical role of cultural certitude in any social struggle or planning.

But to return to Ousmane Sembene, and especially to his *God's Bits of Wood*, a work which comes closest to the harmonization of cultural status and security of traditional African society with a visionary outlook in the evolution of a contemporary African society, resulting in the transformation of the New African. The process of *elicitation*, of Sembene's as opposed to the more common and less assured iteration of traditional values, mostly static, gives his work a permanent relevance to society in any phase of its development. We may take as reference a seemingly anti-humanist pronouncement by one of Sembene's characters: 'The kind of man we were is dead, and our only hope for a new life lies in the machine, which knows neither a language nor a race.' A tradition-hostile view, seemingly, and a not totally inaccurate expression of Sembene's socio-historical bias. Only, in relation to this avowal, indeed, in a dynamic complementarity to it, we are presented with a traditional society of such organic coherence that it is apparent that the transformation could not conceivably take place without the pre-existence of those traditional values.

This is the sociological paradox at the heart of Sembene's work, one which indirectly asserts the importance of a living culture as a precondition for the progressive transformation of society. The dualist sociology of the railway communities of the Savannah turns out to be perfectly 'natural', and transformation is revealed as more intrinsic than external. Thus, in the railway, that mechanistic superreality which has come to affect the life of the people in a most profound way, we observe simultaneously both a concrete focus of contemporary reality, and a passive technological phenomenon which must be dominated and exploited by the collective will, forged in the pre-eminence of an organic community.

The railway is translated into the pulse of that community, even as it is manifested as the life-guaranteeing device for maximizing their productive potential.

It is instructive to contrast this with the industrial superreality of the mine in *Mine Boy*, where the organic index of society is zero, and the black individual is irredeemably alienated from this dependency creation of the human hand. Significantly, the path of redemption which Peter Abrahams outlines is thoroughly artificial and extrusive; it does not spring from within a cultural matrix of forces which alone can confront the machinery of oppression, and for this obvious reason – a matrix of organic forces does not exist in that environment. The oppressed community, lacking the security of its own culture, does not even possess its own means of interior social control. It has no life outside the cultural *diktat* of the oppressor. Such rules as are adopted by the community for its own integral regulation are not expressions of its autonomy, but are reactions to the exterior controls placed upon the community.

Franz Fanon has elaborated sufficiently on this point, and the quality of violence in *Mine Boy* is only one more illustration of his analysis. So has Amilcar Cabral; his memorial lecture for Eduardo Mondlane in Princeton College, United states, titled 'National Liberation and Culture', remains one of the strongest affirmations to date of the pivotal role of cultural autonomy, not only in liberation struggles, but in the simultaneous reformulation of society. And the crucial difference in the contrasting portrayals of two societies of black peoples in *Mine Boy* and *God's Bits of Wood* is the absence of a cultural autonomy in one, and its cohering presence in the other.

I suggest that it is a pursuit of this 'cultural autonomy' which will enable us to overcome the complexities, paradoxes and pragmatic challenges posed by black scholars and revolutionary leaders such as Franz Fanon, Agostinho Neto (who must be constantly recalled as both poet and statesman), Amilcar Cabral and others; a continuing critique which can be accurately summed up in the following extract from Cabral's aforementioned lecture:

> Culture, the fruit of history, always reflects each moment the material and spiritual realities of the society of individual man, and of man the social being, confronted by the conflicts which put them into opposition with nature and the imperatives of life in a community. Further, every culture is made up of essential secondary elements, strengths and weaknesses, values and defects, positive and negative aspects, progressive and stagnant or regressive factors. Further, culture – the creation of the society and the synthesis of the equilibriums and solutions which society engenders for the resolution of the contradictions which characterise it at every stage of history – is equally a social reality independently of the will of men, of the colour of skin, or the shape of eyes.
>
> Undoubtedly, the denigration of the cultural values of the African people based on racialist prejudices and on the aim of perpetuating their exploitation by foreigners, has done much harm to Africa. But in the face of the vital necessity of progress, the following acts and practices will be just as harmful: undiscerning praise; systematic exaltation of virtues without any criticisms of faults; blind acceptance of cultural values without considering the negative, reactionary or retrogressive aspects it has or can have; confusion between that which is the expression of an objective and material historical reality and that which seems to be a figment of the mind, or the result of a specific nature; the absurd linkage of works of art be they valuable or not, to claimed characteristics of a race; and finally the unscientific critical appreciation of the cultural phenomenon.

To concede the entire content of the above – just for the sake of the argument – is however to acknowledge the right of any community or people to determine what constitutes the progressive or retrogressive aspects of its own culture. Further, it is to accept the preliminary responsibility of ascertaining and bringing to knowledge every aspect of society that has gone into the creation of its periodic cultures. Finally, it is to impose upon the creative intellects of that society the task of re-interpreting, through their contemporary experience and visionary acuity, the material and lessons of those cultural properties – *without the dominance of external preconditions*! This process constitutes what we have described as the assertion of a cultural autonomy, of which, as already stated, Sembene's *God's Bits of Wood* provides a most apt illustration, making it indeed 'a novel for our times'.

That the 'machine' appears to replace man or nature in this work should not be allowed to obscure the ultimate deductions, which state that the communal strength from an organic culture dominates the dynamics of conflict in the work. The earlier impression tends to simplify the relation of man to nature within the African traditional world-view, to imply that 'naturalness' in the primitive, Rousseauian sense can be paralleled by what we understand as culture. That would be false.

When and how does the writer arrive at this certitude? How does he, while asserting his ideological convictions, avoid the trap of writing a mere tract – a predictable outcome because it is undistinguished by that unique rootedness which constitutes the non-quantifiable element in any socio-historical drama? For this appears to be the critical direction of visionary commitment for the contemporary writer – unless of course he is content to reproduce works which are programmed into, and executed by, a computer. We have to begin, of course, by agreeing on social directions, which is obviously the reason for the selection of Sembene's *God's Bits of Wood* as our focal reference. If we were content to occupy ourselves with culture in the purely historic-artistic sense, there would be equally viable but inert examples to choose from: from Ola Rotimi to Cheik N'Dao's dramatizations of historic events; the various modern renditions of the Soundiata epic; the poeticization, deification, titanization of the remarkable Shaka by authors from the novelist Thomas Mofolo to the poet Léopold Senghor; the solemn to irreverent evocators of the past – Chinua Achebe, Mongo Beti, Daniachew Worku, Jomo Kenyatta, Hampate Bâ, Camara Laye, etc. Even Hamidou Kane's *Ambiguous Adventure*, that beautifully-sculptured confrontation between the philosophies of two contending cultures, would have to be regarded as constituting part of the relatively inert cultural armoury of the continent, waiting to be practised upon – if only reflectively – by the proponents of the search for the 'new African'. This is not to deny the cultural autonomy so implicit in, for example, Camara Laye's *The Radiance of the King*. The pertinent observation is that, aesthetically fulfilling as this work is, we cannot claim for it the same propulsive cultural autonomy which is infused into the localisation of Sembene's *God's Bits of Wood*, and which thereby strikes the mind with its rational relevance to the future of the continent, and the cultivation of the 'new African'.

The above recognition in no way reduces the aesthetic achievements of the listed authors and works, or the imaginative enrichment which they yield to any mind with the slightest pretence to sensibility. They embody even a critical significance: they demonstrate the seminal potential of cultural selectiveness, even cultural exclusivity, and thereby argue a case for an encouragement of the genre. In other words, Sembene's future-thrusting *God's Bits of Wood* derives from the confident, 'undialectical' culture-scope of *The Dark Child*, and the danger which the latter work faces today, in common with a thousand others yet incubating in the minds of black writers, no longer resides in the hands of the denigrating racist, but with the strident neophyte ideologue who fails to recognize the complementary nature of the varied strands of these literatures. Close upon the 'radical' damnation of the 'decadent, reactionary' nature of *The Dark Child*, *The Legend of Soundiata*, *Ambiguous Adventure*, follows, I suspect, the preliminary death-rattle of the *ijala* chanter, the traditional historian or art critic, the Xhosa poetaster and traditional folk dramaturge. Is there perhaps some deep-rooted cause in the intellectual sub-stratum of the modern African critic and analyst which makes him shy away from the category 'classic' and its fundamental place in the repertoire of African literature and life?

Only the school of 'Vulgar marxism' would insist today that the *Odyssey* or the *Iliad* be expunged from the literary repertoire of progressive European education, yet it is remarkable that parallel works in Africa to those seminal epics, which even made immense contributions to a European revolution, the Renaissance, have not yet found their place in a library of African classics, or provoked one into being. These works are still not generally known. A hermetic regionalization of the various cultures of Africa, induced and encouraged admittedly by the plurality of colonial languages, limits what should be standard 'classical' reading in black pedagogy and even literary pleasure. The corpus of Ifa poetry (the gnomic pronouncements of Yoruba Oracle) remain also within a limited circle, while the fevered utterances of the madman Nietzsche (*Thus Spake Zarathustra*) are deeply probed for meaning at the university level in 'with-it' faculties. New poetic forms owe their genesis as much to the constant availability of such religious or ritualistic liturgical modes as to the frenetic scramblings of the rare, original mind. To switch to a different creative medium, the Russian Revolution has not been retarded one step by the continuing presentation of 'Swan Lake' or 'Sleeping Beauty' in the repertoire of the Bolshoi Ballet; and Mao Tse-Tung unabashedly insisted on the infusion of the most embarrassing treacle-sentiment into contemporary Chinese opera; yet fashionable literary criticism on the African continent today attempts to stifle the yet inchoate definition of an existent classical tradition. The sculptures are fortunate, since they constitute their own ineffaceable record.

Apart from being a record of traditional creativity in itself, the classics of traditional literature, including the oral, provide the same kind of sustenance, a mine for creative quarrying, as European and Asian writers have obtained from their classics – the legend of *The Ring*, *The Viking Saga*, the *Bhagavad Gita*, *Gilgamesh*, etc., not to mention the Bible, from whose bottomless history metaphors have been drawn for man's modern-day dilemma. From such sources literature maximizes the involvement of the oral, traditional specialist in the creative processes and concerns of the modern writer. Additionally, they serve today as a corrective on the contemporary reader, whose mythological horizons are still too remotely stretched, except of course for the predictable folk-tales of his locality. The heroes may be dead, but imagination is not; their literature constitutes an essential dimension of the educational development of the 'new African'.

XI

Theatre in African Traditional Cultures: Survival Patterns*

Even where other resources of pre-colonial society are unevenly shared, culture tends to suggest a comparatively even-handed distribution or – perhaps more simply – mass appropriation. This may help to explain why it is always a primary target of assault by an invading force. As an instrument of self-definition, its destruction or successful attrition reaches into the reserves of racial/national will on a comprehensive scale. Conversely, the commencement of resistance and self-liberation by the suppressed people is not infrequently linked with the survival strategies of key cultural patterns, manifested through various art forms. The experience of West Africa has been no different. The history of West African theatre in the colonial period reveals itself therefore as largely a history of cultural resistance and survival. Confronted by the hostility of both Islamic and Christian values, in addition to the destructive imperatives of colonialism, it has continued until today to vitalize contemporary theatrical forms both in the tradition of 'folk opera' and in the works of those playwrights and directors commonly regarded as 'Westernized'.

We must not lose sight of the fact that drama, like any other art form, is created and executed within a specific physical environment. It naturally interacts with that environment, is influenced by it, influences that environment in turn and acts together with the environment in the larger and far more complex history of society. The history of a dramatic pattern or its evolution is therefore very much the history of other art forms of society. And when we consider art forms from the point of view of survival strategies, the dynamics of cultural interaction with society become even more aesthetically challenging and fulfilling. We discover, for instance, that under certain conditions some art forms are transformed into others – simply to ensure the survival of the threatened forms. Drama may give way to poetry and song in order to disseminate dangerous sentiments under the watchful eye of the oppressor, the latter forms being

* First published in *African History and Culture* (1982).

more easily communicable. On the other hand, drama may become more manifestly invigorated in order to counteract the effect of an alienating environment.

Nigeria offers a valuable example of the dual process of cultural attenuation and resurgence. For example, theatrical professionalism was synonymous, by the middle nineteenth century, with the artistic proficiency and organisation of a particular theatrical form which had emerged from the burial rituals associated with the Oyo monarchy, the *egungun*. The question of when a performed event became theatre as opposed to ritualism is of course a vexed one that we need not bother about in this context. It is, however, commonly agreed that what started out – probably – as a ritualistic ruse to effect the funeral obsequies of an Oyo king had, by the mid-century, evolved into a theatrical form in substance and practice. From an annual celebration rite of the smuggling-in of the corpse of that king and its burial, the *egungun* ancestral play became, firstly, a court re-enactment, then a secular form of performance which was next appropriated by the artists themselves. Its techniques were perfected by family guilds and township cults. About this time, however, Islam had begun its push southwards. The Oyo empire, already in disintegration from internal rivalries and other stresses, found itself under increasing military pressure from the Hausa-Fulani in the north, a situation which came on the heels of a rebellion of tributary states to the south. The fall of Oyo took down with it the security which the theatrical art had enjoyed under its patronage. The Muslims, victorious in northern Yorubaland, banned most forms of theatrical performance as contrary to the spirit of Islam. The *Agbegijo, Alarinjo* and allied genres, with their dramatic use of the paraphernalia of carved masks and other representations of ancestral spirits, came most readily under religious disapproval. It did not matter that, by now, they had lost most of their pretence to the mysterious or numinous.

Southern Nigeria and its neighbouring territories were, however, only temporary beneficiaries from this disruption of political life in the old Oyo empire. The Christian missionaries had also begun their northward drive, usually only a few steps ahead of the colonial forces. The philistinic task begun by the Moslems was rounded out by the Christians' ban on the activities of suspect cults. The Christians went further. They did not content themselves with banning just the dramatic performance; they placed their veto also on indigenous musical instruments – *bata, gangan, dundun* and so on – the very backbone of traditional theatre. It was into this vacuum that the returned slaves stepped with their Western (and therefore Christian) instruments, their definitely Christian dramatic themes and their Western forms.

Another historical factor aided the temporary eclipse of indigenous theatre forms: the slave trade and its supply which involved inter-state wars, raids and casual kidnappings. The missionary compounds often offered the securest havens from these perennial hazards, just as did (in West Africa) submission to the protective spheres of the Muslim overlords. It is difficult to imagine a group of refugees from the old Oyo empire encouraged by their Muslim or Christian protectors to revert to the ways of their 'pagan art'. The records do not reveal any such acts of disinterested artistic patronage. Artistic forms might be appropriated, but only in the cause of religious promotion; thus, for example, the appropriation of musical forms by the nineteenth-century Christian missionaries in Buganda for hymns. This, however, was only a later refinement, a sensible strategy for rendering the patently alien words and sentiments less abrasive to the indigenes by coating them in traditional harmonies.

It is difficult to trace, at present, the effect of the Oyo *egungun* dispersal on the development of theatrical forms in neighbouring areas. This is always the case with any situation of artistic hiatus – a period, that is, when a particular form of art goes underground or disappears temporarily, especially under the pressures of a dominant political and artistic ethos. The records simply ignore them, or treat them merely as isolated nuisances. The substitution of new forms belonging to the dominant culture takes pride of place in records, and this is the situation we encounter in the development of Western 'concerts' and variety shows in the colonized territories of West Africa.

At this point, therefore, let us clarify in our minds what theatre is. That this is more than a merely academic exercise is easily grasped if we refer to a sister art, sculpture, an achievement which the missionary-colonizer pioneers found convenient to deny to the African. The redressing assessment was made by other Europeans – the artists themselves, notably the Expressionists; they had no overriding reasons to deny the obvious, to ignore what was even a potential source of inspiration to their own creative endeavours. The vexed question of what constitutes drama and what is merely ritual, ceremony, festival and so on, while it continues to be legitimately argued, must always be posed against an awareness of early prejudiced reading of the manifestations encountered by culture denigrators, definitions which today still form the language of orthodox theatre criticism. To assist our own definition we need look only at any one cultural event within which diversified forms are found, forms which – through their visual impact – tend towards the creation of differing categories for a comparative description. In other words if, within one performance or cluster of performances (say, a festival or a celebration) in any given community, we discover consciously differing qualitative enactments, we are obliged to rummage around in our artistic vocabulary for categories that reflect such differences. Thus we find that, sooner or later, we arrive at the moment when only the expression 'drama' or 'theatre' seems apposite, and then the search is over. We will take an example from the Afikpo masquerades of south-east Nigeria.

A contrast between the *okumkpa* event and the *oje ogwu*, both being components of this Afikpo festival, actually furnishes us with the basic definition we need. This masquerade, which is the professional handiwork of a male initiation society, varies, we discover, from basically balletic sequences as contained in the *oje ogwu* to the *mimetic* as contained in the *okumkpa*. The latter is indeed performed as a climax to what appears to be the prominent *oje ogwu* turn by the masqueraders. Both are basically audience-oriented – in other words, we are not really concerned here with the complication of a *ritual* definition but one of performance and reception. The audience plays a prominent appreciative role in this outdoor performance, judging, booing or approving on purely aesthetic grounds. Whatever symbolism may be contained in the actual movements of the *oje ogwu* is of no significance in the actual judgement. What the audience looks for and judges are the finer points of leaps, turns, control and general spatial domination. The poorer performers are soon banished to the groups sessions – which demonstrates the importance given to individual technical mastery.

The *okumkpa* event, by contrast, consists of satirical mimesis. Masks are also used but the *action* forms the basis of performance. This action consists of a satirical rendition of actual events both in neighbouring settlements and in the village itself. Personalities are ridiculed, the events in which they were involved are re-enacted. In short, events are transformed artistically both for audience delectation and for the imparting of moral principles. Additionally, however, one standard repertoire consists of the taking of female roles by the young male initiates, this role being of a rather derogatory character. The satirized female is invariably what we might call 'the reluctant bride'. As the young actor minces and prances around, sung dialogues accompany him, built around the same theme: 'How much longer are you going to reject all suitors on the grounds that they are not sufficiently handsome/strong/industrious etc., etc.?' Competition is keen among the initiates for the honour of playing this central female impersonator. The various sketches in this vein are rounded off in the end by a massed parade of the various actors in the *njenji* where the less accomplished actors have their own hour of glory and the entire female world is satirically lectured on the unkindness of keeping the male rooster waiting too long.

We will not examine the sociological motivation of this kind of drama except to point out that this example is actually more rewarding, in our search for an explanation of man's motives in *dramatizing*, than, for instance, the theory of the origin in the Oyo masquerade. Clearly, in the Afikpo masquerade we encounter a male-prejudiced device. It ensures man's claim to social superiority and creates guilt in the woman for not fulfilling on demand man's need for female companionship. It is of no more mystifying an order of things than, for instance, the disparagement by male undergraduates in their press of female undergraduates who have not submitted to their own desires – except, of course, that traditional society imposed heavy penalties on libellous fabrication (which is, by the way, a reliable indication of artistic barrenness). What we obtain from one, therefore, is genuine art; from their modern progeny, alas, only dirty pictures and fevered fantasies. The *okumkpa* provides us with drama – variety, satire. We are left with no other definition when we contrast it with its consciously differentiated companion piece – the *oje ogwu*.

Similarly, festivals such as the Ogun or Osun (River) festivals in Yorubaland provide us with multi-media and multi-formal experiences within which it is not at all difficult to find unambiguous examples of dramatic enactments. The high point of the festival of the Yoruba hero-deity Obatala is, for instance, undoubted drama, consisting of all the elements that act on the emotions, the excitations of conflict and resolution and the human appreciation of spectacle. We begin to understand now why dating the origin of African drama, locating it in a specific event, time and place is an impossible task –

indeed, a meaningless one. In the study of art forms, it is clearly more appealing to look into extant material for what may be deduced as primitive or early forms of the particular art, noting along the way what factors have contributed to their survival in the specific forms. Festivals, comprising as they do such a variety of forms, from the most spectacular to the most secretive and emotionally charged, offer the most familiar hunting-ground. What is more, they constitute in themselves *pure theatre* at its most prodigal and resourceful. In short, the persistent habit of dismissing festivals as belonging to a 'spontaneous' inartistic expression of communities demands re-examination. The level of organization involved, the integration of the sublime with the mundane, the endowment of the familiar with properties of the unique (and this, spread over days) all indicate that it is into the heart of many African festivals that we should look for the most stirring expressions of man's instinct and need for drama at its most comprehensive and community-involving. Herbert M. Cole renders this point of view in penetrating terms:

> A festival is a relatively rare climatic event in the life of any community. It is bounded by a definite beginning and end, and is unified thereby, as well as being set apart from the above daily life. Its structure is built on a core or armature of ritual. The festival brings about a suspension of ordinary time, a transformation of ordinary space, a formaliser of ordinary behaviour. It is as if a community becomes a stage set and its people actors with a battery of seldom-seen props and costumes. Meals become feasts, and greetings, normally simple, become ceremonies. Although dependent upon life-sustaining rituals, the festival is an elaborated and stylised phenomenon which far surpasses ritual necessity. It often becomes the social, ritual and political apotheosis of community life in a year. At festival time one level of reality – the common and everyday – gives way to another, a more intense, symbolic and expressive level of reality.[1]

What this implies is that instead of considering festivals from one point of view only – that of providing, in a primitive form, the ingredients of drama – we may even begin examining the opposite point of view: that contemporary drama, as we experience it today, is a contraction of drama, necessitated by the productive order of society in other directions. That is, drama undergoes parallel changes with other structuring mechanisms of society. As communities outgrow certain patterns of producing what they require to sustain themselves or of transforming what exists around them, the structures which sustain the arts are affected in parallel ways, affecting in turn the very forms of the arts. That the earlier forms are not necessarily more 'primitive' or 'crude' is borne out by the fact that more and more of the highly developed societies are turning to the so-called 'primitive' forms of drama as representing the significant dramatic forms for contemporary society. These societies, which vary from such ideologically disparate countries as the United States and East European countries, are re-introducing on stage, in both formal theatre structures and improvised spaces, dramatic forms such as we have described, from the macro-conceptual (as represented in festivals) to the micro-conceptual, as ritual may be held to epitomize.

In this vein, what are we to make of the famous Return-to-the-Village Festival of the Koumina canton in Bobo-Dioulasso, Upper Volta?* Here we encounter a people who, like many others in West Africa, have experienced the culturally disrupting influences of Muslim and Christian cultures. The traders came first, the Mande traders, in the early sixteenth century. In their next significant migration, the mid-eighteenth century, they were accompanied by Muslim clerics, with the cultural results with which we are by now familiar. By 1775 proselytization had become so successful that an Imamate had been established by the famous Saghnughu family of scholars. The late nineteenth century saw the take-over by colonial administrators and Christian missionaries. Yet under this double assault, Bobo traditional arts have survived until today, and nowhere are they given more vital expression than in the 'Tagaho' season festival which marks the return of the Bobo to their village after their seasonal migrations to their farmsteads. The festival, which has for its core the funeral ceremonies for those who died during the period of farmland migration, has a far more important function for the living: the re-installation of the cohering, communal spirit and existential reality. Costumes are elaborately prepared, formal patterns both of 'ritual' and 'pageant' worked out and rehearsed, individual events enacted by masked figures for a delayed participation by the community as one entity. It is all of course a conscious performance, informed and controlled by aesthetic ideas, by the competitive desire also of 'showing off' dramatic skills. Simultaneously it is an affirmation of social solidarity. Can this form of theatre, considered in its most fundamental purpose and orientation, be viewed much differently from the theatre of 'happenings' which began in American and Europe in the sixties and is still encountered in parts of those societies today? To be sure, the former is more disciplined, formal and community-inspired, which are all attributes that we experience from unalienating forms of theatre.

At this point, it may be useful to consider instances where an art form evolves into another art form in one geographical/cultural area but fails to do so in another. The heroic tradition is one that is common to most parts of Africa (and, indeed, to most societies). Within this tradition may be grouped, at any level of its development, the epic, saga, praise-chants, ballads and so on, but here we are concerned with the performance aspect from which dramatization most naturally evolves. East, Central and South Africa are particularly rich in the tradition of the heroic recitative. Among the Luo of Kenya and Uganda, for instance, we may note the form known as the *pakrouk*, a kind of virtue-boasting which takes place at ceremonial gatherings, usually to the accompaniment of a harp. The individual performer emerges from the group, utters praises of his own person and his achievements, and is replaced or contended with by another. Similar manifestations are found among the Ankole tribes, while further south,

* Now renamed Burkina Faso. (W.S.)

among the Sotho and the Zulu, sustained lyrical recitations on important historical events have become highly developed.

Among the Ijaw people of south-eastern Nigeria, however, the same tradition has actually developed dramatic variants, has moved beyond the merely recited to the enacted, a *tour de force* sustained by a principal actor for over three days. The saga of *Ozidi*, the principal source for J. P. Clark's play of the same name, is an example. By contrast, the history of the performance arts in Central and Southern Africa reveals a tendency towards virtual stasis of the putative dramatic elements. Even the dramatic potential of such rituals as the *Nyasi-iye*, the boat-building and launching ceremonies of the Luo, with its symbolic cutting of the 'umbilical cord' as the boat is freed from its moorings, even the abundant parallelisms with nuptial rites, have somehow failed to move towards a truly dramatic rendering of the significance and life-intertwining role of the boats in the daily pre-occupations of the Luo. One need only contrast this with the various rites and festivals of the coastal and riverine peoples of West Africa, where both religious observances and economic practicalities of the same activity have taken on, over the centuries, a distinctly dramatic ordering. One may speculate at length on the reasons for this contrast; the reality remains, however, that drama as an integral phenomenon in the lives of the peoples of Central and Southern Africa has followed a comparatively meagre development.

Well then, let us, using one of our early examples, follow how traditional theatre forms adjusted or re-surfaced from the preliminary repressions of alien cultures. We find that the 'pagan' theatre ultimately withstood the onslaught, not only preserving its forms but turning itself consciously into a base of resistance against both dominating systems. We are able to witness the closing of a cycle of cultural substitution in a curious irony of this slavery-colonial experience. Having first broken up the cultural life of the people, the slave era, now in its dying phase in the first half of the nineteenth century, brought back the sons of the land with a new culture in place of the old. The returnees constituted a new elite: they possessed after all the cultural tools of the colonial masters. But – and now we emphasize the place of theatre among these cultural tools – even where they were fully assimilated into the cultural values of their erstwhile masters (or saviours), they found on their return company servants, civil servants, missionary converts who belonged in the same social class as themselves, but were culturally unalienated. These stay-at-homes had had what was more or less an equivalent colonial education, yet had also acquired a nationalist awareness which manifested itself in cultural attitudes. As the nineteenth century entered its last quarter, the stay-at-homes were able to provide a balancing development pattern to cultural life on the West coast which came predominantly under the creative influence of the returnee Christians, despite the latter's confidence in the superiority of their acquired arts and their eagerness to prove to the white population that the black man was capable not only of receiving but also of practising the refined arts of the European.

The cultural difference between the settlers of Liberia and Sierra Leone on the one hand, and the coastal societies of Ghana and Nigeria on the other can be translated in terms of the degree of cultural identification with, and adaptation of the authentic resources of the hinterland. To the former – mostly returnee slaves – the indigenous people remained savage, crude and barbaric, to be regarded only as material for missionary conversion and possible education. The converts who had remained at home, however, set off a process of schisms within social and religious institutions whose value-system was Eurocentric, delving again and again into the living resources of indigenous society. Naturally there were exceptions on both sides, but this dichotomy did hold in general. The direction of *new* forms of theatrical entertainment therefore followed an eastward pattern from the new returnee settlements; inevitably it received increasing native blood-transfusion as it moved further east away from the bastardized vaudeville of the 'Nova Scotians', so that by the time it arrived in Ghana, Dahomey (now Benin) and Nigeria, both in form and content, a distinct West African theatrical idiom had evolved.

'Academies', to begin with, were formed for the performance of concerts which were modelled on the Victorian music hall or the American vaudeville. The Christian churches organized their own concerts, schools were drawn into the concert rage – prize-giving days, visits of the District Officer, Queen Victoria's birthday and so on. The black missionaries refused to be outdone; Rev. Ajayi Crowther was a famous example, a black prelate who patronized and encouraged this form of the arts, while the Rev. James Johnson turned the famous Breadfruit church in Lagos into a springboard for theatrical performances. The Brazilian returnees added an exotic yet familiar flavour, their music finding a ready echo in the traditional melodies of the West Coast and the Congo whose urban suppression had not occurred long enough for such melodies to be totally forgotten. At the turn of the century and in the first decades of the twentieth century, Christmas and New Year saw the streets of the capital cities of Freetown and Lagos transformed by mini-pageants reminiscent of Latin fiestas, of which the 'caretta', a kind of satyr masquerade, appears to have been the most durable.

Cultural nationalism was, however, constantly at work against a total usurpation by imported forms. Once again religion and its institutions provided the base. Unable to accept the excesses of the Christian cultural imperialism, such as the embargo on African instruments and tunes in a 'universal' church, and the prohibition of drumming on tranquil Anglican Sundays, the breakaway movements began. The period 1888 to the early 1930s witnessed a proliferation of secessionist movements, mostly inspired by a need to worship God in the cultural mode of the forefathers. And now began also a unique 'operatic' tradition in West Africa, but especially Lagos, beginning with church cantatas which developed into dramatizations of biblical stories until it asserted its independence in secular stories and the development of professional touring troupes. The process, reminiscent of the evolution of the 'miracle' or 'mystery' plays of medieval Europe, is identical with the evolution of the Agbegijo theatre (then temporarily effaced) from the sacred funeral rites of the Alafin of Oyo to court entertainment and, thereafter, independent existence and geographical dispersion. From the genteel concerts of classical music and English folk songs by the 'Academy' of the 1880s to the historical play *King Elejigbo* of the Egbe Ife Church Dramatic Society in 1902, a transformation of thought and sensibility had recognizably taken place even among the Westernized elite of southern Nigeria. The Churches did not take kindly to it. They closed their churchyards and schools to the evolving art. Alas, they only succeeded in accelerating the defiant erection of theatre halls, specifically designed for the performing arts. It was in reality a tussle between groups of colonial elites, fairly balanced in the matter of resources. By 1912 the secularization of theatrical entertainment in southern Nigeria was sufficiently advanced for the colonial government to gazette a 'Theatre and Public Performance Regulations Ordinance', which required that performing groups obtain a licence before going before the public. In the climate of cultural nationalism which obtained in Lagos at that time, it is doubtful whether this disguised attempt at political censorship would have worked; it is significant that the ordinance was never made into law.

Ironically, yet another breakaway church, the Cherubim and Seraphim movement, swung the pendulum back towards a rejection of traditional forms and was followed shortly by other emulators in the Christian re-consecration of theatrical forms. The furthest these churches would go in the use of musical instruments was the tambourine; local instruments which had created a new tonality in the operettas now touring the West Coast – sekere, dundun, gangan, and so on – were damned as instruments of the Devil. Secular stories, even of historic personages and events, were banned and the new theatre halls, church halls and schoolrooms echoed once more to the Passion of Christ, the anguish of Nebuchadnezzar, the trials of Job, and other dramatic passages from the Bible. The Aladura, Cherubim and Seraphim, and their adherents did not however stop there. These 'prophetist' cults spread rapidly along the West Coast waging a crusade against all 'pagan' worship and their sacred objects. Descending on the provinces of the established churches, they ignited bonfires with their hot-gospelling in which perished thousands of works of art, especially in Nigeria, Cameroons, Ghana and the Ivory Coast. The vision of a fifteen-year-old girl, Abiodun Akinsowon, about 1921, was to prove a costly dream for the cultural heritage of West Africa, the heaviest brunt of which was borne by Yoruba sculpture. This period may also be justly said to constitute the lowest ebb in the fortunes of traditional theatre, participation in the cultural life even of the villages being subjected to lightning descents from the fanatical hordes of the prophetic sects. In the physical confrontations that often took place, the position of authority was predictable. Embarrassed as they sometimes were by the excesses of the sectarians, the European missionaries and their black priests had no hesitation about their alliances – and their voice was weighty in the processes of imposing the colonial peace.

But the 'vaudeville' troupes prospered. Names of groups such as we encounter in 'Two Bobs and their Carolina Girl' tell us something of the inspiration of much of these. Master Yalley, a schoolteacher, is credited with having begun the tradition of the vaudeville variety act in Ghana. His pupil Bob Johnson and his 'Axim Trio' soon surpassed the master and became a familiar figure on Ghana's cultural landscape, also later in Nigeria. More important still, Bob Johnson's innovations must be credited with having given birth to the tradition of the 'concert party' of Ghana, groups which specialize in variety routine: songs, jokes, dances, impersonations, comic scenes. However, the most notable achievement in the sense of cultural continuity was their thrusting on to the fore-state of contemporary repertoire a stock character from traditional lore, the wily trickster Anansi. This quickly developed into a vehicle for social and political commentary, apart from its popularity in comic situations.

The Jaguar Jokers, for example, transformed Anansi into the more urban character of Opia, while Efua Sutherland's more recent *The Marriage of Anansewa* takes this tradition into an even more tightly-knit and disciplined play format – the term 'disciplined' being employed here merely in the sense of reducing the areas of spontaneous improvization, without however eliminating them. Those who saw this piece during Festac 77 will have observed how attractively the element of formal discipline and free improvization blended together to encourage a controlled audience interaction. By the middle 1930s, Bob Johnson had become sufficiently established to take his brand of vaudeville to other West African cities. West Africa in this decade could boast of a repertoire of shows displaying the most bizarre products of eclectic art in the history of theatre. Even cinema, an infant art, had by then left its mark on West African theatre: some of Bob Johnson's acts were adaptations of Charlie Chaplin's escapades, not omitting his costume and celebrated shuffle. And the thought of Empire Day celebration concerts at which songs like 'Mini the Moocher' formed part of the evening musical recitals, side by side with 'God's Gospel is our Heritage' and vignettes from the life of a Liberian stevedore, stretches the contemporary imagination, distanced from the historical realities of colonial West Africa.

Again, another irony of colonial intentions: while Bob Johnson was preparing his first West African tour and Hubert Ogunde, later to become Nigeria's foremost 'concert party' leader, was undergoing his aesthetic formation from the vying forces of a clergyman father and a grandmother who was a priestess of the *Osugbo* cult, a European educationist, Charles Beart in Senegal, was beginning to reverse the policy of European acculturation in a leading secondary school in Senegal. The extent of this development – including also an appreciation of the slow pace of such an evolution – will be better grasped by recalling the educational charter of assimilationism, spelt in diverse ways by the publications of such dedicated African Francophiles as the Abbe Boillat, Paul Holle and so on. Boillat, in spite of extensive sociological research (*Esquisses senegalaises*),[2] the result of his examination of the culture and philosophy of the Bambara, Sarakole, Wolof, Serer, the Tukulor and Moorish groups in Senegal, found no lessons to be drawn from African society for modern cultural development, no future but to witness the fall of all those 'gross, if not dishonourable, ways known as the *custom of the country*'. If his addresses to the metropolitan centre of the French world did not become the cornerstone of French assimilationist policies, they undoubtedly played a key role in their formulation. Against this background, and ensuring decades of such conservatism, the Ecole William Ponty was founded. A famous teachers' college, it served Francophone Africa in the same way as did Achimota College in the Anglophone West and Makerere College in East Africa. They were all designed to provide a basic European education for would-be teachers and low-echelon civil servants. Such humanistic education as came into the curriculum of the Ecole William Ponty was of necessity French – French plays, poetry, music, art, history. Charles Beart, during his principal-ship, embarked however on a new orientation of the students' cultural instructions. From 1930 onwards the students were encouraged to return to their own societies for cultural directions. Assignments were given which resulted in the students' exploration of both the form and the substance of indigenous art. Groups from every colonial territory represented at William Ponty were then expected to return from vacation armed with a theatrical presentation based on their researches, the entire direction being left in the hands of the students themselves. Since the new theatrical sociology did not confine itself to the usual audiences of European officials and 'educated' Africans, nor to Senegal alone, its influence spread widely through different social strata of French-speaking Africa. Was it, however, a satisfying development of the culture from which it derived?

The answer must be in the negative, though the experiment was not without its instructive values. It would be too much to expect that, at that period, the classic model of French theatre could yield completely to the expression of traditional forms. The community represented by William Ponty was an artificial one. It was distanced from the society whose cultural hoard it rifled both in qualitative thought and material product. The situation was of course not peculiar to William Ponty since it also obtained in the other schools and institutions set up by the colonizer for the fulfilment of his own mission in Africa. Thus the theatre of William Ponty served the needs of exotic satisfaction for the community of French colonials. Even when it 'went to the people', and with their own material, it remained a curiosity that left the social life and authentic cultural awareness of the people untouched.

We will conclude with the 'new' theatre form which has proved the most durable; hybrid in its beginnings, the 'folk opera' has become the most expressive language of theatre in West Africa. What were the themes that mostly engaged the various groups spread along the Coast? The Nigerian Hubert Ogunde provides a convenient compen-dium, since he does appear to be more consistently varied in his dramatic fare than any comparable group to date in West Africa. His repertoire ranges from outright fantasy through biblical dramatizations to social commentary and political protest, both in the colonial and post-colonial era. A comparative study of the repertoire of the Jaguar Jokers, the Axim Trio, or the current Anansekrom groups of Ghana for example would reveal that these concentrate almost exclusively on social commentary, mostly with a moralistic touch – the evils of witchcraft, maladjustment in the social status of the cash-crop *nouveaux riches*, generational problems, changing status of women in society, sexual mores and so on, all of which also preoccupy the pamphlet drama of the Onitsha market literateurs. Hubert Ogunde explored these themes in his plays and more. His biblical adaptations became in effect a vehicle for direct commentaries on contemporary society.

Reference is hardly necessary to those plays which have earned him the ire of colonial and post-colonial governments: *Bread and Bullets*, a play not merely on the famous Iva Valley strike by miners in eastern Nigeria but on the general inequity of labour exploitation; and *Yoruba Ronu*, an indictment of the corruption and repression of the government of the then Western Region. Both plays were proscribed by the affected governments. They have entered the lore of theatrical commitment in Nigeria.

And additionally, Hubert Ogunde exemplifies what we have referred to up until now as the survival patterns of traditional theatrical art. From the outset of his theatrical career, Ogunde's theatre belonged only partially to what we have described as the 'Nova Scotian' tradition. His musical instrumentation was all borrowed from the West, movement on stage was pure Western chorus-line night-club variety. Nevertheless, the attachment to traditional musical forms (albeit with Western impurities) gradually became more assertive. Encouraged no doubt by the appearance of more tradition-grounded groups such as Kola Ogunmola and Duro Ladipo, Hubert Ogunde in the early sixties began to employ traditional instruments in his performance, his music delved deeper into home melodies, and even his costumes began to eschew the purely fabricated, theatrically glossy, for recognizable local gear. Rituals appeared with greater frequency and masquerades became a frequent feature – often, it must be added, as gratuitous insertions. Ogunde's greatest contribution to West African drama – quite apart from his innovative energy and his commitment to a particular political line – lies in his as yet little appreciated musical 'recitative' style, one which he has made unique to himself. It has few imitators, but the success of his records in this genre of 'dramatic monologue' testifies to the responsive chord it elicits from his audience. Based in principle on the Yoruba *rara* style of chanting, but in stricter rhythm, it is melodically a modernistic departure, flexibly manipulated to suit a variety of themes. Once again, we find that drama draws on other art forms for its own survival and extension. It is no exaggeration to claim that Hubert Ogunde's highest development of the chanted dramatic monologue can be fixed at the period of the political ban on his *Yoruba Ronu*. Evidently all art forms flow into one another, confirming, as earlier claimed, that the temorary historic obstacles to the flowering of a particular form sometimes lead to its transformation into other media of expression, or even the birth of totally different groups.

This survey stops at the emergence of the latest forms of traditional drama. The finest representatives of this to date have been the late Kola Ogunmola (comedy and satire) and Duro Ladipo (history and tragedy). Their contribution to contemporary drama and their innovations from indigenous forms require a far more detailed study, just as Moses Olaiya (Baba Sala) demands a chapter of his own iconoclastic brand of theatrical wit. The foregoing attempts to highlight ways in which artistic forms return to life again and again after their seeming demise, ways by which this process emphasizes the fundamental unity of various art forms and the social environment that gives expression to them; how certain creative ideas are the very offspring of historic convulsions. Finally, while for purposes of demarcation we may speak of Nigerian,

Ghanaian or perhaps Togolese drama, it must constantly be borne in mind that, like the economic intercourse of the people themselves, the various developments we have touched upon here in drama and the arts do not obey the laws of political boundaries though they might respond to the events within them. The various artistes we have mentioned had, and still enjoy, instant *rapport* with audiences far from their national and linguistic boundaries. Their art finds a ready response in most audiences since their themes are rooted in everyday experience, fleshed out in shared idioms of cultural adjustment.

NOTES

1. Herbert M. Cole in *African arts*, VIII (3).
2. Abbe Boilatt, *Esquisses Sénégalaises*, 1858; new edition, Paris, 1984, Editions Karthala.

XII

Shakespeare and the Living Dramatist*

Your statement is an impudently ignorant one to make. . . . Do you really mean no one should or could write about or speak about a war because one has not stood on the battlefield . . . ? Was Shakespeare at Actium or Philippi . . . ?[1]

That tart response from Sean O'Casey to Yeats will be familiar to many. O'Casey is not of course a 'living' dramatist, but I am certain that no one here expects a coroner's interpretation of that expression. O'Casey could have picked no worthier defender of his arguments; the universal puzzle of Shakespeare's evocative power often leads to speculations – in various degrees of whimsy – about his real identity. That is only another way of questing after the unrecorded things he actually did in real life – especially in the area of travel. If Shakespeare was never at Actium or Philippi contemporaneously with the events which he dramatized on these sites, he must have stood on their ruins or visited their living replicas in his wanderings – preferably press-ganged into one of those notorious merchant ships while he was hanging around the theatres, waiting to audition for a small role. Is it any wonder that the Middle Eastern poets and dramatists claim that he must, at the very least, have been a sometime visitor to North Africa and the Arabian peninsula? How else, for instance, could he have encountered the legend of Majnun Layla which he transformed – albeit without acknowledgement – into *Romeo and Juliet*? And so Ali Ahmad Ba-Kathir (who died in 1969), an Indonesian-born poet who became a naturalized Egyptian, restored to his adopted race what belonged to Arab literature in the first place – he translated *Romeo and Juliet* into Arabic free verse.

One interesting poser for Ahmad Ba-Kathir arose from the fact that, in the legend of Majnun's love for Layla, there was no history of family feuds; not only that, Arabic custom prevents a Romeo-style declamation of love even into the empty expanse of the desert – this is bringing dishonour to the girl and ruining the name and reputation of

* First published in *Shakespeare Survey*, 36 (1983).

her family. The fate of an Orlando caught in the act of hanging love-sick verses on tamarind trees is better left unimagined – still, such are the impieties to be expected when a gifted Arab like Shakespeare loses his roots among the English infidels!

The difficulties encountered by Arab dramatists as a result of the opposing nature of much of the conventions and mores of Arabic culture, not to mention the actual intervention of language for these poets and dramatists, heighten the phenomenon of the fascination of Shakespeare for Arab-speaking authors, both those who turned naturally to classical (i.e. literary) Arabic and others, like Gibran at the turn of the century, and the contemporary dramatist Tawfik-al-Hakim who have revolutionized the concept of Arabic literature with their adoption and enrichment of colloquial Arabic.

But I should make it quite clear that I am not about to speak on Arabic writers or their adaptations, about whom I have only very superficial knowledge. The phenomenal hold of Shakespeare on modern European and American dramatists and directors is however not merely well-known but accepted as natural. The ideological interrogatories which a Marxist playwright like Brecht injects into his versions of Shakespeare, such as *Coriolanus*, are normal developments in European literary and dramatic sensibilities – Shakespeare is over-ample fodder for the creative browser. Indeed, the search for a moral anchor among the literary-inclined leads sooner or later to the vast arena of unresolved moral questions in his works and sometimes life. Thus, for Edward Bond, it was not enough that Shakespeare's *Lear* should be reworked through some ideological framework, however vague and ultimately cosseting. Clearly Bond's interest in *Lear* was only a temporary holding device for his real subject, William Shakespeare himself, whom Bond sees – despite some rather 'nice' disclaimers – as a petit-bourgeois Lear:

> Shakespeare's plays show this need for sanity and its political expression, justice. But how did he live? His behaviour as a property-owner made him closer to Goneril than Lear.

The explanation for this bizarre claim is that

> He supported and benefited from the Goneril-society – with its prisons, workhouses, whipping, starvation, mutilation, pulpit-hysteria and all the rest of it.

Like me? And you? Introductions and Prefaces are not of course the most helpful clues to an author's intentions or even thoughts, not even in the case of Bernard Shaw. The basic declarations of intent by Bond are valid enough.

> I wrote *Bingo* because I think the contradictions in Shakespeare's life are similar to the contradictions in us,

complemented, for our purpose, by

Part of the play is about the relationship between any writer and his society.

That that relationship, in the case of Shakespeare, is closer to Goneril's than Lear's carries for me, I must confess, the air of one of those paradoxes which all writers – especially those with a poetic bent – like to indulge in from time to time. Artfulness is indeed a stock-in-trade of the self-conscious moralist; from Edward Bond we are instructed, in similar vein that 'Shakespeare created Lear, who is the most radical of all society critics'. Well, Shakespeare's countryman should *know*, I suppose; so on that note I shall return to Shakespeare's distant cousins and demand, like Hamlet: 'What's Hecuba to him, or he to Hecuba?'

Among other statistical and factual details of this fascination is this: between about 1899 and 1950, some sixteen plays of Shakespeare had been translated and/or adapted by Arab poets and dramatists. They include plays as diverse as *Hamlet*, the ever-popular *Julius Caesar*, *The Merchant of Venice*, *Pericles*, *A Midsummer Night's Dream*, *King Richard III* and – need I add? – *Antony and Cleopatra*. There will have been others by now because even the government of the United Arab Republic, fed up with the number of embarrassingly inaccurate and inelegant translations, set up a committee to produce a scrupulous and complete translation of Shakespeare's works. So much for statistics, for much of which as well as for other details I am indebted to an essay by Professor Bushrui, formerly of the University of Ibadan, and to Dr Kole Omotoso, of my own University and department.

But the Arab world was not content to adopt or 'reclaim' Shakespeare's works. M. M. Badawi, in an article in *Cairo Studies* (1964) titled 'Shakespeare and the Arab World', states that the matter goes much further. Apparently it was not simply that Shakespeare stumbled on to an Arab shore during his unpublicized peregrinations; he was in fact an Arab. His real name, cleansed of its anglicized corruption, was Shayk al-Subair, which everyone knows of course is as dune-bred an Arabic name as any English poet can hope for.

Well, on our side, that is, in our own black Africa, we know that Julius Nyerere did translate *Julius Caesar* into Kishwahili and I believe there has been one recent adaptation of another of Shakespeare's plays – I think it was *The Taming of the Shrew* – into a little-known language, also in East Africa. But I have yet to hear of any claims that Shakespeare was a suspected progeny of a Zulu or Fulani herdsman or an Ashanti farmer. A young Ghanaian cineast did adapt *Macbeth* for the cinema, setting it in Northern, pastoral Ghana, but I believe the matter was taken no further.

Well, there are the historical causes. The experience of colonized North Africa has been one of a cultural struggle between French and English cultures – beginning with their educational systems – wherein the literature is always centrally placed. Then there is the history of Arabic literature itself on which the Islamic culture placed a number of constraints from which the European culture became not merely a liberating but, in certain aspects, even a revolutionary force. At the heart of that literary culture – the European that is – stood Shakespeare, with his limitless universal themes, themes which were congenial to the Arabic epic – or narrative – tradition, promoting the romance of lyrical language for its own sake, as a tool of elegant discourse, formalized social relations and pious conduct. Arabic is the conscious vehicle of Islamic piety. The English language, even of King James's Bible, is not tied to any kind of piety; the Shakespearian use of it, however, makes it the very homeland of moral beings – we can see why the Arab poet felt an instant affinity with this language. It should be emphasized that modern, colloquial Arabic is so distinct from the classical that it makes a practitioner of both virtually bilingual – it was this classical form that was considered for a long time the only poetic vehicle fit to bear the colossal weight of Shakespeare, only this language could map the moral contours of the minds of tragic and romantic heroes and heroines, and their judges.

Earlier, in listing the plays which have been transformed by the pen of Arab dramatists, I gave a special kind of note to *Antony and Cleopatra*. Much of course is correctly made of the universality of Shakespeare's plays; here, I find myself more concerned with a somewhat less usual particularity, one with which, I am convinced, the Arabic, and most especially the North African poet simply could not fail to identify. How could he? O'Casey makes a case for the art of the dramatist by reminding us that the greatest poetic illusionist of all, Shakespeare, did not require physical participation in the battles of Actium or Philippi; to the North African dramatist, especially if he is also a poet, *Antony and Cleopatra* must appear to belie O'Casey. Shakespeare, it seems, must have sailed up the Nile and kicked up sands in the shadow of the pyramids to have etched the conflict of Egypt and Rome on such a realistic canvas, evoking tones, textures, smells, and even tastes which were so alien to the wintry climes of Europe. This is a theme with which I find myself in more than a little sympathy.

Some years ago, I watched a production of *Antony and Cleopatra* at the Aldwych, by the Royal Shakespeare Company – and winced throughout the entire night. We all have our prejudices of course, but some of these prejudices are the result of experience. Perhaps the RSC knew that it had a problem in persuading even an English audience to accept any interpretation of Cleopatra by an English actress – so the actress sent up the whole thing – a sort of 'Look at me, we both know that this Cleopatra is not a character for real'. The production was very much of that order – a sort of variation of the play-within-a-play, only, this time, it was a director's critique-within-a-play – this Cleopatra was 'neither fish or flesh; a man knew not where to have her'. If there was one female character that Shakespeare knew damned well where to have, it was Cleopatra. Come to think of it, I recall that my mind continually drifted off to a not too dissimilar occasion – this was the erotic, gastronomic orgy so sumptuously designed by the director of the film of Henry Fielding's *Tom Jones*. But at least that actress was trying her hardest, only I could not help superimposing on her performance the face and body of the actress Anna Magnani, one of the few European actresses of my knowledge who are truly endowed with a natural presence of erotic vulgarity. Shakespeare foresaw the problem, mind you:

> Saucy lictors
> Will catch at us like strumpets, and scald rhymers
> Ballad us out o'tune; the quick comedians
> Extemporally will stage us, and present
> Our Alexandrian revels; Antony
> Shall be brought drunken forth, and I shall see
> Some squeaking Cleopatra boy my greatness
> I' th' posture of a whore.   (5.2.213–20)

The other side of the balance sheet however is an ironic one. The near-unanimous opinion of the Arabic critics themselves on the translations and adaptations of their 'compatriot' Shayk al-Subair's masterpieces is that they were, in the main, the work of 'scald rhymers' who 'ballad him out of tune'. But I am not qualified to pronounce upon that, knowing no Arabic beyond 'Salaam ailekum', a benediction which we must pronounce on Shakespeare's motions in his grave if what those critics say is true. The special fascination of Arabic literature with Shakespeare however, mends all, at least for those of us who are safe from a direct encounter with the early consequences.

Quite apart from language and colonial history, other theories have been offered, theories closer to the content of literature. For instance, it is claimed – as one of the reasons for endowing Shakespeare with Arab paternity – that only an Arab could have understood or depicted a Jew so 'convincingly' as in *The Merchant of Venice*. Similarly, the focus is sometimes placed on *Othello* – the Moor's dignity even in folly has been held up as convincing proof that no European could have fleshed out this specific psychology of a jealousy complicated by racial insecurity but a man from beneath the skin – an Arab at the very least. This of course would have to account for the unpredictability of a full-blooded Arab who suddenly turns against his kind in the portrait of Aaron in *Titus Andronicus*, reducing the representative of that race to unprecedented depths of savagery and inhuman perversion. No, I find that my judgement inclines to giving most of the credit to *Antony and Cleopatra* for the full conquest of the Arab poet-dramatist, and the reasons lie of course with that universally seductive property of the best dramatic literature – a poetic ease on the ear which, in this case, has been drawn to the service of a specific terrain. Throughout his career, this terrain held great fascination for William Shakespeare. I do not speak here of an inert geographical terrain, but of the opposing and contradictory in human nature. It is not entirely by accident that the physical terrain in *Antony and Cleopatra* was the meeting point of the Orient and the Occident – for Shakespeare, these had come to represent more than the mercantile or adventurers' stomping-ground; they are absorbed into geographical equivalents of the turbulences which the poet observed in human nature, that play-ground, and warring-ground of 'humours', of performance and intent, will and emotion: Angelo is the unfinished paradigm in *Measure for Measure*. The transfer by Shakespere, obsessed apothecary, of the unstable mixture called humanity into the Elizabethan (i.e. European) exotic crucible of the Middle East was inescapable – the signs are littered in images throughout his entire corpus, and the Arab world acknowledged itself as the greatest beneficiary even when its dramatists held up the same models through opposing viewpoints.

Ahmad Shaqui, the poet laureate of Egypt who was hailed 'the Prince of Poets' and 'Poet of Princes' by his own peers is often credited with introducing poetry into Arabic drama. Was it just a coincidence that the play in question was *Masra' Kliyupatra* (The Fall or Death of Cleopatra), and that it was inspired unequivocally by Shakespeare's own *Antony and Cleopatra*? It is true that he used material both from Egyptian and Arab-Islamic history but he did set out, according to our sources, to rewrite Shakespeare's own play. Fired by the Egyptian struggle for independence from the British, he recreates Cleopatra as a woman torn between her love of her country and her love for a man. In the end she commits suicide. For Shaqui, Shakespeare's Cleopatra was unacceptably unpatriotic, even a traitress, since she appeared ready to sacrifice her country on the altar of love. The emendations are predictable; they are of the same political and historically conscious order as, for example, the reversal of relationships which takes place when the theme of Caliban and Ariel is handled by anyone from the colonial or slavery experience, most notably in the West Indies. The case of the Arab world is however very different, owing its primary response not simply to politics or history, but to an order of visceral participation in the humane drama of its politics and history.

When one examines the majority of Shakespeare's plays very closely, there really is not much overt respect paid to 'local colour'. If anything, the colour is not infrequently borrowed from elsewhere to establish a climate of relationships, emotions or conflicts: 'Her bed is India; there she lies, a pearl' (*Troilus and Cressida*, 1.1.99). Where we encounter a localized immediacy we are wafted instantly away on a metaphoric bark to nowhere:

> Between our Ilium and where she resides
> Let it be call'd the wild and wand'ring flood;
> Ourself the merchant, and this sailing Pandar
> Our doubtful hope, our convoy, and our bark.
> (1.1.100–3)

Nestor finds Achilles' brains as barren as the banks of Libya while Ulysses considers it kinder fate that he parch in Africa's sun than be withered by the arrogance in Achilles' eye. Beyond two or three boastful and mutual admiration lines from Ulysses to Hector in Act 4, scene 5, however, it is remarkable that in a war no less celebrated, no less legendary than Antony's scrap with Caesar, very little of the terrain of struggle is actually conveyed in Shakespeare's lines. I do not suggest that we miss it; on the contrary. The absent hills, moats, turrets and physical *belonging* all pass unnoticed thanks to the clamour of *machismo*, the conflicts of pride, the debates of honour and schemes of war. The atmosphere is replete, nothing appears missing. In *Coriolanus* we experience the city state as a corporate entity against which one man is ranged, while the Rome of *Julius Caesar* could be anywhere, and the arguments of both, unchanged.

Compare these examples with the other remarkable exception, *Macbeth*:

> DUNCAN: This castle hath a pleasant seat, the air
> Nimbly and sweetly recommends itself
> Unto our gentle senses.
>
> BANQUO: This guest of summer,
> The temple-haunting martlet, does approve
> By his lov'd mansionry that the heaven's breath
> Smells wooingly here; no jutty, frieze,
> Buttress, nor coign of vantage, but this bird
> Hath made her pendent bed and procreant cradle.
> Where they most breed and haunt, I have observ'd,
> The air is delicate   (1.6.1–10)

Shakespeare, drawing local colour into the service of fatal irony. The colours of *Antony and Cleopatra* belong however to a different segment of the spectrum and are applied on a more liberal canvas – after all, the whole world is up for grabs. But note that even where we encounter no more than what may be called a roll-call of names, there has been prior fleshing-out, so that the discomfiture of Octavius Caesar at the rallying of former mutual enemies behind Antony is real and problematic. It is historical personages that are summoned centre stage of the tapestry of events, not more exotic names and shadowy figures from legend:

> He hath given his empire
> Up to a whore, who now are levying
> The kings o' th' earth for war. He hath assembled
> Bocchus, the king of Libya; Archelaus
> Of Cappadocia; Philadelphos, king
> Of Paphlagonia; the Thracian king Adallas;
> King Manchus of Arabia; King of Pont;
> Herod of Jewry; Mithradates, king
> Of Comagene; Polemon and Amyntas,
> The kings of Mede and Lycaonia, with a
> More larger list of sceptres.   (3.6.66–76)

The prior setting for what would otherwise be a mere catalogue of titles is contributive to the emergence of real figures from a mere bas-relief. For this is Caesar caught in a domestic dilemma involving his sister, using the arguments of war to get it into her head that she is neither an Emperor's wife nor an ambassador but, quite ordinarily – a rejected woman. Caesar's passion is both that of a condemned protector of a weak woman, and a contender for empire on a larger-than-historic scale. And these empires become accessible, reduced to a human scale because of what Antony has done with the accumulated panoply of power: 'He hath given his empire/Up to a whore . . .' The whore? Cleopatra. Her other names – queen, whore, gipsy, Egyptian dish, the serpent of old Nile, ribaldered nag of Egypt, etc., one whose every act, whose every caprice, every clownish or imperious gesture confirms that she deserves every one of these accolades and more. And thus the kingdoms and empires which she draws into her fatal net through Antony partake of this same personal quality and expand our realistic conception and dimension of the drama being waged for possession of the world. Not without cause does Octavius Caesar envision, when the scale of war turns firmly in his favour: 'The time of universal peace is near.'

Shakespeare's enlargements of the ridiculous through sublime prisms are deft and varied; the process happens at bewildering speed, resolving seeming improbabilities through the credible chimeric qualities of the tragic heroine of the piece. Who can quarrel with the steely patriotism of Cleopatra even in defeat? Confronted with the stark choice between death and humiliation:

> Rather a ditch in Egypt
> Be gentle grave unto me! Rather on Nilus' mud
> Lay me stark nak'd, and let the water-flies
> Blow me into abhorring! Rather make
> My country's high pyramides my gibbet,
> And hang me up in chains!   (5.2.57–62)

Ahmad Shaqui, poet and patriot, had most of his work already cut out for him; there really is not much left to do in mending whatever else appears to contradict this poise of nationalist dignity. Even the repulsive imagery has been turned to good account; the worst is evoked, and embraced – if that should be the only choice. How much more those other passages of contrasting physical evocation, those sumptuous, festal passages upon which Shakespeare has poured such haunting sensuousness. Have they not driven later poets and dramatists – notably T. S. Eliot – to an ambiguous relationship with their own literary heritage?

> The silken tackle
> Swell with the touches of those flower-soft hands
> That yarely frame the office. From the barge
> A strange invisible perfume hits the sense
> Of the adjacent wharfs. The city cast
> Her people out upon her; and Antony,
> Enthron'd i' th' market place, did sit alone,
> Whistling to th' air; which, but for vacancy,
> Had gone to gaze on Cleopatra too,
> And made a gap in nature.   (2.2.213–22)

Does the palate tend to cloy a little? Possibly. But by now Egypt, whom all, including Octavius Caesar, have made us identify with Cleopatra totally, is quickly manoeuvred towards reassurance that we are still in command of our faculties of judgement, then acquitted absolutely. Admittedly the foreman of the jury is none other than a prejudiced Enobarbus, but we know him also for a blunt-spoken soldier. Most importantly, that habitual juxtaposition of harsh lingual rigour with lines of ineradicable sublimity leaves no room for doubt that an objective assessment has been fairly concluded. In short, the advocate acknowledges faults, but witness how he praises the extenuating circumstances:

> Age cannot wither her, nor custom stale
> Her infinite variety. Other women cloy
> The appetites they feed, but she makes hungry
> Where most she satisfies; for vilest things
> Become themselves in her, that the holy priests
> Bless her when she is riggish.   (2.2.239–44)

That Cleopatra should match, in her final hours, the dignified poise of humility with a final thought (and abandonment) of defiance against the jealous gods is, in my view, both dramatically expected and aesthetically satisfying:

> No more but e'en a woman, and commanded
> By such poor passion as the maid that milks
> And does the meanest chores. It were for me
> To throw my sceptre at the injurious gods;
> To tell them that this world did equal theirs
> Till they had stol'n our jewel.   (4.15.73–8)

But the awesomeness of the lines that follow can only be fully absorbed by an Egyptian, or one steeped in the esoteric cults of Egypt and allied religions, including Islam. Cleopatra is speaking figuratively here of the house of death, and then again, she is not. She is evoking the deeper mysteries of the cult of Isis and the nether kingdoms of an other-existence, and it spreads an eerie quality over the final tableau – unlike any comparable end in all of Shakespeare.

The following recites like any article of faith in the Resurrection:

> I have believed in Allah, and His angels, and His books, and
> His messengers, and the Last Day and the decree of its good
> and evil from Allah-ta'alla, and in the Rising after death.
>
> (*Islamic Book of the Dead*)

But the Arabic script that transcribes this *ayat* from the Hadith is composed like a high-prowed gondola with a crew of ritualized (hierographically speaking) rowers.[2] What

Islam in fact opposes in the 'Kafir' cults of Osiris and Isis have merely been transposed from their elaborate structures with all their sacrificial rites to a mystic opacity of liturgical language – in the Islamic exegesis of death, the kinship remains blatant. Their neighbours, the pagan Greeks, who borrowed from them much of their cults and religions in any case, would have no difficulty in identifying the Osiris-prowed Hadithic boat of death with Charon's canoe, scything through the River Styx. Islamic injunctions, prayers and invocations on the theme of death more than compensate the exhortations to funeral meagreness by their endless liturgy and lyrical wealth of going, and the aftermath of dissolution.

Cleopatra, whom we have watched throned as Isis, imbues the approach of death with a measured ritualism that is suffused with the palpable shadowiness of the crypt. Not just her contemporary worshippers at the shrines of Isis and Osiris, but their descendants, born into the counter-claims of Islamic religion, would therefore share more than a mere metaphor of language with Cleopatra's demand: 'Then is it sin/To rush into the secret house of death . . .?' We can hear its echo in the following lines also from the *Islamic Book of the Dead*:

> It is said that every day the
> graves call out five times:
> I am the house of isolation . . .
> I am the house of darkness . . .
> I am the house of earth . . .
> I am the house of the questioning . . .
> of Munkar and Nakir . . .

I know of no parallel echo in the Christian offices of the dead. Arabic 'classical' poetry is however full of it, and of Shakespeare's sonnets, the ones which seem to attract the finest 'classical' poets among the Arabs seem to share this preoccupation with the imagery of death as a place of physical habitation. Sometimes they are outright translations but more often they are original compositions inspired by a specific sonnet of Shakespeare. And we find a consistency in the emphasis given to one part of Shakespeare's variations on the theme of love as against the main theme itself. Comparatively underplayed is the defiant sentiment:

> Not marble nor the gilded monuments
> Of princes shall outlive this pow'rful rhyme;
> But you shall shine more bright in these contents
> Than unswept stone, besmear'd with sluttish time.
>
> (*Sonnet* 55)

The humanistic verses of Omar Khayyám are considered worse than irreverent – they are termed heretical and subversive; nor does the graveyard humour of an Andrew Marvell hold much appeal for the true Islamic poet:

> The grave's a fine and private place
> But none, I think, do there embrace.
> ('*To His Coy Mistress*')

No, it is essentially the grave as a place, an abode in time, that taxes the poetic genius of Shakespeare's adapters, not as a spur to the demands of love, presented as an end which is worse for overtaking its victim loveless, against which is held the imperishable products of the Muse or the talisman of immortality in love's offspring. Elias Abu Shabbakah's 'The Song of Death' is aptly titled, though it derives from Shakespeare's Sonnet 71, 'No longer Mourn for me when I am Dead'. The contrast, despite the opening abnegation, is revealing:

> My will, which I want you to remember, is to forget me when I am dead.
> And, if memories move you one day and your affection chooses to remind
> you of me, take the guitar of my inspiration into the dark night and go to my
> tomb in silence, and tap the guitar once; for it will let you hear a moaning
> sigh such as mine.

The unearthly moisture of suicide, the aspic's trail of slime on fig-leaves transports us to this totally alien earth, and I mean alien, not from the view of Shakespeare's culture alone. This is yet another world opening inwards from the mundane one into which we have already been inducted by some of the most unnerving imageries in poetic drama: a yoking of approaching bodily corruption with the essence-draining paradox of birth and infancy closes the fatal cycle of the union of opposites that began with the aspic's slime:

> Peace, peace!
> Dost thou not see my baby at my breast
> That sucks the nurse asleep?   (5.2.306–8)

In this dark ceremonial, the crown which Cleopatra dons becomes not just a prop for composing herself for death as befits a queen, nor her robe the final cover for a soon-to-be-hollowed vessel, but ritual transformation steps towards the mystic moment of transition:

> Give me my robe, put on my crown; I have
> Immortal longings in me. . .
> I am fire and air; my other elements
> I give to baser life. So, have you done?
> Come then, and take the last warmth of my lips.
> Farewell, kind Charmian. Iras, long farewell.
> Have I the aspic in my lips? Dost fall?
> If thou and nature can so gently part,

The stroke of death is as a lover's pinch,
Which hurts and is desired.   (5.2.278–9, 287–94)

Iras has now preceded, and in that calm recital of Cleopatra,

The stroke of death is as a lover's pinch,
Which hurts and is desired

is heard the reprise and conclusion of that death aria which we have earlier described. It commenced in the penultimate act, 'The crown o' th' earth doth melt. . . .' (4.15.63), and winds into the awesome darkness at the Osiric passage:

Then is it sin
To rush into the secret house of death
Ere death dare come to us?   (4.15.80–2)

In sustaining its threnody through one more act, despite the triumphant boots of Caesar and entourage, punctured by the country yokel humour of the aspic-hawking Clown, it becomes clear that our playwright has already inscribed *Finis* on the actual historic conflicts of power and passion. The crown of the earth has melted, and there is nothing left remarkable beneath the visiting moon. But in this setting, is that all? Beyond it? And beneath earth itself? The spectral power of Shakespeare's poetry remains to lead us into the 'other side' of the veil whose precedent reality, which is now seen as merely contingent, gives awesome splendour to the finale of an otherwise butterfly queen. The rest of *Antony and Cleopatra* is our excursion into that world, one which lies more innocently on the Egyptian reality of that time than on the most stoical, self-submissive will in the inherent or explicit theologies of Shakespeare's other drama:

I am dying, Egypt, dying; only
I here importune death awhile, until
Of many thousand kisses the poor last
I lay upon thy lips.   (4.15.18–21)

Contrast this with the death of the genuine Moor whose folly was of a more excusable circumstance than Antony's:

I kissed thee ere I killed thee. No way but this –
Killing myself, to die upon a kiss.   (*Othello*, 5.2.362–3)

One dirge-master is understandably Shayk al-Subair, the other William Shakespeare. Here most noticeably, the cadences of death in Shakespeare's tragic figures are as crucial to his poetry as his celebration of life, even when the celebrants are flawed and their own worst enemy of life. It is difficult to underestimate this property as one which the Egyptian dramatists identified in their own world, for in *Antony and Cleopatra* Shakespeare's sensuous powers climaxed to evoke not merely the humanity of actors of a particular history, but the glimpsed after-world whose liturgy of resolution imbued them with their unearthly calm at the hour of death.

There are other minor but no less critical touches to the realistic evocation of a credible Egypt even within its very mythology. One need only examine the comparative sociologies of Shakespeare's stock characters – the Soothsayer for instance. In *Julius Caesar*, he simply comes off the street like a disembodied voice, and sinks back into urban anonymity once his dramatic role is fulfilled. Cassandra in *Troilus and Cressida* is a hysterical weirdo who, if anything, mars her cause with a melodramatic manner of revelations. Is she a member of the household? We do not really experience her – all these are not pejorative remarks, merely contrastive for a point of view. The Soothsayer in *Antony and Cleopatra* is an individual, a solid, recognizable persona. He follows Antony to Rome as his personal soothsayer and emerges more in the role of a shrewd psychologist than a mere mumbo-jumboist digging in eagles' entrails and seeing portents in the clouds. His analysis of Antony's psyche is as detachedly clinical as Antony's own lecture on the scientific achievements of his adopted home, which he delivers as a cool, observant voyager to a curious stay-at-home:

> Thus do they, sir: they take the flow o' th' Nile
> By certain scales i' th' pyramid; they know
> By th' height, the lowness, or the mean, if dearth
> Or foison follow. The higher Nilus swells
> The more it promises; as it ebbs, the seedsman
> Upon the slime and ooze scatters his grain,
> And shortly comes to harvest.   (2.7.17–23)

This mixture of clinical information on human beings and the cultivated soil alike makes the earth of Egypt dominate Rome and take over the half-way house Misenum, making one suspect that Shayk al-Subair cannot wait to get back to his own soil where his genius for this story resides. He compromises by transferring a touch of Egypt to the no man's land of Pompey's ship in Misenum. Between Enobarbus and Antony – with a little help from Lepidus – the essence of Egypt continues to haunt the concourse of Rome, the Mediterranean and its buccaneers. Does Shakespeare lavish any such comparative care in preserving the smells, sounds, and allied definitions of a yearned-for home? We are not speaking now of rhetoric, even of the pathetic kind old John of Gaunt expends in *Richard II*:

> This royal throne of kings, this scept'red isle,
> This earth of majesty, this seat of Mars,
> This other Eden, demi-paradise,
> This fortress built by Nature for herself
> Against infection and the hand of war,

> This happy breed of men, this little world,
> This precious stone set in the silver sea . . .   (2.1.40–6)

nor of the philosophical, disinterested speculations on land and Nature in *As You Like It*. No! To a people to whom land, fertile land, is both worship and life, an Egypt of Shakespeare's *Antony and Cleopatra* cannot be served by such rhetoric or abstract morality. And like morality, even so those qualities that grace (or disgrace) humanity cannot be rendered in the abstract but must be invested in characters and the affective community – we need only contrast the following with Portia's peroration on the quality of mercy:

> For his bounty,
> There was no winter in it; an autumn 'twas
> That grew the more by reaping. His delights
> Were dolphin-like: they show'd his back above
> The element they liv'd in. In his livery
> Walk'd crowns and crownets; realms and islands were
> As plates dropp'd from his pocket.   (5.2.86–92)

This, then, is the soul we recognize in Antony, so generous in giving that he loses all judgement. His rejection of pettiness over the defection of Enobarbus, his agonizing concern for the safety of his followers after defeat – these small redeeming features approve his humanity and contribute to a suspicion that our judgement of him may be lacking in that generosity which was his one redeeming grace. And what proud Egyptian, especially a poet, will fully resist the anti-chauvinist fervour of a one-third shareholder of the world, one who – no matter the motivation – declaims, both in word and deed:

> Let Rome in Tiber melt, and the wide arch
> Of the rang'd empire fall! Here is my space.
> Kingdoms are clay; our dungy earth alike
> Feeds beast as man.   (1.1.33–6)

'Here is my space.' John of Gaunt's rhetorical flourish does not do half as much for the Englishman as Antony the Roman does, in that brief speech, for the land-proud Egyptian. The conqueror is himself conquered by the land in the person of her capricious Queen, the same land whose foulest ditch she would rather inhabit, upon whose highest gibbet she would rather hang, than be taken to grace the triumphal march of a conqueror (albeit a new one) in Rome. 'Here is my space' – it is at once a hint that the land has doomed him, and a taste of the largeness of a man whose bountifulness – as we come to know this – imbues our space with a heroic grandeur, even when events are trivialized by the humane weaknesses of our kind.

Only Shakespeare could contract the pomp and panoply of love and royalty into a gastronomic experience, yet unfailingly elevate both into a veritable apotheosis without a sense of the ridiculous or the inflated. Enobarbus, in Rome, unerringly predicts that Antony 'will to his Egyptian dish again'. The Egyptian dish herself boasts 'I was/A morsel for a monarch' without a hint of self-mockery, indeed with pride and womanly preening. When things go sour,

> I found you as a morsel cold upon
> Dead Caesar's trencher.   (3.13.116–17)

Food, wine, violence, sexuality and putrefaction – both qualitatively and in sheer quantity – this is a different landscape of human activities from the more familiar settings of Shakespeare's. A moist land and visceral responses. The transitions from the physical to the metaphysical are unforced, and this is in no small measure due to the magnitude of extremes with which the human vehicles are imbued. Is it not through the same lips of the lustful gipsy, tripping credibly because it is made the active response of any jealous woman, that we are led into the self-apotheosis of an irrepressible pair?

> Eternity was in our lips and eyes,
> Bliss in our brows' bent, none our parts so poor
> But was a race of heaven.   (1.3.35–7)

With such a subject, is it any wonder that Shayk al-Subair reveals again and again that he cannot wait to escape home from the land of a 'holy, cold, and still conversation'? In *Antony and Cleopatra*, Shakespeare's borrowed imageries finally come home to roost. That the *terra firma* of his choice happens to be Egypt may be an accident – it could easily have been India. It was nearly the Caribbean but Shakespeare chose there to employ stage effects deliberately and thus denied his island that specific dimension of richness which comes from a physical and human identity. Moreover, in *The Tempest*, Shakespeare is concerned not with history, but with enchantment. By contrast, Alexandria (or Tripoli in this case) is the home of that tantalizing glimpse of the topography of Achilles' frazzled brains, it is the demythologized context of Othello's romantic yarns, the source of all those secret potions of love or death-like sleep from *Romeo and Juliet* to *A Midsummer Night's Dream*, the destination or port-of-call of those rich argosies that billow through the pages of *The Merchant of Venice*, and even the unseen crusader ship of Shakespeare's history plays.

Only if Ahmad Ba-Kathir, Ahmad Shaqui, Khali Mutran, Gibran and a host of others had failed to recognize this, would the history of this relationship have been astonishing. Their fascination with Shakespeare is not in the least surprising after all; the skepticism of some of their fellow-poets and dramatists about Shakespeare's claim to an English ancestry is simply a passionate compliment to those qualities in Shakespeare, a few of which we have touched upon, but above all the paradox of timelessness and history, a realism evoked – simultaneously – of time, place and people

– with which he has infused *Antony and Cleopatra* more deeply than any of his plays except perhaps *Macbeth* which is a horse of an entirely different colour.

Sean O'Casey may be proved only partially right – I return to his rhetorical question – regarding whose answer there is nothing rhetorical in the stance of Shakespeare's Arab co-practitioners in the field of drama. The Shayk was born too early for Philippi, or indeed for the battle of the Nile, but the Nile did course through his veins. Personally, I was left with only one problem to resolve – if the Shayk was indeed an Arab, who was his wife? It seemed to me that we could not dispose of one problem without the other – such being the power of documents in our time. Those documents insist that our William was well and truly wived by someone whose name was recorded as Anne Hathaway. Perhaps there were others, but even Othello had imbibed sufficient European influence to content himself with only one wife, so why not his very creator, Shayk al-Subair? Being a monogamist does not therefore destroy the case for Shakespeare's Arabic origin. Well then, I consulted my colleague in Arabic Studies and our assiduousness was rewarded. Anne Hathaway proved to be none other than an English corruption of Hanna Hathawa. The first name stands for 'to dye red'; the second, Hathawa means 'to scatter, to disperse', someone who disseminates. The puzzle was resolved. Shayk al-Subair's spouse Hanna Hathawa, a high-coloured lady, came to life in her own right, a little-known theatrical agent whose publicity activities on behalf of her husband will, I hope, provide endless preoccupation for at least a dozen doctoral theses.

In the meantime, one acknowledges with gratitude the subjective relation of other poets and dramatists to the phenomenon of Shakespeare, for even the most esoteric of their claims lead one, invariably, to the productive source itself, and to the gratification of celebrating dramatic poetry anew. That Shakespeare may turn out to be an Arab after all is certainly less alarming a prospect than that he should prove to be Christopher Marlowe. No one has yet begun to ransack the sand-dunes of Arabia, shovelling aside the venerable bones of Bedouins in the hope of disinterring the bones of the author of *Antony and Cleopatra*. By contrast, that talented but junior brother of his genius, the author of *Tamburlaine*, has not been permitted a peaceful sleep in his grave, especially at the hands of yet another group of ex-colonial enthusiasts, this time, the Americans. Happily, for the majority of Shakespeare-lovers, those other secret lives of the Shayk which remains to be uncovered outside *Bingo* or the *Arabian Nights*, will just have to wait, until his tomes have yielded up the last of their treasures.

NOTES

1. Quoted in *Sean O'Casey: A Collection of Critical Essays*, ed. Thomas Kilroy (Englewood Cliffs, NJ., 1975) p. 115.
2. A marvellously preserved carving of the Egyptian 'Boat of the Dead' in the Pushkin Museum, Moscow, demonstrates most glaringly the relationship of the transcription to the funerary craft.

XIII

The External Encounter:
Ambivalence in African Arts and Literature*

Let us briefly animate two sculptural representatives of several African figures which find themselves neighbours in an unusual setting. To be a little more precise, Dresden, Berlin or Paris, 1886 onwards. One, a Bakota Ancestral Guardian figure from the Dan peoples, its head bears a vague suggestion of the frontal view of a Sphinx, impacted, so that it is almost two-dimensional like a relief scooped out of its ancient moorings. The trunk is little more than a geometrical figuration, a rectangle turned round to rest on its diagonal so that a point serves for the neck, then thrusts vertically down through its opposite angle to provide the massive extrusion, which, without a hint of representing the lower limbs, serves as its earthing device.

It is not however, one of those figures which are conceived in the round. The eyes bulge outwards, near-independent entities from mildly recessed cavities. Those cavities are diamond-shaped, echoing the dancing rectangle on the diagonal axis of the copper plated highlights, wrinkles it seems, of the forehead. The eyes stare beyond the present.

This Bakota guardian of ancestral shrines with its emphatic angularities is not, however, nearly as numinous in its affectiveness as our other presiding figure, not so massively *dynamique* – nor is it meant to be. The Nimba mask of the Baga peoples, true to its function, which brings it out at night in massed procession with its companions, rising eight to twelve feet tall in a clearing in the woods, the Nimba is a pure expression of organic dominance. It threatens and encroaches on the viewer's sense of adequate being, leaving no route for the individual except to weld his ego into the security of that community of being, of which these metaphysical symbols are both part and completion. Their ponderous eruption is an embodiment of the numinous world, bearing down on earth on paradoxically tenuous limbs, yet reflecting the cosmos in oval and spherical masses and voids, whose spatial relations provide an infolding aesthetic. The head echoes the lower world-womb. Together they constantly reproduce the unseen. The

* Lecture delivered at Cornell University (1985).

breasts – and here we obtain yet another contrast with other African sculptural idioms, such as the Yoruba – the breasts do not thrust out exponentially; it is the head whose thrust into space so massively defies gravity that it has led more than one enthusiast – William Fagg and Margaret Plass for instance – to speculate that African sculptors discovered the exponential principle long before their European scientific counterparts.

> It may be that when the new-found implications for man's life of the
> technological changes inspired by mathematical physics in our time are more
> fully understood, some new movement in art – let us say Exponentialism –
> will arise to do justice to them. If so, it seems likely that the new ground will
> be found to have been reconnoitered long before by the intuitive artists of the
> world.

Again of course, we encounter that problematic 'explanation' – intuitive. We shall come back to it in another context. The breasts, we were saying, part company from a number of other African traditions by resigning that exponential configuration to the head, merging instead with the thighs to encase a huge cavity. The now unified ovum bears down onto a four-legged support which breaks the final link with even the limited realism that would have been implied by a sum of recognizable parts.

And yet, despite the threat to individuation, despite the abundant tyranny of this mass, the final experience is one of a lofty serenity, a quiet, enfolding haven to all who participate in what would otherwise be an insupportable burden of thought-procreation. This figure does not even see with its eyes which are mere lumps, does not evince the slightest hint of a capacity for sensual perception: it absorbs the world directly into this head, then envelops its people in the plenitude of its womb.

What then do they see, exiled in this alien space, the Nimba with its unsighted eyes, the Bakota with its diamond pools of darkness? Surrounded by a sea of Teutonic faces in Dresden, Berlin – for this is where we shall first chance upon them – what sensations course through their ancestral minds in this world of strangers, a world still flexing its industrial muscles towards the close of the nineteenth century, with a dissident minority seeking new humanizing directions to counter the threats of ossification that came in the wake of an increasingly complacent bourgeoisie?

> You with your face of pain, your touch of gaiety,
> with eyes that could distil me any instant
> have passed into some diary, some dead journal
> now that the computer, the mechanical notion
> obliterates sincerities.

Lines from a flesh-and-blood exile, Arthur Nortje, a South African poet whose lines often appear to be sculpted from the same muscular rhythms as inform the sculptures from a vastly different, socially conditioned part of Africa. His images come effortlessly to mind as exemplifying part of that altered reality, the paradoxical transformation which all products of culture undergo even on their own terrain as their society transforms itself in new productive ways. Arthur Nortje's poetry belongs to that corpus whose agonized cry confesses an intense poetic sensibility that finds itself in forced exile. Restless, rootless, Arthur Nortje eventually committed suicide in 1970 through an overdose of drugs. He resolved his anguish like that other poet Rabearivello who however, constituted himself an exile on his own soil, Madagascar, self-exiled through his unresolved impatience and passion for his Cultural Mother, France. The emotions were different – Nortje agonized over a form of impotence, that cruel situation of the unwilling exile from a situation which, in any case, internally constituted a form of exile – what else is human negation but that? Exiled from self-realization – culturally, socially, economically, politically and – historically. That above all else: negated historically. Arthur Nortje's new-found home was not uncongenial. This was a poet who easily absorbed the English mores and norms, its middle-class collegiate and social pleasures, its vices and the destructive self-indulgence to which its artist class is sometimes prone. Apartheid and Pretoria prison cast a shadow on the memory pools of his mind, but the artistic community, the genteel amity of Oxford lawns and neutered comradeship constituted a solace. He found kin-sensibilities in poets like Sylvia Plath, on whose death he wrote two moving poems. He was sufficiently part of the popular culture of the sixties to write a poem to the Beatles. And of course, he never forgot, nor failed, to express his mulatto being – part white, part black – but poems such as 'Winter, Oxford' indicate quite clearly where his inner sensibilities allied him, creatively:

> Winter in a mini-skirt, thin-faced, will come
> in white boots up to the thirteen bleak
> steps to the door of the Radcliffe Camera.
> The pinnacles lose their honey colour
> recorded by a million tourist lenses,
> and water drips through the canvas rigging while
> a man hidden in the scaffolding calls
> above the green ripple of grass for a rope and a bucket.
> The old stone dies, and nothing is restored

Not until the very end of this poem of three short sections is an autobiographical note inserted, as if the poet reluctantly concedes that this deeply felt, deeply etched environment is after all, only an exile's temporary haven:

> You, chill-faced winter, fellow leering along
> the trail of gobs that weigh my cobwebs down.
> On porcelain thrones of cubicles I've sat
> to think away an exile long impoverished,
> who can pay for my safety now,
> and why is it so ineffable.

But all that precedes, as with the major part of Nortje's poetic output, is an environment re-created with the inside sensibility of a native of that environment, not even of the 'hybrid', as he occasionally refers to himself.

Rabearivello on his part was simply crushed by the weight of a distant cultural longing. Self-taught, but coming down finally with Mallarmé and Baudelaire as his principal mentors, he identified himself fully with the French poetic legacy, and by implication, France. What was worse, Rabearivello felt isolated from his peers, the latter-day Negritudinists who were in France, drinking directly from the much desired spring. Again and again he struggled with the French colonial officers to gain that beckoning land of his Muse but failed. Frustrated, he exiled himself permanently from this world. Rabearivello was, through his conscious Surrealism, a more 'authentic' poet than Nortje, authentic being a reference to the fact that his imagery recalls presences of his black sources transformed from the particular objective stimulus to a more integrating, all-embracing, animistic evocation. These stanzas from the cycle of seven poems called 'Night' evoke the numinous territory of those figures we have temporarily left in the galleries of Dresden – this time the goddess Yemoja of the Rivers, or the legendary 'Mammy Wata' of the creeks:

> Here is
> she whose eyes are the prisms of sleep,
> whose eyelids are heavy with dreams,
> whose feet are sunk into the sea
> and whose sticky hands emerge
> full of corals and blocks of sparkling salt.
>
> She will put them into little piles near a foggy bay
> and dole them out of naked sailors
> whose tongues have been cut out
> until the rain begins to fall
> Then she will be visible no longer,
> only her hair scattered by the wind
> unwinding like a reel of seaweed
> and perhaps as well as some tasteless specks of salt.

What would our far-seeing ancestors, their fellow-exiles, make of Arthur Nortje, of Rabearivello the internal exile, given their own history, and the irony of their forced presences in the exhibition halls of Dresden, Berlin, London, Paris? Let us shift our geographical focus for a moment as we indulge our ancestral fantasies.

It is now seventy years later. We are in Ibadan, Nigeria. A number of Nigerian artists and designers – both the modern, experimenting in new forms, new techniques, *and* the traditional, re-animating the old forms, idioms and subject matter – form part of the viewers at the Mbari Arts gallery during an exhibition. This cross-section of the populace filter through reproductions of some foreign artists gathered together under the common title of German Expressionism. And they find little problem empathizing with the woodcuts and sketches of Karl-Schmidt Rotluff, Kirscher, Kandinsky and some lesser-known members of the *die Brücke* movement which, together with *der Blaue Reiter*, were the main branches of Expressionist avant-garde in European arts at the turn of the century. This 'returned compliment' had been organized by a cultural self-exile, the German-Austrian Ulli Beier, who had the useful idea of bringing back to Africa a few products of that earlier inspiration which had been provided by those very ancestral figures which we encountered earlier. It was not just the artists and intelligentsia who responded to this exhibition. Mbari was located in the seething heart of Ibadan, peopled by traders, motor mechanics, junior clerks and accountants from the surrounding banks and business offices, factory workers, school-teachers etc. They passed through, responding in various ways, recognizing, criticizing and of course, in some cases, mystified. But in general, they found that the distortions on realism were not very different from the scarifications and deliberate grotesqueries which are part and parcel of the aesthetic armoury of African masquerades, votive figures, caryatids, housepost sculpture and panel art. The correspondence of these graphic forms to other forms of art – the dance and polyphonic musical rhythms – seemed obvious and familiar. I do not know however what they would have made, for example, of the expressionist theatrical extremisms of an Oscar Kokoschska, whose appropriation of African ritualism led mainly in the direction of sadism, sexual perversion and other excursions into self-gratification – all in the name of human liberation. Introduction to the ritual form was indeed one of the by-products of that African encounter, but an atavistic misunderstanding led the would-be artist beneficiaries in a Nietzschean direction, full of self-induced ecstatic rage and apocalyptic summons. (A similar trend was to take over the American stage in the late sixties, with the same incoherent results.) Nor would our viewers, I suggest, have confronted the character of The Poet in Reinhard Sorge's 'The Beggar' with anything but a condescending amusement, such ego-postures being foreign to those values which produced and are housed within those figures we have designated our representative guides at the beginning. Predatoriness, murder and sadism as sanctified tools for the liberation of man are alien concepts to the ritual process for such viewers. Fortunately, however, this particular return encounter on African soil was limited to the saner repertoire of graphic and plastic idioms.

The rapport between our viewers and the absent artists, a rapport with the products of an alien culture, could not therefore fail to take the mind back to the initial end-of-nineteenth-century encounter, formulating unavoidably the fundamental question – what was it that happened exactly in those few decades – that is, between the eighteen-eighties and the nineteen-twenties? What kind of transformation had taken place within artistic sensibilities of the West that enabled its avant-garde to respond – never mind the confusions and distortions – to a culture that that other world had, after all, been well acquainted with in a quantitative dimension for at least four centuries? The very artifacts of that society were all around Europe. They had been brought back by missionaries, traders and company gents and later, colonial servants. A number of museums – like that in Ulm, Germany – had vast collections of these works. They had been sketched, painted and later photographed by explorers, discussed in learned conferences and stored in private collections. Matisse was one artist who had one of the largest private collections of African art, viewed (with some curiosity) by fellow artists; neither he nor his fellow Impressionists – at least not until Cézanne – appeared to have permitted any form of influence from these idioms in their works. Cézanne, we may claim, began the transition.

But it was not only the artifacts which were familiar. The entire culture, the very premise of an African or several African civilizations was subjected to anatomical dissections. The ontological existence of the blackman, both as speculation and as concrete reality, was at the fore of scholastic concerns, hardly surprising, as the encyclopaedic approach to knowledge could hardly excise the subject of that vast reservoir of cheap slave labour and raw material. Thus, in 1741, that is, some ten years before the first in the series of Diderot's *Encyclopaedia*, the Academy of Sciences in Bordeaux, bored perhaps with its oenological pursuits, called an International Conference on the subject of the black colour of the Africans. We will not bother to go much further back, tempting as it is to recall the 'Summary of the Antiquities and Wonders of the World ... out of the Sixteen Books of Pliny,' published in 1556, to which a veritable black bestiary constituted the African cultural contribution. That would be far too distracting. We are more concerned here with the revolution which took place in the admittedly scientific, not the primitive phase of European mind, a development which even governed its way of perceiving not only its own, but the reality of other societies, one which enabled it suddenly (or eventually) to overcome its blinkers in some respects. Just one notorious example: the Egyptian practice of representing the human eye frontally even when the entire human body is seen in profile. From a condescending point of view which concluded that the Egyptian artist had simply not mastered the trick of representing the eye in profile, the stunning illumination descended – the Egyptian was simply concerned with representing the eye as eternally watchful, keeping a jealous eye on the treasures of the funeral chamber.

So let us turn, once again, to our guardian presences in the draughty galleries of Dresden and Munich, their organs of sight even more 'ineptly' represented than those of the presumed Egyptian amateurs. What blinding insight could they have inflicted to disperse the dark shadows of superstition whch ruled the famed Black Forests of Friedrich William Hegel's birthland, to which, we must presume, Hegel's own mind owed its racial conditioning? I am content merely to pose the question, to highlight the enigma. Thus, did Vassily Kandinsky, unquestionably the most lucid of the theorists of abstract Expressionism in painting, certainly the most mentally stable and productive of them all, ever wonder at the irony of fate which made his nephew Kojeve, professor of philosophy, introduce Hegel to the Expressionist generation in Paris? Hegel, in company with matching and mismatched bedfellows such as Freud, Karl Marx, Bakunin, Nietzsche, cocaine and free love would provide the philosophic fodder of these cultural revolutionaries who, gravitating around even more charismatic figures of Otto Gross (quite mad but brilliant) and Franz Jung (no relation to Karl), would take Expressionism to apocalyptic regions of the mythical New Man. If African art and philosophy had any truthful authentic contact point with the Expressionist movement, it is probably through the Russian Kandinsky, not too surprisingly perhaps since – unlike, shall we say, the Oskar Kokoschkas of that movement – his theoretical pronouncemnts appeared to be tempered by an apparent Russian spirituality, underplaying the superman rhetoric in the common onslaught on a reactionary social condition. The kind of 'community' later embraced by Otto Gross and Richard Ohring in what appeared to be later conversions from Nietzschean supermanism – these were embedded from the very beginning in Kandinsky's vision of the Expressionist man. Guardian figures of the Bakota, Nimba, Yoruba, Dogon, Dan, peering into the hearts of the Teutonic, Nordic, Gallic and other Aryan faces which marvelled at their originality – how could they fail *not* to concede possible symbiotic relations – with profound qualifications – with that Slavic voice which insisted:

> It can be maintained altogether without exaggeration that a science of art
> erected on a broad foundation must be international in character: it is
> interesting, but certainly not sufficient, to create an exclusively European art
> theory.

Kandinsky went on to declare that this science of art will lead to:

> A comprehensive synthesis which will extend far beyond the confines of art
> into the realm of the 'oneness' of the human and the 'divine'.

Kandinsky appears to qualify in that quote almost as the mouthpiece of these alien presences. The severity of the Nimba chin, I fancy, dissolves in amity beneath those baroque chandeliers. For this art anticipated Friedrich Hegel by centuries, embodying in their being, so belatedly recognized by the Expressionist, that paradoxical:

> falling to pieces of Art, a process . . . which was due to an imitation of the
> objects of Nature in all the detail of their contingent appearance . . .

a form, 'coming in direct knowledge of itself'.

And therein lies our irony, and the insistence on my question. This Art as symbolic product of the mind, marvelled at by Brancusi, Picasso and company, has emerged from that same race to which Hegel, from whom that very last quote has been taken, denied even the capacity of Reason. His fellow-philosopher David Hume was just as racially chauvinistic.

> I am apt to suspect that the negroes, and in general all other species of men
> (for there are four or five different kinds) to be naturally inferior to the

> whites. There never was a civilized nation of any other complexion than
> white, not even any individual element either in action or speculation. No
> ingenious manufacturers amongst them, no arts, no sciences . . .

How, I wonder, did Kandinsky resolve this issue, placed as acknowledged head of a movement that opposed internationalism and universal symbolism to the narrowness of fascist isolationism? As he joined with Brancusi, Modigliani, Gaugin, Picasso and others in worshipping at the shrine of these African and Polynesian revelations, did Kadinsky or any of the others actively speculate on what role these philosophers had played in the warping of the world-perception of their predecessors? We must take a few more examples of these highly authoritative philosophic 'verities', both in order to appreciate the extent of the revolution in sensibilities which took place at this period but also, more importantly, to gauge the consequences for contemporary Africans who after all are the real legatees of those unwilling intruders into a hostile cultural milieu. Not that Hegel, Hume and company had it all their own way. We must, for the record, give due credit to humanists such as the Abbé Grégoire who tirelessly reminded his compatriots of the achievements of 'men of colour' as they were known at the time. He pointed out the examples of Ignatius Sancho, Gustavus Vassa (also known as Olauda Equiano), a prolific writer and social activist. There was Antonius Guilielmus Amo, a freed slave born in Axim, Gold Coast, then professor of philosophy at Halle University, Germany – in short, a colleague of our learned philosopher Friedrich Wilhelm Hegel. Nor was David Hume without a contemporary; he found it obviously impossible to ignore Francis Williams, professor at Cambridge University, England, but there was no problem in getting round that, among other notable scholastic rivals. The Abbé Grégoire's grounds of contestation were neatly eroded by proving the rule through the exceptional:

> Indeed in Jamaica they talk of one negro as a man of parts and learning; but
> tis likely he is admired for very slender accomplishments, like a parott who
> speaks a few words plainly.

Case dismissed! These instances are cited only to remind us that an argument, a disputation did exist.

It is not however just for the love of paradox that I insist that our venerable guardians of the shrine (in exile), listening to the Aryan intellect of Hume, that those presences nodded sagely, evincing neither surprise nor condemnation. No blame attaching to David Hume, they suggest, nor indeed to Francis Williams, Guilielmus Amo, nor to yet another famous black in the courts of Europe, Jacobus Capitaen, also a freed slave and a distinguished poet, a professor at the University of Granada and personal friend to the King of Spain. If any blame attached to anyone, it would be to the Abbé Grégoire and other defenders – black or white – of the black intellectual cause who accepted the grounds of cultural valuation from the racial deniers. If we are truly to understand the underlying remote causes of the major contemporary movements in African literature and the arts, we have to approach them, in part, as motivated by the desire *not* to repeat the mistake of the well-intentioned Abbé Grégoire. When the Negritude movement came to be, in the student clubs and the sidewalk cafés of Paris, it should not come as a surprise that the riposte delivered to the long history of racial and cultural calumny would be one which was plucked from a philosophical frame. The philosophers had proved the principal culprits, naturally, since it is the mission of philosophy not merely to frame, but to phrase the world. Thus, rejecting the endocentric parameters which had, to the satisfaction of those philosophers, placed even Jacobus Capitaen, Guilielmus Amo, Francis Williams etc. outside intellectual history, they chose Descartes as the scapegoat of their own complementary rejection and declared: I feel, therefore, I am. And thus, ironically yet again, a new round of ecstatic man, a neo-Expressionism in the arts and poetry was born in the studios of Paris and transported back to the intellectual soil of Africa and the Caribbean. It was also a movement of human liberation which glorified the intuitive man, proclaiming war on black bourgeoisification, letting loose the unrestrained, poly-symphonic man, one which like its forebear, tried to replace the empirical drift with communalistic faith, intensity of emotions and ethical intuitions. Jean-Paul Sartre sums up, without employing any Expressionist reference, what these two movements had in common – that is, as far as the evident creative forms are concerned, not as any valuable commentary on the race since it is, in common with other 'manifestoes' of this movement, basically reductionist:

> The being-in-the-world of blacks (according to Sartre), covers all the ways in which the black experienced his condition in the world: through rhythm, sexual pantheism, a cosmic sense, the indissoluble unity of suffering, the erotic, and joy.

Is this really much different from the manifestoes of the Expressionist revolt? True, Surrealism was the path elected by some of the poets. It was indeed the path proclaimed by the seminal organ of Negritude, *Légitime Défense*, which identified as pointers the European Surrealists André Breton, Tristan Tzara, Louis Aragon, Salvador Dali etc. But the Negritude movement itself, the totality of that rhapsodic embrace of the self re-discovered, re-aligned to the inner depths and spaces of communal and mystical self-realization – this was what made it twin to the European Expressionist adventure. It exploded impressively in every medium, including even a Renaissance of Tapestry art in Senegal whose flaring, defiantly unrestrained colours were rather reminiscent of Fauvist paintings in France. The sculptures were massively conceived, a return to traditional boldness, expressions of black racial strength finally freed from the coldness of European intellection. In wood, metal and stone, they strove to inscribe on the landscape the monumentality of Nature itself, and the ability of the black man to abstractly monumentalize his history. The Festival of Negro Arts in Dakar, 1966, represented the culmination of that movement, memorable mostly in the exhibitions of paintings and sculptures – and the tapestries – which synthesized the Negritudinist, neo-Expressionist spirit. But it is the poetic output which, till today, exists as the record of that uneven phase, its sweeping rhythms which gather into heedless torrents, tearing down the artificial dykes of reason in their ecstatic, race-glorifying abandon. How inner-directed, how autogestive was this movement, and its forms of expression? Lilyan Kesteloot claims:

> From the general viewpoint, the situation did not necessarily imply the presence of whites. This is why, with Senghor, we can speak of a 'negritude of the sources', which existed before the arrival of Europeans. It is true that blacks BECAME AWARE of their 'being in the world' upon contact with whites. The black man recognised his negritude but did not create it in response to whiteness.

Alas, that penultimate sentence, 'became aware of their being in the world upon contact with whites,' – never mind how it appears to be cancelled out, modified, contradicted and generally made irreconcilable by and with all that went before and came after it – that position is the ontological condition accepted and projected through the larger part of the poetry of Negritude.

And those eternal watchers, the ancestral guardians who, like the Negritudinists, had bestridden the two worlds and presided over a similar revolution of sensibilities – could we presume that they were truthfully projected from within their innermost sensibilities, from within a coming-in-being that that was coeval with self-apprehension? Did they perhaps consider Negritude a more appropriate statement than Olauda Equiano's, Amo's, and others who chose, or rather had no choice but to frame their worlds in the language of those other worlds? Not if Yambo Ouologuem had any say in the matter! We shall see in a moment how justified or extreme his position is.

The European Expressionists had fallen victim to a Nietzschean delirium that glorified Man as primal beast, demolishing the soulless prettified walls of bourgeois society, and thus re-constituting Mankind in a blaze of creative energies. With only a limited understanding of its contextual genesis, they saw African art as a signpot. They viewed it, groped towards it as the true expression of man who seized the essence of being in the act of coming to knowledge of himself.

> pressing forward to its true form of existence (where) consciousness will come to a point at which it lays aside its semblance of being hampered with what is foreign to it, with what is only for it and exists as an other; (where) it will reach a position where appearance becomes identified with essence.

In place of the 'primal beast', the neo-Expressionists, that is the black Negritudinists, substituted, alas, the primal child. For the universalism of the Expressionists, a cultural exclusivity of essence was preached but not one, let us hasten to add, which shared the fascist chauvinism to which Expressionism was itself a reaction. On the contrary, its chauvinism was seen as a humane complementarity to the European mechanistic thesis, reaching towards a new synthesis of a universal humanism. This response of Negritude was not however the only option, nor did it remain so. Other writers, secure in the actuality of their environment, confident – or rather – unquestioning about the validity of their heritage occupied themselves with literature which was not a response, one which refused to acknowledge the claims of any reacting imposition or else, responded with a lofty iconoclasm.

Yambo Ouologuem's *Bound to Violence* simply exemplifies this very last. It turns racist history on its head and reverses the cultural claims of the erstwhile deniers – rejecting the thematic and stylistic ambivalence represented by the Negritudinists. That mixture of attraction and objective rejection had, as we have seen, committed the error of the reductionist, in its determination to secure a complementarity for black reality within the universalism that had finally opened its doors through Expressionism. Ouologuem actually portrays this tendency critically in the persona of his main protagonist – the hybridized Raymond Spartacus Kassoumi. He thunders with the outraged voice of those presences, wreaking historic revenge on the instruments of their original denigration, a process which is not resolved totally even at this moment – not by a long chalk – and which certainly formed part of the armoury of yet another Africanist, two or three decades after the conversion – by illumination – of the vital, minority spirit of European creativity. At the very moment that Kadinsky's nephew, Kojeve was introducing Hegel to his students in Paris, and Kadinsky himself was producing his African-Arts influenced abstractions and manifestoes, a certain Leo Frobenius, leader of the German Inner Africa Expedition was, in 1905, in Ile-Ife, spiritual home of several of those ancestral guests trapped in the salons of Paris, London, Munich. And what is Frobenius doing? Digging away in a desperate search for the lost city of Atlantis. And in his own blundering way, he became the apogee of that critical phase of European intellectual xenophobia, honed to the nth degree. For how else does one describe the workings of the mind of a searcher, an explorer who, confronted with material evidence of a culture, *in situ*, surrounded by living progenies of the culture that produced such artifacts, by custodians and manifestations of the cohesive totality of human experience of which those artifacts are a mere part; how explain the mind of an enquirer which, faced with this massive reality that embraces its mythologies of which, again, these artifacts are symbolic representations and/or celebratory instruments; how explain a mind which, faced with this evidence of an integrated world-view, still insists on his own mythology of cities lost in the mists of Etruscan or Phoenician antiquity to account for the unified reality whose feast is spread before him! Ouologuem's savage satire on Shrobeniosology and its fellow travellers becomes tame when we consider the stubbornness of this twentieth-century mind. Of course, certain personal frustrations in his acquisitive obsessions had something to do with it, but it can hardly be held to excuse this final effort to commit the wholesale robbery of a people of their history, even at the moment of rifling and carting away the material evidence of that history to join our pioneer presences in the museums of Berlin. Leo Frobenius, was, admittedly, generous in the main. He did often give the devil his due. But not even that radicalized ordering of the Teutonic mind could, when the credit for this is awarded to the watery ghosts of the lost city of Atlantis, be considered adequate consolation for such attempted dispossession – never mind the language of racist spite:

> There is an element of typical rigidity in the Ilifian [Ilifian is the name
> Frobenius gives to the indigene of Ile-Ife] and his intellectual poverty struck
> me repeatedly as being his most distinguishing quality. This, naturally,
> appears uncommonly strange to the historian of culture, and may at first
> seem surprising and unintelligible, on remembering that Ile-Ife is the
> religious centre, or as its people call it, the 'navel' of Yoruba socio-religious
> existence, the city of the Priest King, the actual Rome of all the Yoruba
> realm. This may sound contradictory, for the priesthood of a nation may,
> indeed, be reactionary, but it is very seldom deficient in thought. The kernel
> of the conundrum offered by this singular African city is this, namely, that
> these people are managing an hereditary estate, whose creation is spiritually
> quite out of touch with their present conception of life. The people of Ile-Ife
> lie like a slumbering dragon over the gold of a prehistoric treasure-house.
> Poverty-stricken in mind, because of their ignorance, they guard the old city
> which lends them respect, lofty position and religious supremacy because
> they reside in it, because the blood of its original founders and builders has
> been dissipated and evaporated by diffusion, but, most indubitably, not
> because the salvage has come down to the present in the external form of its
> original antique creation in an era of productive intellectual activity.

I add Leo Frobenius to our list for very good reasons. If, except in one or two instances, and largely through the disputed Egypt-Greek-Roman route, African cultures *appear* to have contributed little to the mainstream of world civilization – always remembering of course that, for the African, this is a purely academic subject, not a matter for his spiritual or intellectual validation – it is important to recall even a fraction of the catalogue of Europe's chances, of the morbid pathology of its own scholars and explorers which called forth even in the twentieth century the compulsive denial of creative and intellectual continuity on the very soil that manifested the end-products of an enquiry.

Leo Frobenius – is it necessary to add? – did not speak a word of the language of these 'degenerate guardians'. The spare time he should have taken to master at least some significant idioms of the language he spent reading Goethe's romances aloud to his companions – and they to him, when they were not occupied with negotiating for the sale of artifacts and tangling with the interests of the British colonial officers and their spies, under whom this part of the divided continent had fallen. Judging from his choice of imagery in the earlier quoted passage – the slumbering dragon over the gold of a prehistoric hoard – it is not hard to imagine also what musical parameters he would employ when his Wagnerian ears were bombarded by the music of the Ife people. But far more relevant for now is the paradoxical effect on African writers and even would-be aesthetic theorists, blithely unconscious how their instincts have been shaped by centuries of European historicism and intellectual canons for which the African reality provided only the occasional, marginal, race-motivated fodder. To go back to our manifest presences in that gallery, how would they respond to Leo Frebenius if we could but render their essences mortally animate for a moment – a conceit, I readily admit, but a legitimate one since we are regularly confronted by other, and certainly slanderous animators of far more dangerous ghosts. Would these figures respond, for instance, as the play objects nostalgically requested in these lines of Léon Damas?

> Give my black dolls back to me
> so that I can play with them
>   The simple games of my instincts
> instincts that endure
> in the darkness of their laws
> with my courage recovered
> and my audacity
> I become myself once more
> myself again
> out of what I used to be
> once upon a time
> once
> without complexity
>   once upon a time
> before the uprooting came.
>
> Give them back to me
> My black dolls
> Black
> dolls
> black black
> dolls

Hard on the heels of this kind of 'poetry' develops, inevitably, an aesthetic of African poetry which demands that the African poetic landscape be no more than:

> a landscape of elephants, beggars, calabashes, serpents, pumpkins, baskets, towncriers, iron bells, slit drums, iron masks, snakes, squirrels . . . a landscape portrayed with native eyes to which aeroplanes naturally appear as iron birds; a landscape in which the animals behave as they might behave in African folklore, of animals presented through native African eyes.

This debasement of the African poetic province – an infantile regression, no less – has been set by self-avowed African critics, products of this living generation, black, not by a Hollywood scriptwriter of the forties. We have a name for them, not very easy to forget, nor difficult to guess – the neo-Tarzanists – lazy, undialectical interpreters of their own society, choosing the line of least resistance.

There is more for them in another place.* Addressing their sociology however, let us note that it is invariably the uprooted, the culturally alienated who turn back to the roots with the fierceness of the long deprived – and with its corresponding ignorance. Well, perhaps ignorance is an inaccurate word. They do know something. They know Tarzan of the Apes, and they have an abject conditioning coated in intellectual liquorice from the legacy of Hegel, Gobineau, Hume and company. Lacking the resources to challenge such elevated ignorance, they take refuge in glorifying the cultural retardation which has been assigned them as their maximal development, turning it into a 'principled' aesthetic. Unlike those theorists, indeed, in spite of them, Léon Damas for his part did write far more accomplished poems than that unfortunate example and the major Negritudinists did, later on, gracefully modify their positions, acknowledging their original stance to be nothing more than a phase, a reaction, the erection of a combative banner. The pitfalls of the dialectical process ensnared them, so that they fell prey to the lure of a universalist synthesis which, however, relegated them to the junior position in the formulation of a new humanism. Well, let us not even say *junior* position, let us simply say: *assigned* position. This school of poetry committed the fundamental error of imagining that they had willed their position and that this position which, to the racist view of civilization is negative could, by dint of their creative will, by their act of celebration, be turned into a virtue.

'Reason is Greek, emotion, African,' claimed Léopold Sédar Senghor, at the height of his Negritudinist fervour. And, translating this Hegelian position into a paean to self-reduction, to the vitiation not merely of the whole man but of the whole history of man, of all men, Aimé Césaire also rhapsodized his unfortunate corroboration of the thesis of David Hume:

Hurrah for those who never invented anything.

What would they have made of the programme of Johannes R. Beecher who in his Expressionist delirium swore, not only to 'invent the swiftest aeroplane', 'think up the most phenomenal automobile', 'prove Fermat's Last theorem', 'discover new poles', but went on to declare, some fifteen years before Negritude, in his 'Introduction to my New Book of Verse': 'Analysis! Analysis! Analysis! Island of despair, you'd vanish. Ithaca's silvery shores are shimmering: Oh thou island of pure deliverance!' Reconcile that effusion, whoever can, with: 'Reason is Greek; emotion African.'

For some of the Negritudinists of course, Léopold Senghor especially, the ambivalence of their literary product went beyond a mere entrapment in the dialectics of the master race. France held a mystic hold on them, like Rabearivello who was never part

* See 'Neo-Tarzanism: The Poetics of Pseudo-Tradition'. (Ed.)

of the movement, a hold which was translated, wherever they attained political power, into political and socio-economic strategies that bordered on race abandonment. This is no place to go into those aspects, especially as the examples of most other non-Francophone ex-colonial territories indicate that the differences have been only a matter of degree, the result being, with near uniformity, a second expropriation of the African masses, a continuation of the experience of slavery in a different form, of dehumanization and neo-colonial exploitation under a new set of hob-nailed boots shodding black feet. It is the poetry of Senghor which fascinates one, so full of a studied resonance which almost seduces one to the claims of Negritudinist inspiration, only to repel by the nature of the content:

> Black prisoners – or rather French prisoners
> – is it true then,
> that France is no longer France?
> Is it true then that the enemy has taken her face
> from her?
> Is it true that the malice of bankers has bought
> off the
> strength of her steely arms?

It will be difficult, if not impossible, to find an anglophone poet, of any level, approaching Senghor's competence or reputation, who would wring his or her lyric hands over the fate of a former colonial master. And why, why this following coyness, this racial apologia for an assignment that no one ever asked of the poet in the first place? 'Women of France' is the title of the poem which commences:

> Women of France, and you, daughters of France
> Give me leave to sing of you. For you the clear
> notes of the sarong.
> Take them, though their rhythm is barbarous and
> their harmony harsh
> Like a peasant's milk and his coarse bread, pure in
> his clumsy, calloused hand.
> You, beautiful trees, upright under the shelling
> and the bombs
> The only arms in days of despondency, in days of
> panic despair.
> Proud towers, proud steeples under the arrogance
> of the sun in June
> Clear echo to the cry of the gallic Cock.

Barbarous rhythm ... harsh harmonies ... clumsy, calloused hands ... Why! Even Frobenius accepted a 'classic loveliness' in Ife bronzes! Alas, Léopold Sédar Senghor is the true griot with a false vocation. He is a nature poet, an open-air sensibility in whose veins the seasons of black Africa run their course with animistic ease; every breeze trills his tongue in epical tones, the heroic tonalities of the born griot. He paints with bold strokes, delineating the shades and highlights of experience, spraying on the patina of the eternal, of the secured communal (and ancient) reality. His incantations stretch the transient moments and emotions to rouse the ancients in their homes, joining the spiritual to the sensuous:

> Young girls with upright breasts, sing the rise
> of the sap proclaim the Spring
>
> A drop of water has not fallen for six months,
> not a tender word, not a budding smile
> only the fierceness of the harmattan, like the
> fangs of the viper
> At best only a swell of the sand, only the
> whirlwind of dust and straws and rubbish and
> wingsheaths
> Dead things under the fierce erosion of reason.
> Only the East Wind in our throats like the cisterns
> of the desert
> Dry. But this clamour in our limbs, this rousing of
> the sap
> swelling the buds at the groin of the young men,
> waking the pearl-oyster beneath the mangroves . . .
> Maidens, listen to the song of the sap rising to
> your upright throats.

This is the Senghor we prefer to remember, the one we wish someone would award the Nobel Prize for literature so the rest of us African writers can rest in peace for the next twenty years.

Well, we have touched on two strategies, two forms of reactions – one the reductionist context of Negritude, the other being the iconoclastic – that is, Yambo Ouologuem's which cries: A plague on both your houses! The 'second house' is the Islamic, for Ouologuem is equally unsparing of the Islamic world, which he adjudges just as guilty of an active denigration of the African world, its cultures and its socio-political integrity. This view, unpalatable though it is to many promoters of a unified Third World, does happen to be a truthful view of a pattern that began with the earliest Islamic invasion of the black Egyptian world in the seventh century AD.

Mongo Beti – *The Poor Christ of Bomba* etc, – employs a subtler wit, but no less effective, in his demolition acts on Euro-Christian claims to the civilizing mission. With these writers, in company with Sembene Ousmane, Alex La Guma, the South African Marxist writer, Ngugi wa Thiongo, Ayi Kwei Armah, Lenrie Peters and a host of other African writers, it is difficult to find any trace of that kind of nostalgia for the Western world which sometimes – admittedly – provides a creative tension in the literature of Negritude, but generally attenuates a conviction in its internal cultural security. Writers of the ambivalent strain embrace nearly all Negritudinists. Even when the subject-matter is the assertion of a tangible self-validation, the overall response which their works evoke – the poetry especially – is: Methinks the lady does protest too much.

At the bottom of the spectrum, way way down below even the primal child syndrome, is the aesthetic of infantile regression already referred to, one which holds up the following verse, in print believe it or not, as the truthful and authentic voice of the African poetic Muse, and confronts those who call them buffoons with the opportunist flag of cultural decolonization:

> In our little village
> When elders are around
> Boys must not look at girls
> And girls must not look at boys
> Because the elders say
> That is not good.

There is yet another genre of writing however, one which seizes wholeheartedly on the factual basis of an African reality, but insists that it must be interrogated through a conscious ideological framework. An unmediated past, accepted as such, it claims, leads inevitably to a rationalization of social sytems and beliefs, however reactionary, and writers like Sembene Ousmane, and more recently Ngugi wa Thiongo, and lesser-known ones like Femi Osofisan and Niyi Osundare in Nigeria, have engaged such assumptions creatively, either by providing contrasting social (ideological) options in the midst of a social upheaval – as in Sembene – or, like Ngugi, exposing the inherent contradictions which became structured into the 'spoils of victory', the appropriation of exploitative colonial structures by a new class, the true beneficiaries of what has been a massed anti-colonial struggle.

This specific ideological thrust, overtly stated or actively induced from the interplay of characters and situations, has become lately prominent, in the service of which past mythologies and hero-concepts, once taken for granted, are restructured through a Marxist framework. The results are naturally varied. On the one hand, there is the extreme ultra-leftism which commits the same alleged sin of a non-analytical indiffer-ence as the mythifiers, denying on their own part any virtues of progressive potential to the past. One such critic, a foreigner, earning his living in my own univerity in the Philosophy Department – it is interesting how philosophy appears to breed the most racially warped of commentators on the African world – this neo-Humist actually dismisses the material of the African past as:

cracked, chipped and useless pieces of antique porcelain.

Elsewhere in the same essay this critic sweepingly insists that it is the duty of African writers to treat traditional thought-systems in terms of 'false-consciousness'. It is a credit to the liberal traditions of that university in particular that such a 'scholar' is still permitted to earn a living on African soil.

However, some African writers have themselves, as already stated, begun to re-write their own history through the spectrum of class-analysis – or, to be more accurate, do set out with this laudable intent. We will examine what constitutes some of the pitfalls of this exercise through the play *Morohuntodun*, by one of the younger generation of writers, Femi Osofisan. Moremi, the hero of this play, was a real historic personage. Before Femi Osofisan in fact, she has been a popular subject with a number of playwrights, most notably the late Duro Ladipo. Her story is straightforward enough. Moremi, a Yoruba princess, became concerned by frequent incursions into her father's kingdom by the Igbo. These incursions were frequently successful because the Igbo had a secret weapon, a terrifying horde of strange, inhuman figures who erupted from the bushes and demoralized the city defenders by their very appearance. The latter simply threw down their weapons and fled. Moremi decided on a simple strategy. On the next invasion, she permitted herself to be captured. Her beauty attracted the interest of the commander of the Igbo troops who married her and even had children by her. Patiently, she studied the battle strategies of the enemy, eventually discovering that the so-called supernatural beings were just ordinary soldiers who wore fiendish masks and make-up, and spread terror among the Ondo peoples. Once that secret was in her hands, she escaped back home. Of course when the enemy next invaded, the Ondo people were waiting.

This legend in its historical details had often been performed as folk-opera in the Nigerian repertory. Femi Osofisan now took the same legend, transferred it to a contemporary situation and gave it a class twist. He took a revolt of the Western Nigerian peasants in the late sixties – known as the Agbekoya Uprising – and made Moremi the daughter of a wealthy trader who is forcibly kidnapped by the Agbekoya. From a haughty, privileged attitude towards her captors and the villagers where she is lodged, she comes to understand their plight, the justice of their cause ... in short, another Patricia Hearst. Before long, she is a full-fledged revolutionary – she has also fallen in love along the way – and soon she is leading the equivalent of bank raids and caps her career by raiding the police headquarters, freeing prisoners and turning the tables on her pursuers.

The really striking part of Osofisan's treatment is his flashbacks to the real Moremi myth. The new Moremi is seen actually dreaming herself a reincarnation of the historical figure, then, finally breaking with her, having come to the conclusion that that former Moremi was nothing but an oppressor. Her sacrifice was not for her people but a commitment to perpetuating her class control within an oppressive feudal system. The patriotism and heroism of the historic Moremi is thus summarily dismissed, her act was nothing but an act of self-interest, dedicated to a retention of the domination of one class over the masses.

It is, in fact, a valid thesis – but only on the surface. And only if one is prepared to join – in a different vein – in the game of traducing one's history for ideological gains. If Osofisan had been content to use the Moremi theme as base for examining the class genesis and conflicts of the Agbekoya Uprising specifically, the issue would be straightforward. We would have, as already remarked, a sort of Patricia Hearst saga with an unarguable ideological resolution. It would be seen to proceed logically from the objective social reality and the psychology of the individual under stress, and as an intellect responding to new ideas. In short, we would observe an educative process. William Sassine's novel, *Wiriyamu* deals more persuasively with this theme, with the kidnapped victim as the son of a Portuguese commander brought to an understanding of what the Mozambican war of liberation was all about. Not a very accomplished novel, the famous massacre of the villagers of Wiriyamu is treated in an episodic style that dilutes the specific horror and fails generally to equal the heroic dimensions of the imperatives of that struggle. But the sections which deal only as a sub-theme with the 're-educative' process of the captive are certainly more convincing. A dialectical process begins from that moment when the initial shock and the subjective, that is – conditioned – reaction have passed, and the individual objectively assesses the antithetical product of his or her privileged existence as manifested in the reality of the captors' existence of absolute commitment and self-sacrifice. Action – as in the case of Patricia Hearst – may follow – a result of intellectual conviction or, again, thanks to the individual's psychology, as a product of fantasizing.

Fascinated with myth and history, clearly, is Femi Osofisan. This heritage obsesses him – nearly all his works – *Once Upon Five Robbers, The Chattering and the Song*, etc. testify to this. But an ideological conviction and the aesthetic of theatre which he attaches to it places him, in company with a number of a new generation of writers, in a confused, ambivalent creative existence towards the past. It results, as in this instance, in throwing out the baby with the bathwater, denying even the virtues in his history – a strange position for a writer to find himself as interpreter of his own culture, whose very capacity to procreate has been so constantly at issue. It is as if such writers are still wrestling with the options of socio-political development, in dynamic interaction with race-culture, a phase never totally resolved even by their precursors in the original Negritude movement, in arguments which raged in Manifestoes, in the journal *Légitime Défense*, and the combative *L'Etudiant Noir*, affecting choices in stylistic approaches and political adherence. Was it not the same agonizing which led Aimé Césaire to join, then quit the Communist Party after some ten years, declaring:

> I am now convinced that our ways and those of communism do not blend . . .
> we coloured men have become aware of our entire range of uniqueness . . .
> the uniqueness of our 'condition in the world,' which can be compared with
> no other . . . both the political and cultural paths, are not ready made; they
> are still to be discovered and the route to this discovery must be ours alone.

Others of course made a clear choice from the very beginning: the significant fact is that none of them was a creator, certainly not of the same originality and craft as Césaire, the Diops or Damas.

Osofisan was therefore not content with the Agbekoya theme, a dramatic event in recent times with enough material to sustain several plays and socio-political dissertations. When a playwright makes that kind of a choice, we have to accept his goal – in this case, the central subject is mythification, and the specific, the myth of Moremi. The Agbekoya setting has been introduced solely as a critique of the facts of Moremi as received and celebrated by society. Now, those facts have already been stated. Within those facts, and even in prior representations there is no hint that Moremi was ever an oppressor either as an individual or as a type. Wicked princesses exist, we know, in fairy-tales, so do pathetic, oppressed Cinderella-type princesses. And a vast number of variations in between. The question therefore resolves itself thus: would Moremi's action have been acceptable (or correct) *only* if she had been a peasant? The issue here surely is patriotism and self-sacrifice. Nothing in the myth of Moremi suggests that she was anything but an accident of birth which, even in Marxist theology, is not an original sin. Was Lady Godiva saved, despite her albatross of birth? Or did she have to undergo some cleansing in an ideological Purgatory? Her sacrifice of modesty on behalf of the populace oppressed by her husband is easily interpreted as a panacea to keep the serfs quiet and devoted – she certainly made no effort to break the social mould which cast her in the ruling class and kept her there. Any myth or history can be revised – but to what end? What we have in short is a will to ideological respectability which offers its own heroic myths up as sacrifice on a would-be universalist altar by a deliberate and gratuitous distortion. Icons can be positive or negative; a blanket iconoclasm is an undialectical proceeding on a par with blanket fetishization of myth and history. At a critical period of the Russian history, Stalin found it necessary to resurrect folk heroes who had, until then, been banished to the 'evil bush' of history. They had become necessary for a renewal of national pride and belonging. Their legends, epics, poetry and statues were refurbished, parents were encouraged to give new babies the names of these heroes and heroines – never mind that a strict class analysis might prove them actual reactionaries, not merely convenient feudalists in revisionist history. Brecht surely provides a more rational approach, one which cuts the ground from either extreme by situating the dilemma in its own thematic terms:

Unhappy the land that has no heroes. Unhappier still the land that has need of heroes.

But we canot afford to end on yet another playwright of some ambivalence, for Brecht himself was not entirely free of this in his works, and most specifically, for our purpose, in *Baal*, that moisture deity of (probably) Mesopotamian and, further back, North African (Nilotic) ancestry, whom Brecht exhumed to close the torrid chapter of Expressionist excesses. For those who insist that 'Baal' was a satire on the raging beast of the Nietzschean awakening in that movement, it is necessary only to ask that they look closely at the poetry of that dramatic progression of the Amoral Superman. Certainly the portrait of Baal is not meant to be anything but repellent but – such nature lyricism in the service of exposing the nature of Expressionist Depravity – in capital letters – does not emerge from a total vacuum in attraction, or fascination. Was Brecht himself a victim of the dark influence of those guardian figures – even at a second or third remove, an influence filtered through the many frenzied directions of painting, sculpture, poetry, manifestoes and theatrical exuberance during his own formative period? Certainly we know that he was in the heart of it all, registering his disquiet, settling finally for the more disciplined Marxist portion of the ingredients that went into the melting-pot constantly boiling over in the creation of the 'New Man'. Perhaps he merely got carried away by his own war against the hypocrisy and sterility of the rising middle class. We know that he did cast widely for thematic illustrations to his didactic theatre – *The Caucasian Chalk Cricle, The Good Woman of Setzuan*, etc; it is therefore not a totally idle speculation that the atavistic, willful celebration of Life and Nature in the poetry of this play was a dimension wrung out of him in spite of himself. The literary evidence would appear to support it and, for our silent guardians in the galleries and museums of Berlin, let us at least permit them that final knowing smile at the expense of the disciplined, radicalized stylist.

I propose therefore to give Ouologuem the last word; for me, his poem 'Tomatoes' sums up the satirical wisdom of those figures also – we have touched only on their virtues of self-apprehension and symbolic repletion, not so much on their silent, cosmic laughter and creative mockery, virtues which their moral creators are the first to acknowledge and exemplify. A virtue, I might add, which the European Expressionists, and their Negritudinist counterparts appeared to lack in any remedial sense. So let Ouologuem redress the balance, and at the same time, annihilate, with its mordant wit, the entire history of racist literature and propositions, and the ambivalent need of those literatures it has provoked – consciously or unconsciously – into being, in the strategies of refutation, veering from the willed imperatives of specificity to the folds of universalism and back; exploiting but negating their own myths and history; courting and shying from ideologies. I think the world-womb of our Nimba presences must be near premature delivery from the – no pun intended – belly laughs produced by these surrealist lines whose 'cannibal joke' is, this time, on the alien humourist:

Tomatoes

People think I'm a cannibal
But you know what people say

People see I've got red gums but who has
White ones
Up the tomatoes

People say there are not nearly so many tourists
Now
But you know
This isn't America and nobody
Has the money

People think it's my fault and are scared
But look
My teeth are white not red
I've not eaten anybody

People are rotten they say I scoff
Baked tourists
Or maybe grilled –
Baked or grilled? I asked
They don't say anything just keep looking uneasily at my gums.
Up the tomatoes

Everyone knows in an agricultural country
    there's agriculture
Up the vegetables

Everyone knows that vegetables –
Well you can't live on the vegetables you grow
And that I'm quite well developed for someone
    underdeveloped
Miserable scum living off the tourists
Down with my teeth

People suddenly surrounded me
Tied me up
Threw me down
At the feet of justice

Cannibal or not cannibal
Answer

Ah you think you're so clever
So proud of yourself

Well we'll see I'm going to settle your account
Have you anything to say
Before you are sentenced to death

I shouted, Up the tomatoes

People are rotten and women curious you know
There was one of these in the curious circle
In her rasping voice sort of bubbling like a saucepan
With a hole in it
Shrieked

Slit open his belly
I'm sure father is still inside

There weren't any knives
Naturally enough among the vegetarians
Of the western world
So they got a Gillette blade
and carefully
Slit

Slat
Plop
Slit open my belly

Inside
Flourishing rows of tomatoes
Watered by streams of palm wine
Up the tomatoes.

XIV

Climates of Art*

The title is of course deliberate. It is meant to trigger off those associative devices we all utilize at will, so that 'Climate of Fear', 'Climate of Terror' and so on, will surface in the mind without much conscious effort. These, I regret to say, are not inaccurate readings – from my local meteorological station – of the creative spaces we mostly inhabit in these times – in varying degrees of course. In some spaces, the climate is unrelentingly torrid. Artists suffer instant heat-stroke for opening their windows just to let an air of reality into their secretive closets of creative avowal. They are charred to cinders, atomized by invisible laser-beams of state controls. They join the swelling army of *desaparecidos*. At one of the other extremes, there is never any suggestion of human or technical agency – visible or invisible. The official temperature having been set at Minus Zero, the artist is frozen out of the productive world – sent to Coventry or Siberia – it all depends on the location of one's observatory – where he is at liberty to warm up his toes by setting a match to his canvases or manuscripts which neither the system nor the commercial controls approve. At such moments a sculptor in wood, operating in wintry climes, may be accounted luckier than his colleagues who have opted for the medium of bronze or iron junk: no matter, sooner or later they all discover that mere inspiration has distinctly limited combustion or dietary levels. The poor wretch is discovered, years later, in a lonely garret – death by hypothermia, which – translated in the dictionary of this talk is – death by the cold shoulder.

We shall shortly abandon all effort to be faithful to the metaphor of this discourse. For now however . . . in between our extremes are those variable weather conditions where the artist basks in tolerable warmth one moment, then finds himself put on ice to take his creative ego down a degree or two. That tantalizing, balmy territory, the even, temperate zone beckons in silent reproof – if only you would sing the praises of occasion, or observe the silences of convenience, the permanent residence permit would

* The Herbert Read Memorial Lecture delivered at the ICA, London (1985).

be yours. The trusted indigenes are conspicuous as exemplars, elegantly robed and delicately perfumed, golden goblets refilled even before the concession of emptiness. Their supercilious smile, the scornful turn of the lip says, distinctly: He is the architect of his woes, he knows what to do to gain or regain entry into this congenial belt. On their rather distended chests are pinned ribbons and medals proclaiming national honours and citations. Commissions, pensions, estates and sinecures are obtained at the stroke of a pen. They are chairmen or members of every lucrative board, delegates on every government commission.

Of course the climate can change unexpectedly but that is no problem. These are the salamanders of mythology whose skin, breathing and blood circulation adapt to inconceivable extremes of climate. The Vicar of Bray – let that historic personage be finally given his due – the Vicar of Bray was no mere prelate but a consummate artist.

And yet, such is the brutal immediacy, the absolute lack of options in certain situations that those who are privileged to be on the outside, mere observers, find it an abuse of that privilege to pass judgement. I think of Ben Kawadwa, the first martyr of Theatre under Idi Amin, and his colleague Dan Kintu, both playwrights and directors. And others of their company. After their horrible deaths, does one not secretly wish that they had had the facility of a Robert Serumaga who did manipulate Idi Amin for as long as he could, succeeded in staying alive longer than any artist under that psychopath, creatively active under the nightmarish regime, identifying with great prescience when the tightrope had sagged beyond recall and leaping off to safety? We met at Victoria Station on his last trip home to evacuate his wife and family and he confessed: 'You know, once, you knew what to say or not say in order to stay alive. You were careful in your choice of plays, what to put on and what to leave alone . . . now all the rules are gone. What saved you yesterday may prove your death-warrant today.' Robert had the satisfaction at least of joining up with the Liberation forces and seeing the ogre put to flight before he died of an illness. At such moments one indulges in useless regrets – is it possible that Ben Kawadwa could also have survived with a little more sagacity? It is a useless question because the answer is NO. This is not a concession to fatalism but a realistic recognition of the nearly unique 'variable weather' conditions of Idi Amin's Uganda. Robert Serumaga was right; the only difference is that he was a more capable weather forecaster.

That situation must be near-identical with that of the thousands of tight-rope walkers in former Argentine, post-Allende Chile, Ayatollah Khomeini's Iran among others. The South African climate where the downward 'wind of change' was supposed to have threatened miracles, still dominates a unique landscape of its own. It manifests an apparent confusion of indications which only disguises a diabolical cunning, the cynical opportunism of a minority which internally exiles its own black artists while paying lip-service to other black artists – and sportsmen by the way – as long as they are outside that country's borders.

Picture this moment in the privacy of one monitoring post. The writer in his study, tuning his radio at random for news from foreign stations. He is arrested by the sound of his own name on some as-yet-unidentified airwave. He stops, naturally. What have I been up to lately? But it is alright really, just a critic reviewing some books by African authors. And do you know what strikes the listener all of a sudden? Not the fact that the reviewer is meticulously analytical and, as it happens, very favourably disposed to all this writing. No. It is the tone of exaggerated respect, an almost fawning, apologetic, unctuous respect which stubbornly detains his attention. MISTER Chinua Achebe. MISTER Amos Tutuola. MISTER Lenrie Peters, MISTER Ngugi Wa Thiongo, MISTER Wole Soyinka etc. etc. There is such weight of protocol upon this ordinary trapping of formal, egalitarian distance, such implicit rejection of any patronizing familiarity that our listener is arrested by a statement beyond mere literary opinion. Something more is being promoted by this Mister language, something whose essence is trapped in the sonorous accentuation of that – 'Misterious' – prefix. Finally, all is made plain. The review ends, and behold, the station our listener has stumbled upon is Radio South Africa. The lie is exposed. 'We respect black people, we treat their writers just like any other writers' – that is the message. 'Whatever else you may hear about us, weigh it against this uttermost respect we accord writers of black skin and kinky hair.' Did I use the expression 'internal exile' for the South African black writer? My apologies, I should have said, the state of non-existence. The status of non-persons. And I do not mean simply that legal mechanism of pronouncing those troublesome voices – white or black – banned persons: Don't publish. Don't mention. Don't associate with. Don't publish photo of . . . etc. etc. I refer to the deeper excision of the creative value of black writers from the pale of total humanity.

But now, by contrast, we other black writers are coralled into instruments of refutation of the true internal status of black South African writers. Having accorded us this status, in keeping with the bleak logic which also informs the strategy in the creation of 'honorary whites', should it surprise anyone that when Chinua Achebe for instance writes his address to fellow Nigerians which he titles *The Trouble with Nigeria*, it would be reviewed in South African newspapers even before neighbouring black African countries knew of its existence? The anomalies which distort the national character of that black African country, Nigeria, outlined by an indigenous writer of that country – a writer whom an 'objective' reviewer has regularly accorded honorary equality – naturally provide proof of the need for suppressing the will to self-determination which the black majority of the South African polity express through every means, including that most pervasive medium of art and literature.

If all the preceding sound somewhat exaggerated you must excuse me. It is no straightforward matter to attempt to enter into the mind of a regime which, having denied me – among others – a visa to respond to the call of a black writers' group in the South African ghetto of Soweto, proceeds, through its international propaganda medium, not only to provide the world with a respectful review of my works, but actually refers to me and other racially inferior humans – as decreed by such a regime – as Mister, and Doctor, and Professor. The mind, as P. G. Woodhouse would put it, the mind absolutely boggles!

But, transcending the negativity, what a developed African self-awareness since the beginnings of the South African struggle! That we were unable to respond to the reaching out of the Soweto poets and theatre artistes became of secondary importance to the fact that they reached out at all – not to Europe East or West, or to America North and South – but to writers from African nations. How many years, after all, was it since the Madagascan poet Rabearivello committed suicide? A mixed-up, identity-confused poet of potential genius, Rabearivello became an extreme victim of the colonial psychic divide which could not reconcile itself with a seeming rejection by that suffocating cultural mother of the Francophone writer-intellectual, France. He was not alone, but he was an extreme instance, singled out by his obvious talent. That psychic divide was made possible or at least accentuated by the conscious policies of 'assimilation' and colonial divisions which effectively isolated each colonial grouping by language imposition, a jealous territorial imperative based on the principle of honour among thieves, and the manipulations of pre-colonial rivalries. Indeed, often by a conscious formenting of totally artificial rivalries. If the poet Rabearivello, whose genius was of that nature which could not bear the constrictions of a tiny island, had had recourse to the comradeship of creative minds which were then beginning to re-define their own identity, and exercised that potential extension which was interrupted by the colonial misadventure, if he and others like him had been secured in a creative fraternity that filled the vacuum of ruptured individual identities, it is more than likely that that life – and other talents – would not have been wasted.

And so, belatedly in the late fifties, the *cordon sanitaire* drawn around colonial African nations began to buckle and tilt. Even before they moved into the other clime of discontent, the winter of exile, the manuscripts of poets like Dennis Brutus were being smuggled out of South Africa, to receive publication by the MBARI Writers and Artists publication arm in Ibadan, Nigeria. *Sirens, Knuckles and Boots* spoke a different language from the already absorbed realities of Apartheid which did surface from time to time, especially through the medium of that popular and racy magazine, *Drum*. With Alex la Guma's 'A Walk in the Night', scores of poems and short stories and other escaping material, the trickle did not become a flood, but it was at least a rivulet which opened into a new climate of awareness, new creative relations with a vast section of oppressed humanity. A family was becoming creatively extended, recovering a unique reality hitherto sentimentalized by works like Alan Paton's *Cry the Beloved Country*.

This breakdown of boundaries did not limit itself only to South Africa. The Boers' intransigent, primitive and canonical brand of racism was indeed only one of the many conditions of Apartheid, Portuguese colonialism being one of the – if that was possible – even more 'Misterious' proponents of the divisions between black and black in the fifties and sixties. The Portuguese did not have to go far afield to find their 'Misters'. They created them from within, employing a different technique of depersonalization of artists and intellectuals through the process of 'assimilation'. Honorary Portuguese, just like Honorary French. Honorary whites. If Agostinho Neto, not so well known in his own right as a poet as he is as a revolutionary leader and Head of State – if

Agostinho Neto had been content to be accepted as an Honorary Mister Poet and Intellectual black Portuguese, the history of Angolan decolonization would certainly have been qualitatively altered. Other poets like Mario Andrade, even in translation, brought a new music to the language of African poetry. In the plastic arts, I recall the revelation we received of the existence of the surrealist painter, Malangatana, from Mozambique even before the beginnings of the liberation struggle initiated by FRE-LIMO. From the Horn of Africa, other geniuses like Ibrahim el Salahi, Skunder Bhogossian crashed through the conventional restrictions of Islamic taboos and created new forms from Arabic calligraphy, Bhoghossian in particular going on to evolve unsettling images of procreation as he pushed his experiments towards a probing of foetal formations. And there were also physical contacts. Ezekiel Mphahlele (*Down Second Avenue*) with the covert aid of some of that same tribe who froze him out down under, actually turned up in Nigeria to participate in a writers' workshop, staying on to lecture in universities.

The erasure of transatlantic boundaries proved the most dramatic of all, thanks to the activities of some Afro-American organisations which turned out, ironically, to have been sponsored by some vaguely CIA-connected foundations for that organisation's very tortuous, generally impenetrable motivations. We are concerned here mainly with effects however. What the CIA got out of it, we still do not know after twenty-five years or more, but what we got out of it we know only too well – I suppose we could call it the fall-out benefits of Anglo-American political and cultural rivalry, there being no doubt that the United States of that time was only too ready to poach in the previous preserves of European colonial acculturation.

From this distance, one can only wonder at the belatedness of the discovery that Brazil – with Bahia as focal point – was a West African cultural survival source, despite all syncretic variants in its artistic actualities. As if by determinist will, Antonio Olinto, a novelist with a strong sense of African belonging, would be the Cultural Attaché at the Brazilian Embassy in that post-independence Nigeria, with his linkage novel *The Water House* ready for gestation. This work would take a Yoruba family to Brazil and bring it back onto contemporary West African soil. His wife, Zora Zeljan, beginning to strengthen her already manifested Yoruba sensibilities – her journey back home would result in the play *Oxala*, or *The Festival of Bonfin*, a Passion Play of an African deity which, without any extrusive thesis, universalized a Yoruba Ritual aesthetic – with its transatlantic adaptations – that only emphasized the replete self-sufficiency of the original. Duke Ellington's massed band invaded our *agidigbo-atilogwu-sakara* sounds in company of those blues heavyweights, Mahalia Jackson, Odetta, and their modernist counterpart Nina Simone. The voice of the Harlem tribe, Langston Hughes . . . from the Caribbean, Aimé Césaire, Nicolas Guillen . . . all, either in their own person or on pages of the linkage journals – *Black Orpheus, Odu, Présence Africaine* and others – altered the climate of exclusion with their indigo scented breezes which wafted over and settled periodically over Lagos, Ibadan, Enugu, Jos and Zaria. Those cultural centres – mostly British Council Centres – and indeed student campuses which were formerly monopolized by Tennysonian assonances and the cadenzas of Mozart, Beethoven etc. – or, on the more popular level, the maudlin strings of Victor Sylvester or the skiffle-band pot-pourri of Lonnie Donnegan with his bland, synthetic clichés of Leadbelly – these centres of cultural consumption were enabled to compare the authentic originals with the anglo-transmited pallid imitations. Harry Belafonte's Banana Boat Song was easily relegated to its toast-and-milkwater level beside the calypsos of Lord Kitchener or The Mighty Sparrow. The lyric pathos of Leadbelly, with its internalized history of survival under American racism, challenged the commercial exploitation of the British skiffle school of masqueraders. Billie Holiday, Bessie Smith, Ella Fitzgerald . . . history, our history in the Diaspora was retrieved for us after decades of selective winnowing through the tepid sieve of British colonial policies. The fake art which had postured for so long as the entirety and quality of black contribution to Europe and the 'New World' of the Americas could now be seen in all its rags.

Let me make this concrete by my own personal encounter, something which presented to my mind an appreciation of that experience which the Japanese call *satori*. After years of listening to English bands play 'Irene Goodnight' at student hops, I heard, for the first time, the original version of that song by Leadbetter – known more commonly as Leadbelly. This could not be the same song – that was my thought. This cry from a ghetto of pain, of humiliation, mixed through some magical formula with an affirmation of tenderness, hope and yet harsh despair, surely this threnody, counter-pointed by the downbeat chords of a twelve-string guitar, was not the same song as the treacly, deodorated 'Irene Goodnight' with which those English bands ended their ball-room dances. But of course that *satori* was the product of other educative passages – we shall touch upon some in a moment.

We do know that the effect of the artistic product is not always one which is limited to and is fulfilled exclusively by the composition of the artistic object itself. Sometimes the work of art commences its function and extends its objective properties through experiences outside the artistic object – other encounters, forms and properties of other spaces of imagination and – Reality. Leadbelly's 'Irene, Goodnight', and even more pertinently, Billie Holliday's 'Strange Fruit' or Odetta's 'Deep Blue Sea' cannot produce the same degree of empathy, cannot evoke the same sense of a communal poignancy – never mind how deeply steeped one is in the history of racism – if one were not, above all, a member of that race which constituted the object of that historic racist exploitation and dehumanization. All black peoples know of the harrowing history of the slave trade but not many in the fifties and early sixties – at least in my part of the continent – were aware of the continuing forms of slavery which still obtained in many parts of the United States. Few Africans were aware that, even in the sixties, it was still not totally safe for a mixed couple to walk arm in arm on the streets of New York. Racial discrimination in the United Kingdom and in other European countries was a notorious fact – indeed, racial discrimination in some West African countries was still a regularly contested actuality, but few, even among those battling for racial equality on their own soil, knew that blacks were still being lynched without any repercussion, in a number of states of the US of A. The revolution of the sixties – heralded and accelerated by the poetry, drama and novels of Ralph Ellison, Langston Hughes, LeRoi Jones (later Imamu Baraka), Ed Bullins, Sonia Sanchez, Haki Madhubuti etc., etc. – took many by surprise. This was only to be expected, as the attention of the continent was focussed on the tempo of events closer home – the Mau-Mau Liberation war in Kenya, the commencing contestation of Portuguese colonialism, Lumumba's death-struggle in the Congo, the tightening noose of Apartheid girding itself against the 'barbaric hordes' descending from the successful conclusion of all the above. How ironic it was, that it was largely those who escaped from the undeclared censorship of British educational policies within the colonies into the heartland of that colonial power itself that were enabled to receive – not quite at first-hand but close enough – the literary testimonies of those others in the burgeoning liberation struggle of the black race within the United States. Nothing, absolutely nothing could have equalled the educative impact of that classic of the literature of racism, *Scottsborough Boy*! For those who are not familiar with that text, *Scottsborough Boy* is the biography of one of two black youths who were sentenced to death in the infamous deep South of the United States for allegedly raping a white prostitute. It was however one of those miraculous times, miraculous in the sense of the tempo of activation of a world-wide conscience – for that time, and in particular within the European world on behalf of two unknown black individuals.

How shall I put it? In the struggle against European colonialism, the United States, with its history also of an anti-colonial struggle, had come to stand as an alternative goal of emulation to British development qualities. It is difficult to explain how this came to be so, but the rose-tinted accounts of students who pursued – to use our popular Nigerian expression – 'The Golden Fleece' in the United States rather than in Europe had much to do with it. Even slavery managed to get blamed more on British greed and inhumanity than on the self-interest of this amorphous society called the United States. And then, suddenly, *Scottsborough Boy*! A horror story to beat all sadistic inventions, transcending all pornography of violence. An indictment also of the medieval prison conditions of that country, of the system which upheld it, thrived on it, indeed appeared to be sustained on it.

But this digression is really about creativity – its genesis and the responses generated by its products. It is mere background to a certain heightened response which certain products from a specific history and milieu wrench from their consumer. After *Scottsborough Boy*, the music that emerged from that collective, ravaged psyche takes on near-intolerable complexities. Employing a new subjective language, dating from my reactions to that book, the horror of enforced prison sodomy, of sexual bestiality, the hammer-blows of the chain-gang, of the pitiless sun in that shared tropical climate, the black glances flashed conspiratorially from beneath clouded brows – these become the strident images that emerged from the slide of the trombone in a blues accompaniment, vivid in the bitter-sweet dissonance of the singing of Leadbelly, or in the tortured, latterly drug-ravaged voice of Billie Holliday. When, in the sixties, those skies finally erupted and lightning shattered the centuries old complacency of their tormentors, we could dance naked in the ensuing rains to the strains of those long violated guitars.

Malcolm X it was, I believe, who said, on the occasion of one famous assassination, 'The chickens are coming home to roost,' evoking torrents of condemnation, predictably from American John Birch sectors but also from liberal whites and even from among his fellow black combatants in the anti-racist struggle. There were others however who did recognize that that was an ouburst, not so much of Malcolm X, as of American and European history – of which very little, if anything, could be blamed on black contribution. Malcolm X in my view was the unconscious medium of the ghosts of American history. The problem however, for us in this age, a problem which did not really exist before, is that that very climate of undirected violence, a more generalized product of the history of these same nations, has become expanded and undiscriminating – both in potential and actuality. The issue of guilt or innocence has become largely academic – the fall-out of the gathering cloud guarantees its odious bounty to every corner of the globe.

It is not possible, peripatetic as one's profession makes one to be, to feign ignorance of the more global fear which has indeed found expression in works which vary from the so-called 'serious' art – that is, the kind which end up catalogued and hung like condemned criminals in some prestigious gallery – to the instant, commerce-directed canvasses which are displayed along the Left Bank of Paris, outside Ikoyi Hotel Lagos, or along Bayswater Road every weekend. Quite recently I encountered one such canvas; it was given the unambiguous title 'Holocaust'. It did not refer to Hitler's pogrom. We are also variously aware of numbers of artists – poets, playwrights, novelists, musicians, painters and sculptors – who have chosen to 'opt out' of the present world as it were. So convinced are they of the inevitability of the unleashing of a nuclear war by the superpowers or, in the view of others, the possibility of a terrorist organization realizing the neo-nuclear terror by assembling and detonating a do-it-yourself kit, that they have fled from urban existence altogether and embraced the doctrine of ecological survival at its most primitive. I know of one such who has created a small commune in one of those Penepolysian islands. There, its members grow all the food they need, including, I must add, an East African brand of marijuana which constitutes their sole export trade. As for painting, which is his real métier, his attitude is: Paint? For whom? For which generation? Others, more fatalistic – for our former example does plan after all for the survival of himself and his clan – others have merely clammed up, downed their tools and resigned themselves to the inevitable nuclear deluge. Central to their defence mechanism is the absolute refusal to have children. They are not about to breed children whose children would fulfil the vision of a Hieronymous Bosch or turn the familiar object identities of their world into a Salvador Dali nightmare. So to the chickens ... from an attitude of 'let the chickens roost where the eggs were laid,' I confess that I moved quickly back to a position of concern from which, not so long before, I did start out at the time of the first anti-nuclear Aldermaston March. The change occurred quite simply, quite subjectively. France had just tested her first atom bomb in the Sahara, ignoring, with that then fashionable Gaullist arrogance, the cries and protestations of Third World countries, and of the African nations in particular. My outrage found outlet in a poem which formed part of a Royal Court Theatre poetry-cum-drama night:

> We whom you super powers condemn
> To vague, unmeaning, future fears
> Regret we cannot sooner favour you
> By dropping dead.

Those verses which, I am certain, no African head of state ever heard of – since they were not in any case published beyond that Sunday night reading at the Court – obviously had nothing to do with reactions from African heads of government, but I was personally gratified to find that a number of them, including my own, broke off relations with France over the explosion. France, that is Charles de Gaulle, was rather surprised – and offended – at this assertion of a continental sensitivity!

I claimed earlier that the artistic object does not always rely for its effect – or even meaning – on the specific properties of composition. External reality or experience, especially of a powerful and pervasive character, can appropriate the work, accentuate aspects of its statements and even distribute meanings through its parts. Here is another instance that was born of that Gallic egg, laid callously in my backyard.

When I first encountered the paintings of Francis Bacon, I was struck in a way in which few modern artists – of Europe especially – had ever affected me. There was an odd familiarity about his specific scheme of image distortion and of course it did not take too long to recognize the source. Those who are familiar with the representation of the numinous in African mask will perhaps recognize this similarity in the use of distortion. Indeed I possess an *egungun* mask which is almost a replica of one of Francis Bacon's self-portraits. Dennis Duerden, in *The Invisible Present*, has written perceptively of the aesthetic of movement which is assumed by the traditional artist whose medium is the mask. The mask, he accurately insists, is really incomplete in itself. The aesthetic completion is already inserted – invisibly – in the modalities of distortion, but the full harmony of linear relations, and even colours, can only be apprehended in motion even though it is of course already present in the static, artistic conception. Bacon's faces – the distorted postures of some of his seated figures – appeared to be, for me, almost an attempt to capture an essence of that mask in motion – but without the numinous dimension. You could say that the figures I refer to are a profane idiom of the total aesthetic of the mask in motion. So much for the phase of innocence which coloured that reception of Bacon's images. Is it necessary to add that later, as I plunged into the other phase of subjectivity, aroused by events like the atomic explosion over the Sahara, Bacon's faces should assume projections of the future of humanity? The intentions of the artist become secondary in such interpretations – of course. But then, if Malcolm X was the unconscious medium of history's ghosts at the moment of an individual, yet universally symbolic moment of violence, could artists such as Francis Bacon not be accounted the unconscious medium of the ghosts of a future world?

I was recalled to the example of Bacon by what, I can assure you, was a pure coincidence. A year or two ago, my childhood biography *Ake* was published in paperback by Random House, New York. I found the cover very striking. Everything about the painting by an unknown artist, seemed totally familiar, yet removed. Then suddenly it was all clear. It was yet another trick of distancing from the familiar mask – à la Francis Bacon. Instantly the three artistic frames – Yoruba Mask, Francis Bacon and this new artist fused in a recognizable matrix. The newcomer, Wendy Hoyle, revealed to me that she had selected as motif a scene from *Ake* in which I had tried to describe my earliest sensation of speed – a human propelled by sheer wind and borne off into a permanent absence by that incidental fear that had first propelled him. The book cover remains one of my favourites. I could also identify – I like to believe – the distorted mask from which it was drawn, unseen, by someone from a totally different culture. Let me draw out, for a little longer, this phenomenon of identification parallels.

Perhaps you have read 'Abiku' – a poem about the myth of our 'recurrent child' syndrome – known in medical parlance as infant mortality. However, in my society – to extend the expression of yet another culture – once is happenstance, twice is coincidence but, thrice is definitely mythology. When a child dies to a mother twice or thrice, it becomes the same child returnee, whose 'earthing' can only be guaranteed by sacrifices and rituals in propitiation of the obstinate child or, in confrontation with his or her siblings on 'the other side'. Their wiles of seduction, it is presumed, are often responsible for the child's constant disappearance.

Colin Garland was – still is of course – an Australian. He shared a flat in Notting Hill with a West Indian actor, Lloyd Record, in the sixties, which was how I met him. I came into his studio one day and – there it was – a painting of 'Abiku'! I entered the studio, stared and shouted: *Abiku*! He stared back at me, not knowing what the hell I was talking about.

Of course there was nostalgia. After all, I had been away from home – for the first time ever, and for over three years at that time. Any object, voice, smell, sky-line, was available for conversion to my catalogue of missed or repressed images. But then, the ensuing symbolic conceit, an extension of Abiku's mythic metaphor: when I returned a few weeks later, believe it or not, Colin, that familiar figure of the struggling artist who can ill afford paint, brushes and canvas, had cleaned out the painting and was using the canvas for a totally different subject. I think that the moment he admitted what he had done was the closest I had ever come to a *crime passionnel* at that time. I felt that his parents deserved to have an *Abiku* in their family, so they would understand the dimensions of his cultural crime. No matter, there was little else that could be done; a few weeks later I consoled myself by writing the poem 'Abiku'. Sometime later still, Colin read the poem and – truly remorseful and better informed, I like to think – painted something else around the same motif. *Abiku* was indeed repeating its accustomed role even in an alien clime, staging its petulant rounds of appearances and exits to a surrogate artistic mother. The cruelty is part of the mythology of *Abiku*, the sadism of incomplete consciousness – indeed I should have pitied the artist who had unwittingly been made an instrument of the wilful child. The new painting was certainly not the original, but the understanding, the sensibility was there. It remains my very earliest acquired painting – Colin let me have it for – think I remember the exact figure – thirty-five pounds, which I thought extortionist since it was not the very painting I had responded to so instantly and completely. However, since I only paid him ten pounds down, and he is yet to collect the rest after these twenty-five years, I consider myself having come off best in the exchange.

How tempting then to use *Abiku* as a metaphor for the phenomenon of creativity. The only problem is – would it be an optimistic metaphor or an expression of doom? The atomic bomb is, after all, part of man's creative works. So, will *Abiku* remain appropriated by Salvador Dali's nightmares even at their most consciously self-parodying or exhibitionist, or Francis Bacon's figures which also threaten with their masquerade of mutations? Are these the human and objective realities of an inevitable holocaust? Will the creative hand earth *Abiku* once for all, or has the world been handed over to Dr Strangelove – Third World or Netherworld, no difference? The problem is really whether one sees, on the cover of an *Ake*, an idyllic image of recaptured childhood, or a figure fleeing in terror from an uncomprehended disaster. Both readings are consequences of a global reality which either restores or denies the innocence of the world. Unfortunately, I do not really believe that we in the so-called Third World have much control over the lime droppings of the chickens when they come to roost; true, we did not lay the eggs – at least, have not yet done so. And what is truly painful – and this is the essence of my excursion into the climates of passive 'innocence' – is that the moral right of indifference – even if it were possible still to be immune from the effects – these moral rights are being eroded by a common climate of fear which is engendered by internal acts of states against the humanity of their citizens.

In short – have I a moral right today, being the citizen I am of present-day Nigeria, do I have the moral right to write verses condemning atomic tests in the South Pacific? Is this still a priority of my creative concerns?

I have ceased to find it curious that the outside world which, as I hope I have sufficiently indicated, is not that much outside, since our various climates meet so easily on a creative terrain – I have ceased to find it curious that the outside world pretends to know nothing of all this, or at best, finds it convenient to insist that silence best serves the course of silence – for we are speaking of the effective silencing of that sort of creativity which retains relations with the real world of living, experiencing and organizing. For those of us who broke through the colonial barriers to reach the Ethelridge Knights, the Ben Caldwells, the Dennis Brutuses, the Alex la Gumas of the embattled ranks against racism, these names were inseparable from the socio-political situation that sought to dehumanize them and render non-existent their contribution to the productive history of humanity. When the Generals took over in Greece, the persona and the music of Theodorakis were inseparable from the fascistic context which thrust him on the attention of the world. By contrast, when a Fela Anikulapo-Kuti is gaoled in present-day Nigeria, there is no attempt, repeat, NO ATTEMPT whatever to understand and address the acute socio-political context which made such a travesty of justice conceivable, much less possible. The misfortunes of an exotic maverick under a 'serious, anti-corruption' regime – that appears to be the summative attitude. And therein lies the heart of the problem, for me personally. I have conceded this quite unambiguously – on hearing the music of a Billie Holliday, I experience the horror of *Scottsborough Boy*. On hearing that poignant Irish folk-song, 'Oh the praities they are small', the horror of the Irish famine and depression, population shifts and general social alienation are the images which are readily evoked. Does the outside world – when it hears of the imprisonment of Anikulapo-Kuti, does this world, on hearing his music, submit itself to this contextual projection? I doubt it. Nothing is understood, no contextual curiosity is aroused. Just a musician whose records sell popularly by reason of a general, undirected iconoclasm. But what specific icons are assailed by this general maverick music? What system do they operate? And what other victims of these 'undirected creative energies' are affected by the paranoia of these icons? As long as those questions remain merely peripheral, the protestations, no matter how ardent and committed, remain at best, merely sentimental.

It is a situation, in effect, where life does not really appear to have caught up with art, where those links which arts from different climes find so readily in one another have not really been extended, universally, to the producers and the productive conditions of such arts.

One final personal recollection: Fela Anikulapo-Kuti was a principal musician – together with Ambrose Campbell, another Nigerian musician – when I had that Sunday night poetry-cum-drama stand at the Royal Court Theatre in December 1959. I recall that he supplied the musical background for the reading of my two 'Immigrant' poems, and also for the poem I have already referred to, my versified outburst against the explosion of the French atomic bomb in the Sahara. I have never forgotten his trumpet improvisations on all of those themes.

Art is unavoidably linked to its formative – or at the least, inspirational – realities, so if we concede that the realities which confront us today breed a certain concurrence of response, which I have tried to insinuate is a climate of fear, then it is surely time to take general stock, and present a concerted front against the causative or responsible factors of these aberrations. It is surely no coincidence that a wave of fascism or right-wing 'nationalism' has taken hold of Europe and America over the past decade. Is it conceivable that the resultant regimes, whether in power as in England and America or striving for power as in France, do not, or will not ally with similar interests in the so-called Third World? The anti-racist and anti-fascist manifestations which France has recently witnessed are encouraging signs, I admit. They are at least an acknowledgement of the reality of this menace; our only problem, in my part of the world, is the failure of such embattled species to recognize that this phenomenon is not limited to Europe, that the agents of its atavistic philosophies are to be found even among the leaders – in their own homes – of those very minorities who become the target of fascist violence and dehumanization in European countries. Until this is understood, until this finds expression in the very same forms and intensities that one witnesses in other societies both through daily communication means and as components of the artistic expression of a global menace, as real and immediate as the threat of atomic holocausts, the climate of fear and despair will continue to overwhelm the will to recreate humanity.

The paradoxical child, *Abiku*, having been successfully snuffed out in Greece, resurfaces, gloating, in spheres as far apart as the coast of West Africa and Latin America, wearing its mask of death and sadism. This malformed consciousness of contemporary power expands without curb, ignored by those whose sleep is too deep or whose roosts are too distant to be affected, they think, by its petulant snarls. But this particular chicken has arbitrary roosting tastes. No one ever thought, before the take-over by the Greek generals, that such a retrogade event could take place, in that birthland of European democracy. Today, the same endangered species insist on believing that it is not taking place in other countries – not even after the experience of Idi Amin. I regret to disappoint you. We inhabit the same climate of terror – only the agents are different. Whatever fails to survive a nuclear holocaust will not survive, in different climes, the depredations of insane power, and the insanity of power recognizes no specificity of boundaries. Sooner or later, a choice must be made. In the ironic words of one of our power contenders, a failed coup-maker in my nation's recent history: 'We are AL-L-L-L-L together.'

XV

Of Berlin and Other Walls*

It seems only yesterday that the self-styled free world – the Euro-American portions of it, that is – uncrated their bombers and cargo planes from premature beds of mothballs and flew continuous sorties into the beleaguered sector of an ancient, half-devastated city. This time, their mission was not to drop tons of TNT or fragmentation bombs, but sacks of flour, fruits, potatoes, clothing, drugs – raining milk, wine, and oil on the desperate inmates of that city. They flew through a specially demarcated airspace – I believe it earned the name of a corridor – that, by some strange arrangement, these former enemies, now welcome conquerors, could legitimately call their own. All land access had been closed. The Berlin Blockade, one of the many facets of the Cold War, was being challenged, and neutralized. A little over a decade later, the physical wall itself was erected. It would be several years before I experienced the wall in person, not the concrete structure which ran through the heart of Berlin, but the continuation of it along the ideological divide of Germany.

My encounter took place about a year after I had myself been disinterred from the graveyard of Nigerian prison walls. Overwhelmed with a need to vanish into some kind of creature retreat, I asked my brother – who was a product of German universities – to use his old contacts to find me a peaceful chalet to rent in some isolated part of Germany, preferably in a mountainous area. I cannot now recall the name of the village but it was not very far from a town named Fulda. I had no idea how close it was to the East-West divide until I took a stroll one evening along a narrow street. Suddenly I came up face to face with a roll of barbed wire. On the other side of that wire was a sentry-box guarded by some two or three soldiers, armed in quiet menace. Some distance away, another soldier patrolled the perimeter of the fence with a fierce Alsatian dog on a leash.

I had, it appeared, selected quite by chance the hour for the enactment of a daily

* A version of the Padmore-Nkrumah-Dubois Lecture delivered in Accra, Ghana (1990).

ritual. Just as I was about to turn back, a trickle of people emerged from the other side of the barbed wire. Then I heard footsteps behind and around me and discovered that others, from my side of the fence, were also approaching where I stood. Those from the opposite side stopped about fifty yards from the fence while those from our side walked right up to the barbed wire. Arms were raised in greeting, hand-waves exchanged. A baby was raised above adult heads and encouraged to wave to those on the opposite side. An old man's gaze was directed somewhere in particular. With some difficulty he succeeded in making out the form he had perhaps tottered out to see. The wrinkles on his face dissolved in a beatific smile; he raised his walking-stick in greeting.

And so it continued. The spoken greetings were rationed, mostly monosyllabic. It struck me that perhaps those expressionless guards across the barbed wire had set a limit on the currency of conversation that could be exchanged, and that the participants were keeping strictly to the arrangement. My guess was later proved correct. It did not come as a surprise to learn also that some other guards permitted an exchange of parcels – usually a one-way affair, I was told – and of more spirited conversation. The fifty-yard limit was, it would appear, a variable one; it all depended on the temperament of the guards.

Was this further back in time than yesterday? The suddenness with which these images have been reversed pulls them into a closer focus than time would normally accord them. It is also chastening, and on many levels. Certainly, it sends one back to school, if only for a reconsideration of the 'human condition' both in the particular, and in the general: in politics, culture, religion, in social theories and practice. Given the enormity of what has occurred, those who have been outside the gathering of forces towards such a testamentary moment can only relate its lessons to aspects of their own existence, both individually and collectively.

Travellers on West African roads may have encountered public transportation – taxis and passenger lorries – the so-called 'mammy wagon' decorated with both graphic and verbal motifs. One favourite epigram on such contraptions reads: 'No Condition is Permanent.' I believe Heraclitus had earlier proposed a more or less identical sentiment; no matter, the Berlin Wall is the latest reminder of that ultimate truism of the human condition. Perhaps one gate at least should be preserved intact from the rubble, bearing such an inscription over its archway. Humanity needs much reminding, regrettably, even of this most banal deduction from its historical evolution.

Alas, claimants to absolutism over the relationship of man and society still cling to authority, and with ever increasing aggressiveness. Religion is one such claimant. And unless we examine this phenomenon of mind-closure at every fresh turn of events, we may find ourselves victims of new dogmatisms that have been quick to identity a vacuum, and just as quick to fill it. The activity of the intellect that results in the artistic product, indeed, the cultural totality of social being, is the most prominent victim of any closed system: this is an acknowledged tendency, and still-living generations have been its victims. Those who took pains to follow the path taken by the Chinese cultural revolution will testify to the forms of art and literature that were first banned, then 'rehabilitated' once the 'Gang of Four' had fallen. It was an aberration at once comic and tragic. I remember turning up at the Chinese Embassy in a distant country in search of a specific text from the Chinese classics to which an article had referred, and being met by a blank stare by the cultural attaché, a man who had earlier presented himself as being most knowledgeable in Chinese literature. When I was pursued into my classroom by some dozen consolation volumes of the 'correct' type of literature, programmed, produced (I dare not say, written) in an almost identical, lifeless style, as substitute for the works I had requested, insult was added to deprivation. But the ultimate experience was to receive, only a few months afterwards, coincident with the fall of the 'Gang of Four', handsomely chased copies of that 'non-existent' classic by the embassy's special courier, autographed by that same cultural attaché: as a reversal, that truly boggles the mind. Will Salman Rushdie's *Satanic Verses*, one distant day, be available in Iranian Embassies all over the world, if only to demonstrate how Islam rose above the 'diabolical construct' of one individual imagination?

We are addressing, in short, the lived effects of ideological walls raised against humane pursuits. The Bamboo Curtain did not fall in Tiananmen Square in 1989, but it has been rattled, and the flattening of the anthills of discontent by armoured tanks cannot disguise the fact that the surface protrusion is only an infinitesimal portion of a subterranean network of workers, thinkers and artists.

Once, the reaction of the 'hard left' to such events as took place in China would have been predictable. It would have been firmly on the side of the brutal manifestation of state power, since this had become synonymous with the revolutionary duty to seal up the slightest breach in an ideological paradise. Third World ideologues were usually to be found at the forefront of such hurrahs, incapable or unwilling to relate the predicament of the dissidents in such societies with their own condition – and the attendant brutality of repression – under various forms of absolutism. Afraid to be found sharing sentiments of 'liberal, bourgeois revulsion' with the 'decadent west', they would prefer to undergo the most tortuous rationalizations for a horrendous reality. Indeed, the strategy was never to address the event itself, but to address reactions of others to the event. A much cruder ploy was indeed to deny the event altogether, pronouncing it a figment of the liberal imagination. Thus as a student, during the twilight years of Stalinism, I had the instructive experience of encountering passionate reconstructions of reality in the Soviet Union by Third World ideologues, whose intensity of advocacy often suggested that they were witnesses to events which, in their same argument, never did take place. The fiercest of these were of course to be found among nationalists from the colonized countries. Then came the miracle of Nikita Krushchev, a premature John the Baptist to the advent of Mikhail Gorbachev . . .

There are, of course, understandable causes for this. As victims of a specific European intervention, and products of partial – and in some rare cases, total – cultural and political conditioning, they could not long defer a moment of internal reckoning, whether it was undertaken on the level of individual awareness or as a public ideological debate. Of course, this is to concede that there really was a period of total submission to the invading world view. For my part, I do not believe that a people can immerse themselves in the totality of the thought-womb of another, becoming, in effect, 'born-agains' of a new motherland; such a people simply have never existed. There are periods of *apparent* suppression and/or total submission, but a dialectical current will always traverse the wider, seemingly enveloping stream of the dominant culture. When an individual confronts irreconcilable elements from within his own recollected beliefs and values or, when he encounters actualities that contradict logical expectations from the torrent of the usurping values, it is a rational option to proceed to identify alternative catechisms also from within that 'other' world, to seek social codes that have challenged and in some cases, successfully routed the canonical claims of the self-proclaimed masters of its own world. Both the experience of slavery and of dispersal, and the structured variants of colonialism that ensued – that is, both settler and surrogate colonialism – were products of, or sustained by 'reasoned' apologias by some of the giant intellects, secular and religious alike, of Western Europe. These intellects, moreover, were the producers of the philosophical temper of their own race. Since they and their forebears were the architects of the ethical justification of the very condition of the exploited, the exploited, seeking total liberation, may adopt the strategy of reviewing that external, self-justifying ethos, taking it to pieces, and comparing it with other rival precepts, almost exclusively from without. Marxism was historically fitted for this role.

And if today we can readily deduce the limitations of such recourse, we can equally see how deeply affecting it must have been at the time. Behold, then, the colonial intellectual, emerging into the thought-structures of the dominant culture, buffeted by its confident rationalizations even of his, the African's, condition, yet prevented by imperial effacement from reaching into the humanistic structures by his own anterior culture. His encounter with a new and even more holistic value system can have only one result. The alternative – the alternative of contesting the resented dominant reality with the suppressed autochthonous one – is an exercise that the colonized can undertake only from a position of weakness. When yet another contending value system therefore presents itself from some other part of that other world – a system that speaks to the aspirations of the oppressed, and in seductively universalist terms; that challenges the predatory view of the human condition, that explains the workings of history, the processes of social development, the stratification of social groups and the causalities of social deterioration and conflict; that dares, even while pronouncing itself coldly analytic, to be prophetic and millennialist – it is quite understandable that the oppressed should see, within this ethos, the path of their own salvation.

But ideas, theories, are one thing; practicalization is another. And the terrain that produces such ideas, the orchestration of historical events – both in predictable development and by the fortuitous (often uncredited) historical incident – are never the same in two separated localities of the globe. The practical strategies for the implementation even of a commonly shared idea must therefore necessarily differ in locales with different histories, resources, and cultural usage. To revert to my originating metaphor, it is an extreme and risk-laden undertaking to break free from a walled-in arsenal of ideological assumptions by walling oneself within another, attempting from within that total enclosure to replace, in entirety, all aspects of instruction, perception and application which can be traced to that earlier, rejected or discredited arena. Sometimes, this wholesale self-immersion is gradual, even subconscious. That it translates itself into a near tangible, hermetic construct in the practical acts of political power is a feature that is common to those African countries that were compelled to undertake armed, liberation struggle – such as Angola or Guinea Bissau. Simultaneously with the armed struggle, leaders of these struggles sought to supplant the fascism of Portuguese colonialism, and its rapacious capitalist ethic, with an attempted organic irradiation of a socialist ethic that commenced with grass-roots, village organizations, and utilized, in some cases, the traditional communal structures of the society.

In other instances – and Matthew Kerekou's Republic of Benin is our most notorious example – this transformation has been purely rhetorical. The ideological curtain or 'cordon sanitaire' drawn around the Beninois was a cheap, opportunistic, and unsuccessful walling-in of an entire population for the very obvious purpose of consolidating power. The trappings, the recitations, the programmed invocation of Marxist-Leninist phraseologies at every apposite and irrelevant opportunity, the mammoth images of the giants of socialism – Marx, Lenin, Mao – figures that, to the majority of the people, could have been visitors from Mars or Jupiter, the stream of ideological jargon over the radio to which no one, not even the script writers ever listened ... all this was an obvious attempt to corral the populace into a state of abject docility. It was a totalitarian project based on nothing but the incantatory power of incomprehensible verbiage.

Those who have travelled through West Africa will admit that between Benin's next door neighbour, the Togolese Republic, which unabashedly espouses a free-enterprise economy, and the former self-styled Marxist-Leninist Republic of Benin, there was not one pinpoint of difference either in class relations or in the social attitude of the average citizen. Indeed, in terms of the glorified personality cult and the proliferation of hoardings, marches, uniforms and drills, both are clones of the same social aberration: the fantasy of power that appropriates the handiest instrument in order to manifest and realize itself – be such an instrument ideology, religion, or social discontent. Was anyone surprised when, barely months after the definitive collapse of the Berlin Wall, Matthew Kerekou became the first 'Marxist' African leader to publicly renounce Marxist-Leninism? The difference between the positions of Angola, for instance, and that of Benin is quite remarkable. Even before the Gorbachev effect truly began to manifest itself, Angola had begun to readjust its more dogmatic positions to current Angolan reality. The ruling party had begun to relax its theology on a number of economic strictures that went by the text but against observed relations between state interference and potential productivity. It had begun to redefine the role of the party in the political direction of the nation. By contrast, Matthew Kerekou simply threw in the towel with a resounding sigh of relief. When you have ensconced yourself within a purely rhetorical hermeticism, erected a protected wall of ideas that are neither yours nor have been organically tested or translated through the reality of your own terrain, it does not matter which direction you turn to for inspiration – you are bound to read the writing on the wall.

We must constantly remember that the African has never been allowed to enter fully into the European's consciousness, not in a fundamentally affective way, as yet another segment of the human family. And the African himself? I speak now of leadership products of that 'other'-denying European, his ideological product either of the Left or the Right. The principal test applicable to this quandary is the test of power relations, the issue, in short, of perception of the ruled by the rulers. Do they see us as mere integers in an exercise of social engineering? Or as sentient beings of corporeal and spiritual dignity? If the quantitative loss of humanity, the permanent brain damage to millions of famine-afflicted children, the trail of skeletons along desiccated highways, the mounds of corpses in deserted villages, and the mass graves in refugee camps; if the lassitude and hopelessness of those emaciated survivors crowded in refugee camps and even in forced 'resettlements' dictated by ideological formulae: if these images evoke the trails of slave marches, the coastal fort dungeons and stockades, makeshift markets filled with black human merchandise; if, as each succeeding year closes in on the symbolic challenge of a new century, these vistas persist, then we must accuse a leadership that refuses to come into knowledge of itself, of its own kind, and the expropriation of a continent that is again betrayed, but this time from within.

Will the dependence of socialist Ethiopia on the humane concerns of the pop-music industry accompany the African continent into the twenty-first century? Consider this humiliating concert of charity for a continent that does not lack in material and mental resources: surely Bob Geldof may claim that he, not Mariam Mengistu, is the intelligence that holds the Ethiopian people in humane knowledge, that the yearly processions of destitution across the Ethiopian landscape are fully comprehended by his real conception of the human family.

During the feudal reign of the Ethiopian monarch, Emperor Haile Selaissie, a magazine which I then edited from Ghana, *Transition*, was nearly alone among African journals in denouncing the royal neglect that had resulted in the devastation of large sections of the population, especially in the Tigre provinces. The monarchy persisted in its regal denial of any such human calamity. I reall that, to dramatize the situation, we resorted to obtaining a copy of the menu for a banquet hosted by the emperor for a visiting delegation, and printing it, imperial crest and all, side by side with reports of the human tragedy unfolding in the provinces. Nearly twenty years after the 'revolution', the magnitude and cyclic certitude of the occurrence is multiplied a hundredfold! I have not bothered to obtain the standard menu of Comrade Mengistu and his cohorts, but I note that they do not appear too ill-nourished in photographs. And that Marxist regime has of course proved more than a match for the feudal Emperor both in its denial of the truth and in its incompetence in the organization and distribution of relief. A wall of ideological self-righteousness, festooned with its spurious anti-Western phobia and persecution complex, entombs hundreds of thousands whose fate is to watch their offspring waste away before their eyes, before they themselves finally succumb to a fate they had barely avoided the previous year.

'We are the world'! What a rich sound from the throats of those who *have*, and who also possess the grace to be concerned enough to *give*. It is, however, a bitter pill for any race that possesses an iota of pride. For we are not speaking here of any sudden, unexpected calamity which justifies the 'brother's keeper' obligations of the rest of our global village. No, we speak here of a sustained management of resources, of planning and priorities. We speak here also, by a fortunate coincidence of our theme, of the entire issue of liberty, or self-determination. The resources expended by the Ethiopian Dergue every month to prosecute the war against Eritrea are over and beyond whatever amount was collected by the global musical linkage organized by Bob Geldof.

Under a feudal regime, Eritrea sought its freedom. The early support which the Eritrean people gave to the advent of Mengistu's regime was predicated on a clear policy statement by that Ethiopian revolutionary movement that it would restore to Eritrea what it was unjustly robbed of, first by Italy and then by the Ethiopian monarchy. Incapable of learning even from such examples as the British Raj in India following on the Second World War, the new masters forgot their pledge and insisted on perpetuating the role of the feudal colonial master.

But it was not only the Eritreans. What of Ethiopian youth itself? The paved courtyard of one of the building complexes of the Ethiopian university still bore – at least when I first visited it some twenty years ago – the well preserved stain of the blood of students mown down in cold blood by the Emperor's soldiers. It was fenced off and preserved as a shrine, a point of reference for both visitors and students seeking to liberate their future from a predatory, unproductive and impossibly distended aristocracy. When the so-called 'creeping revolution' began, those students embraced it wholeheartedly. They were at the forefront of the movement; indeed, they could claim that they were the real initiators of the revolution. But when the revolution finally succeeded? Once again they were at the forefront of the casualties – this time at the hands of Ethiopia's new masters. At least Haile Selaissie had the decency to permit a decent burial to the students; the Dergue, by contrast, piled their corpses high in the streets and left them to rot for days, in the company of other so-called counter-revolutionaries, as a lesson. Boastfully, these new rulers declared that they were implementing their own version of the Red Terror, an embarrassingly crude parroting of past revolutions in eighteenth-century France and early twentieth-century Russia.

The students were hunted down, slaughtered, and left exposed to vultures – all in order to preserve a text-book model of revolutionary will. Peasants, workers, intellectuals all became fodder for the insatiable machinery of this so-called revolution. Dressed-up terminologies echoed the paranoid season of Stalin. Since classes were not so acutely developed, apart from an obvious feudal aristocracy, they were of course invented, for the rhetoric of class war required some base material, however synthetic. One after the other, erstwhile comrades were eliminated. A mere inclination towards clemency for the doomed, merely doomed the suppliant in turn. High-ranking comrades were confronted with no stronger evidence of guilt than a tapped telephone conversation regretting the execution of one of their ranks – and found themselves next on the firing range. In the name of 'revolutionary discipline', 'adherence to party line', 'internal criticism', 'anti-deviationism', and other clichés, the cream of Ethiopia's intelligentsia was wiped out or sent into exile. The black aspirants to the cardinal's hat had become holier – and bloodier – than the Popes of the Inquisition.

Let us descend for a moment from tragedy into bathos. Seeking ever the approbation of the acknowledged exemplars of Marxist purism, mimicking the superficies as always, instead of carving out its own unique humane socialist character, the Marxist Dergue once decreed, no differently from the client-capitalist and utterly corrupt regime of Mobutu's Zaire, that its civil servants should rid themselves of personal (that is, individualist and reactionary) forms of dressing and wear instead some kind of uniform, shorn of every vestige of personality. Clothing is of course one of the commonest forms of control, and the new revolutionary masters were not slow to exploit that route towards wholesale depersonalization. They remained convinced that they had scored a huge success – until recently. Defections, reverses on the Eritrean front, and finally the attempted *coup d'état* of 1989 all contributed to a slight movement toward the relaxation of some state controls. Nothing dramatic, but rhetoric proved not only inadequate; it had become suicidal. The Dergue began to talk to the opposition, or more accurately, to the several oppositions. And among the minor sequels of this re-examination of reality was that the regime rescinded the sartorial stricture. Not that this was altogether annulled, no; it was simply made optional. The hope remained that the majority would demonstrate their commitment to the revolution by voluntarily retaining this outward symbol.

We have all heard, I believe, the expression 'voting with your feet'. In this instance, the Ethiopians voted with this dress. Not one single worker turned up in official garb once the statutory obligation was lifted. Not one! This was after nearly two decades of intense ideological bombardment, 'scientific' programming, intellectual and spiritual compression into a common mould. Two decades of complete control over the lives and fortunes of the populace, two decades of exemplary lessons meted out in the gory compilation of corpses in public squares – all enemies of the revolution. In the end, not a single figure of consolation in the symbolic attire of a Marxist utopia.

The issue of power – and, its corollary, freedom – will, I believe, occupy the twenty-first-century man, on the level at which ideology has preoccupied us, the nations emergent from colonial domination. It is inevitable. Indeed, with the removal of the mantle of infallibility from any one ideology, I foresee no viable successor for the intellectual avant-garde. No projection for a holistic approach to the renewal of our interrupted and submerged world-view can evade this challenge, not if we wish to rid ourselves of the past legacy of excusing, ignoring or even justifying leadership atrocities and betrayals, simply because they are of the 'left'. And what a chequered 'left' it has been!

Did not Field-Marshal Idi Amin Dada, multiple murderer and cannibal, also proclaim himself a radical and socialist? Our relations in the Diaspora and indeed within the continent itself need to be reminded of these distressing facts, for many of their intellectuals, remote from the hideous actuality of the tormented Ugandans, found it convenient to simplify the phenomenon of Idi Amin Dada. For them, every negative revelation was an effort of Western propaganda, designed to tarnish the image of authentic black leaders. A high-powered black intellectual caucus from the United States even visited Uganda to 'verify' the truth or falsehood of disseminated reports. They received, naturally, a red-carpet welcome from the 'genial giant', were treated to his lavish hospitality and regaled by his buffoonery. They returned home full of glowing reports of this avuncular leader, so maliciously vilified for his pan-Africanist, progressive stance against the rapacious, patronizing, capitalist West. I recall this period as a depressing, frustrating one. For us on the continent, directly in touch with events, it even smacked of insensitivity and arrogance that our intellectual kin from the Diaspora should seek to impose, with such intolerance of dissent, their own interpretation of the events that were directly lived by the Ugandan people. As for the late Master-Sergeant Doe, the Liberian people have been yet again doomed to a bloody fiesta of liberation.

But the global political scene is gradually being clarified. That may appear an over-optimistic assessment, especially as, in the opinion of many, the events of Eastern Europe and the Soviet Union have merely thrown the ideological arena into turmoil. That is, however, the very heart of these historic lessons. When a dike is smashed that has held up the clamour of ocean tides for decades, the result is indeed turmoil, even disasters and devastation. Even so with dams and the pent-up energy of interrupted rivers. Consider those measured, sectioned, meticulously irrigated holdings, gardens, farmsteads, and plantations, chemically fertilized, sustained with synthetic nutrients, furrowed, manicured into geometric shapes by the latest models of tractor technology, bombed by insecticides, protected by satellite predictions from invasion of locust and kwela birds, sown, pruned, and harvested by computerized orders – what happens when these artificial controls of the organic reality and natural imperatives of the authentic environment are suddenly swept away, an event triggered off perhaps by no immediately visible cause, but one which may become clarified ten or twenty years later, as science catches up with nature through further advances into backward causation? We may discover today's event to have been the result of shock-waves that began their unhurried, even meandering course from a distant volcano or an earthquake, muted by the earth's crust some four thousand years away. Or perhaps it was prompted by some undetected stellar explosion in a remote galaxy – these scenarios, I understand, are constantly being plotted retroactively, and may one day unravel not only hitherto inexplicable phenomena, even the mystery of how we all come to *be* in the first instance, and on this particular planet.

With such an infinity of imponderables, how can any one system of thought lay claim, and with such murderous assertiveness, to a definitive explication of the laws of human association and development? The human entity is only one – and a minuscule part at that – of the infinite element of universal phenomena: and it is a universe of not only stable forms but also, more humblingly, of infinite mutation. The simple amoeba, we know, is capable of infinite self-reproduction; and who knows what properties the AIDS virus will prove to be capable of, when a new breakthrough is achieved in genetic engineering in another year, decade, or whenever? So once again, let us interrogate any such presumption: how can any system of thought – of whatever colour or creed – claim to have attained the definite explication of the human condition, its potential and eventual direction? What system of thought dare insist that no further enquiry, negative or positive, futile or productive (for we can never really know in advance) is pursued in the exercise of the human mind, that faculty which, above all else, distinguishes humankind from the majority of other living species?

And my fear today, based on recent global rampages over the past few decades, is hinged on what is both a scientific claim and a philosophical acceptance: Nature, it would seem, abhors a vacuum. The capitalist ethos, one could argue, has been largely discredited. I know that this sounds like an exaggeration, especially from the point of view of Western Europe. As I suggested earlier, however, the search of African nations for alternatives in the socialist world was predicated on the realization that capitalism was synonymous with exploitation. If only attachment, therefore, you could arguably propose that capitalism had been largely discredited as a humane ideology. Now Marxist-Leninism – and indeed, communism – is taking its turn for a battering. And we have to remind ourselves yet again that Gorbachev's perestroika was only a bold, impeccably-timed definition of various motions that have been taking place within the socialist world for a number of decades. Even in the twenties and thirties, various economic experiments, such as the New Economic Policy initiated by the Bolsheviks under Lenin in 1921, and even patchily by Stalin in 1934, suggest that the dogmas and economic catechism were always open to pragmatic adjustments. Yet millions of Russian humanity were liquidated on the authority of these theological annotations!

As a holistic world-view, therefore, one which encompassed, or was continually expanded to encompass, the entire productivity of the human society – intellectual, artistic, technological, and spiritual – the Marxist world-view, which, for many intellectuals virtually equated itself with a religious creed, has taken a battering even more severe than the capitalist, which had the grace to surrender the trappings of absolutism over the decades. What happens next?

And this where I believe that the new African comity – at least we who lay claim to intellectual leadership – have failed, and have placed ourselves outside the propulsion of a historic moment. I tried earlier to explain why the theoretical formulators of our world embraced so completely the alternative world-view of the European 'other', having rejected the social precepts of the imperialist world. I implied, deliberately, that our philosopher statesmen – with only a few exceptions – Amilcar Cabral and Julius Nyerere come readily to mind – did not make a committed, convinced effort to address their own supplanted social systems and world-views in the search for alternatives to alien structures violently or insidiously imposed on African societies.

Let us be honest with ourselves: the progressive ones among us have been too concerned to earn the approbation of that alternative world. We substituted acceptance by Western intellectual caucuses with an equally imitative and self-abnegating posture before the world-view of Eastern communism, even when, as we knew very well, certain laws – both of separate histories and environments – made a wholesale transplant of those ideas onto our own actualities impracticable. In short, we intensified the game of role-playing. The handful who resisted – persisting, through their works, in that exploration of the supplanted world-view, for good or evil – had to combat, additionally, hostile, negative, and distorting interpretations of their concerns. Retrograde idealists, romantic throwback reifiers of the ineffable, reactionary enemies of the materialist (i.e., the only correct) interpretation of society – these are some of the milder of provoked epithets. I have dealt at some length with this intellectual entrapment in previous exchanges. My purpose here is not to resume that argument; certainly I take no pleasure in mocking the dilemma of a newly created community of ideological orphans. Our concern is the issue of power and freedom, and of the abandonment of originality. We became submissive components in the creation of mental satellites, heliocentric to one sole source of intellectual energy. The more domestic metaphor employed by Isaac Deutscher in his biography of Stalin is probably even more apposite for appreciating the way the average Marxist ideologue applies his theory, at least in my own personal encounters:

> The semi-intelligentsia from whom socialism recruited some of its middle
> cadres enjoyed Marxism as a mental labour-saving device, easy to handle and
> fabulously effective. It was enough to press a knob here to make short work
> of one idea, and a knob there to dispose of another. The user of labour-
> saving gadgets rarely reflects upon the difficult research that preceded their
> invention. Nor does he reflect upon the disinterested and seemingly
> impractical research that will one day make his gadget obsolete. The users of
> the intellectual gadgets of Marxism, perhaps not unnaturally, treated their
> possession in the same narrowly utilitarian fashion.

It may prove that we stand on the threshold of a tragic irony, that as we move into the twenty-first century, we discover that it is yet other 'labour-saving gadgets', such as the uncompromising face of state-structured codifiers of the 'ineffable', the anti-materialist kingdom, that will step into the gaping space left by the demise, or at least the atrophy, of the twentieth-century contenders for ideological supremacy – symbolized in the collapse of the Berlin Wall. I refer to the blood wedding of religion and power, the no-compromise edifice of spiritual imperatives which, fictive though they are, prove ruthlessly effective instruments of mind control, and of a more tenacious kind than any political ideology. The zombies of the twenty-first century, the army of the Fifth Horseman of the Apocalypse, may well be the creatures of religious fanaticism. This movement began long before the evident collapse of that ideology, Marxism, that turned itself into a religion. The gradual rise of religious fanaticism began at least two or three decades ago, releasing a venom that now percolates into the blood-streams of unsuspecting, complacent nation communities. It is a slow-acting venom, fatal nonetheless, and it is coursing quietly through the nerve cells of several nations. Mine is no exception.

The corruption, venality, hypocrisy, and megalomania of much Third World leadership, its arrogant neglect of, and alienation from, the people they are meant to serve, the contrast of their life-styles with that of the productive majority, and, above all, the lip-service they pay to whatever secular ideology they profess, be it of the left or the right, bankrupting in the process the positive or productive properties of the ideology itself, has led, in no small measure, to a disillusioned people's desperate embrace of religions that lay claim to the very holistic virtues of those ideologies that named themselves, however indirectly, religions. It may be that the global bid for power will be mostly manifested by religions that, with increasing boldness, now name themselves ideologies. Both appropriate to themselves the right of prescription and intervention in every aspect of human life and act, and thus, the faculty of thought.

The European world, by its total disruption of all previously conceivable transformational, even revolutionary tempo, has clearly begun to address the question of power and freedom – and I do not mean on the accustomed level of philosophical wordplay and evasion. It has taken the unprecedented step of unmasking ideology as a sometime opportunistic and unprincipled usurper of popular will, which represents freedom. Freedom remains the antithesis of power, that historically proven corollary of enslavement. Obviously, power can only be made manifest with the act of enslavement of some other. What then of the Third World, captive and client of the two ideological estates – socialism and capitalism – even as it has been, and still holds itself in thrall to two other alien contending religions, Christianity and Islam? Both these religions in their turn operate globally in mind-boggling, fluctuating alliances with the two main ideological scaffoldings, left and right, yet constantly strike out in their own specific authoritarianisms, often of the most destructive, anti-humanist nature. Are we bound to continue the errors of passive indentureship? What happens when one or the other chooses also to dissolve itself – an unlikely event admittedly, but quite a legitimate exercise of projection. Revisionism is a form of partial death, an admission of fallibility, and those major religions do periodically revise themselves, splitting into mutually and implacably hostile sects, thereby admitting errors that have cost millions of lives and impeded human progress across our own societies. And sometimes these very revisions are bloodily inscribed, scorched across the landscape, annotated on human flesh. Are we doomed forever to await the coming-to-terms of these various fountain-heads, with their own contradictions, their own self-deceits, granting them an eternity of aggressive certitudes, conceding the substitution of 'revelationary' for 'scientific' impregnabilities? Are we permanent prisoners of other Berlin Walls that we have actually assisted others in building around ourselves?

Let those who wish to retain or elevate religion as a twenty-first century project feel free to do so, but let it not be done as continuation of the game of denigration against the African spiritual heritage. Even as it is irrational to ask individuals and communities in the Third World to turn their backs totally on any one ideology because it has proved itself partially wanting, even anti-human in parts, so would it be a waste of time, both impractical and obtuse, to insist that the African world reject any form of spirituality which, despite its negative incursions on Africa's proper history, yet speaks to the continent in any positive way and has enriched its existence. The task is really much simpler; it involves that very simple strategy of becoming far more knowledgeable of oneself, not being caught flat-footed in the rubble of intellectual *and spiritual* walls that we have erected around ourselves with alien brick and straw. Let me use this occasion yet again to remind the world that religions do exist, such as on this continent, that can boast of never having launched a war, any form of jihad or crusade, for the furtherance of their tenets. Yet those beliefs have proved themselves bedrock of endurance and survival, informing communities as far away as the Caribbean and the Americas.

Is there, or is there not a lesson for our universe in this? Is there no lesson for these dogmatic, over-scriptured and over-annotated monumentalities whose rhetoric and secular appropriations far exceed the ascertainable, inner verities of their spiritual claims? The religions of this continent rescued us as a conscious race in the Diaspora, preserved our identity and, what is more, infected even those claimants to a superior knowledge of the Supreme Deity – those religions whose exalted high priests sometimes claim to be on a first-name acquaintance with their deities, on whose personal authority they mete out diabolical punishments to unbelievers, even for secular activities. Such elaborate beliefs, truths or fantasies, should be allowed to exist in their own right, but *in their own place*. This, in the sphere of religion, constitutes the ultimate challenge of the twenty-first century mind. It is not a new project; it dates back to the beginnings of man and has probably claimed more martyrs than most causes of human liberation. The dismal records of the Roman Catholic Inquisition are available to us, and the iconoclasm of Protestant missionaries on African soils, as are the unspeakable cruelties perpetrated on African humanity in the name of Islamic conversion or the preservation of the 'purity' of sheer spiritual intuitions.

I must not be misunderstood. I extol, indeed, I partake with creative and humane enlargement, in the inherent and productive values of all religions, their monumental legacies to the world, their piety and unflagging spirit of the search for truth. I acknowledge that the world would be a much poorer place without the phenomenon of religion. But wherever any religion parades or enlarges itself through the tactics of denigrating autochthonous values, or indeed, obstructing the very search of others for truth, then we are compelled to remind the purveyors of such aggressive 'truths' of their own historic errors, contradictions, and human diminutions. It is our duty to remind them of the horrors they have inflicted on other peoples, of their costly spasms of intolerance, some of which continue, even till today. Africa must remain the elephant of history; her memory should be accounted legendary because she has much to remember.

Her scars are not just part of her general history; each scar is labelled, catalogued, and visible.

Let all religions therefore call their proselytizers to order, or we, whose temper of piety is the most quiescent, will call them on this continent to strict accounting.

We know that no people can escape their history. It is not merely a geography that is physically invested by conquerors, but a cultural and philosophical actuality that then becomes weakened in turn by the very erosion of its geographical and economic autonomy. We would be content to leave the past alone, stay within our secure spirituality, and proceed with our future. But even this passive, forgiving or accommodating sense of realism is not permitted us by some of our contemporary African scholars who, deliberately or unwittingly, have been drawn into the service of the racial traducers of a pre-existent African world. A not so recent example deserves special attention, because of its pervasive medium – television – adopted for this exercise. In a thirteen-part series[1] that Professor Ali Mazrui filmed and narrated for the Public Television Service of the US, Mazrui adopted the explicit thesis that the contest for the African soul, on African soil, between Christianity and Islam, took place over a virtual spiritual vacuum. Even though, as a scholar, he was compelled to pay lip service to African religions and social systems, a quite unsubtle slant of denigration of the African past was effectively introduced, leaving the African values with no narrated strength or validity to contest or rationally accommodate the invading beliefs or retain any substance, depth, or relevance to African contemporary needs. A series which, we were informed, was designed to redress the appalling ignorance and misrepresentation of a vast continent ended up as yet another expensive propaganda for furthering the claims of the racial-religious superiority of two other structures of human superstitions which were imported into Africa and forced down the throats of its peoples, and with an unembarrassed bias towards Islam.

For those who are interested in this theme, a salutary view is provided in microcosm by Ousmane Sembene in his film *Ceddo*, and with an epic sweep in Maryse Condé's historical novel, *Sequ*.

That African social values and religions did undergo an attenuation under the onslaught of rival socio-religious groups from East and West must, however, be kept constantly in mind. When we are moved to recall history, however, it is not in order to institute courts for the determination of guilt or of altruistic errors by Africa's physical, spiritual, and intellectual invaders; it is to remind ourselves that the promotion of myths of cultural superiority have never really ceased. The consolidation of such myths through seemingly objective and opulently 'researched' documentation is not new, and merely continues its purpose of reducing targeted peoples to secondary, even tertiary levels of contribution to the pool of human civilization.

The Berlin Wall remains both symbol and point of departure. On its ruins, the writing for future is most dramatically embossed. It is our duty to seize every opportunity to impress on our peoples the unnaturalness, the inherent insult and denigration of our humanity, of the very imposition of any form of dictatorship under whatever colour, purpose, or ideology. The era of shameless opportunism is over. The rhetoric of seductive ideologies must not be permitted to obscure the act of robbery which underpins all forms of imposed governance, most criminally of all from our own kind. It is a calumny which must cease to attenuate the productive potential in a truly liberated humanity, certainly before the beginning of the next century.

After more than two centuries of indentureship to one school or another of alien world-views, leading in this century to authoritarianisms which are founded and perpetuated on nothing but the deeds of succession and a legitimacy of theoretical derivation from those same external sources of social ordering, nothing will serve us but a clinical, unsentimental operation which takes all claims to pieces, re-examines their components, histories, records, their territorial presumptions either of this world or of the next, their material and theoretical structures, and even their self-breeding abstractionist games. Above all, face squarely the issue of Power and Freedom and strip them of the glad rags that have obscured these fundamental axes of human striving since the earliest known community of man began, even when every such striving lacked the ability to name itself. Identify and proclaim where mythification has ensconced itself and permeated historical reality, where it is camouflaged by robes of revelationary authority, or the equally spurious claims to 'scientifically derived' theoretical laws which demand total submission of the laity and obedience to their findings.

That distant event, the disintegration of a human divide in Berlin does lay special claim on the African imagination, and on our vision. It is a centennial verdict on our relations with the European world since that arbitrary deed of cession that echoed, across centuries, the agreed division of territorial spheres of interest among the Christian kings of Europe. The nineteenth-century offspring, the formal annunciation of European colonization of Africa took place, you may recall, in Berlin itself, almost a century ago to the year. Such is the poetic mischief of which history often proves itself capable. A century after the partitioning of the African continent at the Berlin conference, Berlin is itself liberated and reunited in one of the most dramatic moves initiated by a European power in this century. On this seemingly global wave of liberation rode also the now iconic figure of Nelson Mandela, and with him the hope, the sheerest thread of hope that even the white atavists of South Africa may be poised to break down the wall that shields them from reality, and thus proclaim, and attain, their own liberation. It is of course preferable that this (apartheid) and other forms of tyrannical aberrations be voluntarily dismantled, otherwise they shall be forcibly. The issue of freedom and power has been stripped, definitively, of all further possible mystification. We must remain alert, however, to would-be usurpers of rationally abandoned ramparts, those who would don the masquerades of proven scarecrows stripped by the fury of the wind, would-be sowers of the tares of mind-enslavement on evacuated terrain. The final spike has been driven into the stone heart of dogma, and the monster of infallibility pronounced clinically dead. Its pall-bearers have been named: they are Humanity, Secularism, and Democracy. There is a fourth, however, whose name has been soiled by the opportunism of power. Let me describe it for now as the lawful heir, the legitimate heir-apparent of a theoretically humane ideology which was debased by unspeakable cruelties, appears globally discredited, yet remains the hope of impoverished millions on their own continent.

It may become necessary for each community to find a new, self-regenerating expression for that fourth pall-bearer which some of us still recognize and describe as socialism; perhaps even that name will continue to serve as a general foundation for the humanistic striving of African nations, since it is not an alien concept, whatever claims are made by others in that. It predates Marx, Engels, and Lenin. The term 'socialism' therefore still qualifies to serve, convincingly, as the expression of social operations which place social man at the centre of all state strategies for the attainment of the supreme quality of life for every individual. What we have always insisted upon, and what has been proved in such an irreversible manner, is that dogma should not, should never have usurped the humanistic goals of mankind, should never have become an alibi for raw, naked power lust and contempt for the mass of humanity.

Permit me to appropriate a statement by Trevor Munroe, the Jamaican communist, made in the wake of the disarray of communism in Europe, and the consequent internal reassessment of the Jamaican Communist Party. It appeared in the *Sunday Gleaner* in February 1990. Trevor Munroe must, however, be absolved from any unintended implications of my quotation, which is taken out of context.

> What we must keep and never lose is our social conscience, our concern for freedom and for social justice, our determination to find ways and means to facilitate the upliftment and the improvement of all the disadvantaged. In a sense, this conscience, this concern, and this determination were there before we became Communists; they have continued since then. More recently, even with our constitution and rules being inoperative, they have continued and found expression in the many ways each of us, despite personal pressure, has continued to serve our people, to fight against wrongs, and to help those in need to help themselves. These are the fundamentals which brought us together originally and on which we now need to fall back.

I repeat my (obsessive?) *fin de siècle* call: A definitive end to all forms of dictatorship on the continent! I had only this message for my fellow writers and intellectuals, who gathered in Lagos in May 1988 for a literary celebration of the transfer of the Nobel Prize in Literature to the African continent.

I re-issue the challenge with increased conviction: let all creative and polemical skills be directed toward hounding all forms of absolutism out of historic existence, before the end of the century. Existing dictatorships are also once again exhorted to set a firm date, well before the end of the century, for dismantling their totalitarian apparatus and commencing a dialogue of restitution for usurped political choice to the people. Those who have already commenced this process are to be loudly commended, stridently encouraged, so that they are not tempted to backslide!

This intuitive computation of the tempo of popular self-recovery has been reinforced by the seeming coincidence of response across the continent over the past year, one which has overseen the collapse of one dictatorship after another, and overtures from former intransigent heads of state towards their populace. The symbolic deadline is rapidly proving a reality.

The theocratic face of this imposture was similarly addressed at a meeting in Paris some months earlier, in February 1988 – significantly well before the self-aggrandizement of a priest and mortal declared its mission in a 'death sentence' passed on the writer Salman Rushdie for alleged blasphemy in a work of the imagination. It is this '*fatwa*' which constitutes the act of blasphemy against humanity, probably against Godhead itself – but I do not claim familiarity with the thought processes of the unknown and unknowable. Global theocratic terror being yet firmly entrenched and unrelenting, it is poor consolation that the priest has preceded the writer to the Great Beyond, accompanied by two (and perhaps unannounced) others? who immolated themselves in 'heretical' London, preparing the anointed device that would send Salman Rushdie to eternity. The powerless but symbolic figure of a global plight has won at least a temporal dimension of the unspoken wager. The contest must however continue until the tocsin of secular determination breaches the hardiest fortifications. Millennial or instinctual, benevolent or tyrannical, secular or theocratic, military or civil, the apparatus of repression embedded in governance without choice is an anachronism, a denial or truncation of self-knowledge of the human polity. It should not be permitted to linger on into the twenty-first century.

NOTES

1. The appearance of this essay in *Transition* magazine (US) provoked such a virulent *ad hominem* response that I urge the reader to ignore my comments on these series and refer, instead, to Hailu Habiu's 'The Fallacy of the "Triple Heritage" Thesis: A Critique' in *Issue*, no. 13, 1984. This meticulous essay examines in depth both the television series and Professor Mazrui's 'The Semitic Impact on Black Africa – Arab, Jewish Cultural Influences.

XVI

New Frontiers For Old*

I must begin by acknowledging that this talk is a belated response to two widely-spaced stimuli, spaced indeed over a number of years. The first was a PEN conference which had for its theme: 'The Writer at the Frontier'. I could not attend, but I found myself for some time afterwards quite fixated on the notion of a 'frontier' inhabited by writers masquerading as Customs and Immigration officials – that kind of waking nightmare in which roles are reversed. I never visited the United States during the McCarthy lunacy, but I believe that the familiar format of questions for any long-haired or bearded, that is, artist or seeming intellectual breed was, 'Who have you got in your luggage?' Denials of the spatial improbability of such contraband as humanity only increases suspicion that you are an importer of dangerous or subversive literature. You are taken into a special room, and even without actually arriving at the underpants, the dreaded book is fished out in triumph – Aha! Arthur Koestler's *The God that Failed*! An atheistic invasion of God's own country?

About the same time, the frontiers of the United Kingdom were also closed against a slightly different breed of immigrants, identified not so much as the ideological subversive as a sex-maniac called D. H. Lawrence. That he was a native son made no difference – he had 'gone native' in the Americas, which was worse. Back to my home front, using Africa's Malawi as sample, the frontier is closed to the most bizarre assortment of writers – from Karl Marx through D. H. Lawrence, Franz Fanon, to Walters Rodney, Ngugi wa Thiongo, Chinaue Achebe, etc. My records do not indicate what is the official position regarding Salman Rushdie; I doubt if the censors have yet heard of him!

This background should explain why even the rare delighted smile of recognition by an immigrant officer, who has just seen and recognized your name on a passport, is not necessarily an occasion for joy. The smile looks genuine enough to begin with but, it does not preclude a sudden transformation into the Medusa mask. 'Ah, you are so-and-so?' A mawkish grin acknowledges guilt. 'The writer?' Quickly you try to recollect

* A revised version of the Judith Gleason Lecture, Cambridge University (1990).

whose frontier this is – which is not as easy as it sounds if you have been up in the skies for quite a while and have crossed a number of date-lines. Still, the truth must be acknowleged and so again you gulp an affirmative, as cheerfully as you can. The risks tumble over one another, internally. What did you last write? Whose right to write did you last insist upon but, even more frequently, on behalf of which inmate in that immediate territory did you last invoke the code of Fundamental Human Rights? In Eastern Europe, until these past dramatic years, these were not idle considerations. In several countries on the African continent, such 'interfering pens' have occasionally been compelled to taste the same harsh hospitality as their beleaguered colleagues in their own native lands.

And thus, whether as one of the pernicious breed itself – the writer – or simply as the innocent, or not so innocent consumer, those creative frontiers remain territories of hazardous navigation for the voyager, thanks mostly to the writer – and his products – who tends to remain there in permanent or fluctuating residence, a suspect emigré in a refugee camp whose status of semi-exile undergoes quite arbitrary forms of articulation.

You may have gathered by now that I have come to a more than mild suspicion that there are few creative terrains more congenial to the writer – among the many creative species – than the frontier. If there were no frontiers either in his exterior or interior being, the writer would probably erect one. Communication – and this was the other stimulus I earlier referred to, a conference on communication (for journalists) in which I participated – communication itself must be regarded as a primary frontier between the artist and the rest of humanity. Certainly it is a fixture of the most elementary import. Commencing with the material which we all share in common, artist and non-artist, this material being reality, we can only question what makes the mission of the artist different from that of the next member of society. At first, one is tempted to say that it is *Reality* that constitutes the primary barrier that must be transcended; certainly some schools or periodic movements in the arts imply as much. 'Humankind cannot bear too much reality' etc. – such alibis have been elevated to manifestoes and tend to obscure what I fear is the artist's primary frontier – that of communication. For it is here that we come face to face with that instinct to transpose the 'fable' onto reality, a reality which, we know, does marshal overwhelming forces against such threatened negation – tactile, olfactory, visual forces ... the full resources of the infinite. The question then is, why? Faced with this formidable, incontestable statement of itself, the totality, even repletion of being of the 'real' world, why do we encounter loiterers at its frontiers, seeking the rights, rites and 'writes' of passage, fragmenting and recomposing, or operating 'through a glass, darkly'? Why present a winnowed down essence, or an opaque, dense-textured version of what is apparent to all as a simple text of real life; delaying, suspending or augmenting direct apprehension through a barrier of communication strategies, pawing such an 'open' text for the texture.

It was, as I have already hinted, in the process of reviewing the occupation of the journalist, during that communication conference, that I began to wonder if the secret was not really one of that very shared function – communication. That perhaps we must dredge the marshlands of primordial being or instincts to recover lost clues to the act of creativity, in the motions of communication. This came about from a sober recognition of the fact that the journalist, in my part of the world at least, and certainly also in others, often seems indistinguishable from the self-convicted writer of fiction. I began to wonder whether the 'reportorial slant', that mild expression for outright fiction, or grey 'faction', was that much different, really, from the creative writer's real vocation. Since this tendency to augment, or complicate reality applies to both, I began to look for some common denominator which went deeper than a mere problematique of the more obvious frontier of *reality*. And that fundamental accomplice, the common denominator, appeared to be – communictaion. What, after all, is the artist – writer, painter, or sculptor – but another member of the tribe of information gatherers and disseminators, scavenging within the common pabulum of reality? If one truly moved the frontier a few yards inland from maturity, groping backwards into the interior and hinterland of primary consciousness . . .

Think for a moment of the pathetic, even masochistic image of an infant attempting to speak. It is almost as if that infant came into the world with no other mission but this – to speak. Here is a barely formed tissue of consciousness; no sooner is it out in open air than it takes a huge gulp of the polluted stuff and lets out a bellow. From then on, it is one continuous proto-language hurled indiscriminately at the ceiling and other still or moving objects, sometimes at nothing in particular. Even alone in its crib, this activity never ceases. Nothing will do until it has succeeded, after titanic struggles, in fusing its own primitive womb syntax with that of the exterior landscape, abandoning the protective capsule of incomprehensibility with which it was blessed from the very beginning. The frustrations, the jerks and spasms, uncoordinated gladiatorial lunges in every direction, the weeping and gnashing of gums as it struggles to utter the first plosive! What, I have often asked myself, what is the hurry? Why all this compulsion? This desperation? Considering all the tribulations that await it once the adult world accepts that it can now be admitted into conversation, one can only agree with the experienced eye which takes one look at such an object, shakes its head sadly and pronounces: 'That child, 'e no get sense!' I have come to near certainty that watching a baby committing such a crime against itself is justly described as watching it exhibit all the symptoms of a writer!

Or the painter? By chance we are once again at an epochal frontier, another *fin de siècle* or centennial ending when the significance of a passing, purely symmetrically reckoned era, is probably at work again on the creative psyche to produce motions that either return us to beginnings, or will thrust perceptivity in seemingly innovative directions. The last *fin de siècle* produced, you may recall, what I like to refer to as the first formal Declaration of Indpendence for the Arts. 'Art for Arts sake' remains certainly one of the memorable expressions that were actually launched during this period. However negatively it is painted today – and no pun is intended – it nevertheless attested to a kind of liberation of the human imagination, perhaps unprecedented in the course of European arts and art criticism. Liberation? Some would say, 'abandon'. Self-indulgence. Dionysianism would be carrying the phenomenon a little too far but, irreverent, blasphemous, etc., were all applicable to its manifested attributes. Decadence is another favourite expression – these are all judgemental and therefore contrary to the spirit of that epoch.

But even those who decry the excesses, the negativity, even the self-destructive reaches of that movement, acknowledge that unprecedented experiments in tonal compositions, in painting, pigmentation, even the elevation of chromatism to a primary, near-autonomous value in itself – thanks to a renewed attention to Chinese masters – did become, for the European art scene, an irreversible advance in the perception of, and statements on reality. Rather in the spirit of that children's story of the elephant and the blind men, the elephant of reality was being yet again itemized, and while the part was not exactly being promulgated for the whole, it was being accorded its own replete existence in the ontology of appreciation – and not merely in the area of pure abstractions.

How ironic that a full century after that self-liberation in European arts, one in which the celebrated encounter with African art was manifested so robustly in the works and artistic manifestoes of Gauguin, Kandinsky, Brancusi, Cézanne, Picasso, etc., African arts should still almost routinely encounter today, and be compelled to surmount one of the most vulgar frontiers ever raised against the creative impulse – namely, Authenticity – captial letters! Yes, that is indeed one of the main parameters of proscription which African writers and artists still have to undergo even at the tail-end of the twentieth century! Ironically, the most strident of such immigration officers are themselves Africans, but they also give themselves the name of critics. These guard the frontier with a list of permissible imagery – everything outside that list is disallowed. Here is one of the most notorious; I take morbid pleasure in reciting the obscene litany at every possible occasion – understandably, I think. After all, the author not only parades himself as a critic but as a school of criticism in his own person, the principal conservator of African values, authenticity, etc., and is a favourite on lecture circuits both in Europe and Ameria, especially in the latter, very much in the latter. Even the *Times Literary Supplement* of England has more than once opened its pages to his magisterial opinions. Here then, without apologies to anyone who has encountered my pet reference before, is this critic's delimitation of the African poetic landscape, if its denizens would be adjudged anti-colonial, unpretentious, unaffected, faithful to African creative traditions. Such poetry shall remain, declares our literary pontiff, within:

> a landscape of elephants, beggars, calabashes, serpents, pumpkins, baskets, towncriers, iron bells, slit drums, iron masks, hares, snakes, squirrels . . . a landscape portrayed with native eyes to which aeroplanes naturally appear as iron birds; a landscape in which the animals behave as they might behave in African folk-lore, of animals presented through native African eyes.

But just in case that definition proves too complex for the consular officer from whom a visa has been requested, our would-be dictator of the zoo-platonic republic also provides an actual sample by which the simpleton may compare the kind of poetry which seeks admission at the border. Here it is, titled, with appropriate coyness, 'Life in our Village'.

> In our little village
> When elders are around

Boys must not look at girls
And girls must not look at boys
Because the elders say
That is not good

Even when the night comes
Boys must play separately
Girls must play separately
But humanity is weak
So boys and girls meet

The boys play hide and seek
And the girls play hide and seek
The boys know where the girls hide
So in their hide and seek,
Boys seek girls,
Girls seek boys
And each to each sing
Songs of love.

It is by no means an exceptional attitude. It informs the receptivity of even theatre directors and critics – I have had personal experience of this – to contemporary African works, one which, fortunately, can always be balanced – for the sake of one's blood pressure – by a quick recall of far more perceptive and sensitive analysts of African arts, such as William Fagg and Margaret Plass, Ladislas Segy, Dennis Duerden and dozen others.

Let us proceed for now with the chosen medium of creativity itself, which also constitutes a barrier against which the African artist has to contend – in the zoo-platonic republic of one kind or the other. Sometimes it is never directly acknowledged but – 'Well you know, the *novel* for instance, is really alien to African forms of expression. After all, when did the form actually develop in the more advanced European world? Poetry, especially the epic, and theatre – of a rudimentary, mostly ritualist kind of course – yes, perhaps. But not the novel. And certainly not painting – a totally alien form to the African artist. Sculpture, of course. Wood and metal ornamentation – quite admissible. But painting? Definitely a western affectation.'

In the foreword to an exhibition of contemporary African art at the Harlem Studio, New York, I observe that dismissing such restrictive views of the province of African plastic art forms is a simple enough process, and not merely through reference to the so-called primitive rock and cave paintings uncovered on the African continent. There is also the art of body decorations, mask paintings which prefigure three-dimensional expressions of the many possibilities of the colour medium. Bark painting is indigenous to Central Africa and Australasia. 'Bead-painting' (an expression coined, I believe, by the art critic Dennis Duerden) has been brought to the highest state of mastery in the Cameroun. The wall-paintings of Mbari shrines in Eastern Nigeria and cult houses in the Republic of Benin, the *asafo* houses in Ghana – the *mural*, in short – all these ancestors of the 'canvas' easily accuse a narrowness of definition, just as the African oral narrative questions the ontology of literary forms of the verbal art as named in Western terms. Where, for instance, does the debate lead us if we switched to the expression 'prose fiction?' Is the 'alienation' crime restricted to the creative effort or does it embrace consumption? And of course, in the case of painting, which constantly seeks to destroy its 'surface' in order to penetrate reality more meaningfully, developments such as collage, pointillism, action painting, drip techniques and even cubism often strike one, in their results, as a 'return to source', and with what vengeance!

The confusion is obviously a product of sensibility. The context in which the modern work (or indeed religious or secular traditional art) is encountered today is the museum or exhibition gallery, for which the precise canvas appears to have been especially tailored. Today's preference for, and architectural evolution of airy, 'natural light' gallery space, and even the more socialized café or restaurant galleries, are the modern counters to this dubious legacy of the spirit of artistic 'hoarding', enshrined by those ponderous baroque and other privileged edifices which commenced the museum tradition. If we wished to be generous, we would say that the critical *nay-sayers* in question merely object, subconsciously, to this 'constriction', this 'elitism' of the museum gallery in relation to the freer, more 'natural' and organic encounters with works of art in their traditional setting such as shrines or community huts. This umbrage is then transferred, perhaps unconsciously, to the canvas itself as medium of expression.

Alas, it does not always end on this note. From the genre of the canvas that is the framed expression develops yet another delimiting critique – this time of style. Innovative directions (i.e., any form outside realism) are deemed – and here I quote from that same school earlier cited – 'sterile imitations' of European art forms, a hardly surprising attitude, since the medium itself – painting – has already been deemed a European affectation. Entire chapters have been devoted to this theme, ironically enough, in exercises undertaken in defence of the purity of African creative genius. I have dealt with such labour of race amputation in creative fields in other places. This school, which we usually give the obvious name of neo-Tarzanism, eventually slips into the position of unsolicited but welcome apologists for regimes which, waving the opportunistic rag of 'authenticity' as a banner, suppress forms of literature, or other art forms that may present a reality outside the glossy brochure of state, especially where, for the sake of prudence, such a reality is veiled, coded, seeped in self-protective nuances and ambiguity. Derek Walcott provides the Caribbean face of such state-induced sterility, this time with economic motivations:

In these new nations, art is a luxury, and the theatre the most superfluous of amenities.

Every state sees its image in those forms which have the mass appeal of sport, seasonal and amateurish. Stamped on that image is the old colonial image of the laughing nigger, steel-bandsman, carnival masker, calypsonian and limbo dancer. These popular artists are trapped in the state's conception of the folk form, for they preserve the colonial demeanour and threaten nothing. The folk arts have become the symbol of a carefree, accommodating culture, an adjunct to tourism, since the State is impatient with anything it cannot trade.

Pumpkins, calabashes, baskets . . . calypso and steel drums!

But there are also worthier frontiers, one such being classicism. No one who seriously responds to the aesthetic dimensions of man's productivity will deny the impact of travelling exhibitions of past glories such as The Treasures of Tutankhamen, Suleiman the Magnificient, A Thousand Years of Nigerian Art or the Heritage of India, all of which, quite apart from their unqualified success outside, have opened even the eyes of the heirs of these artworks anew to the heritage they take for granted or, of which many had remained blissfully unaware. But the very challenge of such classic power, the productive conditions of which have now vanished, or have become attenuated, can only be answered by the evolution of new artistic forms which, in their turn, reflect the experiences – travails and triumphs – in short, the spirit of our own age, and serve as graphic documentation of the sensibilities of our time.

The Muse for our times is indeed one that truly celebrates the bounty of styles, themes and exploratory verve from a continent where every act or product of the imagination is always conveniently summed up by the word 'African'. Yes indeed, there is an entity called 'Africa', but the creative entities within its dark humus – fecund, restive and protean – burst through the surface of a presumed monolithic reality, and invade the stratosphere with unsuspected shapes and tints of the individual vision! And there, we know, the ancestors join in the festive dance to rhythms that have always lain latent in their veins, awaiting the solar eruption of new harmonics from their uninhibited, space-tuned offsprings.

Part of the foregoing will be found in my programme notes to that exhibition, and what applies to the plastic forms in Africa apply equally to the literary. The writer remains the permanent child who will not accept that it has at any time succeeded in crossing the frontier of communication – in any language. I believe this is true of the writer in any culture, indeed I am more than ever persuaded that this is what defines the breed – living the paradox that embraces, even interiorizes the barrier, yet insists that the barrier should not be there. And thus, charging at, manoeuvring past, slithering through, hurling imprecations and shaking the fists at . . . simply insisting that the frontier be shattered, that the barricades be lifted, that human communication be not controlled, constricted or manipulated. For this activity takes place on all fronts – it is both elemental and social. Political. And this last results not infrequently in the writer himself finding the barricades sharply lifted at a critical moment of contest; the momentum carries him forward and, by the time he has regained balance, he finds himself across the frontier, the barricade neatly, definitively or temporarily lowered behind him. He is compelled to learn the language of the space beyond the frontiers, the mores, customs, taboos . . . in short, he encounters the new language of the frontiers of exile, its joys and anguish, its challenges. This tension has proved, over the ages, a life and death recurrence.

The conjunction of both the physical and the elemental frontiers has surely never been more dangerously expressed, at least in this century, than in the yet ongoing drama of Salman Rushdie and the Satanic Regime of Iran. For Rushdie, the physical frontier has contracted while the elemental remains – within the imperatives of creativity – innately expansive. Does Salman Rushdie himself know this, much less accept it? His most recent act of abnegation appears to confound this assertive reading but I do insist that this self-compensating actuality is the potent environment of the writer's mission.

Is this a perennial condition? Consider again the writer's conditioning, the rules, the modalities of his vocation. The frontiers of perception and representation constitute at least a portion of the paradoxes most deeply embedded in the subconscious of the average writer – from the most deceptively simplistic to the most tortuous stylist. This certainty that the writer cannot exist without frontiers to cross, that indeed, frontiers are the first condition of the writer, implies sometimes that the writer's vocation obliterates the distinction between his functions and those of an explorer, the physicist, atomic or space scientist. Indeed the social activist. Perhaps, to revert to my constant metaphor, the artist is simply another being impelled by that unique god of the Yoruba pantheon, Ogun, who led all other deities in slashing through primordial chaos to the world of man and the ordering and expression of experience, utilizing a technology that, until then, had rested in the limbo of knowledge, in the world's womb. Such dare is of a parallel order with that of the ocean explorers of the so-called European Dark Ages who wrested the decision on the shape of the earth from the hands of superstitious clerics, necromancers and alchemists and simply, literally, sailed over the edge of the world but somehow climbed up again – up the galactic waterfall? – to regain dry land, none the worse for wear. But the obverse is also true. It is part of the artistic alchemy that the writer, without a shade of embarrassment, also claims kinship even with the heirs of those very necromancers, such as the admirable adherents of the Flat Earth Society, and with thousands of cultures all over the world which insist that Night is the after-dinner belch of the primal Dragon, that the ancestral realm is co-terminous with ours who claim to be the living, that the moon is the glowing navel of the eternally pregnant sky-mother, whose labour-pains replenish the world with trees, seas, rivers, beasts and humans. Who, in short, is truly content with the frontiers of the empirical, against whose constrictions the writer constructs not merely eponymous histories but elaborate assault towers? Like the scientist, is the writer not really upset, irritated, intrigued, and challenged by the arrogant repletion of objective reality and experience?

Much of the process of creativity, and its results, are therefore an effort of brinkmanship – stretching the frontier of human imagination or perception as far as is – inhumanly – possible. I consider now the nature scene spread with generous foliage outside my window as I write this. What do I perceive? A friend? A companion? A conundrum? A chance encounter? Of indeed, a hostile experience? Of course it is potentially all of these, but not if one were content to let it be just as it appears in its itemized detail, in the sum of its parts. The writer defines his being, one may suggest, when he suspects a case of mere appearances, an affront of frontiers erected by nature against its innermost, and most rewarding secrecies. It is the tale of Adam and Eve all over – do not probe beyond the veil of seeing – they broke the taboo and found a complicated world beyond the frontiers. Opinions may differ about the perfection of that earlier secretive terrain, but knowledge, we are informed, was thereby inflicted on the world.

Yes, those alleged forebears of humankind – after their brutal expulsion from paradise, would the apple, the serpent, the tree – any tree – and finally, the fig-leaf still remain to them the apple, the serpent, the tree and the fig-leaf? Is it conceivable that the pair would advance no further than the ability to discern in any tree no more than a dual latency – knowledge and ignorance – the former denoting Big Trouble, the latter, bliss? We know what purpose the fig-leaf continued to serve for artists in later millennia, especially during those European puritanic spasms – ages after the fall from grace. And not just the fig-leaf as that triangular piece of verdure, but their several 'incidental' variants, pressed into service for fear of giving offence to patrons or a new political order, or transgressing periodic codes of permissiveness – the piece of drapery for instance, which always just happens to cover restricted areas of the human anatomy. In other canvases, a bunch of fruits, a wine-jar or just the edge of a piece of furniture, even a clump of shrubbery upstaging the coy variant on the model as she steps, alluringly surprised, out of the pool or stream where she had just taken a swim – the canvases and tapestries even on classical themes are full of these improvizations on the morality of the fig-leaf. Was the expression, 'I don't give a fig!' first uttered, I wonder, by some artist reprobate in a Benedictine monastery in ancient times?

We do know of course that such fig-leaves were not always the artist's device but the politician's, usually wearing or hiding behind a cleric's garb. Politicians and allied upholders of public decency and morality have left their imprint, literally, on public statutary by ordering artisans, or indeed any available dauber, to cover up specific areas of the human anatomy on those art works inherited from 'pagan' times, with fig-leaves, preferably in gold-leaf or gold paint, for reasons I have never understood. Anyone who has actually encountered these historic hybrids can hardly be blamed if they become instant converts to the doctrine that the devil always finds work for idle hands – but also that the cleric, of whatever religious persuasion, is his most faithful servitor. I like to think of this particular devil as the painter's devil, named after the more familiar fall guy, the printer's devil, that gremlin which, long after the writer, editor and compositor have done their duty and put the journal to bed, creeps into the print-shop and inserts just that incongruous word or punctuation mark, which renders the original text meaningless, contradictory or even libellous. In those periodic orgies of sanitization of the arts which appear to affect most societies, look out for his signature – the punctuation mark of the fig-leaf over the human genitalia. If the director of the Cincinnati gallery had only studied his art history he would have saved himself a lot of hassle over his Mapplethorpe exhibition by replacing those 'Sold' stickers with a different sign and stuck them on the contumacious spots.

But enough of this enticingly prurient digression. The original question was – how would Adam and Eve have perceived the fig-leaf (or apple) after their expulsion from paradise? To put this another way, would their perception of paradise itself have altered in any way? Would this idyll have remained paradise-as-was? But we must take the event further back – *what* was paradise to Adam and Eve after the revelation of Satan as reptilian both in shape and purpose?

On one level, probably more significant than the next, sits the awareness of the unstable nature of this being – which, within the limited context of that phase of existence, constituted a fifth of the entirety of beings – its capacity to manifest itself in alternative forms and shapes. Related to this, but of a different dimension, is the complication of the perception of reality, and illusion, the 'apple effect' if you like. It ends the habit of presumptions, shatters the serenity acquired by their one-dimensional conception of their own being, and perception of the exterior world. Then follows the trauma of exile, dispersing ever wider the shards of innocence, fragmenting their once hermetic notions of existence.

So, afterwards, does paradise continue paradise-as-was? Will the aspects of shame and guilt exist in their own clinical patches, affecting the filtered recollection of, and mode of expression of paradise-that-was in no novel manner? And the continuing relationship between Adam and Eve, the blame passing, the newly aroused sensibilities towards each other – all of this, not to mention their final image of the garden of Eden, an image which indeed is not the garden at all – the garden has by now vanished – but the towering figure of the deportation officer, the angel with the flaming sword, cancelling their residence permit with a majestic flourish as he slams the gates of paradise behind their fig-clad posteriors.

On encountering another creature from outer space, or even crouched within the confined purgatory of each other, blubbering to each other about this traumatic curtailment of a shared idyll, can we, in the name of that, or any other god, conceive of Adam or Eve narrating the event in the 'unspoilt', 'authentic' language of:

> In our little garden
> When angels are around
> Boy must not look at girl
> Girl must not look at boy
> Because the angels say
> That is not good . . .

I must consign the rest of that stimulating transposition to the whimsical extravagances of any interested listener. Even from this distance, paradise does not lack mystery. My theory is that the game of hide and seek, so profoundly injected into the earlier cited poem by our exemplars of pristine authenticity, holds for such critics the key to all conceivable mystery of any paradisial idyll. Milton's agonized effort to 'justify the ways of God to man' is justly rebuked. He should have stuck to the model of 'our little village'.

The loss of paradise is a recurrent fable, the morality tale of the colonized world, of the very experience of colonization, not simply of expulsion and exile. For colonization is indeed a state of internal exile at its most spiritually debilitating. To fully appreciate this condition, one needs only examine the human temper, even today, of the victims of successful colonization – be it in the Caribbean or certain sectors of the African continent. The quality of this experience predates Shakespeare's own memorable variation on this theme, and not in *The Tempest* alone. The theme of exile occurs and recurrs in several of Shakespeare's plays – *As You Like It, Timon of Athens*, etc., etc. This becomes clearer if we recall that the experience of colonization involves seemingly contradictory but indeed complementary motions: for instance the sensibility of entrapment, not only physical entrapment but entrapment within a recollected but receding idyll. Simultaneously it is the shattering of barriers, a brutal thrust into an extended world from within whose expanded reality, the rendering even of the prior experience now takes form and resonance. And of course, we do not speak here of a purely physical distension. However determinedly rooted the colonized remains within the same circumscribed anterior world, the dynamics of that physical reality have changed, irreversibly. Yes, the reality remains intact because, the totality of culture is one matrix within which reality takes shape and form. But the rendering of that very assailed cultural reality cannot evade the dynamics created by the intrusion, however undesired and resented. In the truly sensitive artist, that anterior reality continues to permeate the present, but without sentimentality or mawkishness. Its evocation, involving 'autochthonous' cultural attributes, is heightened through the prism of the total apprehension of the present. The fig-leaf, in short, is not denied. It is not, however, stubbornly retained in its crinkled form, desiccated through time and usage, like a leaf pressed between other leaves of the literary product of modern technology, perhaps even the latest computerized desk-top publication. Indeed, paradise can be regained; again and again, the artist does regain paradise, but only as a magical act of transformation of present reality, not through the pasting of a coy, anachronistic fig-leaf over the pudenda of the past in the present.

This magical act of transformation is readily recognized in the works of many new generation African writers such as Ben Okri, whose collection, *Stars of a New Curfew*, enmeshes that reality of pumpkins, iron bells etc. in metaphysical evocations. In these tales, the mind is constantly pulled towards a 'place of things remembered', a timelessness of human suffering, self-destruction and the paradox of the survivalist will. The genre is as familiar as the work is unique, stamped with the ease of a truly original imagination which acts on the singularity of a terrain's evocation – the aftermath of war, devastation, the nightmare of hopelessness, the individual's incessant effort to break through the cul-de-sac of life's defeats and enervation. It bears affinity with the fiction of Wongar, the Australian aborigine, in its evocation of landscape desolation which however has been imbued with an interior pulsation of its own, once the author, through a violence that is itself a symbol and reflection of the real world, has broken through the mirror that hides this other world. And we then proceed to pick our way through a new order of reality and fragmented time, through nightmarish images that are at once disorientating, yet strangely calming in the delineation of their acceptance by the denizens of this ulterior world. A fusion of realism, harsh, violent realism and the fantasy of dreams.* You will encounter it in Toni Morrison, in Partap Sharma, the Indian playwright, Garcia Marquez, Amos Tutuola, etc., and obviously not in literature alone. It is present in the landscapes of most surrealists, products of the process of imagic transparencies – the effect of slide transpositions which transform or distort impressions of multi-faceted realities. And of course we recognize it abundantly in the surrealist cinematography of an Ingmar Bergman, as in the recent film *Yeleen* by the West African cineaste Sulyman Cisse. We speak here of artists who penetrate one reality to expose another, structured upon its own inner logic yet contingent on the original reality that gave it birth. I would add Robert Wilson, indeed, I do include Robert Wilson and more specifically his production *Deafman's Glance*, but this theatrical denizen of the timeless frontier demands a very special kind of attention, all of his own.

For realities are indeed multiple, even the realities that we take for granted in our daily, material existence. Back in Nigeria, for instance, usually around February, it has become customary to encounter a tourist advertisement on the pages of national newspapers, reminding Nigerians that the Carnival season is once again at hand. Naturally, this advertisement is meant, not for all Nigerians, but for a small but steadily growing class of our affluent countrymen and women who have discovered the seasonal attraction of Brazil. I have seen films of this festival; it is truly lush, extravagant and overwhelming. It is the very pinnacle of decorative art in motion, a dionysiac celebration of the peacock in man. It is a visual feast on a scale which, even on celluloid, overwhelms you, batters your senses into numbness until all the colours, plumes, imitation gems, contours and textures fuse into one another to create a totally new, unheard-of material form, like a new synthetic product, a fiesta wrapped up in a swathing of remorseless, percussive polyrythms of the samba and haunting diminished chords. Within this chariot of the senses the viewer is borne off into a world beyond recognition, past definition, totally submissive. What it must do to the spectators physically present at this tumult of colour, sound and motion, one can only wonder. All we do know is that year after year, this spectacle of the senses is paraded through the streets of Rio de Janeiro. And even before one is over, the next is already under way in the competitive lust of its producers.

It is, apparently, impossible for the average Brazilian to envisage life without the Carnival. One would-be reformer, a president, thought differently. He found the Carnival symptomatic of the torpor and unserious life attitude of the Brazilian and he proposed to abolish it. He was forced to change his mind very quickly.

So much for one reality, the reality which makes the opulent Nigerian invade Rio, in some cases, on annual pilgrimage. But there is of course that other reality, that which the ill-starred president saw, lamented, and sought to evoke in his crusade against the orgy of escapism. It is a reality which was caught, to some extent, in the film *Orfeo Negro*, by the Frenchman Marcel Camus. But, as you will observe from the title itself, Camus merely superimposed another level of reality – the mythic – onto the Carnival.

* Ben Okri has since taken this fusion to extravagant dimensions in his densely textured novel, *The Famished Road.*

The story of Orpheus and Eurydice, that perennial allegory of the lover pursuing his beloved even into the netherworld – in short, the inner defiance of mortality by the will to life. Camus' images were however faithful to the truth of the barrios, those infamous hillside shacks, the ghettos of despair and squalor from within which life, or a semblance of it is extracted through the sheer will to survive. This was the underlying reality of the Carnival, creating a paradox which of course does not concern – why indeed should it? – the spectator who has flown through some thousand miles to wallow in this monumental escape from the rigours of existence.

That Carnival, under a variety of names – Play Mas, Mardi Gras, etc. – is indeed a way of life in much of Latin America, the West Indies and in New Orleans in Southern US of A. And one writer who has captured the interior reality that appears to confound the surface, yet all-engrossing self-abandonment is Earl Lovelace. In *The Dragon Can't Dance*, the countdown towards the Trinidadian brand of this annual explosion is explored through the miniscule interstices of actual life, the betrayals of social relationships, poverty and hunger, and that tragic syndrome of mutual predatoriness among the oppressed of society. Violence is the currency of social exchange, it would appear, and yet tenderness is by no means devalued. On the contrary, we are enabled to experience love and affection as the cementing bond of humanity whose self-expression is constantly embattled by the material conditions of those to whom this is, demonstrably, a sustaining value. The struggle for the very means of life underscores, pitiably, the sacrifice made towards this life-affirming spirit of the Carnival – a mind-boggling irony which however, throughout the pages, asserts itself as a universal truth of existence.

From one crucible of the imagination, alchemists of the temper of a Lovelace, George Lamming, Chinua Achebe, Charles Dickens, Tolstoy, Emile Zola, wa Thiongo, Camara Laye, Banumbir Wongar ... from yet another, a Garcia Marquez, Amos Tutuola, Verlaine, Rimbaud, Genet, and again Banumbir Wongar and Camara Laye ... fundamentally one material world, one physical reality. Yet, in different degrees, our sorcerers construct and communicate wildly separated yet coherent structures of a new reality, implying a refusal to accept that the empirical datum of reality is all there is – or else, why write? So they create neo-beings, agents of new histories, new experiencing, new vectors of communication. I have just stopped to check that word 'vector' in the dictionary (Chambers), and permit myself a nod of contentment. It translates as 'a directed quantity, involving both its direction and magnitude, the course of an aircraft, missile, etc.' but, additionally, as 'a carrier of disease or infection'. Very good. A perfect expression – until I can think up a better one – for the communicable disease from an artist's vocation.

In this paradoxical act of celebrating (even unconsciously), while eroding, the frontiers of his vocation, is the artist inching the world towards an abandonment of the frontier mentality? My concluding remarks will expose my bias. What seems inescapable, from whatever point of view, and whatever is the intention of the artist, is an obsession with frontiers. Or perhaps since we can only deal with any degree of certainty with the result, the created work itself, we should limit ourselves to saying that the artistic act of communication, whatever else it does or fails to achieve, certainly diminishes the effective existence of one frontier or another.

In his attempt to place Kandinsky, Klee and Mondrian within the template of artistic impulses, the art critic Gombrich described these artists as 'mystics who wanted to break through the veil of appearances to a higher truth'. It is a familiar expression, and I believe that the emphasis should be placed on the word 'attempt', the vision, not on the more contumacious issue of whether indeed a higher truth exists beyond reality or appearances, and whether or not any artist glimpses, much less attains it. Gombrich had in mind a particular kind of artist however, whereas I am occupied here with the very vocation of the artist, *sui generis*. My conception of the veil is therefore not so elevated; it is simply that of communication, the frontier of communication. That Gombrich should also employ the analogy of the child is however most comforting. He writes:

> I suppose the true reply is that the modern artist wants to create things. The stress is on create and on things. He wants to feel that he has made something which had no existence before. Not just a copy of a real object, however skilful, not just a piece of decoration, however clever, but something more relevant and lasting than either, something he feels to be more real than the shoddy objects of our humdrum existence. If we want to understand this frame of mind, we must go back to our own childhood, to a time when we still felt able to make things out of bricks or sand, when we turned a broomstick into a magic wand and a few stones into an enchanted castle.

From my commencing analogy, it is clear that I prefer to place the struggle much earlier, to suggest that it began before the instinct to make or transform, and reaches into the much earlier phase of human development, which is communication. This surely is where it all started, and it is at this very frontier that the rest of humanity parted company a long time ago, and left its 'lunatic fringe' still struggling to communicate, to be later described in kindly fashion as artistes.

The image of the child seeking to communicate is not far-fetched or indeed, fetched, I assure you. Take Dadaism. Did not the Dadaists themselves flaunt it as a banner before the world? They may have tagged it 'primitivism'; again, I consider 'primordialism' a more accurate description. Gauguin explicity asserted his need to go backwards from the horses of the Parthenon to the rocking-horse of his childhood, and the 'da-da' of the movement was an expression of that masochistic child we have referred to, struggling to communicate with a far better linguistically equipped world. Gauguin and company merely retreated from the contest in order to engage in a dialogue – on a different level admittedly but, nevertheless a dialogue – with the 'adult' world. For 'adult' in this instance, we must read of course institutionalism, be this identified as 'feudalist', 'social-realist', 'religious', 'bourgeois', 'proletarian' or 'politically correct'. Fashions change, and so naturally, does anti-voguism.

What will it be, this '*fin de siècle*', at this twenty-first century frontier? Dadaism was not strictly '*fin de siècle*', but it was a child of that movement; it was suckled at the same teats. So, Dadaism the last time round; Mamaism this time? We may expect some revisionism in art history which indeed insists that it really was 'Mamaism' all the time – trust the male chauvinistic pigs to alter what is the authentic first sound of the masochistic infant! Justification would be found in centuries of European artistic trends and criticism which, admittedly, have been lamentably misogynist – 'sexist' being a world I religiously avoid because of its debased currency, its pompous, neuterist agenda. It is, in our current environment, a sound note on which to end, a warning note against the new breed of immigration officers.

One taboo falls, another is fabricated. The erstwhile liberationist is transformed into the tyrant of a new orthodoxy where words, even syllables and phonemes are scrutinized and sanitized to ensure that they pass the self-righteous neuterism of over-assiduous immigration officers. The quirks of language that distinguish one stylist from another are held up as deep-seated proofs of the closet sexist or homophobe, as evidence of their primitive 'crimes against humanity' which are excoriated in the seminar rooms of literary Nurembergs. To be 'politically correct' – that presumptuous, catch-all, intellectual labour-saving expression of American with-itness – you have to be, among other criteria, a closet heterophobe or a breast-thumping feminist, preferably without the breasts. A new, guilt-propelled literary ideology is born; its manifesto is the emasculation of language – and that pun is definitely intended – its methodology a sanctimoniousness that preens itself to exceed the worst banalities of moralistic proletkults. The dominant temper of this century and of some societies – the United States, yes, especially the United States – often appears to involve a special aptitude for leaping from one frontier to another, for crushing one frontier only to erect another, walling out balance, rationality and even history, competing for authority with descredited totalitarian claims not only on political ideas and eonomic strategies, but on the sciences, the arts and even human relationships.

Does the foregoing sound somewhat exaggerated perhaps? I do not believe so; the evidence is overwhelming, not merely within the circles of academia, those sterilization units for creativity, but in the trendy theologies of literary conferences and art journals. The warning is therefore more than timely. The artist has need, more than ever, to rise in defence of his true territory, resisting the erection of new frontiers and assailing the deception of enslaving 'verities'. Let the new breed of censors therefore tread warily and remember that, like politicians and clerics, ideologues and pundits, they too merely come and go, and that their passage traverses that elusive terrain of the untamable frontier being rootless, yet citizen of a protean universe, indestructible, because his territorial authority is ultimately not of the world of seeming but of the liminal.

XVII

The Credo of Being and Nothingness*

I do not claim to know what has been the experience of others but, as a child, I found myself frequently indulging in a rather exotic mental exercise. It was an exercise which originated from my attempts to come to concrete terms with the christian myth of the creation of the world. In the beginning, claim the christian scriptures, there was Void. Emptiness. My imagination insisted on conjuring up this primeval state and ended up by evolving this quite logical exercise: I would shut my eyes, shut off my mind, then try to enter that primal state of nothingness which the world would have been, before the creation of anything, animate or inanimate. It became quite a compulsive indulgence. I found myself impelled by a curiosity to experience the absolute state of non-being, of total void – no trees, no rocks, no skies, no other beings, not even I.

All I can recall today from that phase was the experience of dizziness. My head would begin to spin and I became somewhat scared. It did not stop me putting myself through the same cerebral wringer over and over again. I can only wonder, at this distant remove, how I would have been affected at that impressionable age, by the knowledge that adults have actually constructed complex philosophical and religious systems, in which all material life, including all those dynamic processes for the reproduction of life which in fact constitute our social consciousness or value of being, are actually conceived as a programmed reversion towards that very state of nothingness, the primal zero, which I then tried vainly to experience. Obviously I should have saved myself the trouble and waited until I could read it all in books, heard it in sermons and glimpsed it through guaranteed meditative routes such as those prescribed in buddhism. How was I to know that sages and visionaries of various persuasions had already perfected their own spiritual paths towards that individual, or collective state of negation?

This exercise must not be confused with a related kind which is far more common

* Delivered as the inaugural lecture in the Archbishop Olufosoye Lecture Series at the University of Ibadan (1991).

among children, that being the attempt to experience death. My shared recollections of childhood games, shared with some colleagues in mature life, indicate that this is quite a popular childhood indulgence. Sometimes it even results, accidentally, in the real thing. The child locks himself in a dark cupboard, trunk or disused refrigerator and simply suffocates to death. No, the exercise to which I refer is quite different. The latter, the death mimesis, is a *game* which is played against the accepted reality of existence. The former, by contrast, attempts to deny or efface existence altogether. This former, I would recognize much much later as being akin to what buddhists undergo as part of their spiritual training – empty your mind, shed your flesh, your beingness . . . dissolve in the void itself and experience – Nirvana.

What christians and moslems share with buddhism is not so much Nirvana as its universalized state – Mahapralayi. This expression offers a loose distinction which I had better qualify. I do not deny that there are states of individual contemplation in christianity and islam which approach the ideal of Nirvana. Certainly some of the fundamentalist sects – even of a cultic temper – in either religion, indulge in this exercise of intensive inward dissolution which parallels the buddhist Nirvana. But the orthodox bodies do not encourage them; indeed, they are viewed with suspicion, as deviant and dangerous, even diabolic. The Universal Day of Judgement, guaranteed by both, is the concept I can propose which comes closest to the condition of universal nothingness, the in-folding of the world as we know it into its original womb of darkness, or more accurately, non-darkness and non-light. The main differentiation between Mahapralayi and Day of Judgement is however a crucial, even cheerful one. The material world we know disappears, in the latter case, but it is revived on a different plane, as Paradise, Purgatory or Hell. In the islamic Book of the Dead, it is expressed in language not that disimilar from the christian creed of Resurrection:

> I have believed in Allah, and His angels, and His books, and
> His messengers, and the Last Day and the decree of its good
> and evil from Allah-ta'alla, and in the Rising after death.

Mahapralayi, by contrast, is a return to the primal void. To transcend present existence therefore, we need not wait for the equivalent of Mahapralayi, the Final Day of Judgement, or All Souls' Day. All we need to do is die, having led a good life, and we shall be wafted to another state of being. In some cases of course, especially in aspects of islamic preaching, it also helps to have died fighting a holy war. That way, transition into paradise is instant. The christians appear to be more procedural – there is a temporary halt at the gates where your credentials are checked. After that there is also the half-way house called – Purgatory.

At one conceptual level or the other, therefore, deeply embedded as an article of faith, is a relegation of this material world to a mere staging-post, awaiting the drop of the final grain of sand into the lower half of the hour-glass, then universal negation – gently or cataclysmically. Existence as we know it comes to the end that was preordained from the beginning of time. Indeed, time itself comes to an end. In the solitary confinement of prison, when time weighed heavily on my mind and showed no inclination to come to a desired end, I found myself contesting that very element, Time, by reverting to my childhood exercises, the negation of existence. Of course on this occasion, I was armed with the knowledge of others. I even had the grisly trigger of the sound of a number of condemned men walking towards their last moment on earth, their footsteps receding into a permanently fading echo in the mind. Without too much effort, beyond the simple routine of fasting, I found myself drifting into this curious state of the incorporeality, not only of myself, but of the surrounding world. It resulted in the poem 'Mahapralayi'. Hopefully, you may share some of that projection in the following lines from the poem:

> a spring is touched by appointed fingers
> and whirlwings fold into the dark.
> a glacier mind of all-being
> slows to a last enduring thought
> a deadweight seal of silence sways
> upon the secret – at this wake
> none keeps vigil, none.

That background is necessary to understand why I, for one, failed to understand why my fellow Nigerians, especially of the christian persuasion, got so excited when the great intellectual, sage, philosopher, religious leader and man of peace, Sheikh Gunmi, uttered his memorable words: 'Christianity is nothing.' Now I know that christians will say that I can afford such detachedness because I am not a christian, but they would be wrong. The truth is simply that, having raised myself as an experimenting spiritualist of nothingness since childhood, graduating, under prison conditions, into even deeper illumination into the profundities of nothingness, I was able to grasp at once that Sheik Gunmi was paying christianity one of the most enlightened compliments in the calendar of piety. We have to recall his exact words: 'Christianity is nothing.' An objective, deeply thought-out statement. Compare it, if you like, to these words from the buddhist mystic Malarepa, words which I recited as lines of self-abnegation in a section of 'The Man Died':

I need nothing. I seek nothing. I desire nothing.

The similarity, not the difference, is clear. If Gunmi had said, 'Christianity is nothing to me,' that would have been a subjective, even provocative statement and christians would have been correct to demand that he be publicly crucified – not metaphorically, I mean literally. In a moment, I shall point out which particular cross I would have recommended. But let us continue. The semantic purist might insist that Gunmi should have said, 'Christianity is nothingness,' that is, christianity is the harbinger of the eventual state of nothingness of being. I would be inclined to agree, except that we do not really know in what language Sheik Gunmi was thinking; we only know in what language he spoke. Translation from one language to the other is difficult enough, how much more, translation of profound spiritual intuitions from the abyss of the mind into the spoken world. 'In the beginning was the Word', and Sheik Gunmi had gone back, not only to the beginning, but to the predicated end of the very purpose of christianity and other religions. The Word as end and beginning was pronounced but, alas, his listeners were caught in the middle. That is their shortcoming, not Sheik Gunmi's.

The great Persian poet, Astronomer and Scientist Omar Khayyam, patron saint of all agnostics, has given us the definitive word on the theme:

> The captives of intellect and of the nice distinction
> Worrying about Being and non-Being, themselves become nothing
> You with the news, go seek out the juice of the vine
> Those without it wither before they die.

Omar Khayyam, native of Naishapur in Khorasan, lived in the eleventh century of the christian calendar, but I often think that he should be living in this age, and in this country. He was dubbed a heretic by some, but that is always a subjective point of view and what this nation needs with its current rash of possessed born-again christians on the one hand, and their partners in islamic extremism on the other, is a corrective presence of an Omar Khayyam, preferably in large doses. For these are times where piety has become equated with ostentatious religionism and even elevated, in certain recent instances, to the status of state policies by public servants whose private practices would hardly bear the rigid test of their own religious precepts. We are speaking here – to cite one example – of attempts to introduce religious separatism through the uniforms of schools pupils, and hospital nurses. Who knows, it would then be only a matter of time before a Minister for Police Affairs decides to create separate religious categories of uniforms for the Police Force, then the Army, the Air Force, the Navy and – why not – even overalls designed for workers on construction sites and in factories. But the greatest attempted crime, in my view, was the 'duoform' policy for schools, a most pernicious device for depriving children of that phase of humanistic oneness to which they are entitled, as an essential dimension of their positive knowledge of human society and the development of their sense of community.

We must take leave of these shores for a moment – we shall be back soon enough. My task today is to bring the two religious warring tribes of this nation to an understanding that they represent only a part of the many global strains of spiritual adhesion that constantly threaten to bring the world to that presumably blissful condition of nothingness, or Mahapralayi. Israel and India provide us with chastening examples, at least, those of us who still claim a capacity to think and to relate the experience of others to the latent threats within our community.

Israel represents, for me, a tragic instance of a people who fail to learn from their own history. The Jewish race, a people whom I have described in a different context as being endowed with an unfair proportion of the world's productive genius, persist, paradoxically, in demonstrating to the world that its people are just as enlightened as Sheikh Gunmi in their appreciation of the social and political consequences that attend religious insensitivity. The most recent penalty for this obtuseness, exacted from the largely moslem population of Palestinians, was twenty-seven lives in one fell swoop, the result of a provocative act by Jewish fundamentalists. When one considers, quite dispassionately, the height of arrogance entailed in the attempt, by those Jewish extremists, to lay the foundation of their own temple on a site considered as one of the holiest, possibly the second holiest of the moslem faith, it become quite easy to understand why even quite enlightened moslems all over the world genuinely feel and pronounce themselves under siege, why they even go as far as to accuse the rest of the world of a global conspiracy that threatens the very existence of their religion.

As if to lend further credence to this conspiracy theory, half-way across the globe in Northern India, a parallel event was taking place at the same time. The hindus made equally fanatical efforts to demolish an ancient mosque, nearly five centuries old. Their project was to build a hindu temple on that very site which, they claimed, was the birth-place of the hindu god, Rama. In a dramatic simultaneity across the globe therefore, two well populated and ancient religions, judaism and hinduism, were attempting to concretize their own variant of Sheikh Gunmi's credo. They were declaring and acting: 'Islam is nothing.' The international community, led by the United Nations, rose in unambiguous condemnation of such a credo, understanding quite well what its consequences would be. At the risk of losing his hold on government, the Prime Minister of India rejected such a divisive manifesto, sent in armed police and troops and sealed off the contested area. Over ten thousand hindus poured into the state of Uttar Pradesh; over a hundred were killed. And these were not simply illiterate, shirtless fanatics. They were led by an articulate parliamentarian whose party, the Bharatiya Janata, was a crucial partner in the coalition government of Prime Minister Singh. Mr Kishen Advant, leader of the coalition partner, gave his ultimatum to Singh: Demolish that mosque; Islam is nothing. Other equally articulate, scholarly men dissented. There was no evidence, as claimed by the hindu militants, that a hindu temple of any sort ever stood on that spot now occupied – for over five centuries – by the mosque. And of course no one, living or dead, could possibly offer proof that the god Rama was actually born on that spot. Well, a caution there. That very statement, for some, would constitute blasphemy. For the hindu to whom Rama is Rama, the beginning and the end, such skepticism would amount to saying, 'Hinduism is nothing.' To be caught even looking such a sentiment, within that stressed cauldron of Uttar Pradesh, would of course earn such an unbeliever instant and grisly death.

No one knows for certain what the ultimate death-toll was in the conflict between the secular imperatives of the state and the self-enclosed mandate of religion. The political casualty was predictable – the Bharatiya Janata withdrew its support from the government and Mr Singh fell as Prime Minister. Those who have followed the sanguinary course of religious conflicts in India will recognize, however, that this was only one of many such skirmishes. We are speaking here, alas, of a country whose industrial progress has been a source of envy to much of the so-called Third World, and indeed to several stagnant industrial economies of Europe. We are referring also to a nation which has led nearly all ex-colonial nations in exemplifying democratic principles in governance and made non-alignment a viable policy in global relations at a time when non-alignment was a truly crucial factor in preventing the Cold War from heating up and catapulting the world into that already prophesied state of Mahapralayi. Successive Indian governments however have found themselves unable to resolve definitively this upsurge of atavism among the many religious groups, a situation in which religious atrocities have become routine. A passenger bus on a highway; two or three armed men appear from ambush. The passengers are forced to disembark and separate into their religious persuasions. One group is machine-gunned on the spot – women and children are not spared. Or they are ordered to remain in the bus into which grenades are then thrown while the survivors are machine-gunned to death. There is not much point going into several other refinements to torture and brutaliza-tions which one feuding religious group inflicts on another – sikhs, hindus, moslems and others still, who do not care one way or the other about any of these upholders of spiritual dogmatism, those to whom religion is well and truly – nothing, but are trapped within the resultant social chaos. That grenade, rocket or fragmentation bomb is not yet born that can distinguish between sikh, christian or atheist – peek into the vortex of horror unleased on Sri Lanka through the unhealable breach between hindus and moslems, and you will be tempted to conclude that, in terms of indiscriminately inflicted atrocities, our own experience of civil war was nothing worse than a friendly football riot.

How sane and wise the agnostic irreverence of Omar Khayyam must be adjudged, when read against the literature of such pious savagery, how serene and humane its litany contrasted with the liturgy of dehumanization that insults the beasts of the jungle when we appropriate such expressions as bestiality to convey the depth to which humanity has sunk and continues to sink in upholding the unprovable, the merely imbibed or intuitively experienced. The poetry of Omar Khayyam and, of course, its pantheistic philosophy, its sublime iconoclasm, are infinitely more humanistic than any scriptures which tolerate, indeed promote the denial of human value or the sanctity of human life. Much, much saner to scoff at the reifications of what is ineffable, especially when centuries of contestation between sects and religions have succeeded in establish-ing nothing beyond the elaboration of their structures, and at such enormous human expenditure. Said the poet:

To be free from belief and unbelief is my religion.

Yet his accomodating spirit of communion results as well in the following suspiciously christianized lines from the Rubaiyat, full of sublime mischief:

> Wine is the liquid ruby, the flask the mine
> The cup its body, the wine the soul
> That crystal goblet laughing with the wine
> Is a tear, the heart's blood hidden within it.

Omar Khayyam's humility which stresses the uncertainty of knowledge, and the imperfectibility of the human mind as instrument for grasping the ineffable are virtues which are often obscured by his unapologetic celebration of *joie de vivre*, by his Epicurean vitality. These virtues are however of crucial relevance to our global religious plight, and we can do worse than resurrect such questing tempers of mind from centuries' neglect. Omar Khayyam's sense of inner harmony, translated into imperishable lines, may be the kind of music needed to rescue us from the cacophony of the warring sects and religious extremism:

> Would but the Desert of the Fountain yield
> One glimpse – if dimly, yet indeed, revealed
> To which the fainting Traveller might spring
> As springs the trampled herbage of the field.

Our institutions need to promote extra-curricula studies of the agonistics, for the terrain of learning should be that paradox of 'the desert and the fountain', its ideal denizen the 'fainting Traveller' pursuing the 'dim glimpse' of Truth.

Erase that temple! Demolish that mosque! Obliterate that cathedral! Flatten that shrine! Each major religion and even sect within the same religion appears periodically incapable of finding its own centre except by the act of reducing the other in some form or the other to nothing. It is very convenient that this lecture is taking place on this spot which, not so long ago, resounded to just such a rallying-cry of mindless intolerance. Suddenly, a cross, the christian symbol of faith which could claim to be nearly as old as this university, became a cause of spiritual debilitation for some moslems in the academic community – both students and lecturers. Ultimatums were delivered, protest marches were held. The moneyed fomentors of religious discord got in on the act and invaded Ibadan campus to address rallies, threatening armageddon if the cross was not removed. The Minister of Education summoned the Vice-Chancellor to Lagos; some day, I suppose, we shall have a truthful record of what actually transpired between them.

Let us not gloss over this shameful episode in the life of our premier university which even stirred christians to form vigilante groups and hold a wake around their cross to ward off any act of vandalism. It split long friendships, soured long established neighbourliness, poisoned collegiateship and implanted suspicion among colleagues. May I suggest here that these militants did not go far enough? They should have insisted that even the sign for Plus (+) in Mathematics should have been abolished because it looks like a cross. And the other side should have responded by abandoning the use of the bracket because it is suggestive of the symbol of the crescent. The passion which was aroused over this menace is perhaps best exemplified by a colleague in the Humanities, one of the gentlest and most urbane of beings you could wish to meet across a convivial or seminar table, not overly political nor overtly religious. 'I am a pacifist,' he said to me, 'and I cannot really call myself religious but, over this issue, I shall pick up a gun and fight.' What a relief to enter this campus a few years later and find that a plinth, bearing the islamic symbol of the star and crescent, has been erected close by the contumacious cross, and that no earthquake or other earthly convulsion has been reported within those holy grounds.

Violence appears to be the one constant in the histories of all the major religions of the world – a primitive aggressiveness, violence – despite the lip-service which their tenets pay to the need for tolerance, peace and understanding. We are concerned here with the practice, the manifested presences of these religions, not the scriptures which we know can both condemn and extol holy hostility towards non-believers within the same chapter. Even today, as we approach the end of the twentieth century, a century in which man has broken almost all the frontiers of the universe and challenged Nature in its preeminence over phenomenological ordering, yes, even today, we need only pick up any journal or tune in the radio or television to any corner of the world, and you may depend upon it – a new inhuman act, some new destructive conflict is certain to have surfaced somewhere, one that is tracable to one or other or the so-called major religions. It is time that these religions took stock of themselves, re-examined their social tendencies in the light of a constantly evolving world and resolve to transcend their violent histories. This act of re-examination will, however, remain incomplete if it is wholly self-centred. By this I mean that it is not enough to examine their own course in world history but to equally re-examine the very nature of other beliefs with which they have interacted in their passage through history, including those which they do not accept as religions. We are referring here, to put it mildly, to the reality of structured ignorance – not merely intolerance – but ignorance and misconceptions of other systems of beliefs whether as philosophies, religions or world-views. Even when some of these religions – such as christianity, islam, etc. – have been affected, or infected by aspects of other beliefs, and religious practices, it is my contention that such religions have failed to grasp the essence of those other faiths which now constitute 'impurities' within their own spiritual blood-stream. They prefer to persecute manifestations of such realities, to excommunicate or indeed exterminate them, thereby depriving themselves of the most rudimentary knowledge of the other. Not that they ever read this attitude as one of deprivation, on the contrary. You cannot deprive yourself of the knowledge of what does not exist. It is always far, far simpler to proceed along the Gunmistic dictum: the other is nothing. Nothing is there. Whatever appeared to be there is mere appearance, Satan-induced illusion, a nothing being.

Is it surprising therefore, that when the real estate of this very campus was being parcelled out, at the inception of this university, the christians got theirs, the moslems got theirs, but not traditional religions? The falling out between these two favoured monopolists of campus religious stakes three decades later therefore provided me only malicious pleasure and, if the security of academia and indeed, the entire question of religious tolerance on a national level were not involved, would have left me totally indifferent.

By the time I returned to this campus in 1960 after an absence of four years, the anglican, the roman catholic and islamic commuities had erected their places of worship on campus, but no one appeared to have given thought to the righfulness of indigenous religious presence on the soil of Nigeria's premier university. I began a campaign which ran straightaway against the ramparts of the Gunmistic dictum manned by both christians and moslems: 'Traditional religion is nothing,' they declared, in loud and clear terms. That campaign petered out on Abadina soil with my departure, but I was able to resurrect it at Ife when I transferred there, succeeding eventually in obtaining land allocation for a unified place of worship of African deities which we named *Orule Orisa*. Whether that shelter has been erected or not I do not know, but at least, recognition had been accorded a spirituality that was marginalized by the aggressive, often bloody intrusion of christianity and islam onto this continent, a spirituality which, despite its seeming effacement, has continued to spread across the globe, providing sources of spiritual strength to our kin in the Diaspora and acting as a rallying-point in their struggle for liberation and human dignity. I seize every occasion to call attention to the resilience and vibrancy of these religions; I shall do so again today employing extracts from statements I have made before. Their validity remains unchanged and the repeat a necessary warning against the unrepentant in this stubborn reiteration of the Nothingness credo against African spirituality. He must constantly remind the world that . . .

> . . . religions do exist, such as on this continent, that can boast of never having launched a war, any form of jihad or crusade, for the furtherance of their beliefs. Yet those beliefs have proved themselves bedrocks of endurance and survival, informing communities as far away as the Caribbean and the Americas.
>
> Is there, or is there not a lesson for our universe in this? Is there no lesson here for those dogmatic, over-scriptured and over-annotated monumentalities whose rhetoric and secular appropriations far exceed the ascertainable, inner verities of their spiritual claims? The religions of this continent rescued us as conscious race in the Diaspora, preserved our identity and, what is more, infected even those claimants to a superior knowledge of the Supreme Deity – those religions whose exalted high priests sometimes claim to be on a first-name acquaintance with their deities, on whose personal authority they mete out diabolical punishments to unbelievers, even for secular activities. Such elaborate beliefs, truths or fantasies, should be allowed to exist in their own right, but *in their own place*. This, in the sphere of religion, constitutes the ultimate challenge of the twenty-first century mind. It is not a new project; it dates back to the

beginnings of man and has probably claimed more martyrs than most causes of human liberation. The dismal records of the Roman Catholic Inquisition are available to us, so is the iconoclasm of Protestant missionaries on African soil, as are the unspeakable cruelties perpetrated on African humanity in the name of Islamic conversion, or the preservation of the purity of sheer spiritual institutions.

I must not be misunderstood. I extol, indeed, I partake with creative and humane enlargement, in the inherent and productive values of all religions, their monumental legacies to the world, their piety and unflagging spirit of the search for truth. I acknowledge that the world would be a much poorer place without the phenomenon of religion.

I do not refer here merely to their architectural and artistic legacies but even to the inspirational value of their scriptures, the lyricism in which they are frequently couched, and the intellectual challenges of their exegeses. You will find this a frequently recurring theme in previous essays and lectures. In *Myth, Literature, and the African World*, for instance, the following typical passages will be found in a chapter which deals with the works of Hampate Ba and Cheikh Hamidou Kane:

> In colonial societies which constantly seek a world-view to challenge the inherent iniquities of any philosophy that can be associated with colonial intrusion, we naturally encounter works which make a point of claiming that Islam – a very effective organised challenge to Christian cultural authority – is one religion whose ethics, philosophy and forms of worship reconcile races and encourage universal fraternalism. Hampate Ba's *Tierno Bokar* is a very persuasive biography of a Muslim sage, the Sage of Bandiagara. At the basis of Tierno Bokar's teaching is the simple message of a universal humanism, a belief in an eventual tolerance and mutual generosity of sufficient strength to transcend historic memory.

And again, on Cheik Hamidou Kane's *Ambiguous Adventure*:

> That quality of the language of the Koran which Kane describes as a 'sombre beauty' he tries consciously to capture in his own prose. The quality comes out even in translation, cleanly sculpted, yet mysterious and often elusive, suggestive of much that is left unspoken, layers of perception that need paring away.

There is hardly one religion in the world which fails to extol godhead as truth, or beauty. God is truth, we are consistently reminded. God is truth; god is beauty. Well then, if these properties of godhead are universally acknowledged, can we not then simply agree among ourselves there wherever we find truth, then an element of godhead is present? That where there is beauty, and wisdom, there indeed exist aspects of godhead? We need not go so far as to conclude that wherever we find truth, wisdom and beauty there also exists godhead, no. For the sake of present argument, it will be sufficient to accept that wherever we find truth, wisdom and beauty in their purest essence, we have indeed glimpsed fundamental attributes of godhead. After all, religion itself preaches and illustrates this goal of human striving, urges mankind to approach, emulate or be worthy of godhead by assimilating and demonstrating these qualities in mundane activities, in social relationships and in the manifest creativity of the human mind. The architectures of various religious tempers separated in time and space are evident attempts to capture the immanence of godhead in mundane but creative language, arbitrated by the cultural idioms of various human communities. If, therefore, we, as sentient beings, can respond with a sense of elevation to the enduring islamic architecture of a Suileman the Magnificent, to the flaring Gothic cathedrals of European medieval churches, to the Dorian temples of the Greek pantheon, the elaborate temple of Anghor Wat in Cambodia, the ancient shinto temples of Japan, the extravagant hindu temples which litter the Asian continent, the caryatid-studded shrines of African *orisa* whose profoundest creative responses to the mysteries of godhead are scattered all over the museums of the world and in numerous private collections ... we merely respond to essences of the intuition of beauty which becomes elevated to the status of godhead.

The ungodly in any religious conception are not therefore those who respond to the commonality of the intuition of godhead in a way different from ours, but those who set about the destruction of such manifestations whose idioms they do not understand. The Khmer Rouge in Cambodia for instance acted as barbarians, as no better than mean-spirited thugs in their conduct towards the spiritual treasures of Cambodia. We need not be hindus to recognize this, and to dub the Khmer Rouge ungodly iconoclasts for their 'pogrom' of the hindu gods. Similarly, both christian and moslem invaders on the African continent share the inglorious resoponsibility for their pogrom of Africa's spiritual heritage. And we must call attention here to a singularly blasphemous contestation between these two, one which is long overdue for terminal dismissal: this blasphemy is summed up in the proposition, so well beloved of their proselytizers, that one or the other of these two religions is obviously indigenous to the continent, while the other is alien, or foreign. Indigenous? Indeed! It is a purely self-serving rhetoricism which belongs in the same school of 'reasoning' that claims that Arab enslavement of Africans was more humane than European enslavemnt, or vice versa. We must request that this gratuitious justification of any form of imperialism – spiritual, political or cultural – be restricted to the privileged circles of those whose ancestors were the slave raiders and merchants; it should not be uttered within earshot of those who are yet surrounded by the evidence of their historic dehumanization. For those who are truly interested in the subject of comparative religions, and the purely academic issues of compatible features, three distant religions come easily to mind which may boast certain truly significant aspects of some African religions. One is that of pre-islamic Egypt; another is that of ancient Greece, and a third is the hindu religion. When you recall current practices of some of these religions however – take the case of the goddess Kali in hindu religion – you will understand why I am not over-anxious to draw too much attention to such similarities. Let us leave the subject purely in the academic realm. It is enough to emphasize the obvious truth: before either islam or christianity can propose that that it is tailor-fitted for the nude body of African spirituality, it should first take a spiritual journey through ancient Egypt, ancient Greece and the Far East of hinduism.

Nearly everly religion develops sects, even cults, which then proceed to act contrary to the fundmental precepts and articles of faith within that religion. It is sad that many of those who comment on African religions are ignorant of the differences between religions and cults in general on the one hand, and between religion and those specific cults which spring up in relation to certain observances within that religion. Far too many inanities are uttered in this respect. To such an extent has this mind-closure developed that such commentators do not even permit themselves to take account of the empirical evidence manifested in the continuing, public celebrations of such religions. The last annual festival of the river goddess Osun attracted such sadly typical responses, the most notorious of which came from one *ewi* singer based in this very city, Ibadan. The festival of Osun remains one of the most community-cohering events of a spiritual dimension in the Yoruba calendar. Those who are so blinded by the prejudices of imported religions that they cannot share, even vicariously, in its emission of joy and communal well-being are to be pitied, but they should at least spare us the negative, unreflective predictability of their pronouncements. We know of course that much of their intervention derives, not from any deep spiritual impulsion, but from a hunger for notoriety, a trend which is identifiable among extremists of every religion. The business of assuaging such hunger should not, however, be undertaken at the expense of the sensibilities of others who contain themselves within their own spiritual serenity and do not interfere with the faiths of different believers. The competitiveness for public attention has become the hallmark of so-called piety in our society, leading even to the obscene development of self-declared seers of the future, who trigger off and feed upon the anxiety neurosis of their fellow men and women. Let me make myself clear: I see nothing intrinsically evil in any claims to foresee the future. What we must deplore is the crude attempt to bring individuals or their circle of friends or family under the power of any spiritualist pretender, by strewing their paths with fictitious disasters. The purpose is childishly evident; the expectation is that such public targets, or their relations, would come running to you, monsters of prophetic impudence, placing themselves under your presumed spiritual protection in order to ward off imminent evil. Unfortunately, there is enough insecurity in society, in the lives of many, for some to succumb under this transparent ploy.

We need to spell this out in distinct terms. There is an implicit assault, which should be actionable, in the publicized prediction of illness, misfortune or death for any individual. Those who wish may go further and call it a psychic assault. Certainly, it contains elements of psychological warfare, not simply against the named individual –

and this is what needs stressing – it is an assault not merely against the specific individual but against his friends, colleagues and relations. The individual himself is usually quite indifferent; it is the orbit of his relationships, usually far more susceptible, that vulnerably protective extension of the individual against whom the barrage is principally directed. We need not dwell too long on this brand of religious opportunism. Let me call your attention to my play *Requiem for a Futurologist*, written about eight years ago, in which I focussed attention on this escalating tendency. I recommend it to all acting companies, amateur or professional, schools, universities etc. You do not even need to write me for permission to stage it. I donate the play, in entirety, in excerpts, quotes etc. to be used for Nigerian stage performances, so as to prune these merchants of anxiety to banal dimensions. Since, when *Requiem* was written, our media prophets had not even remotely approached their present level of presumptuousness, it should be clear that it is I, not they, who can claim from evidence of these current developments, to be the genuine prophet. Read that play, *Requiem*, and see whether or not you agree with me.

But enough of these localized disgressions. Let us make an attempt to summarize the ironic history of man's spirituality, ironic in the sense that even while nearly all religions that we know of pay lip-service to the concept that man is, in his most fundamental being, spirit or soul, it is the very realm of that common denominator of man's spirituality, or soulfulness, that man has insisted most fanatically, and self-destructively, on remaining most humanly divisive. It is a contradiction that does not speak highly of the rationality of *homo sapiens*, yet, ironically once again the causes may be found in the very rational processes undertaken by man to arrive at a satisfactory definition of his being. I suspect that this is due to a tendency of man to short-change his species by embarking on this definition, this attempt to capture the essence of his being, through an isolationist procedure. That is to say, isolating, then consecrating what appears to be man's most distinctive function at any given phase of the development or evolution of his species. As a function of human reason, this compulsivenss to grasp and express the beingness of ourselves is of course inevitable. What am I? Who am I? Why am I? These are fundamental questions of thinking, feeling and sensing being, and the first – What am I? – we can safely state, is the commencing question for human self-apprehension; certainly it has preoccupied sages and philosophers since our knowledge of the evolution of today's human species.

The hidden corollary of that first question however, manifested in patterns of what we may term 'otherness exclusion' has been – 'What is the other?' I do not say for a moment that it is an ineluctable component. I accept, indeed, I insist that the question 'What am I?' was, in fact, a quest for the totality of the species. In short, it stood for: What are we? Who are we? Why are we? – not 'What is the otherness of – that one?' At some point in human evolution however, certainly a point which must remain permanently lost to us, the 'otherness' of the other half of community became a critical issue. On the individual level it must have occurred very, very early. The mere contest between one primitive ancestor and another for a fruit or shiny piece of stone, or a shelter, must have consecrated, for all time, in human consciousness, the distinction between 'I' and 'the other'. With the honing of the rational processes through constant reflections upon the exterior, material world, and the arbitration of a new challenge with the deductions of a prior encounter, we may further assume that even the exchange of notes between two primitive ancestors on reality would not always remain identical, and would lead, eventually to at least a suspicion that 'I' am in some ways different from 'that other'. The question 'What am I?' or 'Who am I?' becomes progressively ego-centred.

That same process of differentiation applies even more obviously in primitive encounters between communities, or between an individual and a newly encountered community. The evolution of xenophobia, racism and other programmes of exclusion in human relationships owes much indeed, to what really may be accounted an innocent intellectual pastime, the instinct towards self-apprehension. It is not therefore the question that is at fault but the answers, and here I must take you back to the observation with which I commenced this revision exercise, namely, that humanity does tend to short-change itself in its effort to grasp, and to express the complexity of its functional being. This intellectual tendency did not begin with Descartes, though we cannot deny him credit for its axiomatic popularization: 'I think; therefore, I am.' Stripped of all pretentions however, such premises are little more than philosophical constructs which mimic a familiar figure of speech termed synecdoche, the metaphor which substitutes a part for the whole. A linguistic conceit makes no rigid claims on truth however, nor does it even insist on literal correlations; it is merely a convenient or ornamented way of naming names, whereas its structural relations in the philosophies do tend to limit our intellectual range by their dogmatic assertions, especially once they acquire the patina of time, reverence and ancestry. It is always best to regard most philosophical claims as figures of thought, nothing more, simply figures of thought on which rational edifices are mounted just in the same way as the architecture of an aesthetic product may create or sustain an ethical structure, operating through what we have already described as a metaphorical device. Perhaps one of the most famous examples of this particular deployment of the synecdoche is to be found in that well-known poem, 'Death the Leveller':

> Sceptre and crown
> Must tumble down
> And in the dust be equal made
> With the poor crooked scythe and spade

I have of course invoked that example in a spirit of bias. It enables me to proceed to other figures of thought which once derived from, then held sway in actual social relationships, and still do in some societies. 'Sceptre and crown' versus 'scythe and spade': I rule, therefore I am. 'You do not, therefore you are not.' The pattern of division of the species, class or functional definition, innocent or prejudicial, oppressive or indifferent, overt or implicit, will be found indeed to have a long history, a history as old as the habit of reflection in the human species. Long, long before Descartes, neolithic man had come to his own practical suspicion that 'I make, therefore I am.' The articulating voice of man the rudimentary technician may have been muted, since he simply expressed his being in his artifact, through the process of making, but that does not deny him a self-consciousness attained through the act of making things to enhance and even reproduce his existence. To transfer rapidly to contemporary times, need I remind you that Leopold Sedar Senghor took on Descartes and his thesis of rational (racial?) exclusivity by proposing his negritudinist credo of: 'I feel, therefore, I am.' My position on that proposition is already notorious; I shall not rehash it here.

My interest is really to call attention to what is perhaps the most insidious of all such exclusivist dicta, a religious one, whose stridency both historically and in contemporary times, has taken on aggressive and territorially rapacious proportions. For me, this dictum is the most persistent credo that militates against the evolution of a harmonious, all embracing human community. Permit me to hold you in suspense long enough to observe that the marxist world had obscured this particular dictum most effectively, with its own economic deduction – 'I produce, therefore I am' – a dictum which it opposed to the human alienation of capitalism whose pernicious credo may be summed up as: 'I have, therefore, I am.' We do have to spell out its anti-thesis: 'You do not have, therefore you are not, you are less than nothing,' to grasp the obscenity embedded in this specific schism between affluent being, and impoverished nothingness. Let those who wish celebrate the present blunting of the marxist tool; the battle to eliminate that distinction will continue to occupy societies as long as inequality is manifested or enthroned as a principle of social ordering.

The force and persuasiveness of marxism's economic approach to history and social development must, ironically, take a lot of the blame for underrating the force of this last reductionist dictum which has so successfully eroded the goal of a single comity of man, always remembering that, as I have emphasized already, it is the implicit or expressed anti-thesis of every such dictum that wreaks the havoc: 'I believe, therefore, I am.' 'You do not believe, therefore you are not.' No doubt the 'believers' of every so-called major religion will claim that they do not deny humanity to 'unbelievers' but, history, even contemporary history, gives them the lie. The dictum is embedded in their daily pronouncements, their daily activities, exhortations, disseminated precepts, social attitudes etc., etc., but, most critically and dangerously, even in their political acts and pronouncements. When all else fails, and even before all else has been attempted, it supplies the fuel for the machinery of tyrannical political schemes, social advantages and other forms of opportunism. 'I believe, therefore, I am.' 'You disbelieve, therefore you are not'; therefore, you count for nothing. You are subhuman. You are outside the pale of humanity, outside the concept of community. On our home front we have watched helplessly as this escalates to the periodic slaughter of 'infidels'.

The tactics being employed by Saddam Hussein in his attempt to turn a straight-forward expansionist adventure gone wrong into a contest between 'believers' and 'non-believers' is our most recent cautionary instance of the vulnerability of humanity – even this late in the century – when assailed by the doctorine of being and nothingness. This lecture, which was conceived before the outbreak of hostilities, will not attempt to address that ongoing drama of human failure; it contents itself simply with drawing attention to the perils of such emotive divisiveness. Anyone is free to engage in the mother, grandfather and great ancestor of all wars, but the world must not be set on fire through cheap recourse to the most primitive of all human instincts – that of religion. Even within the permissible rhetoric of war, such opportunism must be isolated in its own capsule, and tranquilized. As for our own nation, whose several tendencies are so readily susceptible to alien winds, this government has a responsibility to listen carefully to those who, on either side, attempt to cloak this madness in religious gear. Then it should provide them places in the presidential jet, and fly them to the Gulf. And they should wear round their necks, for identifiction purposes, the framed cartoon from *The Champion* of 16 January 1992. It is a cartoon that speaks directly to the current world dilemma.

For the rest, I wish only to exhort you: study the spirituality of this continent. As in all things, selectiveness is the key. To limit myself to that with which I am on familiar grounds, I say to you: go to the *orisa*, learn from them and be wise. The religion of the *orisa* does not permit, in tenets, liturgy, catechism or practice, that pernicious dictum: 'I believe, therefore I am.' Nowhere will you find the sheerest skein of reasoning in that direction to human self-apprehension. Obviously, therefore, you will not find its corollary: 'You do not believe, therefore you are not.' Orunmila does not permit it. Obatala cannot conceive of it. Ogun will take up arms against it. No one *odu* of IFA so much as suggests it. It is not weakness in the character of this religion however, it is not even tolerance. It is simply – understanding. Wisdom. An intuitive grasp of the complexity of the human mind, and a true sense of the infinite potential of the universe.

I shall end with certain precepts which I extracted and formalized from this religion some ten years ago, when, during the battle to establish a place of communion with the Yoruba deities, at the University of Ife, the suggestion was made that this ancient system of belief did not qualify for consideration as religion because it had no written scriptures. Imagine that! The scholars of a society which never ceases to extol its oral culture actually attempt to deny its most fundamental intuitions because they are not printed, annotated and marketed. When convenient, the same academics will make use of that familiar quote: 'When a griot, or an ancestor dies, it is an entire library that vanishes.' Come to religion however, this same breed of intellectuals employs the alien yardstick of their spiritual and intellectual enslavers to annihilate the spiritual heritage of that same society. No matter, I went to work and elicited a set of seven precepts from the teachings of the *orisa*. I shall leave you with them: they cannot be refuted by anything that has come down to us, in lyric, liturgy, or mode of worship from these primordial forces that the concerted might of islam and christianity have failed to crush:

OBATALA fulfils. Purity, love, transparency of heart. Stoical strength. Luminous truth. Man is imperfect; man strives towards perfection. Yet even the imperfect may find interior harmony with Nature. Spirit overcomes blemish – be it of mind or body. Oh peace that giveth understanding, possess our human heart.

SEEK understanding of the signposts of existence. Is knowledge not within and around us? If the Supreme Fount of Thought sought counsel of ORUNMILA in the hour of crisis, why will you by-pass the seer of signposts, O seeker of knowlege? Wisdom may slumber on the gums of infants – lucky that man who patiently awaits the loosening of infant tongues. IFA maps the course through shrouded horizons.

OGUN set the example: follow. Virtue wears the strangest garb – comradeship in strife, meditation in solitude, the hardy route of self-sacrifice . . . Life is multiple and strange. The death of fear liberates the will that sets forth where no mind ever trod. OGUN liberates: Rise beyond his shadow.

JUSTICE is the mortar that kneads the dwelling-place of man. Can mere brick on brick withstand the bloodied cries of wrong from the aggrieved? No more than dark withstands the flare of lightning, roofs of straw the path of thunderbolts. SANGO restores.

HONOUR to the ANCESTORS. If blood flows in you, tears run, bile courses, if the soft planet of brain pulses with thought and sensing, and earth consumes you in the end, then you, with your ancestors, are one with the fluid elements. If the beast knows what herbs of the forest are his friends, what plea shall man make that boasts superior knowledge, yet knows no empathy with moisture of the air he breathes, the juice of leaves, the sap in his roots to earth, or the waters that nourish his being? Man may speak OYA, OSUN, ORISA-OKO . . . yet mind and spirit encompass more than a mere litany of names. Knowledge is ORISA.

ORISA preaches Community: Found it! This, no honest man will deny: man has failed the world or the world has failed mankind. Then question further: What faiths and realms of values have controlled our earth till now? And next: since their gods have failed, may ours not yield forgotten ways that remedy?

THE WILL of man is placed beyond surrender. Without the knowing of Divinity by man, can Deity survive? O hesistant one, Man's conceiving is fathomless; his community will rise beyond the present reaches of the mind. ORISA reveals Destiny as – SELF-DESTINATION.

APPENDIX: RESPONSES IN KIND

Introduction

Would a calling-card inscribed 'Consultant in Medieval Manuscripts' elicit, from the average student or literary scholar, any more than informative interest? I doubt it. Or a notice in the Business Section of a Telephone Directory in which the advertiser has bought space to announce himself a 'Consultant in Sanskrit Religious Scrolls', 'Egyptian Hieroglyphic Literature', etc., etc.? One might, admittedly, wonder if some new discovered hoards in the vaults of some ancient monastery had loosed a collectors' fever on some parts of the world. Beyond that however, it is unlikely that such notices would provoke more than the raised eyebrow of a mildly casual interest. Changing now to a somewhat differing field of specialist interests, it would not be considered unusual if, embarked on a business enterprise, one began by seeking out a 'Business Consultant'. 'Engineering Consultants' abound for those in construction of manufacturing projects . . . and so on. Then why, I found myself demanding some years ago, why did I undergo such a peculiar feeling, bordering on the disordered, on receiving a letter at the bottom of whose notepaper was the rubric: 'Consultants in African Literature'?

What did this signify?

As title of course, one is only too familiar with professional identification in such phrasing as 'Lecturer in/Professor of/Research Fellow in . . . French/German/Arabic, etc., Literature'. But consultants in . . . ? This was new, and strange. I suppose that some of the unformed questions in my mind were: What did this make of African Literature? What did this make of me, as one of the producers of this body of literature? Could it be, after all, that African literature had become a business? A market commodity just like any other? Or maybe even a disease – Consultants in Muscular Dystrophy/African Literature? It would have helped if, in my literary career, I had come in contact with 'Consultants in Armenian, Irish or Russian Literature'. I never had! So what was I to make of this new phenomenon? Had I become, unwittingly, a middleman in a literary version of a renewed flesh trade?

A comparatively innocent example perhaps of the kind of chequered responses which

'African literature' has provoked among critics of all shades of colour, vested interests and ideology since its expression, in *European languages*, noticeably transcended the event of occasional emergence some three decades ago. At the beginning, this literature was definitely the exclusive preserve of a tiny handful of European commentators, not all of which limited company could truthfully claim to possess even the most rudimentary literary analytic skills. Such made up for this deficiency by promotional skills. In the main, their approach was marked by an undiscriminatory enthusiasm which went quite straightforwardly for blanket exposure, uncomplicated by any selective obligations. The successive stages followed quite logical development: territorial competition marked by increasing sophistry and/or sophistication in critical styles. We will not pursue here the mixed career of this new-discovered enterprise – the sweeping generalizations, the impudence of claims which masked disinterest in and/or ignorance of the cultural variants of the African literary products; cavalier imposition of regional and thematic parameters to provide a veneer of studiousness and research. The categorizations, slapdash, facile categorizations which such critics would never dare impose on the literatures of their own societies – all these soon bred a violent revolt among the writers themselves who began to respond in kind, appalled by the – to put it bluntly – literary lies that had begun to gain currency about their works and the environment that produced them.

Of course these matters are never quite straightforward. If the writers strove to recover their material from false alien interpreters, there were also other Africans, usually the non-creative ones, whose sole mission was, like early independence politicians, to wrest the 'authority' of the departing colonial critics and step uncritically into their shoes. This breed, in short, had no interest whatever in literature, only in AUTHORITY. They begin and end their argument very simply on the premise that the non-African has no business whatever pronouncing upon African literature. This of course leaves the field clear for their own round of rape on the literary products of their compatriots.

But how do these black rapists distance themselves from the white act of rape? Alas, only in the gratuitous violence of approach, in the violent appropriation of literary material and its violent mutilation. The criticism of the past decade and a half has been marked by a violence of language and mindless destructiveness the like of which I have yet to encounter in any other literary culture – certainly not in such a sustained intensity. Not even during violent social revolutions when the slightest ambiguity in ideological content of a work is seized upon as proof of dangerous, subversive sympathies. To such an extent has this violence become competitive that a certain school has even proudly labelled itself 'bolekaja' critics, this in order to place its practitioners beyond any form of rules of combat or knowledge of its subject.

'Bolekaja' means, literally, 'come down, let's fight'. The form of West African transport which bears that name, also known as a 'Mammy Wagon' or 'passenger lorry', is an expression of transportation torture on four wheels. Crowded, lethal in accidents – its carriage simply disintegrates like matchwood – it is a form of cheaply constructed, usually unlicensed instrument of death which bears on its front and/or side panels a series of admonitions which alas, are very blithely ignored by the suicide-bent drivers. The competition for passengers – those who have no choice except for this form of transport – is keen and noisy. The *bolekaja* tout has to scream for attention. Sometimes this competition results in a tug-of-war for the luggage or the very person of the traveller. The luggage may end in one vehicle, a toddler in another, while the mother is struggling to extricate herself from the interior of a third. Within the vehicle itself, with humans crushed against one another and against market produce, sheep and other livestock, suffocated by the stench of rotting food and anonymous farts, tempers tend to be short and fights break out even within the cramped space. A character in my play *The Road*, a timber lorry driver who bears the exotic name 'Say Tokyo Kid', comments on the *bolekaja*:

> You take any kind of load. You carrying rubbish. You carrying lepers. The
> women tell you to stop because they's feeling the call of nature. If you don't
> stop they pee in your lorry. And whether you stop or not their chirren mess
> the place all over. The whole of the lorry is stinking from rotting food and all
> kinda refuse. That's a passenger lorry.

Normally of course, 'critics' who identify themselves with the mental abdication of this level of existence should be beneath notice. And so, for a long time, they were. But then of course, stung by the fact that the world of sense ignored them, their lies grew bolder, their noise more deafening. They quickly recognized their very excess as marketable commodities especially on the lecture circuits of American colleges where freaks and seers are accorded equal interest. Not for nothing do the Yoruba observe, *Wèrè dùún wò, kò se e bí l'ómo'.** Even literary magazines of repute began to commission essays from them for a 'alternative view', a 'controversial angle'. In these cases however, such essays ended up being sent to the writers who have been honoured by their attention for their own response, as editorial self-protection against the laws of libel. I have selected among this *bolekaja* school just two local examples which should serve, I believe, for all others who are yet struggling to attain their level of notoriety. Both extremes of the ideological spectrum are covered by this choice – one is from the extreme, reactionary right wing (and accidentally black); the other, a white expatriate's, represents, on the evidence of his writings, the extreme 'radical' left. So, both race and ideology are catered for in this uneasy partnership. It would be unwise to ignore the *bolekaja* squad in a collection like this, as long as they are quarantined, for the health of literature, in their own ghetto, appropriately titled, 'Responses in Kind'.

'The Autistic Hunt' is a response to a lengthy essay by Geoffrey Hunt (twenty-eight pages of foolscap, small print, $1\frac{1}{2}$ spacing) titled 'Two Views of African Culture: Soyinka Versus Cabral'. Its history is noteworthy. After being rejected as a contribution

---

* The lunatic is entertaining to watch, but who prays to have one for a child?

to a periodic literary conference at the University of Ibadan whose theme is 'Radical Perspectives', Geoffrey Hunt began to shop around for a journal that would accept his stillborn child. It should be noted that the reason for this rejection, according to one of the 'editorial collective', was its shoddy scholarship and a language that revolted even the stomach of the radical organizers whose efforts I have dubbed elsewhere as 'The Annual Leftocratic Convention'. Embarassed however by Geoffrey Hunt's campus propaganda to the effect that the leftists had betrayed their cause and were shielding this 'sacred cow' from his Marxist fire, he was encouraged to re-write his text in more acceptable language and re-present it for publication in *Positive Review*, the journal published by the same group which organized the conferences on 'Radical Perspectives'. The result was an even lengthier essay, and with none of its scurrility toned down. In desperation, the editors invited a response from me which they had decided would be published at the same time as Hunt's masterpiece.

In the meantime, Geoffrey Hunt had begun to shop around international leftist journals for a platform for his diatribe. CLIO magazine in the US was one of many which sent the article to me, exactly as did *Positive Review*. Of course, the version sent to CLIO was much toned down. A number of elementary gaffes which I pointed out in my reply (a copy of which had been also sent to him by the Editorial 'Collective' trying to bend doubly backwards to be fair to all sides) these gaffes had been either corrected or placed in a less ridiculous form. Mr Hunt had done his best to eliminate all aspects of ideological illiteracy but there was nothing he could do, since he lacked the training, to hide his yawning ignorance on the subjects of culture and of literature, one of the expressive media of culture. I wrote back to CLIO to state that I was not interested in responding to a bowdlerized version of the original article which was not only in circulation in mimeographed copies on university campuses – Mr Hunt had a one-man evangelical mission to reform the literary perceptions of the Nigerian intelligentsia – but was already cited in his Curriculum Vitae in support of his application for promotion to the grade of lecturer – or was it merely confirmation of appointment? At the Faculty Board meeting, I saw this 'learned paper' listed as either 'being considered for publication' or 'submitted for publication' – I forget which. I, of course, abstained from all discussion on this expatriate's advancement.

And this should have ended the shameless opportunism. *Positive Review*, for reasons, I was told, of the sheer problems of space, would not print the 'learned paper' and its response. Mr Hunt proceeded for the next ten to twelve years to hawk around this essay which he had listed as proof of scholarship deserving advancement, diverging from time to time to put African leaders such as Kwame Nkrumah through his peculiar ideological wringers. Finally, in 1986 to be exact, it found a home in an anthology of African Marxist Criticism,* his lack of credentials balanced in the volume by the credibility of other Marxist thinkers. It is, I find, ridiculous to expect this object of Mr Hunt's attention to keep up with the very latest versions of a twelve-year old odyssey upon

* Georg Gugelburger (ed.), *Marxism and African Literature*, 1986, London James Currey Ltd.

which he strove to ride into academic prominence in a Nigerian university. The original response, written in the same critical style as his, but with far more respect for truth, must represent my offering here to this particular pole of the *bolekaja* axis. My concern is to situate the 'critic' in his sociological actuality, an actuality little known outside a closed 'ivory' circle, an actuality made up of those calculating, trite, opportunistic motivations which lead the critic to abandon – if he ever had one – a genuine concern for the literary corpus or the triggering cultural mechanism of a society.

Chinweizu Ibekwe, *a.k.a.* Chinweizu, but whom we all know in our Nigerian journalistic circles as Chichidodo* is, by contrast an Africanist African. Such is the nominal thoroughness of his black authenticity that he NEVER publicly acknowledges his father's name Ibekwe, which, in case anyone is in any doubt, is as hundred percent an African (Igbo) name as you will find on the East side of the Niger. The Igbo, and other African societies too, have a proverb for a son who does not answer to his father's name, but I shall not repeat it here. Ibekwe can lay claim to the credit of giving the name *bolekaja* to our school of critical writing. He remains, without dispute, the unchallenged exemplar of this genre. The essay 'Neo-Tarzanism' (shortly after followed by a second part) was a response to an essay in *Transition* Magazine in 1974, written by him in collaboration with Jemie and Madubuike. This essay did not merely slander African poesy; its hectoring tone, the crudity of its language and totalitarian presumptuousness demanded that this trio be countered at once on their own terms even as their literary ignorance was exposed. 'Neo-Tarzanism' is presented here as the major cause – for those who have marvelled at the seeming derailment of Mr Ibekwe's rationality – of a thirteen-year long self-destroying obsession of this 'critic' with the works of Wole Soyinka. In several dozens of essays, monograms, lectures on the American college circuit, in newspaper columns, in a book laudably titled *Towards the Decolonization of African Literature*, Mr Chinweizu has occupied his entire productive life with replying to this one essay.

I have not read *Towards the Decolonization* in book form but discussions with those who have indicate – at least that part which deals with Chichidodo's favourite subject – that it has substantially incorporated the contents of a manuscript which he submitted for a Festschrift to which he had been invited to contribute in honour of this very writer. That manuscript, like so many essays of his, was sent to me by the would-be editor, not so much for my response – she had already decided that it was sanely impossible to use – but out of curiosity. Was there a 'history', she wanted to know, behind such evident 'sickness'? The essay has since been published – never all at once but several times over, in bits and snippets, re-hashes, re-arrangements of contexts and changes of departure points, but always with the most industrious repetitiveness. There has never, therefore, been any need to honour Chichidodo with another line of reply,

---

* According to Ayi Kwei Armah (*The Beautiful Ones Are Not Yet Born*), a Ghanian bird which, even as it loudly protests that it is revolted by excrement, nevertheless feeds fat on the worms that inhabit it.

any more than there is to address oneself to his opposite number, the 'Marxist' Geoffrey Hunt, his expatriate fellow tout in the *bolekaja* motor park.

It would however be instructive to 'describe' at least, this master-text from which every word and phrase that Chichidodo has written and uttered in twenty years is taken, and some of its subsequent history – again, in the interest of the sociology of the critic. This contribution to a Festschrift on Wole Soyinka runs to eighty-five pages (!) It was backed by a screaming – yes, screaming – letter to the editor, that not one word, not one comma be taken out. The magnum opus must be published entire! Of these eighty-five pages, five are taken up with footnotes. (One aspect of *bolekajary* which, in reality, craves academic respectability is in the magnitude of its footnotes.) The significance of the footnotes in this particular context will be shortly apparent. The title, by the way, for this author who 'castigates' other critics and writers for indulging in literary references from European works is: 'Soyinkaism: Eliza Doolittle as Ariel'.

On page 4 of this tome, in the introductory section that is, Chichidodo writes:

> In a well known remark he made early in his career, Soyinka declared that he wanted to be a writer, not an *African* writer.

The above attribution then becomes the springboard for the essay, the thematic base for a single-minded hammer-and-tongs assualt but applied most obsessively in that early introductory part where the 'argument' is summarized, and in truly scatological language. Such is the affronted Africanity of this patriot that he examines, in this same spirit of racial defence, the poem, 'To My First White Hairs' and asserts:

> This poem is remarkable for both aspects of blanchitude-blancophilia or a lust for whiteness, and negrophobia or a revulsion from blackness.

The incredible analysis concludes:

> Perhaps these three hairs are ironic to their very roots, but it is clear that at some level or other – deep or superficial – Soyinka is celebrating whiteness and showing disgust for blackness.

If it is thought, by anyone who has read this poem and encounters these lines of critical illumination, that the essayist was suffering from a temporary form of derangement, let us quickly reassure that reader that, as recently as this year, in a Nigerian newspaper *The Vanguard*, where he abuses his weekly astral viewpoint, 'The Observatory' column, Chichidodo rehashed this same commentary from his ancient master-text as a piece of reasoned evidence on the tenor of Soyinka's literary (racial) treachery.

But the ethics of Chinweizu Ibekwe's literary mission are even more thoroughly demonstrated through a recorded interview which took place, on this very subject of the 'well known remark', between a former student of mine and Mr Ibekwe. It is worth quoting at some length:

ILORI: Now there is somewhere, I don't know where I came across it, there you claim that Wole Soyinka is not African, that he doesn't want to be called an African, that he doesn't want to be called an African writer, or something like that.

CHICHIDODO: I don't claim that's what he said. Early in his career. The reference was somewhere or other in . . . I can't remember offhand. What he did say is that he wanted to be a writer, not an *African* writer.

ILORI: Could that be at a particular conference in Philadelphia?

CHICHI: Could be; I don't know. At this point . . . but it was quite early in his career so . . .

ILORI: You were a student then, were you? When he made the remark?

CHICHI: I don't know which year in which he made the remark. Early sixties, I believe.

Ilori later returned to the subject during this long interview which ranged through a number of literary figures and topics.

ILORI: But what of – in a case where you are not sure – let us say in a case where you do not remember now the time he said something about he was not just an African writer but a writer – this universalist claim. You are not sure of the time he made that statement. You are not even sure where to find that quotation. So what does it become? Permit me . . . an error of judgement on your part.

CHICHI: Rubbish. Whatever document it was cited in, you'll find wherever he made the statement – it was a very common remark. People remarked upon it at the time. It was discussed. It's public knowledge. So that's not the issue. To cite it in course of a discussion. It's a matter of public record that he said so. So, if he withdraws the comment, that is a different matter. I've not heard that he has withdrawn the comment. But it was a comment he made at a certain period. That at this moment, where I'm sitting with you and you just come in and start asking me questions, that I can't immediately pull it out doesn't mean it's not there on the records.

West Africans, all too familiar with the tactics of the barracks lawyer, or the high intensity of *bolekaja* logic, will readily concede that this particular experience transcends both and deserves a totally new province of its own – *jankariwo!** This passionate defence of blithe disinclination for verification assumes even greater significance when we recall that the master-text in which this lie was first planted contained five pages of footnotes containing 95 (ninety-five) items, mostly source references, yet not even such academic painstakingness found room for the source of an attribution which formed the basis – to which this essay returns again and again *ad nauseam* – for what must surely rank as the most filth-impregnated essay ever submitted for a writer's Festschrift.

Just for the record, and for the further edification of Mr Ibekwe, it would appear that most writers – of all nationalities – do say something or the other, in certain circumstances which testify to their creative desire to transcend the limitations – of whatever nature – of a particular milieu. One example that comes readily to mind was Christopher Okigbo at the first African Writers' Conference in Makerere, 1962. It was there that he uttered his (yes, well-known) remark that he wrote his poetry for poets, not the general reader. Chichidodo has yet to turn Okigbo's white images into a proof of 'blanchitude' on that acount, though he does accuse him of European stylistics. But even more pertinent to this *jankariwo* logician is the statement by Chinua Achebe:

> My audience is anybody who wants to read. I no longer think of any
> particular group of people although I think that I have more readers in
> particular places – e.g. Nigeria.

Of the nine writers interviewed by Ms Phanuel Egejuru for her essay, 'The Modern African Writer Serves a Non-African Audience', only Chinua Achebe made any statement which could be accounted twin to the 'well-known remark' of Wole Soyinka. Cheik Hamidou Kane who claimed also that, when he wrote *L'Aventure Ambiguë*, he was not thinking about any audience, qualified this by stating that, at the time, he was not writing to publish. By contrast, in the same essay, Egejuru quoted a remark (it was not part of the series of interviews conducted by that writer) which Wole Soyinka made on the reaction of 'the Nigerian masses' to his play, *A Dance of the Forests*:

> What I found personally gratifying, and what I consider the validity of my
> work, was that the so-called illiterate group of the community – the stewards,
> the drivers . . . the really uneducated non-academic world . . . they were
> coming to see the play every night . . . if you allowed them. They felt the
> thing through all the way, and they came night after night and enjoyed it
> tremendously.

It is a curious transposition altogether, and the significance of this kind of Chinweizu ethic has assumed a national dimension as Nigerians, both in the literary sections of the

---

* Jankariwo: Used for (i) cobwebs in disused or neglected buildings which have accumulated filth, dust and dead insects; (ii) strong-arm or con-man tactics; (iii) goods or trade related to (ii); (iv) a generally chaotic situation, lacking head or tail.

newspapers and weeklies, have lately been pushed to the stage where they accuse Chichidodo and other equally notorious *bolekaja* 'critics' of being motivated more by tribal prejuduces and loyalties than by any real interest in literature or academic truth. Certainly the average reader of the Chinweizu Observatory (first in *The Guardian*, then in *The Vanguard*) had finally to come to terms with the obsessional level of commentary and its sectarian direction by this particular group. To paraphrase Chichidodo's fellow Igbo writer, Chinua Achebe, who was writing on a Yoruba political figure, it would appear, in short, that Mr Chinweizu and Company, for all their opportunistic camouflage of black-authenticated passion, are little more than 'tribal chieftains' of the literary profession. James Gibbs has put his finger more accurately on their methodology:

> In their analysis of British and American criticism of African literature, the authors employ with approval a term derived from the name of an American critic, Charles Larson: *larsony*. The term, coined by Ayi Kwei Armah, is defined as 'that style which consists of the judicious distortion of African truths to fit Western prejudices, the art of using fiction as criticism of fiction'. In this paper, I argue that the authors of *Decolonization*, in the sense that they present a tendentious, misleading, and emotive account of events as an adjunct to their literary criticism, are themselves guilty of 'using fiction as a criticism of fiction'. I intend to examine, in the context in which it appears, the passage in which they describe Wole Soyinka's return to Nigeria in 1960. The authors of *Decolonization* have not indicated the sources for several observations, and I have, on occasion, had to make the assumptions about the points they make.

If I may just belabour the major points again: fiction as a criticism of literature, combined with a studious avoidance of sources for several observations. In short, a factory of lies, decontextualization of factual citations, the convenient yoking of matrices separated by time, place and purpose. James Gibbs goes on to conclude:

> Chinweizu, Jemie, and Madubuike use the term *larsony* but, I suggest, their own discourse employs 'larsony', that is, fiction as a criticism of fiction. They use dubious arguments, present fact in heavily emotive terms, slander by association, neglect to examine relevant material, and extend findings quite unjustifiably. This is 'larsony' with a difference, since the prejudices which produce the distortion are not, of course, Western.

It would be wrong however simply to substitute 'Igbo' here, for 'Western', since this would constitute an unjustified slander (by association) of genuine, numerous Igbo critics who, even when they are hostile are objectively so, and would never stoop to employing outright fiction to critique literary material. The reference is squarely to those Igbo revanchists, the mental state of whose flag-bearer in particular has become a source of concern for many of his compatriots and even foreigners who nevertheless invite him to their conferences as a kind of circus freak.* It was not only the wide-eyed editor of the famous Festschrift who had cause, among Chichidodo's foreign readership, to be truly concerned about the rational condition of the *bolekaja* boy. James Gibbs, in the same essay: 'Larsony with a Difference: A Paragraph from *Toward the Decolonization of African Literature*', comments:

> Chinweizu *et al* describe Soyinka as 'This Marshall Ky of African Culture'.
> But this comparison is so far-fetched, so inappropriate, so clearly the result
> of emotional imbalance as to be ridiculous.

The bulk of Chinweizu's Nigerian readership came to a more alarming conclusion ages ago.

Why then, should we waste space on the outpourings of obvious dementia? Simply because, especially in our own society, the printed word still carries some kind of mystique of its own. Also because, quite apart from the freak-seekers who take pleasure in deformity, some foreign journals, scouting for indigenous 'experts' to replace the erstwhile foreign 'consultants' spoken of earlier, tend to make a beeline for the noisiest barrel. Thus, the London *Times Literary Supplement* which handed over a volume of essays on Black Aesthetics to our bright lad for review. What kind of review would you expect from a black mind whose entire aesthetic matrix does not extend beyond 'town-criers, squirrels, snakes and lizards'? Any honest critic would disqualify himself but no, to Chinweizu, the very existence of the volume – written from multiple perspectives by various scholars – constituted an affront. He performed his customary hatchet job on this volume, one which did not oblige him to address the sheerest intellectual proposition contained in the essays.

We have all witnessed variations of the following scene, I am certain, sometime or the other on the streets of Lagos, Kano or Benin: a village idiot, tolerated, even patronized by the community. From time to time he aims his phlegm at an unsuspecting passer-by, or urinates on a bowl of food from which his would-be benefactor has just offered him a piece of meat. He runs away and stops a short distance away, giggling vacuously at his victim's discomfiture, secure in the knowledge of the ethics of tolerance towards his kind among his own people. Until one day he is discovered in a ditch, victim of a hit-and-run vehicle, usually a *bolekaja*. Thus do the gods, applying the principle of poetic justice, relieve the community of an intolerable burden of the untouchable among them.

Is there something unique in the artistic atmosphere of Nigeria which breeds the *bolekaja* spores within both the native and the expatriate? Not if Franco Zeffirelli is to be believed. In a letter of rebuttal to the critique of his production of *Turandot* in the

---

* This assessment was confirmed by several participants at the African Literature Association Conference in East Lansing, April 1986. Their names will be supllied, on request, to Mr Ibekwe – if he agrees to acknowledge his father's name publicly, since this, in traditional psychiatry, may prove to be his first step to recovery.

New York Times, the famous Italian director passes some telling comments on the meretricious image of the critical trade in that journal. It is useful to have these contemporaneous remarks as a response to the *New York Times'* review of my play, *Death and the King's Horseman*. To say that the language of that review, let alone the content, transported me instantly to the familiar terrain of the Chichidodo school is to put the experience mildly. It is instructive that Mr Chinweizu learnt his trade in the United States, in those slack moments away from 'collecting funds for Biafra' during the Nigerian Civil War. One can speculate at length on the unsettling effects of such a traumatic event in one's life, but this would serve no verifiable purpose. Each society must learn to take care of its certifiable population. Suffice it then to extend our gallery with the figure of a certain Frank Rich who obligingly provides an international dimension to this occupational hazard of artists.

Unlike the Italian director, I did not write to the *New York Times*. Others did however, and sent us copies of their expressions of outrage in a gesture of solidarity which greatly boosted the morale of the company for the duration of the performances. None of these letters was ever published by the *New York Times*. By contrast, a letter from Luben Vichey, a former metropolitan opera basso was published alongside that of Mr Zeffirelli. Now it could be that the editorial policy of the *New York Times* requires that the author or director himself 'authorize', through his own participation, the protestations of the patrons of a performance against a scandalous review. I regret that I cannot persuade myself of this explanation. With the politics of an earlier cultural encounter* with the same *New York Times* and other American journals still fresh in my mind, I hope I may be forgiven for insisting that this 'liberal' journal had merely acted in character. In short, I repeat here the same observation which I have made on various platforms against the so-called American 'free press' – namely, that it does practise the most self-serving illiberal form of censorship at par with the media of most nations of the world. This is a subject which deserves to be treated at greater length in another place. For now, back to Franco Zeffirelli on the theme of the New York critics of the liberal arts:

> Donald Henahan's recent account of my new production of *Turandot* at the Metropolitan Opera, while comparable to the contemptuous dismissal of my previous productions of *La Bohème* and *Tosca* in the Times, has caused such an outpouring of unanimous support for me and my colleagues that I feel compelled to suggest that you seriously scrutinize the present policies and practices of your staff in a situation that many people have come to regard as intolerable.

> Mr Henahan's review of *Turandot* not only shows a lack of taste, but is also full of inaccuracies . . .

---

* A response of the American media to my alleged 'censorship' of the British National Theatre's production of 'Animal Farm' when I was president of the International Theatre Institute.

Long ago I stopped taking what most critics said seriously, for in general they are a destructive lot who can gain attention only by producing outrageously condescending affronts to the dignity of dedicated artists.

Citing the histories of world famous artists whose sensitivity had made them easy targets for destruction by reviewers who 'imagined themselves in a competition to see who could be the nastiest', Zeffirelli sums up the sociology of such critics as 'amateurs, eaten by resentment, jealousy and soured ambition'.

Evidently, Zeffirelli's audiences agreed. But what of those who, captives of the 'myth' of the *New York Times*, were kept away by the 'contemptuous dismissal' of its authoritative voice?

W.S.
Abeokuta, June 1987

XVIII

The Autistic Hunt;
or, How to Marximize Mediocrity

Mr Geoffrey Hunt's article is well met – not in any valuable sense, but as further evidence of the University of Ife's simmering 'intellectual' politics – into which, regrettably, the *Positive Review* has seen fit to draw me by surrendering its pages to the blackmail of 'detached objectivity'. An argument which was lost in the Philosophy Department of the University – both intellectually and 'politically' – has been extended, under cover of radical commitment, to embrace the (implied) life-work and philosophy of a writer who, for some circumstantial reasons, the now threatened agents of an imperial intellectual arrogance imagine is the main inspiration of the revolt of African philosophers in the department.

The confrontation is more than welcome. It is a pity that it has to take place on the pages of *Positive Review* since my response, taking its cue from Geoffrey Hunt's scabrous and programmed attack, will not pretend to transcend *all the time*, such a level of devalued academism. This position stems from the conviction that Geoffrey Hunt's demented dribble could not possibly find space in any journal of an international standing. The opportunism is apparent – does not Mr Hunt himself confidently refer to an 'ignorant public'? Mr Hunt knows the easy way to achieve a *succès de scandale:* famous target, reckless, sweeping claims, a heady iconoclasm – all perfect ingredients for shooting the upstart to instant 'recognition'. In responding to such opportunism, there can be no place for inhibition on my part, for I must emphasize that, in recent years, I have not read any attempted *summative* essay on the work and philosophy of any author, living or dead, even in the extremest far-out ultra-left Review which dared to express, in such form, such an 'interpretation' of perverted and decontextualised readings – in theme and place – of that writer's supposed literary evidence of social (ideological) commitments. One thing is evident – Mr Hunt attempts to out-Lenin Lenin in the exercise of power through the tactics of abuse. We shall see, as we go along, that this is about the only quality he shares with Lenin.

From a reaction of incredulity, wondering if we all proceed by any common identifiable intellectual norms, has developed a feeling of mystification. The *personal* tone could not be ignored, a definite *ad hominen* crudeness, raising the suspicion of an *inspired* piece. But by whom and to what end? These questions will wait. Our first task is to demolish, objectively, the pretensions of a racist critic who is persuaded and reveals – unwittingly – that he addresses the same 'ignorant public' as he attaches to his target, Wole Soyinka.

In a different article, a response in *Transition 48* (Ch'Indaba) to what I dubbed the poetics of Neo-Tarzanism – one which Mr Hunt, an avid reader of that journal, chooses to ignore – I proposed the need to scrutinize, very seriously, the sociology of would-be critics. I have no intention of evading that task now, certainly not in the University of Ife context. The game of concocting and *foisting* a sociology on the writer has become a risk-free free-for-all, and Mr Hunt plays it with the gusto of a neophyte. I shall give examples later of his disgusting innuendoes. But I insist now, as other writers are beginning to recognize, that the sociology of the critic is equally crucial to objective social evaluations by the 'dumb' – *pace* Geoffrey Hunt – consumers of critical 'certitiudes' proposed by the most reactionary to the most radical literary analysts. In short, it helps to distinguish genuine criticism from attempts to reinforce hollow analysis with snide throwaways such as:

> Fortunately, this topsy-turvy world is largely reserved for the neo-colonial
> elite who pay week-end trips in air-conditioned Volvos to 'the bush' as rather
> inept visitors at some 'traditional' burial ceremony. (Hunt, p. 11)*

For the reader who knows that the author of this piece of yellow journalism is from the same university as the target, the comment *appears* to be aimed at the writer under discussion even though, literally, the critic can claim that in no place did he refer to that writer, but had merely passed a general remark. But the purpose is to present the writer as a Volvo *voyeur* at the shrine of exotica. This is where the sociology of the critic assists the reader's evaluation of his intellectual honesty. It provokes a re-reading, perhaps of the entire paragraph, then of the preceding sections and raises questions of motivations. So let us go back to what precedes the personal innuendo, and see how one thing is supposed to follow another and make sense:

> Elsewhere Soyinka reproaches Femi Osofisan for making the point that
> animism accomodates natural disaster and so negates social action for
> improvement, or to put it in Soyinkese: '. . . The Marxist view of man and
> history, denounces the insidious enervation of the social will by the tragic
> afflatus' (*Myth* . . . p. 47) Soyinka responds to the charge: 'A little more
> gunpowder and, not only the natives of South America, but their brothers in
> the North would have wiped out the white invaders' ('Who's Afraid of Elesin

---

* Soyinka's page references are to Geoffrey Hunt's mimeographed essay described in his introduction, and do not correspond to those of the revised version of the essay in Gugelberger's collection. (Ed.)

Oba?'). What he does not ask is what kind of social organization and associated culture and beliefs make gunpowder *possible*? To parody the answer let us imagine, for instance, Australian Aborigine hunter-gatherers running after small game with boomerangs all day, to hurry home to quadrophonic Stockhausen in carpetted high-rise apartments as the 4:30 work siren sounds across the desert! Fortunately, this topsy-turvy world is largely reserved . . . (Hunt)

This quotation then continues as in the already quoted Volvo section above. Now, all one can say about this highly mystifying 'sequitur' is that, fortunately, this topsy-turvy analogical 'reasoning' belongs only to scatty minds, totally devoid of the obligations of rationality in the use of parallels. But it goes beyond carelessness; some technological facts and historical truths are cunningly tucked away behind 'aborigine' jokes.

Does the 'ignorant public' of Wole Soyinka know that the boomerang is one of the most intriguing and, even today, scientifically challenging examples of aerodynamic technology? For Geoffrey Hunt, however, it is an achievement to be sneered away as a crude piece of technology belonging to the phase of the hunter-gatherer in human development. Next, the clever diversionary stroke:

What he does not ask is what kind of social organisation and associated culture and beliefs make gunpowder *possible*?

The reason for Geoffrey Hunt's racist clownery is immediately clear: any schoolboy knows that colonial *warfare*, as the colonized and the colonizers experienced it, did not stop to ask what 'social organisation and associated culture and beliefs made gunpowder possible'. And this was the immediate context of that Osofisan-Soyinka exchange. Raw materials of every variety were always acceptable in *exchange* for guns and gunpowder. The level of control and transformation of raw materials (or nature) therefore *did not always* decide the capacity of the 'aborigines' to defend themselves. The greed of European colonizing powers, plus their rival interests were such that they were prepared to and often took the risk – to themselves – of providing the colonized with technological means of defending themselves, sometimes even after serving the interests of the intruders. Political alliances (of convenience) also played their crucial role. I suggest for Mr Hunt an extensive reading of the trade agreements between the European adventurers and kings, chiefs, petty traders, missionary converts, obscure warlords, etc. both on the African continent and the Americas. In short, the pragmatic bargaining, and thus the rise and fall of independent communities obeyed none of the convenient theories that are still, today, pushed around to gloss the reality of European and Arab adventurism on the continent, or the crime, *against their own*, of the African middlemen.

The entire paragraph of Mr Hunt's attempt at racial humour is a gross obscenity. Why does he fail to take into account this fact, that the cupidity of the European exploiters could be, and often was, turned against them to obtain from them the practical weapons of their destruction. I advise Mr Hunt not to attempt the interesting task of comparing the development of gunpowder as an offensive weapon in medieval Europe to its prior discovery in ancient China without a corresponding militarist conversion. Such an exercise would be suited only to one capable of intellectual honesty, one who would not be scared to accord equal places in analysis to socio-economics, philosophy and religion, and the sociology of scientific discoveries and their practical application.

There is more matter to this section however. It affords us an unedifying insight into Mr Hunt's sense of fair summary and rational commentary. Here now is the context from which our critic has plucked his weighty atom of ideological heresy. It is necessary to quote the passage at length, for this sample of Huntian methodology is by no means atypical. On the contrary, the entire essay is built on a desperate concoction of meaning, reference and intent, smeared on to lend academic credence to a straightforward overflow of bile. Osofisan wrote:

> Because the animist world accommodates and sublimates disaster within the matrix of ritual, the Red Indian world collapsed, and so did ours, perhaps with slower speed.

Soyinka responded:

> This analysis does not match the facts of history. The Red Indian and our world collapsed because of technological deficiency. Let us not play ellision games with history. The conquest of the Incas by the Spanish is our classic example of one elaborately structured superstition confronted by another. Cortes won by a mixture of superior armoury and wily politics – formulating alliances with the traditional enemies of the Incas on terrain that was clearly disadvantageous to him. Superstition, within which I, at any rate, group 'animism', 'buddhism', 'roman catholicism', 'islam', 'protestantism' etc. etc. has never yet prevented the rise to technological heights of any society. Other factors must be sought. A little more gunpowder and, not only the natives of South America but their brothers in the North would have wiped out the white invaders. When Femi Osofisan claims, à propos of these false premises therefore, that the 'art that stubbornly weaves around the old mythologies, *unmediated*, prolongs the enfeebled past and is anti-progress' the question has to be asked: prolongs the past for whom? Whose revolutionary commitment does it sap exactly? Whose enfeebled *present* is it that is so threatened that it cannot take a poetic excursion, once in a while, to an *unmediated*, hermeticized moment of history, as lived, thought, experienced, and debated by the personages *of that moment*? Is it by any chance this present in which atomic scientists still go regularly to Roman Catholic Mass? Is it some special dispensation in the theory of 'unmediated-past' 'anti-progress' equation which concentrates, among the adherents of one of the most unliberalized religions in the world – the Judaic – such an unfair proportion of scientific

geniuses in the world? I am surprised to see that *Death and the King's Horseman*, staged at the University of Ife, has not prevented the basing of an Atomic Commission at Ife, any more than it has prevented the agricultural workers from jumping onto their tractors in Operation Feed-the-Nation!

Political (Literary) Commitment and Romanticism

But the foregoing was at least an attempt at a subtle camouflage. Mr Hunt is also at home with the propagandist method of direct, white lies. By the third paragraph of Mr Hunt's essay we already encounter a singularly bold claim:

> Soyinka's writings contain . . . including the explicit rejection of political 'commitment' in literature. (Hunt, p. 1)

A typically bold falsehood to which Mr Hunt cannot possibly produce an 'explicit' proof in any of Wole Soyinka's writings. Hunt's presumed justification for such a claim may be located – in so far as Mr Hunt ever bothers himself with the need for justification – in the quotation from a statement of mine with which he deliberately prefaces the Section (2) which follows upon his absurd claim:

> The truly creative writer who is properly uninhibited by ideological winds, chooses.

'Winds' no longer has meaning in Mr Hunt's radical vocabulary. The rejection by me of a *literary* ideology becomes equated with an 'explicit rejection of *political* commitment in literature' (emphasis mine). Mr Hunt is a most convenient reader and is even more impressive as an expositor of the con-trick of verbal transpositions. Wole Soyinka is thus proved, to Mr Hunt's satisfaction, and in the very next lines, to regard 'ideology' as something extraneous and *dispensable* (again, italics mine). This with equal logicality, renders him – poor sod – a member of the neocolonial agent class 'torn between allegiances to the bourgeoisie of the neo-colonising powers . . .' The cheapness of Mr Hunt's romanticism – an accolade he laboriously bestows on me – is revealed firstly in the gratuitous isolation of the *rural* African as 'impoverished' and their presentation as the alternative choice of allegiance to the bourgeoisie. And the impoverished *urban* working class? The answer is a profound ignorance of the total social situation in which Mr Hunt earns his living, presumes to instruct but elects to romanticize. Let us see what other lessons we can obtain from this mentor of class loyalties.

Now Mr Hunt is not a Romantic – perish the thought. A matter for consideration in attempting to make more precise these convenient terms (of a piece of course with Wole Soyinka's 'compartmentalist slur' on European intellection) is whether the exoticist is not the lowest form of the romantic species.

Mr Geoffrey Hunt is a self-proven exoticist. For proof, we need go no further than the following passage in his diatribe. I shall quote somewhat fully, so as not to appear to quote out of context and therefore open myself to the criticism of employing similar despicable tactics as Geoffrey Hunt:

> If art is ideological, an expression and organ of class rule . . .

A howling reductionism by the way, repudiated by less calcified minds in Marxist criticism. Not *all* art is 'an expression and organ of *class rule*'. Marx and Trotsky – among the giants – conceded as much. That Geoffrey Hunt attempts to pass off this historically dated and increasingly qualified definition of art, in 1978, is yet another index of his contempt for his 'ignorant audience'. Mr Hunt is a master – we will concede that – of slipping in the generalized fallacy while the reader's mind is focussed on the particular. But we must move on:

> If art is ideological, an expression and organ of class rule, then progressive
> art is art directed towards the enlightenment and liberation of the exploited
> class. Such art would be oriented towards influencing certain sectors of the
> petty-bourgeoisie and youth and also towards making contact with the urban
> poor and rural population. This contact would be made in the manner of
> Yoruba travelling theatre groups or the Onitsha Market literature. *It would
> not only reflect the aspirations of the exploited, but would indicate the only
> meaningful way in which these aspirations could be fulfilled* as well as giving
> insights into the class system and the way in which power is exercised. (Hunt,
> p. 3)

Let us examine the italicized section carefully. I choose to ignore, as a predictable rhetorical obeisance, devoid of practical meaning and *practical commitment*, the section that rounds off the paragraph. The italicized section is probably the severest and unanswerable indictment of the claims of Mr Hunt to sheerest acquaintance with the literature which he presumes to engage ideologically. I assert here, very simply, that Mr Hunt has not read *one* pamphlet of Onitsha literature, or else, that he is illiterate. One or the other, or both. Can anyone in his senses dare suggest that the 'aspirations of the exploited' expressed in Onitsha Market literature deserve not only further reflection but are indications of the ways and means in which 'these aspirations could be fulfilled'? Just who is Mr Hunt trying to fool? What ignorant public? The models (style and content) of Onitsha Market literature are a bizarre mixture of Marie Corelli, John Wayne, Cisco Kid, Watchtower instructional brochures, beauty cream literature, Candid Revelations, News of the World, Superman, Indian films, Awful Disclosure of . . ., True Romances, James Bond, Lennards' Overseas Catalogue, etc., etc., plus, of course, the occasional direct and simplistic recasting of political events in black Africa or in the black portion of the United States (such as the deaths of black heroes like Malcolm X or Martin Luther King or the exploits of Muhammed Ali). Any proposal, therefore, from a so-called Marxist philosopher that these 'aspirations' not only be further reflected but fulfilled, is only another question mark into the *sociology* of our critic. What exactly is he? A diabolical mind-warper masquerading as a populist? Or simply an exoticist camouflaging his real tastes under Marxist incantations?

Now I happen, as a matter of fact, to enjoy Onitsha Market literature. Before it became fashionable in Marxist and other culture-entrepreneurial circles, I read, and enjoyed, these incredible pot-pourri of the semi-urban romancier. Long before Onitsha Market literature became yet another opportunity for the Ph.D. aspirant, we pursued the latest titles with unabashed relish, assuming (falsely, it now appears) that other readers recognized in this literature a reflection of a sudden inundation of false values, offering therefore a measure of unconscious humour and robust language. The mish-mash of mongrel aspirations would, we thought, gradually disappear with the development of societal pride in its own right. Now along comes a Marxist philosopher who says that Onitsha Market literature and the aspirations it reflects should be a guiding light to modern African Literature!

If we may descend to parodying the parody of our revolutionary firebrand, we do know that ... the task of mobilizing the forces of production in a neo-colonialist situation so as to raise the level of productive forces and thereby control the means of production in order to destroy the comprador classes and petit-bourgeois agents of international entrepreneurism, thereby situating, in a correct historico-economic per-spective, the interim inevitability of an Idi Amin acting on behalf of the rural impoverished and the lumpen-proletariat against middle-class agents of economic imperialism ... we do know, yes, that this must be a full-time job for Marxist philosophers. *But*, when they step out of this monumental commitment and into Onitsha Market literature we demand that they, at the very least, do their homework by first reading the stuff.

We will not yet depart from the issue of romanticism – which, by the way, I am far from conceding the ultimate, capital crime in the arts, seeing in it only a tendency to be noted where it occurs, and its thematic appropriateness objectively debated. Mr Hunt makes a great play of *The Man Died* which, according to him, had no business being anything but a political manifesto, in the manner of 'George Jackson's prison notes, *Soledad Brother*, or Antonio Gramsci's nine years of prison writings ...' Now I confess here a definite feeling of embarrassment. I always feel embarrassed when confronted by the phenomenon of an intellectual absolutely not 'at risk', calmly asserting what form the account of a prisoner must take. But it goes beyond this.

And I hope this must be my last word on the subject. It will be readily admitted – even by Geoffrey Hunt – that I have tended to avoid engaging critical statements on the book up till now. Geoffrey Hunt is, however, a package deal, and it would be unwise to ignore this particular revelation of the interior sociology of the radical aspirant. First of all, certain statements can be dismissed with utter contempt. No one, to my recollection, not one critic, pro or against *The Man Died*, has ever suggested the contrary to Hunt's brilliant insight which expresses itself thus:

The fact that Soyinka was thrown in prison at the outbreak of the civil war
does not prove that in any meaningful sense he was progressive . . . (Hunt,
p. 8)

Hunt himself uses the expression 'petulant' to describe the writer's attitude in *The Man
Died*. I consider this too mild a word to describe a presumably serious critic who takes
time off, in the midst of graver issues, to sneer at the commonplace misfortune which
befalls any writer in or out of civil war, for the simple reason that he might therefore be
considered a progressive. The depth of Mr Hunt's analysis of man and creative
production is very much of this level: to put it plainly, it is something beyond bad taste.
I confess I can react only subjectively: it makes me squirm. But we can, fortunately,
proceed to more objective observations.

For a man who teaches philosphy, the possibility of a developed philosophy – for an
African – does not, of course, occur. (No claim is made here, *please*, that this is an
African philosophy!) The point is that, in bewailing the fact that *The Man Died* is not a
replica of *Soledad Brother*, Mr Hunt betrays himself as governed by a Christian (stoic)
philosophy without being conscious of it. 'Out of evil comes forth goodness', 'Every
cloud has a silver lining', 'Suffering hones the spirit', 'Turn the other cheek', etc., etc.
ad nauseam. While pretending to a Marxist objectivization even of intensely personal
experiences, what Mr Hunt is really saying is: This famous writer, there he was in this
isolated hell-hole; outside we awaited the message of salvation. The greater we imagined
his privations the more certain we became of the emergence of a masterpiece – political,
of course. The more total his isolation, the profounder must be the ideas which he
spins out of the gossamer sheerness of the empty air!

That is all there is to it, reduced to the layman's demystifying terms. Alas, in this
case, conscious of the *tradition* of prison writings, conscious of the Romantics who
reconcile prison inmates to their lot, extolling them to employ their time usefully, in the
cause of the progress of mankind, who cajole them into converting an absolutely barren
and mind-destroying existence into statements of lofty idealism, programmes for
political salvation which are no sooner published, lionized and exploited than they are
completely forgotten – yes, forgotten and *ignored* – I, in this case, reviewed this Puritan
tradition (never mind the various camouflages) and broke with it consciously and
deliberately. I chose: it is time to counter this monumental deceit! *Soledad Brother*, Mr
Hunt? *Notes from the Underground?* Or shall I remind you of *The Ballad of Reading Gaol*
or John Bunyan's *Pilgrim's Progress?* Embarrassed perhaps that he has since become
Uncle Sam's best apologist and fashion model for Cleaver jeans, I notice that Mr Hunt
does not mention Eldridge Cleaver's *Soul on Ice*. Let me sum it up: nothing is valid that
comes out of a man while he is shackled. He is prey either to messianic dreams, to
reformatory intentions (mostly limited to his environment), or to absolute despondency.
The only thing he is certain of is that he would like to survive – mentally intact. We
know of the conditions of a certain kind of imprisonment – South Africa's 101 days in
total darkness and periodic tortures. We know also of others – television sets, football

games, visits by lawyers, relations, seasonal parcels, access to libraries, to college tuition programmes, etc. Prison conditions vary – Lenin and Stalin in Tsarist prisons enjoyed conditions which post-Allende Chilean prisoners would postively envy. These two revolutionaries led an active life in prison, edited newletters and maintained networks, received books, parcels, even sometimes visitors. Those who care may study the irony of contrasts between the prison conditions enjoyed by Stalin and those imposed on his opponents when he came to power. It was Fidel Castro's anticipated 'day in court' which inspired his *Historia Me Absolvera*. In short, there is no such thing as 'because he was imprisoned' – that is stupid, privileged talk. Even from a prison habitué, it is unworthy language when it refers to another prison experience.

I chose to combat the Sunday School philosophy of the Geoffrey Hunts. The redemption masterpiece for which Mr Hunt waited – even if it had happened in prison – I would have denied its place of origin. You don't write a political salvationary tract when your entire reading list comprised Thomas Merton, some rat-nibbled pages of P. G. Wodehouse, the Bhaghavad Gita – all smuggled in or actually officially loaned me suddenly and without explanation. In any case, it is not your business to write that brilliant political treatise. What are the Geoffrey Hunts at liberty doing? And what, in any case do they need for revolution that has not been written since the 1850s? If ever there was a permanent human fixture to the library of the British Museum – in the fifties and sixties – it was Karl Marx. Before writing one line, Marx consumed volumes of reference. Wole Soyinka, in two years deprivation of books or human contact, is supposed to emerge with a political manifesto fully armed for action. Or, of course, simply to gratify the Romantic Puritans of 'radical' philosophy, to say thank you for solitary confinement which produced lofty reflections from barren material conditions.

The abrupt cessations in recollected conversations in *The Man Died* therefore become a problem for Mr Hunt. It would be preferable if I faked the usual recitals of 'control of the forces of production' etc. to assure the reader that Alale, Banjo, etc. did *mean* socialism. These are snippets – tantalizing of course – of events which were related to my being where I was. Any genuinely curious mind who tries to *deduce* a political orientation from these figures is free to do so, armed, however with a *minimal* knowledge of the various genres of this kind of writing. For a start, such a reader should recognize the obviousness of a certain level of reticence in certain situations, necessitated both by the proximity of events and by the fact that at that time of writing the implications of such events were by no means concluded. Of course there is always the come-back: why publish it at all, at the time? The answer is equally simplistic – why *not*?

But it suits Mr Geoffrey Hunt to pretend that this *claims* to be a source-book of political directions. This is why, with his mouth agape in intellectual horror, he can attempt to warn his 'ignorant public' to seek shelter from a lethal bombardment of conversational lacunæ from a writer who makes –

virtually no mention of the mechanism of imperialism and neo-colonialism (words which are almost totally alien to Soyinka's vocabulary), of past British divide-and-rule politics, of the difference between British colonial rule in the North and the South of Nigeria, of internal differences in religion, culture, educational background and opportunities, of the creation of a rapacious comprador class in the South, or the precise role of the traditional ruling classes, of foreign monopolies, of the causes of urbanisation and migrations, of oil and inflation and ideology! (Hunt, p. 8)

Whoops! A most politically comprehensive man, Mr Hunt knows the socio-political history (and theories) of Nigeria backwards. Alas, we wait in vain for him to write the text which will fill in explanations for a simple accusation – genocide! In seeking to recall the conscience of a nation to a sordid act, I am also expected to provide the socio-political salve: well you know, it is true that you did perpetrate genocide but, you see, that is really a bourgeois-intellectual concept. What actually happened was that you were all victims of the mechanisms of imperialism and neo-colonialism. The radical conservatives never use or understand these expressions naturally, but *we* know why. And then you had this problem of divide and rule politics, and what about that rapacious comprador class in the South, not to talk of the precise role – precise, you understand – of the neo-colonial agent class and the multi-national corporations . . . so you see it is pure romanticism to simply decry genocide, as the bourgeoisie . . .

J'Accuse is a liberal pastime permitted only the European intellectual, naturally. A neo-colonial has far more complicated tasks assigned him from birth and for life!

Chapter XIII of *The Man Died*, from where these vilifications took their root, consists of ten pages. It *compresses* an extensive conversation and veers aside occasionally to the antecedents to that conversation. Naturally, any ideological initiate would feel frustrated and, as Kole Omotoso pointed out – with genuine curiosity and some resentment, not as opportunist grist to prepared smear à la Hunt – what sort of socialism are they talking about? Looking over that chapter, I realize that the duration of the conversation is not even given – I recall that this was no inadvertent omission. Even with all those sources of irritation for those who need the specifics of a purposed impressionist account, there is a real cause for suspicion of motives in such personal venom – spattered all over this tract. For it forces the ideologue to box himself into a textbook corner as constructed by Hunt in the memorable sentences:

And then, since when are armies part of the proletariat? The proletariat consists of industrial and agricultural wage-earners. The army is an element of the state . . . Here is a man telling us that 'socialism' is the only answer when he does not grasp the socialist perception of the nature of the army, the State, the proletariat and the ruling class in a neo-colony.

Well then, let us see where *lived* socialism parts company from its robot aberrant. First of all, the army – in its affective role, social presence, etc. manifests itself *both* as an instrument of the State and as an exploited, indeed, self-identifying part of the proletariat. The consideration of this dual personality of the armed forces has historically determined state policies in times of crisis and even in peace times. In pre-'66 Nigeria, the army was indeed one of the most contemned sub-classes within the proletariat. It was faceless, anonymous. It identified, in effect with the class status of the proletariat since the soldiering occupation was treated with condescension by the petit-bourgeoisie and the colonial aristocracy. All this changed, naturally, after the Jan '66 coup and the changed status became virtually consecrated after July '66. From a faceless, anonymous army which was formerly submerged with the army of workers, farmers, petty traders, etc. – all of which they often were, part-time – they became arrogant overlords, exercised the powers of appropriation, privilege, even of life and death over the rest of the populace.

If this analysis of the Nigerian actuality is a little difficult for a student too close to the militarist examples of Mussolini's armies and fascist Europe in general, I will refer him to the Cuban Army from 1962 onwards and challenge him to assert that the armed forces of Cuba had not become merged with the Cuban proletariat. I cannot, of course, choose a cancellation date as I have not returned to Cuba since then. What cannot be disputed is that, during the early sixties, Cuba did achieve the ideal of transforming its army into just another disciplined, socialized profession within the proletariat. Other nations have gone through similar experiences, however brief – the National Guard of Paris Commune, 1871, for example. Once an instrument of the ruling class, at the critical moment, the *thinking* revolutionaries realized that these 256 battalions were largely composed of workers and the petit-bourgeoisie. They did not stop to consult the textbooks on their objective classification but set about winning them over, exploiting their subjective class reality. As our armchair petit-bourgeois intellectuals are themselves the first to admit.: 'Objectively, I am a member of the proletariat. I have committed class suicide.' It seems strange that a member of the intellectual classes who arrogate to themselves such suicidal tendencies should close his mind both to historical precedents for any other groups and most especially to the right to mass suicide of underprivileged agents of the possessing class.

But finally, it is simply necessary to invite Geoffrey Hunt to read that chapter again, Chapter XXIII, upon which he has the effrontery to base his summation of my understanding of socialism. This chapter, insofar as it deals with any political idea or phenomenon, deals with the question of national boundaries, their meaninglessness, and calls them to question. (Mr Hunt is quite free to seize upon this to label me a Prudhonist, and welcome). The chapter also deals with genocide directly, which the author claims was the answer of the Northern-Lagos Mafia axis to the threat of disgorgement of stolen millions through the resumed activity of probes. It was also a response to the killing of northern leaders but it was organized and fuelled – in three waves – by the aforesaid Mafia axis who needed total chaos to cover their tracks. I do not know where Mr Hunt was marximizing his meagre talents during this period, but it could not have been in Nigeria. Only a fool or a scoundrel would deny the truth of my claim. Hunt is by no means a fool or a scoundrel, so it can only be that he is ignorant of such propulsive accidents of history which set in motion events uncharted even by his unacknowledged genius, and which can be stated baldly, which *need* to be stated baldly without recourse to obscurantist remote causes. That task can be safely left in the hands of doctoral thesisists and neophyte lecturers in Marxist philosophy. (Incidentally, one of the unprobed Ministers is back in business, aiming, no less, for the Presidency of the nation. Since he is only a product of the socio-economic conditions of the mid-sixties, I think if FEDECO* registers his party I shall go and vote for him.)

Cabral and Marxism

But it is time to sandwich a little credit into Geoffrey Hunt's splenetic assault on plain intelligence. This has to do with the arguable 'injustice' done to Cabral's ideas in the speech referred to in *Transition*. As always, of course, Hunt is not content to make a case and let it rest; he has to impute dirty, even libellous motives which are designed to soil the editor with the most sordid attitudes of the opponents of African liberation.

> In an editorial in the journal *Transition* (editor: Wole Soyinka) a fair summary
> is given of the mass-based revolutionary alternative to neo-colonialism . . .
> (Hunt, p. 5)

The following pages then proceed to qualify the 'fair summary', citing examples which, to the fair-minded, do call for an answer. Before that answer is given let us quickly examine the smear technique in operation yet again where, much later on, in the penultimate pages of his essay, with the comparatively objective remarks receded in the mind of the reader, the smear is applied with Mr Hunt's now recognizable delicate touch:

> In view of the whole terms of reference of Cabral's analysis and strategy and
> his continual demand for the 'socialist solution' it is amazing that anyone can
> in sincerity deny that Cabral was a Marxist or socialist, although such a ploy
> is clearly important to the neo-colonial intellectual faced with the *fait accompli*
> of the revolution in Guinea-Bissau. (Hunt, p. 26)

The only question that comes to mind at this point is – is Geoffrey Hunt a student of Goebbels? The intended implication is that the Guinean revolution was indeed a devastating blow to the 'neo-colonial intellectual'; confronted with its *fait accompli* he had to put on as brave a face as possible. Now, let there be no dissembling here: I consider this the one unpardonable slur that can be made on any politicized ex-colonial however thick-skinned. I regret that the epoch is gone when such matters were settled in idioms other than words! There is nothing intrinsically uncivilized about *that* way of dealing with a man who slanders a black man by imputing that, deep down, he prefers

---

* The Federal Electoral Commission, responsible for organising the elections which preceded the return of civilian rule in Nigeria in 1979. (Ed.)

to be enslaved and to see his fellow Africans enslaved. This ignoble accusation which no attempt is made to prove, is brazenly passed off – contextually – as the 'truth' behind the editor's special issue on the Guinean revolution. I must suggest here that this is a particularly cowardly libel whose motivations can only be impure, even sick. I will claim that we are dealing with a dirty little ideologue with no scruples, a raddled intellectual whore to whom decency is a 'romantic' word.

Enough. Back to the championship of Cabral's Marxist purity, and to a further attempt to play on the presumed 'ignorant public' of Wole Soyinka, where Mr Hunt, in his eagerness to qualify the 'faint praise' damnation of the fair-summary passage quoted above, adds:

> But then an attempt is made to put a wedge between the success in Guinea-Bissau and socialism or Marxism. (Hunt, p. 5)

The coupling of 'socialism' and 'Marxism' is no accident. Mr Hunt, with his mythical ignorant public in mind, is convinced that it would pass unnoticed. He knows damned well that socialism is not strictly interchangeable with Marxism – certainly not in such a context where he concerns himself with textual interpretation – and he knows also that *nowhere*, absolutely nowhere, can the claim be sustained that the sheerest wedge is placed between the revolution in Guinea-Bissau and socialism – which Hunt claims he understands. If there is one single passage, ellision or emendation of Cabral's speech in *Transition* or my editorial which does this, I would like it pointed out.

With Marxism, however, the case involves Cabral's Marxist development which is conveniently glossed over by Geoffrey Hunt. Since when, Mr Hunt, did Amilcar Cabral become accepted as a 'correct' Marxist? Since when did the 'pet-dog' tolerance of the 'primitive socialist' in Cabral cease in the most vocal rabid Marxist circles? At a conference in Halifax (Dalhousie University) in 1971 where a large number of Geoffrey Hunt's ideological clan were gathered, we were treated to the most patronizing, condescending assault on Cabral's awkward – yes, awkward – attempts to reconcile the dogmatism of Marxists with the objective realities he had observed, had had to contend with, and conceded a place in the re-shaping of the revolution of Guinea. On several occasions it was flatly declared that Cabral had Marxist pretensions but was no Marxist. Guinea was 'hot' at this time and there were tracts galore by pundits who knew better than Cabral how the Guinea Revolution should have occurred.

Among the handful of objective, even respectful critiques of Cabral's departure from 'Marxism', including his disagreements with *fundamental* principles in the analysis of social development, is Chapter III of Lars Rudeback's *Guinea-Bissau*. I recommend to Hunt a careful reading of the section 'General Ideology and Analysis of Society' (p. 72). Hunt claims to have *read* Cabral's *National Liberation and Culture*; well, we are probably entering the age of scientific miracles. But he certainly does not reveal any true acquaintance with, or understanding of 'The Weapon of Theory' in Cabral's *Revolution in Guinea*, where Cabral upsets the traditional acceptance of the place of class conflict in his conclusions on the motive force of history. If Mr Hunt does understand the significance of Cabral's 'deviation' he would never have attempted to present Cabral as the acceptable Marxist *par excellence* to an intellectual community *without first* admitting why Cabral has remained a theoretical pariah to Marxists, and then explaining his, Geoffrey Hunt's position in a clear, unambiguous way which would put Wole Soyinka's 'dishonesty' to shame. Hunt, however, ever the opportunist hypocrite, hopes that dogmatic assertions, even fraudulent ones, will suffice. His audience is, after all, only the same as Soyinka's 'ignorant public'.

Now earlier, I used the deliberate expression 'awkward'. Mr Hunt himself is not ignorant of a certain 'awkwardness' in some of Cabral's pronouncements of a political-analytic nature. Indeed, this 'awkwardness' is so pronounced that Hunt could not avoid it, and he deals with it in the following passage:

> It is true that Cabral did on more than one occasion say that his party did not find it necessary to label itself 'communist' or 'Marxist' (e.g. *Revolution . . .* p. 55). The reasons for this are simple. Firstly, Cabral was not an academic concerned with the niceties of terminology but an active politician frequently appearing before the United Nations and having to court the assistance of neo-colonial governments in Africa, including for a time such a centre of reaction as Morocco. Secondly, he *does seem to have been worried* by the narrow dogmatism of the Stalinist parties in Europe, although he *may well have been aware* that these parties represent only one trend . . . (Hunt, p. 26) (Emphasis mine)

'Does seem to have been worried', 'may well have been aware'. Dishonest, understated speculative drivel! Cabral – and the quoted section in *Transition* makes this clear – true, opposed certain Marxist interpreters, not Marxism. But he was more than 'seeming' to have been worried. Cabral's 'hedging' was not simply on the *Realpolitik* level, it was analytical! The nerve of Geoffrey Hunt to patronize Cabral! 'Cabral was not an academic concerned with the niceties of terminology . . .'! This disgusting, amoral attempt to 'excuse' the serious thought processes of an intellectual in action, compelled to explain to himself and to his people the contradictions he had noticed between *received theory* and observed reality! Translate 'not an academic concerned with niceties, etc.' how you will, and all you obtain is the supercilious sympathy of the ultra 'Marxists' already referred to who, even while Cabral was living and courageously embattled, had begun to dub him a crude pretender to Marxist theories.

It is convenient now, however, for the purpose of calumniating yet another pretender to rational processes among the African intelligentsia, to temporarily rehabilitate the pure Marxism (albeit with 'imprecise terminology') of Cabral, and to provide a supporting case of a new generation of Marxists and would-be Marxists, some of whom are still struggling with a century's terminological variants on our urgent material reality.

With the crude lesson of the Spanish Revolution behind us, it is pertinent to ask, for whom was the revolution in Guinea-Bissau really an unwelcome '*fait accompli*'? Who really is trying to put a brave face on it? Who is it that has a history of treachery, of callous betrayals in the heat of revolution simply to safeguard purely theoretical ideological splinters? No, not the 'radical conservatives' or the 'neo-colonial intellectuals' but the pretenders to ideological purity trying to befuddle an 'ignorant public'. The Cuban Revolution was similarly beset – hundreds of its ranks betrayed to Batista's goons for torture and death by 'comrades' manipulated by theoretical purists. This attempt to 'rehabilitate' Cabral on the campus of the University of Ife by an extreme, dogmatic Leftist is a contemptuous effort which presumes on the ignorance of his audience – a not altogether unjustifiable assumption – for how many 'intellectuals' even in this country know of the condescension with which Cabral's theories of active revolution were held by Geoffrey Hunt's ideological clansmen? This attempt is therefore not merely opportunist; it is insulting.

And it is with this background that the difficulties experienced in translating Cabral's address can be explained. The version we had was, to make matters worse, a French translation from a version in English. An English version could not be obtained from the PAIGC offices in time for the press and we had to undertake the urgent translation to make the issue. Geoffrey Hunt cannot but have noted – for I assume that he does possess the English text – that the rest of the translation is not the same. What began as a difficulty with language soon became apparent as an awkwardness in attempted reconciliation of ideological positions. We left out the more awkward, convoluted sections, aiming for the clearest 'message'. If bias did come into it – then it was a bias created by the insolent context of Cabral's standing in the then dominant circles of Marxist verbalizers, of which Geoffrey Hunt, on his own showing, is a useful example, one which Cabral himself was aware of and impatient with – an awareness acknowledged by Mr Hunt, unavoidably.

Now let us, with the foregoing in mind, re-examine this crucial passage which we are accused of excising, 'in order to drive a wedge between the revolution in Guinea and Marxism or socialism':

> . . . We agree that history in our country is the result of class struggle, but we have our own class struggles in our own country; the moment imperialism arrived and colonialism arrived, it made us leave our history and enter another history. Obviously, we agree that the class struggle has continued but it has continued in a different way; *our whole people is struggling against the ruling class of imperialist countries* . . . (*Revolution in Guinea*, p. 56)

The underlined section is my own emphasis, but the quotation begins and ends precisely as presented by Geoffrey Hunt. But where is Cabral's emphasis in this pasage? Now, committed as we were to Cabral and to the revolution in Guinea-Bissau, our position was clearly partisan. It still is. Guinea was occupied with internal struggle, yes, but its struggle was also externally directed. The intellectual ruling class of imperialist countries may commit objective suicide as vociferously and as vicariously as they wish – we experience them still as agents of intellectual authoritarianism. If Hunt does not see the awkward hedging between 'history obviously *means* the class struggle' and 'we agree that history in our country is the *result* of class struggle' then he also cannot be concerned wth the niceties of terminology. As translators we were compelled to be. Attempts to arbitrate the 'awkwardness' created by the fundamental departures on theories of 'class', 'class conflict', 'motive force of history', through the other essay 'Weapon of Theory', only led to increasing discomfort – any neophyte to Marxist analytical method and nuances of expression can see why. The location of the 'motive force of history' surely has a crucial place in the liberation strategy of any serious revolutionary – it affects decisions on development, tempo, methods of indoctrination and even external alliances in the conduct of the struggle. When we are in doubt – and we were on this occasion – we side with African progressives and do not risk exposing their ideological flanks to the dubious terminological niceties of uncommitted Euro-centrists – through our inadequacy.

That is the story of the famous Guinea-Bissau feature, but it is not complete without reminding Mr Hunt's readers of some valuable comments from the pen of the genius who began it all – in any comprehensive and systematized way, that is. I refer to the meeting of the General Council and the Communist International of 1866 where the Prudhonists faced the 'Marxists' with their insistence on the de-emphasization of national revolutions in favour of the unions of stateless communes. Marx's comment was that while the French appeared to deny all nationality, they appeared 'to reconcile it with their absorption into the model nation which was France'. In short, international-ism – or anti-nationalism – wears more garbs than ideological purity. Very often it is simply a mask for national chauvinism. Russia later committed the same error, resulting in revolts by former 'satellites' including, of course, China.

Demagogues who remain blinded by specific national models are only too eager to convert original revolutionary minds into piping supports for their intellectual hegemony. A mandatory corollary of this is the undermining of their historico-cultural basis which – as in Geoffrey Hunt's case – frequently takes a racist form. His essay is generous with the required proofs of the racist in the 'universalist'.

Geoffrey Hunt and the Race–Culture Question

The entire nervous system of Mr Hunt jangles with alarm bells because Wole Soyinka states that he is concerned with 'the apprehension of a culture whose reference points are taken from within the culture itself'. This section is from my brief preface to the essays in *Myth* ... The same preface, however, goes on to add that the author admits that:

> ... In order to transmit the self-apprehension of a race, a culture, it is
> sometimes necessary to liberate from, and relate this collective awareness to,
> the values of others. (p. viii)

but criticizes the deified aura which is given to such externalized 'intellectualism'. Hunt conveniently fails to mention this as he also fails to recall that in the same preface, the author warns that:

> nothing in these essays suggests a detailed uniqueness of the African world.

And in the same preface (Preface: summation, statement of intent, even methodology, etc.) I state:

> The persistent thread in the more recent lectures stems from this earliest effort to encapsulate my understanding of this metaphysical world and its reflection in Yoruba contemporary social psyche.

Let us return to the full quotations from Hunt in order to appreciate how he proceeds to counter Soyinka's propositions which, of course, are first distorted:

> . . . Soyinka is concerned always with the 'apprehension of a culture whose reference points are taken from within the culture itself' . . .

Then a brief section in which the same Soyinka is accused, predictably, of:

> going beyond this as a way of excluding progressive analyses.

Some profound distinctions follow about 'understanding' and 'participating' in a culture, every phrase of which neatly cancels the other out – just in case someone notices the gross presumptuousness of some of the claims. However, finally:

> The effect of Professor Soyinka's rejection of external concepts (it is surely too facile to reject them simply as 'alien European') of understanding is to cut off all possibility of recognizing causal determinants of social institutions and activities and cut off the possibility that many beliefs are 'rationalisations'. The philosopher, Alasdair MacIntyre . . .

Let us give praise that, however cutely the racist intellectual thinks to cover his tracks, the disease uncovers itself willy-nilly; such, yes, is the wilfulness of rational pursuit. For Mr Hunt makes two indictments here against the culture(s) which Wole Soyinka engages in this work. Let us reduce it to clear, unambiguous language and let anyone fault, if he can, the precise fairness of the following translation of the above quoted passage including the paraphrased diversionary waffle referred to above:

(i) Participating in a culture is one thing, understanding it is another, and one which requires going *outside* of that culture.
(ii) The rejection of external concepts of understanding means cutting of *all*

possibility of recognizing the causal determinants of African societies and institutions, as well as the possibility of recognizing many of their beliefs as 'rationalization'.

(iii) And if you want proof, just begin with what that *European* sage Alasdair MacIntyre had to say . . .

Other things are implied: we can spell them out *ad infinitum*. There was no evolution of ideas in African cultures until the European came. There was no system of evaluation of beliefs, no evidence of progressive transformation. External concepts of understanding had to come in first before participation could be arbitrated by Reason. We now come full round the Negritudinist circle – if Wole Soyinka is the neo-Negritudinist, what shall we make of Hunt – the ultimate neo-Hobbesian? Perhaps we must go further. Goeffrey Hunt is so free with names of European racists – Gobineau, Verger, Hitler, etc., he trots out such obscenities at the slightest provocation – in a mind-boggling exercise that proves, to his satisfaction, that my writing is a remarkable apologia for them, that my suspicions were early aroused. 'They *also* dispensed with empirical enquiries' is Hunt's equating link of these historic mutants to Wole Soyinka.

Well, it is time to ask what empirical enquiries have been conducted by Mr Geoffrey Hunt before he came to the categorical conclusion that no African intellectual dare dispense with European concepts of understanding before he can determine the causal factors of social institutions or separate rational beliefs from rationalizations. The question here is not of course whether or not *Myth, Literature and the African World* successfully does, or even attempts this. The claim we are making is that a racist opportunist has, under the guise of an objective 'radical' analysis of the works of one African author, made general racist claims which the despicable Gobineau and Company have been making in their confident racial superiority. Only such Africans are saved as genuflect towards 'external concepts of understanding'. Thus, in the opening sentence of that section (4), we learn that, in contrast to Soyinka's 'eternal' and 'immutable' aspects of traditional thought, Cabral's

historical materialist approach makes Reason operative on real conditions . . .

But for the 'external concept of understanding' of 'historical materialism', poor Cabral would have been incapable of Reason, of making it operative on material conditions; without the external concept of understanding, Cabral would be incapable of 'challenging a usurping authority, and reestablishing it in the people as a whole'. No challenges to 'arbitrary authority', no 're-establishing of it in the people as a whole' ever took place on the continent of Africa before the salvation of external concepts. Geoffrey Hunt is to be congratulated – he has outdone Andreski who claimed in *The History of Black Africa* (Akademiai Kiado Budapest, 1966, quoted by Lars Rudebeck) – that we cannot speak of the history of most African peoples prior to the end of the fifteenth century. For Mr Hunt, Reason did not appear in Africa prior to the nineteenth century.

This of course enables us to understand why 'external concepts' from Africa never played a role in the formulation of European understanding (including the Marxist) of their own culture and societies for a millennium – Africa was a conceptual vacuum. It explains why Geoffrey Hunt can confidently teach European philosophy in an African university since he need not make 'empirical enquiries' to explain this non-phenomenon to his students. Reason did not come to Africa until the late nineteenth century – to deny this is to deny that Reason is synonymous with dialectical materialism and to cast oneself with the 'neo-colonial agent class' bent on distorting a radical African leader's 'criticism from within Marxism itself'. Fortunately, today's African thinker is no longer so easily intimidated by cries of 'Wolf' from the vulpine assassins of black minds who decline to accept the commission of race suicide as the price for the accolade of Reason.

This is why, with his contempt for African beliefs – 'rationalisations', etc. – it never once occurs to Geoffrey Hunt to even make comparative references to the more rampant institutional superstitions – Christianity, Buddhism and Islam. Not even as parallel cautionary examples of false consciousness. Yet a serious attempt to relate parellel institutions and beliefs of the black people to their social existence earns a permanent sneer which is almost visibly superimposed on every page – 'cracked, chipped and useless piece of antique porcelain' – a contemptuous dismissal which is still racially impertinent even from one who has exhausted all 'empirical enquiries' – an impossible claim. 'No, African culture sees what the European cannot', sneers Mr Hunt. For centuries the European world claimed that the African did not *see* at all – but that is not the issue. European history of racism plays an insignificant role in *Myth* . . .; that history is referred to only as a warning reminder. Geoffrey Hunt is, however, beyond warning – well, we have a proverb, sorry, not a European proverb although of course I do know, and will quote on demand, a few European expressions of the same sentiment: 'The dog which is destined to get lost remains deaf to the hunter's whistle.' We do claim – without, of course, the *reductio ad absurdum* choice of expression – we do claim indeed that Africa sees what the European does not. The corollary is self-evident. (The expression of a sighted culture is Geoffrey Hunt's by the way, not mine.) And if we feel that the cultures of Europe occupy, till today, the larger part of the curricula of the majority of educational institutions in the world, then there appears to be no logical cause why we, on our part, should not contribute to the task of understanding the underprivileged culture from the way – as far as we can surmise today – that culture apprehended itself. The penalty for this enquiry, this search for knowledge sets off alarms in the breasts of so-called philosophy graduates of assured and dominant cultures, leading to the most ignoble lies and distortions in the presentation of 'evidence'. We will pause briefly and run through a few.

The Goebbelsian Dimension
A few of these lies, such as Soyinka's 'explicit rejection of political "commitment" in literature' have already been mentioned. It is now necessary to go more deeply into the

structure of the lies already mentioned, while we also unmask a few others. We have already referred to Hunt's:

> If art is ideological, an expression and organ of class rule . . . (Hunt, p. 2)

A very big 'if', still rigorously contested. 'All art' is implicit in this premise, and only the crudest, indeed the most ignorant Marxists – ignorant about the various trends in Marxian criticism of art – would have the effrontery to suggest that *all* art is an expression and organ of class rule. We refer to this passage again only because it is the assumption of the artistic and ideological verity of that claim which paves the way for a series of unschooled pronouncements, including the already quoted reference to Onitsha literature as the expression of progressive social aspirations. Next:

> Instead of treating aspects of 'traditional' thought in terms of false-
> consciousness, Soyinka abstracts them and makes them eternal and
> immutable. (Hunt, p. 9)

The first part is answered by what we have discussed so far in terms of Europe's own continuing superstitions. The second part is a blatant lie. It is claimed in *Myth* . . ., obviously, that Africans do weave myths – this assertion runs right through the entire book. It is claimed also that the reasons for these myths vary from internal, 'psychological' compulsions to historic events such as migrations, wars and heroic deeds, plus economic opportunism. (The 'token' mention of the last indicates, very plainly, that the writer does not acknowledge his profession as being in the economic field but in that of yarn-spinning and mythopoetics. When this becomes an intellectual crime, it will only be after we have wiped out the intellectual parasites whose acknowledged field this is, but who expect poets and playwrights to do their work for them.) 'Nowhere in the whole of his writings is there any socially significant programme for action, either overt or implied.' We recognize here the familiar romantic, starry-eyed cry to the author as saviour: 'Lead us, writer, lead us.' Upon which the writer simply passes the buck to where it properly belongs, 'Lead us, paid ideologues, paid socio-economic theorists, paid philosophic carpers, lead us.' In the meantime, have the intellectual humility to *read* us – accurately.

To ensure that this demand for accuracy is not made gratuitously, let us re-read the passage from *Myth* . . . which offers the widest possible opening for insertion of the spurious claim contained in the charge that Soyinka abstracts aspects of traditional thought . . . and makes them eternal and immutable. The 'evidence' for this spectacular piece of idiocy could only come, I surmise, after much bewildered search, from the chapter on 'Drama and the African World-View':

> Where society lives in a close inter-relation with Nature, regulates its
> existence by natural phenomena within the observable processes of continuity

– ebb and tide, waxing and waning of the moon, rain and drought, planting and harvest – the highest moral order is seen as that which guarantees a parallel continuity of the species. We must try to understand this as operating within a framework which can conveniently be termed the metaphysics of the irreducible: knowledge of birth and death as the human cycle; the wind as a moving, felling, cleansing, destroying, winnowing force; the duality of the knife as blood-letter and creative implement; earth and sun as life-sustaining verities, and so on. These serve as matrices within which mores, personal relationships, *even communal economics are formulated and reviewed.* (p. 53)

This of course must be where the crime was committed, to suggest to that minority breed – the Marxist zombie (I do *not*, emphatically *not* refer here to the creative Marxist) – to dare suggest to this vanishing species the possibility that societies did exist which actually had the temerity to organize – progressively as they acquired greater intellectual and technolgical tools – their economic programme in relation to their observed analysis of the material, nature-physical phenomena around them. This section of the chapter actually goes on to insist that

The African world-view is not, however, by implication, stagnant;

goes on to attack the Popperian school of totalitarian conceptualism. The same section goes on to claim, in explication of the constantly expanding social metaphor of myth:

This principle creates for society a non-doctrinaire mould of constant awareness, *one which stays outside the monopolistic orbit of priesthood,* outside any claims to gnostic secrets by special cults. Interpretation, as it does universally, rests mostly in the hands of such intermediaries, but rarely with the dogmatic finality of Christianity or Islam. (New emphasis)

Perhaps this is where the hurt is, the claim that African religions adapt themselves to experience while Christianity and Islam settle for dogma. It is part of the hazards of the literary profession that, with passages as quoted above, I should now find myself indicted for making claims of the 'eternal' and the 'immutable' for aspects of African thought. Of course, it could be that I am barking up the wrong tree, that Mr Hunt does have some more incontrovertible evidence. As with other claims of the Marxist philosopher, we await the references thereof.

Birth and death *are* 'irreducible' phenomena. Now those are immutable and eternal. To the Marxist revolutionary impotent who cannot bear any realist qualifications to the claim that we exist in a 'technologically remediable world', the commonplace fact that you cannot prevent or control – beyond very petty limits – the birth or death of a human being must be very humiliating. We read in this nothing but the familiar syndrome of the megalomaniac. But, delay or prolong the act of birth and death, the phenomenon of coming to consciousness and having extinguished, for all time, that experience of consciousness is a phenomenon which is so subjective to the experiencing human entity that paradoxically – even with the stoutest objective considerations – it is not surprising that it is religionists (theologians, etc.) poets, tragedians, musicians and other artists who make it their exploration ground. The embarrassment felt by ideological immortals at the mention of such irreducible facts of experience is only an index to their dwarfishness in face of imponderables, but also their cowardice which must be sublimated by an obtuse, ego-denying pose. To tag as 'Romantic' this occasional preoccupation is a mere device of intellectual superstition which wishes off bad news with 'scientific' incantations. You, Mr Geoffrey Hunt, will finally abandon consciousness for the last time one day – just lke the rest of us – and you will not be around to insist that the event only exists in the minds of victims of 'extreme individualism and preoccupation with individual freedom and its negation in death'. We will ignore the now familiar Huntian sequitur which, in the same brief paragraph makes this *result* in an 'emphasis on imagination tending to irrationalism and emotionalism and *an inability to make concrete commitments*' (p. 12).

Nowhere, incidentally, does Geoffrey Hunt indicate where in Soyinka's works individual *freedom* finds its negation in death. But it sounds nicely damning.

A few more literary howlers, all from page 15:

> . . . in *Kongi's Harvest* where the 'moral superiority' of traditional kingship is assumed in opposition to Kongi's modern tyranny . . .

> . . . in the novel *The Interpreters* Egbo's choice of the civil service is correctly presented as inevitable, but as certainly cowardly and 'wrong' faced with the alternative of restoring damaged traditions . . .

> Soyinka once made the sound declaration that 'The African writer needs an urgent release from the fascination of the past'. This was made in a much heralded 'radical' speech given in 1967, and then promptly forgotten by Soyinka himself.

Where does one begin? The last item will do, I think. Only thanks to a Nigerian literary popularizer was the notion of Soyinka's 'radical' manifesto ever born and publicized. For most people it was only another conference contribution, with no significance beyond what Soyinka had said before or would after (in spite of 'promptly forgetting it'). I am still interested to know who, apart from the popularizer in question, dubbed it 'radical' or a manifesto. Once the tic has been set in motion by the interior affectation of contempt, diversionary horrors are evoked to explain Hunt's physiological defect.

> . . . The suicide of the western educated Olunde, first son of Elesin Oba, is the medium of the message. (Hunt, p. 15)

I have dealt with this *wilful* cataract on the idiological retina of the critics of *Death and the King's Horsemen* in my paper to the workshop of Radical Perspectives, 'Who is Afraid of Elesin Oba?', 1978; I need waste no further breath on one of the agents of their confusion.

> ... in the *Lion and the Jewel* it was the attractive Sidi's preference for the traditional chief rather than the young educated man who is made to look ridiculous by Soyinka.

Here, a stop must be called. It is clear here that we are dealing with a strange disease – literary autism. (Definition – Autism: absorption in imaginative activities directed by the thinker's wishes, with loss of contact with reality. *Chambers*) Here I must really pause and hand over Mr Geoffrey Hunt to first-year secondary school pupils who confront the figure of Lakunle the school-teacher in *The Lion and the Jewel* for the first time. First of all, you will not find, apart from a handful of the victims of colonial aristocracy and the usual quota of retarded students, any school pupil who sees Lakunle as a young *educated* man. A man, and especially a school-teacher with simplistic ideas of foreign values is not, in these parts, considered educated. He is nothing but a figure of fun. Only Geoffrey Hunt in his innocence or obsessive *hate* – only Mr Hunt could propose, to an African community, the figure of Lakunle as representative of the educated and 'progressive'. To plumb the depths of cultural slumming by Mr Hunt, this section (p. 15) has to be read and re-read, and even after the hundredth reading, it will not be believed. Here, I am certain, even the racist colleagues of Geoffrey Hunt must part company with him, for one thing which they cannot afford is to be caught out being obviously stupid. If this language seems extra strong, I make no apologies. If an illiterate 'philosopher' nerves himself to attempt to pass off such a boob, it signifies not only a pathetic level of literary understanding, but a suspicion that Geoffrey Hunt, whatever he professes, is a fraud, since his profession is one that demands a high level of literacy and he has proved himself incapable of the slightest literary intelligence.

We continue:

> Man's nature is necessarily dualistic for Soyinka: man cannot escape his destructive aspect any more than he can his constructive aspect and this duality traps man in a cycle of futility. (Hunt, p. 9)

Buttressed half a page later by the passage from 'The Writer in a Modern African State' ('It seems to me that the time has come when the African writer must have the courage to determine what alone can be salvaged from the recurrent cycle of stupidity.') Mr Hunt then goes on to conclude:

The general idea is that war, exploitation and social inequalities are inevitable given man's inescapably evil or deficient nature. Hence, Plato and Aristotle and the Ancient Greek aristocracy justified slavery . . . (p. 19)

At this point, I think I must really be excused. This is a demeaning exercise, necessitated only by the effrontery of the assault, concealment of motivations, the attempt to exploit the open-mindedness of a radical-leaning journal, coupled with the sordid rewards of exposure for a desperate mediocrity. How, one must seriously ask, can one reconcile the justification of slavery, exploitation and social inequalities as inevitable, with an exhortation to decide and act on behalf of what alone can be 'salvaged from the recurrent cycle of human stupidity'? Under the guise of preoccupation with dialectics, logic has been given short shrift by Mr Hunt. Logical deduction means *nothing* to this autistic child. The pathetic bungler finally reveals himself as an apprentice armed only with the cookery-book of philosophy, throwing one spice after another into the casserole in the hope that the authentic flavour of a basic ingredient will be forgotten, then mistaken for that of his own obnoxious spices.

Mr Hunt is free to wish off history, but let him not deceive the world that the massacre of students and peasants in 'revolutionary' Ethiopia is any less stupid and reprehensible than the genocide that took place in Nigeria's feudalistic North, or the slaughter of Jews in Hitler's Nazi Germany. We will not obtain the permission of those who prefer to describe these inhuman acts in socio-economic language of optimism before we denounce them in the 'romantic' language of reality, however pessimistic. Nor will we pretend that what is happening today in the world, nearly one and a half centuries after the maturity of Marx, has not recurred repeatedly in various forms since the beginning of human history or that it will not again. We will make a note of it, call attention to it and only then, exhort humanity to combat it – by whatever means, including through socio-economic theorizing and socialist philosophies. Only Geoffrey Hunt is capable of the magical feat of transforming a historical observation into a justification of that observation. Indeed, it is much too kind to suggest that Mr Hunt merely tries to wish off history, he wants to escape from it.

'African' as Expression versus 'European'

Mr Hunt's unhappiness over these convenient groupings can be summarily dismissed. First, they were first employed by Mr Hunt's intellectual forbears, and not necessarily that racist breed which Mr Hunt finds it convenient to isolate. Those expressions are adopted as a means of revaluating the thoughts of such racial identities as are, even today, still conveniently referred to as African. The employment of the 'paradigm' as a means of generalization is valid methodology in most humane disciplines – anthropology, philosophy, sociology, etc. – Mr Hunt should know better than to attempt to obscure this fact. If, however, his schooling somehow managed to miss this, I can refer him again to Andreski's *The History of Black Africa* for a racist's support, but, by preference, to an African philosopher, Willie Abraham and his work *The Mind of Africa*.

As for the inevitable comparison with European thought, I have not spoken lately to the Sicilian peasant though I freely admit that he has a lot in common with the Ibo peasant – it should be obvious that what I refer to is the way European thought articulators have propounded periodically cancelling systems of man's knowledge and understanding of his existence and environment. I know also that the Roman Catholic Sicilian peasant is as superstitious and dogmatic as the university Marxist who is also a Roman Catholic. There are therefore valid areas of philosophical contrast between the thought systems of these two classes of Roman Catholics and the Ibo farmer or Ngoni herdsman locked in his own 'traditional' superstition. Why does one cling with greater desperation to his rosary and bleeding saint in time of adversity, while the other takes out the symbol of his superstition, sets it on fire and picks up another one? I don't know which class the new Pope emerged from but I do know that he comes from a socialist country. I also know that the leader of that nation did not denounce him for accepting to head the world's best organized superstition; on the contrary, he sent him his congratulations. I know that Russia has failed absolutely to stamp out superstition after half a century of socialism. Why then must a Marxist pretend that the Sicilian peasant and his Roman Catholic intellectual compatriot share no common aspects of a world-view? Who is Mr Hunt trying to fool?

'Race' – declares Mr Hunt – 'is a subjective response to an objective class situation, and this applies even to the most extreme cases such as South African apartheid or Israeli oppression of Palestinians' (p. 23). First, Mr Hunt is applying a very similar tranquilizer therapy here – the conflation of the Palestinian struggle with that of the black man in South Africa. This purely theoretical gambit is a political conceit – more extravagant than permitted even poetic licence. To try and blur the external, racial basis of the greatest obscenity ever inflected on any peoples, a national independence struggle is roped in as added measure, in case the purely socio-economic explication fails to satisfy – as it must – the black victims of apartheid. Mr Hunt, warmly cossetted in a non-racial university, white and secure, must feel rather uneasy at the mere mention of apartheid among his hosts. He, plus, of course, a handful of similar *black* radicals who feel they ought to be above subjective identification with the South African situation, also indulge themselves with theorizing out of manifest existence the oppression of the *racially defined* black man in South Africa. Such escapist tactics have the unfortunate effect of spreading a callous over the humane conscience of the 'objective' thinker – humane conscience being of course merely a 'romantic response', not a class-objectivized position. It patronizes the oppressed, in effect, robs him in advance of a number of options against his racially defined oppressor (e.g. the weapon of 'Black Consciousness'), even convicts him of the crime of self-defence at threats to his racially defined existence. Applying Mr Hunt's own loose tactics of free consequences – without descending to his dirty level of incongruities – does Mr Hunt's apologia here not provide the argument for the torturers and murderers of Steve Biko who accused *him* of racism?

An end should be put to blasphemies such as this, for they turn out to be no more than a plea for the objective understanding of apartheid, and therefore of its acceptance – even for a day. The gratuitous insertion of apartheid in this context is opportunist, it is an apologia, and it reveals the sub-conscious of the racist, and his brain-washed black supporters. It has been evoked paradoxically, to confuse the issue of Race which really is not at issue. A visit to the Soviet Union and the Eastern European (Communist) countries renders evasion patently ridiculous. The literatures of these countries, and their proud insistence on the rich rewards of the diversities of races within their boundaries amply document the 'external existence' of race, which Mr Hunt wishes to concede only to 'class'. 'Race does not exist outside men's minds' (p. 23) – this fatuous claim is possible only from a racist conniver, by which we mean, one who, for reasons which are to be found in his own racial temper, seeks to undermine the racial security of others. We do not claim anywhere that social progress should be dependent on the racial factor, or that even the struggle against apartheid should be based on a counter-racism. No, we claim merely that race can be objectively discussed and that the racial factor in culture need not be obscured, else, the discussion of culture remains incomplete.

Technology and Religion

In his spiel on Technology and Religion, Mr Hunt declares:

> . . . thus we find, as a necessary consequent of his abstractiontism, the implication that technology is utterly unconnected with the ethico-religious ideas embraced by a culture, and that religious institutions are similarly sealed off from technical ideas (p. 10)

If our Marxist critic thinks to cover his rear by employing the merely suggestive expression 'implication', he has done his sense of anticipation a disservice. But very seriously now, has Mr Hunt read *Myth, Literature and the African World* at all or has he merely heard it discussed, read reviews and apoplectically browsed blindly through to confirm his suspicions, burrowed out of order for quotes which would sustain a private war of his own (we shall come to that later)? There must be many bemused Nigerians, and foreign readers, who will read this assertion of Geoffrey Hunt and wonder at the standards for employment at the University of Ife. If anything, the complaint is that Wole Soyinka *mystifies* technology by weaving it into mythology, especially in the figure of Ogun, who, in *Myth* . . . is rendered as embodiment of the metallic sciences. Ogun is the musician and farmer also, perhaps that is Mr Hunt's 'compartmentalist' problem – would it help if he employed a mnemonic device? Shall I recommend that light composition by Handel entitled 'The Harmonious Blacksmith' since Ogun – as stated in plain English in *Myth* . . . – is the god of blacksmiths? On page 150, of *Myth* . . ., we encounter the following passages:

> The symbolic artifact of his (Ogun's) victory is metallic ore, at once a technical medium as it is symbolic of deep earth energies . . .

... organising the mystic and the technical forces of earth and cosmos to forge a bridge for his companions to follow, Ogun not only dared to look into transitional essence but triumphantly bridged it with knowledge, with art, and the mystic creativity of science.

And so on. Now, we do know that Mr Hunt is a hard man to please. We know that his scientific soul abhors the 'podgy mysticism' in Wole Soyinka's works and that, maybe, is where the very evocation of the mystic blurs his sight (we dare not say vision). But then he must not make senseless claims which are so effortlessly contradicted by hard evidence. Soyinka creates the *implication* that technology is utterly unconnected with religion and ethics? The very opposite implication is what Soyinka, as in the above and other numerous examples prove, very unabashedly makes. Soyinka does *not* suggest that such a religion is therefore scientific, but he indisputably implies that this traditional religion is inextricably bound with the technological awareness and development of the society of that religion. *The Road* – Mr Hunt affects such a comprehensive knowledge of my writings that he surely must have read this play – *The Road* is about transport workers, long-distance drivers, whose mechanical employment makes them worshippers of Ogun.

Only the desperation of a mercenary hatchet-man could produce the series of contradictions in the entire section on Soyinka's attitude towards technology (pp. 10/11). What was written in one context, and as commentary on a specific example, is upended to make it read, in Mr Hunt's version, as the correct order in which we encounter passages in *Myth* ... Thus, the following Huntian paraphrase from Mr Hunt's page 11:

> ... for the 'African', technology is or can be incorporated in a unitary vision
> so that 'African metaphysics' sees no incompatibility between, for example,
> lightning as a stream of electrons and as the will of Sango. The former is
> simply a wasteful and 'truth-defeating' re-definition of the latter.

The last seeming sentence of that quote is, as usual, removed from its immediate context – a general one which also comments on George Steiner's views on European tragedy – and latched onto Mr Hunt's hotch-potch compression of a number of preceding observations. The full version of the 'truth-defeating' sentence actually reads:

> For cultures which pay more than lip-service to the protean complexity of the
> universe of which man is himself a reflection, this European habit of world
> re-definition appears both wasteful and truth-defeating (*Myth* . . ., p. 49)

Well, when I studied chemistry in my school days, the atom *was* – according to all the chemistry text-books – the smallest *indivisible* unit of any mass. Before I had time to fully incorporate the idea in my scientific armoury, fortunately – for me, not for the

Japanese – the atom was split, with quite spectacular results. It took a few years yet before the fact could percolate to the colonial school curriculum and the frantic process of correcting the text-books began. I suppose even those who built the first atom-bomb were still not sure what had happened. That is one example of European scientific basic certitudes which blew a fuse in recent times. Although the entire world of physics was based upon this fallacy for centuries, I actually believe that no serious harm was done. (Errors are part of science.) That was simply as far as scientific knowledge had advanced at that time, and the European world had fortunately outgrown the age when men would have been burnt at the stake for daring to suggest the opposite.

I think that it is probably 'humiliating' recollections like this which really hurt Mr Hunt's racial pride – for he knows damned well that my statement can be backed by a thousand and one examples from antiquity to the present. Arthur Koestler has indulged in similar views (*The Act of Creation*, Hutchinson); he has not, to my knowledge, been subjected to such obscenities as have been uttered by Mr Hunt. I suggest, therefore, that what really hurts Mr Hunt is that an African writer has dared to suggest that any European periodic system of knowledge may appear, to other Africans, wasteful and truth-defeating.

The key word here is *certitude*, periodic certitude – that is, a contradiction in terms, philosophically at least, if not semantically. Atoms are one thing however, humanity is another. The European philosophers and theologians have defined and re-defined the world with passionate, murderous certitudes for centuries. The European has, in the name of scientific and technological certitude, murdered sages, mathematicians, philosophers and razed entire populations to the ground only to turn round in the next decade and commit intellectual genocide on the former 'correct' survivors. Now Mr Hunt is free to account for this 'periodic certitude' which leads to mass extermination in socio-economic terms backed by conflicting class interests. I hope he will not be so stupid as to deny that, whatever the reasons, the mental 'conditioner' which leads to the events themselves is 'wasteful and truth-defeating'. And I hope he will have the humility to at least consider a proposition that certain non-European 'primitive' societies, instead of chopping off one another's heads over the question of whether electricity is caused by a movement of electrons or by a frown on Sango's face, simply promote Sango to the honorific role of the Demiurge of Electricity, in addition to lightning. Metaphor, Mr Hunt, myth and metaphor! And the key word in this case, which Mr Hunt as usual conveniently omits, is 'essence'. No one suggests that the scientific formula which defines a steam of electrons impacting on Mr Hunt's head in a thunderstorm is 'wasteful' or 'truth-defeating'. 'Essence' is not the same thing as an atomic formula.

Shall we now specify one concrete, unassailable instance of waste and the defeat of 'truth', in human terms? In the cause of a typical 'periodic certitude' millions of peasants and 'kulaks' were butchered by Josef Stalin. Of course, in the next period of 'sub-dialectical' certitude, they were largely posthumously rehabilitated by Kruschev. That makes everything all right, of course – until a repeat performance, as has been enacted in Ethiopia since its revolution. Perhaps Mr Hunt, the philosopher, will inform us which form of superstition is worse – that which demands the liquidation of millions of humanity in the name of a particular *degree* of collectivization, or one which says – well, lightning or electricity? – as long as we install a conductor and sacrifice to Sango. Mr Hunt should now go back to examine what, in addition to what I claim for the 'assimilative' wisdom of the African, I also observe of his pragmatic wisdom.

Puffed by his 'radical commitment' on behalf of the impoverished masses of Africa, Mr Hunt indignantly protests:

> . . . that is, delusions have their psychic uses, so who cares if we are exploited by them!

Mr Hunt should now direct that sanctimonious observation to his own European post-Marxian and contemporary societies, employing a stronger word than 'exploited'.

Now, having said all this, provoked into a seeming defence of Sango against atomic science by the inanities of an apprentice philosopher and by his disregard for truth and logical processes, I hope I can safely backtrack and insist that the foregoing is a position made inevitable by a need to contest Mr Hunt's extravagant strictures by a drastic recall of human history, including scientific history. If I am challenged by references to the foregoing as evidence of a rejection of scientific progress – a simplification technique to which I am now attuned – if the charge persists that it all amounts to a primitive defence of 'delusions' and an attack on scientific materialism, I reply in advance that Mr Hunt has created the opening for misinterpretation through the conflation of myth and science for the purpose of denigrating an entire culture of which myth forms a part. Myth remains valuable in numerous societies for explicating what is as yet unexplainable as a scientific phenomenon but, continues also afterwards as an enriching metaphor of experience which goes into the arts – theatre, poetry, music, painting, etc. In the smallest village in Nigeria there will be found a nondescript motor mechanic by the roadside, skilfully improvizing spare-parts for the latest model of motor engineering. During the Ogun festival, he joins the procession and dances up the hill to sacrifice at Ogun's shrine. In the process of building a modern society, I have no intention of interfering in this unscientific contradiction – at least, not as long as the churches, the mosques, the temples and synagogues remain assertive aspects of the spiritual landscape of this and all other societies, however progressive.

When myth is harmful, where myth interferes with progress, where loss of political will and human alienation is the result – in concrete not in detached, sounding-off, purely speculative terms which only betray an intellectual neurosis – a society decided on progress *will* find a solution. Cabral, so liberally misused by Geoffrey Hunt, was never squeamish in admitting this recognition into his liberation strategy.

The Material Condition of Geoffrey Hunt

It is regrettable that a mere dismissal as an inept Marxist fanatic will not suffice for the case of Mr Hunt. It will not explain why the pages of his paper are drenched in so much bile, why such virulence dominates even his few instances of arguable criticism, why smear and sneer are substitued for clarity or precision of attack. It would be futile to deny that I was not immediately impressed by the *sickness* of his paper, futile to deny that I did set out to enquire into the circumstances of the man.

It would be futile also to deny that I did not immediately suspect motives which had nothing to do with strict disputation in the realm of ideas, of immediate but far-reaching sociological causes which might even be traced to purely human motives such as frustrated ambitions. I could not understand, to name one example, why a Marxist philosopher should attack *The Lion and the Jewel*, *Death and the King's Horseman*, etc., etc., in such compromisingly subjective language, without the slightest iota of respect for literary truth or objective contents when the man from whom he drew his authority, Karl Marx, did not deny the pleasures he derived from the reactionary English poet and playwright, William Shakespeare. Karl Marx frequently attended productions of Shakespeare, kept his works as permanent companion, spent evenings with his family reading aloud from Shakespeare. This did not prevent Marx from criticizing the implicit ideology of Shakespeare. Karl Marx, however, never utilized any form of language which attempted to reduce even the worst of Shakespeare's feudalistic apologia to a facile catalogue of romantic elizabeatitudes. Inevitably, I became curious about Geoffrey Hunt.

On discovering that Hunt belonged to the Philosophy Department of the University of Ife, where some four to five years of policy struggle about the existence or not of an African philosophy finally erupted in the open, in a violent seminar-paper presented by Dr Olu Makinde in 1978, I began to suspect a little of the man's possible motivations. The conservatives of that struggle – in short, the *European* conservatives – lost the struggle, resulting in the resignation of their leader, Professor Robin Horton. His 'boys', among whom was Geoffrey Hunt, began for the first time to feel insecure, and for a good reason. Dr Makinde's thesis was not content with the assertion of the existence of an African philosophy; knowing, from experience, that it did not take long for the expatriate, trained in a particular discipline, to become an authority in a totally different field of that discipline, he questioned seriously if anyone who lacked the *language* of a people could pretend to understand or pronounce on the philosophy of such a people. If his thesis was right, Professor Horton – and by implication a number of the opponents of the existence of an African philosophy – had no right being part of the argument at all!

The implications of this for a largely expatriate-staffed philosophy department are of course incalcuable. I must say here, by the way, that I, in common with many participants at that explosive seminar, did not share Dr Makinde's strictures on Horton; indeed, the language of the paper was severely criticized. But the indication for the future of philosophy at the University of Ife was startlingly clear at that seminar, as indeed it must have been for some time within the department. This was indeed later confirmed. The threat to a comfortable tenure, to easy 'bread', spouting dogma rather than immersing the intelligence in questions, was, to an unknown and run-of-the-mill

Graduate Assistant, quite acute. After all, during the tenure of an expatriate Headship of that department, Mr Hunt was mandated to 'assess' the work of another Graduate Assistant, a Nigerian, for the latter's advancement. The departure of Professor Horton must have been traumatic. I suggest that while the situation did not make Geoffrey Hunt completely lose his reason, it has definitely affected his rational processes.

Since a Colloquium of African Philosophy and the Humanities at the University of Ghana in 1972, at which I delivered a paper which formed the major part of Chapter One in *Myth* . . . (Morality and Aesthetics in the Ritual Archetype), quite a number of former African adherents to the view of an African vacuum in philosophical thought have swung round from their original view. At that Makinde departmental seminar, one such, the Head of a Department of Philosophy in another Nigerian university, admitted this when I spoke from the floor and was about to resume the argument we had had in Accra. The Philosophy Department of Ife had undergone just such a reform in thinking, and the truth of the matter is that, all over the continent, the task of defining and systematizing African philosophical thought has gained in intensity over the past decade. That would have been intolerable enough for the European intellectual supremacist. The really unforgivable aspect of this is that the Euroepan intellectual has been told that – with some self-proven exceptions – the very nature of philosophy precludes him from pronouncing on the subject and, by the same token, calls into question every pronouncement on African thought that has been made by his similarly 'illiterate' European predecessors.

Beneath the radical commitment of the ideologue to universalist progress and commonality of the intellectual process, let us never dismiss the possibility of opportunism, sordid self-interest, and plain intellectual will-to-authority.

There is yet one more statement – a question really – which must sum up the contention, with which I began, that the politics of the world today demand that we also examine the sociology of the critic as complement to the critic's adoption, presumption and projection of a sociological context for the writer. Commenting on Soyinka's vague, ambiguous, unlocated etc., etc., statements of political understanding which occasionally appear in his works, Hunt comments:

> The Nigerian poet is absolutely right, however, in seeing the futility of the
> war, the void of ideas in which it was waged and that ultimately it could 'only
> consolidate the very values which gave rise to the war in the first place . . .'! It
> is a pity that he has no framework by which to interpret and fill in a few
> details. But then, that would make all the diference between ambiguity,
> which has its political convenience, and revolutionary commitment, which has
> its political consequences. (Hunt, p. 9)

Of the many varieties of *ad hominem* taunts flung at the writer by the 'revolutionary' critic, this is of course one of the cheapest. It is time to return the implicit question to the critic. Let Mr Geoffrey Hunt now tell us what political consequences his 'revolutionary commitment' has for Mr Hunt? A life of intense political risk spouting Marxist rhetoric at drinking time in the University Staff Club, sustained by the sweat of the African peasant whose systems of thought he dismisses with such contempt, with no justification, from 'empirical inquiries'?

The question is not addressed to him only, but to our facile black, unproductive colleagues of identical persuasion. The Leninist terror-tactics are totally unsuited – in the main – for today's advancement in Marxist methodology, and verbal terrorism only exposes the revolutionary eunuch that espouses it. We are capable of comparing the feudal oppression that warranted the particular tactics employed at the turn of the century and the early decades of the twentieth century to ensure the success of the Russian revolution. We say confidently, empirically, that the same material conditions do not apply here and now, in this country. The 'ignorant public' is a figment of the salvationist's messianic imagination. The language may be unaccustomed, but they are not awaiting the ignition of the flame of *Reason* in their dark lives, least of all from the electronic lighter of a failed Marxist 'promethean'.

While ideas and acts are inextricably intertwined, we insist that discourse can be conducted in rational accents that do not compromise the revolutionary cause. Anyone is of course free to choose his weapons, but let no one think that the use of any particular weapon is the monopoly of the unprincipled. For the defence of the right to enquire into our material experience, and to formulate concepts from them which have been occluded by a colonial tradition of cowed acceptances, of 'stunning insights' into the formative process of alien societies, we will not hesitate to adopt the very weapons of mind-suppressors, no matter by what title they aspire to intellectual respectability. And no matter their colour, creed or credentials.

W.S.
Ile-Ife, 1979

Neo-Tarzanism: The Poetics of Pseudo-Tradition*

Pretenders to the crown of *Pontifex Maximus* of African poetics must learn to mind the thorns. For a start, especially when their credentials are declared to be a love and espousal of the virtues of traditional African poetry, they must penetrate into what constitutes poetry in traditional art or be contradicted by their own limitations and superficial understanding of this activity of the imagination. Traditional African poetry is not merely those verses which, being easiest to translate, have found their way into anthologies and school texts; it is not merely those lyrics which, because they are favourites at Festivals of the Arts haunted by ethnologists with tape-recorders, supply the readiest source-material for uprooted academics; nor is it restricted solely to the praises of yams and gods, invocations of blessings and evocations of the pristine. Traditional poetry is all of this; it is however also to be found in the very *technique* of riddles, in the pharmacology of healers, in the utterance of the possessed medium, in the enigmas of diviners, in the liturgy of divine and cultic Mysteries (in addition to the language of their public address systems), in the unique temper of world comprehension that permeates language for the truly immersed – from the Ifa priest to the haggler in the market, inspired perhaps by economic frustration! The critic who would arrogate to himself the task of formulating an African poetics – a typical pre-occupation of the European critical tradition, by the way – had better understand this from the start or confine himself to extolling the virtues of European nursery rhymes – a field which appears more suited to the analytical capacity of our critical troika.

An earlier published essay by Chinweizu ('Prodigals, Come Home', *Okike* No. 4) defines the troika's concept of the African poetic landscape with its flora and fauna – 'a landscape of elephants, beggars, calabashes, serpents, pumpkins, baskets, towncriers, iron bells, slit drums, iron masks, hares, snakes, squirrels . . . *a landscape portrayed with native eyes to which aeroplanes naturally appear as iron birds*; a landscape in which the

* First published in *Transition*, 48 (1975).

animals behave as they might behave in Africa of folk-lore, animals presented through *native* African eyes' (my italics). We must add in fairness that Chinweizu rejects the use of such a landscape as 'an exoticism for background effect'; nevertheless it is one which must be moved to 'the dramatic centre of poetry'. I am not at all certain how this proves more acceptable than the traditional Hollywood image of the pop-eyed African in the jungle – 'Bwana, bwana me see big iron bird'. My African world is a little more intricate and embraces precision machinery, oil rigs, hydro-electricity, my typewriter, railway trains (not iron snakes!), machine guns, bronze sculpture, etc., plus an ontological relationship with the universe including the above listed pumpkins and iron bells. This may result in a subtle complication in the 'narration, reflection and resolution' of these phenomena but emphatically denies the deliberate complicating of them. Echeruo, alas, chose his wording most unwisely and Chinweizu & Co. can hardly be blamed for seizing that big stick to hit their unfavourable poets over the head. The trouble is that, being rather unsure critics and superficial traditionalists, they have wielded that stick with a destructive opportunism rather than with an intelligent concern for poetry. Their case is worse than over-stated; it is mis-stated. And it is not only modern poetry by Africans which has been maligned in the process but the very traditional poetry whose virtues they present as examplar. When critics are weaned on, or have chosen to limit knowledge of their own heritage to one-dimensional verses on cassava and yam – not that this form of poetry is in any way belittled, the gods forbid! – and evade even one example of the mildly extra dimensional, such as, for example, the following lines from Ifa's 'Irete Meji', can they really claim true knowledge of the poetic experience of the modern African writer?

> Slender as a needle
> Grimy and frayed as clothesline
> Shiny as fool's gold
>
>> Full purse clinks to the ground
>> Encumbered net slumps down, tightening the
>>> noose
>> Two cocks young: tease and tag
>> Two cocks old: bedraggle themselves along
>> Bony buttocks fall with a dry thud
>
> Made Ifa for My-thoughts
> waterbuck, bush cow
> blocked up riverrun
> who worshipped Our Mother of the Waters at Ido
>> on the day he was using the tears in his eyes to
>> hunt for the good things of life
>
> Can he prosper when everything seems to elude him?*

* Free translation by Judith Gleason: *A Recitation of Ifa.*

Of course, Ifa did not claim to be engaged in the art of poetry when he uttered this gnomic prelude to the full body of response to a supplication. But then, neither did the anonymous author of 'Humpty-Dumpty' who lampooned a public figure in English history in the words of that rhyme. The lines later passed into the nursery-rhyme repertoire of Britain – a fact which our troika may not know. What the rightful inheritors of these delightful lines dared not do, our troika have more than dared – raised 'Humpty Dumpty' to the level of 'great poetry' and equated it not only with William Blake's 'Tiger' but with Langston Hughes' 'Harlem'! Fools rush in . . .

Is this a joke? Or are our critical troika indulging in that mystification of which they accuse other critics and poets?

As a writer, given a choice between the model of 'Humpty Dumpty' and the Ifa lines I have quoted, my creative sensibility opts naturally and effortlessly for the latter. As a critic I find my receptivity more rewardingly engaged, stimulated – even aggravated, yes – but ultimately more enriched by the analytical exercise of sharing my discoveries with my readers: this incidentally is one of the functions of the crtitic, one which Messrs Chinweizu, Jemie and Madubuike preach – No. 2 on their list of a critic's functions – but resolutely refuse to practise where some extra intellectual effort is required.

'Irete Meji' disobeys the major canons laid down by the troika – except perhaps one: it is full of similes, a poetic device that must win their approval, being straightforward and demanding little of mental effort –

> Slender as a needle
> Grimy and frayed as clothesline
> etc., etc.,

But does it all 'read well'? Is it 'smooth'? Has it 'music'? Is it 'pleasurable' or at least 'pleasurable nonsense'?

> Two cocks young: tease and tag
> Two cocks old: bedraggle themselves along
> Bony buttocks fall with a dry thud
> Made Ifa for My-thoughts
> waterbuck, bush cow
> blocked up riverrun

I rather suspect it is 'heavy', 'tongue-twisting', 'difficult to articulate'. And the only reason why it is necessary to bring up this melody aspect of a mere translation is that this is the operational mode of the troika, blithely moving from original composition to translations of traditional poetry and adjudicating these without the least note being taken of the inapplicability of all critical criteria to both categories of composition, musicality most notably of all. This level of criticism lacks acquaintance with the very rudiments of its occupation, requires perhaps a little more practice with nursery rhymes.

But what is the pronouncement, musically, on traditional poetry? Is it all mellifluous? Do we never encounter passages of great internal cohesion yet 'difficult to articulate'? How, in any case, does the troika define 'musicality'? Our critics appear to belong to that school of ethno-musicologists who, until two or three decades ago, brainwashed the European world (including its Africans) into believing that African musical tradition was nothing but a cacophony of sounds, that the polyrhythmic tradition was the original sound of bedlam and choral dirges a wail of jackals in the night. The smooth musicality which the troika wish to foist on modern poetry by Africans as its passport to authenticity is nothing but an alienated sensibility which stems from this curtailed musical education. Yes, poetry is an 'auditory' medium* and instead of pronunciamentos of ignorance from the wilderness, it would profit would-be champions of tradition to actually immerse themselves in recitals of traditional poetry. There is no need to go back to the village to do it. The libraries of Europe and America are full these days of recordings and even attempted notations. The musicality of poetic recitations of the Yoruba people, for example, is *not* the bland mono-rhythmic smoothness advocated by our critics; it is often staccato and deliberately so. Themes are abandoned, recovered, merged with a new arbitary inclusion under the deft, inspired guidance of both reciter and accompanist. The stark linear simplicity of translations should never be permitted to obscure the allusive, the elliptical, the multi-textured fullness of what constitutes traditional poetry, especially *in recital*. And those who read the original lines in cold print do *hear* it, and in the generous intricacy of rhythm and structure. The most faithful expression of this counterplay in the New World is Modern Jazz – the music, not often the lyric.

> Wó ni, alóló alòlò.
> Àtiròrun àkàlà.
> Ojú ro wón tòki
> Ló difá fún olómitútù
> Ti nsobirin Àgbonirègún.
> Èdidi àlò.
> Ifa ò ni polómitútù kó pupa.
> E è ni ba won kúkú òwówò lailai.

'Sprung rhythm', if I may risk faulting for borrowing the terminology of a British poet, is probably the handiest expression to describe the internal rhythm of these lines. I suggest the troika obtain the services of a good Yoruba reciter and listen to the above

---

* The naïveté of any literary critic who actually believes that the visual actuality of print can or should have no formative effect on poetry requires of course no commentary whatever. The phenomenology of the printed word is too vast a subject to be tackled here however; it is sufficient to invite formulators of poetics to direct a small part of their energies to a comparative analysis of written contemporary poetry in the vernacular languages and oral poetry in the same languages. Even radio, which is an oral medium, exerts formative influences on poetic texts as can be testified by anyone with an experience of radio programmes in the vernacular. They acquire traits which are absent from poetry of a purely oral genesis, and lose others. To suggest that the printed (visual) medium will result in identical products of the imagination as the oral, transient form is simply unintelligent.

Ifa utterance from an egungun chant. They might then in wisdom apply their own adage to themselves – 'that I am a man, and older than you are, does not mean I am your father' – and make the discovery that Gerard Manley Hopkins did not invent 'sprung rhythm', nor is its exploitation forbidden to modern Africans who use his language because he so uniquely made it his tool. They might even commence to listen to their own poetic tradition with a new ear, eschewing the simplistic insults under which they ironically persist in burying it. Is the following really the hallmark of traditionalism by which the modern poet is to regulate himself?

> In our little village
> When elders are around
> Boys must not look at girls
> And girls must not look at boys
> Because the elders say
> That is not good.
>
> Even when night comes
> Boys must play separately
> Girls must play separately
> But humanity is weak
> So boys and girls meet
>
> The boys play hide and seek
> And the girls play hide and seek
> The boys know where the girls hide
> And the girls know where the boys hide
> So in their hide and seek
> Boys seek girls,
> Girls seek boys,
> And each to each sing
> Songs of love.

This trite, prosaic, coy, kindergarten drivel which my seven-year-old daughter would be ashamed to write is extolled by the troika critics: 'Markwei's poem(!) is simple and vivid. It conveys the experience of moonlight play, whereas Wonodi's *Moonlight play* is dark and dense.' I hold no brief for Wonodi's poem about which I have indeed grave objections. But to hold up Markwei's jejune prosification as the ideal can only arouse suspicions that our critics have deliberately chosen to scrape the bottom of the barrel and subvert, for reasons of their own, the entire future of African poetry. 'Humpty Dumpty' is at least witty; it stretches the imagination a little, though it is not the 'great poetry' claimed for it by the troika. In what line do Markwei's verses achieve a moment of 'vividness'? Do Messrs Chinweizu & Co. understand the word? Where does it engage the imagination? Or is this attribute of poetry no longer applicable to poems written by Africans? Looking through the window of my study as I type this, I observe and 'reflect':

> Over my neighbour's fence
> A boy
> Throws a rubber ball to a girl
> The girl
> Throws a rubber ball to a boy
> Over my neighbour's fence
> The games and laughter
> Recall the bygone days beneath
> The moonlight in our village square
> When boys must play separately
> Girls must play separately
> The ball separates boy from girl . . .

Balls! There is a limit to self-abasement in the service of uncreative empathy. Also to one's patience with critics who find no room in their kingdom of poetry for both Egudu's 'The First Yam of the Year' and the Yoruba traditional 'New Yam'. What kind of perverse, mental castration is this! Two contrasting approaches, both highly successful. Only an enemy of poetry would seek to exclude one or the other or indulge in evaluative comparison such as leads to this astounding assessment: that Romanus Egudu's poem fails to convey 'tenderness or exaltation or bite' or, merely celebrates emotions 'in the abstract'.

> I have dug it fresh,
> this boneless flesh
> of air, earth, warmth
> and water, this
> life out of the heart
> of death . . .

Restraint is very difficult when one encounters such destructive and inaccurate criticism. I suggest that these critics wash out their ears (and eyes) and listen again. The above lines not only convey tenderness but extend that emotion. They call this poem 'privatist, sterile', a 'laboured and lifeless attempt at nostalgic revivalism'. This is the language of borrowed pedagoguery, barren and meaningless; it bears no relation to and no knowledge of the material it engages. I suggest that these critics read the poem again from the point of view of the involved participant, one who is however not afraid to utilize language that truly reflects the numinous essence of the experience, the social symbolism of the new yam and the metaphysical context both of its celebration, and its seeding and maturation from decay. The Yoruba poem is witty; Egudu does not attempt wit. Egudu's poem is visceral and sensuous; unless our critics, with their noted reductionist tendency find the last line in the traditional poem sensuous, the Yoruba poem attempts to be neither visceral nor sensuous. It plucks its images from the domestic relations (and relationships) of the new yam, it is joyously hyperbolic, irreverent; indeed it fills the mouth with the good satisfying feelings of a morsel of yam. These however are not the only attributes or evocative potential of yam and Romanus Egudu explores some of the other, attempting to enter the deeper and essential association, including the cosmic. He extends the significance of the yam into a parable of the human condition. It appears now that this is a crime and a disservice to African literature and the African heritage. And it earns his poem what can only be best described as a malicious, untruthful analysis.

But I must not, out of fear of personalizing the issue, fail to point out the most glaring and damning indictment of these critics. The charge this time is one of sloppiness (or blindness) coupled with sheer intellectual laziness. This particular example is inexcusable since it has nothing to do with critical evaluation but with truth and falsehood, a deliberate attempt to mislead for the sake of consolidating a position. Abiola Irele, another Nigerian critic, makes the following commentary on the poem 'Massacre', indeed quoting the very verse which the troika have also quoted and grossly misinterpreted:

> Placed at a distance to the scene of events, the poet is not led to a
> reformation of the tragic experience, but rather to a more intimate
> identification. *All the elements of the new environment* enter into his
> consciousness . . . and establish for him a tenacious relationship between the
> new environment and the tragedy he has left behind in Nigeria.*

'Placed at a distance to the scene of events', 'new environment' – now, how is it that this was apparent to Abiola Irele and a number of other critics, including hostile ones, but not to Messrs Chinweizu and Co., who stand alone in achieving a monumental distortion of this verse. It is time, seriously, to question whether these gentlemen understand the language we have all adopted, for below the title of the poem is the brief legend – 'Written in Tegel'. Not that there was need of this specification but it certainly comes in useful now that we know what level of comprehension seems to operate in the ranks of the formulators of African poetics. 'Why does Soyinka find it necessary to "borrow seasons of an alien land" to mourn our dead?' This is literalism gone mad, turned illiteracy! 'In any case why import and then apologise?' Soyinka neither imported nor apologized – read the poem. 'All we are saying is that when the context and setting is Africa and tropical, it is asinine to drag in Spring, snow and other arctic paraphernalia.' Critics who fail a simple literacy test make asses of themselves.

Of course it could be that Africans, being Africans and victims, among other Nature disasters, of a mass leucotomy from some forgotten age are not even permitted to reflect their immediate environment, unless that environment happens to be 2000 BC Africa. It may be that to stare in a lake in Germany and see reflected, side by side with the immediate physical borders of that lake, the border of one's own land thousands of

---

* *Benin Review*, No. 1 (emphasis mine).

miles away is 'privatist' etc., that the authentic African voice should immediately substitute thatched huts and bonga fish for the stained-glass windows and motor-boat exhaust. This delimitation of poetic provinces has not only been exactly proposed by Chinweizu but has been decreed in other ways, largely through the pronouncements on religion and its metaphors, symbolisms and imagery. In African countries where at least sixty per cent of the population are either practising christian or moslem, it is proposed that the intrusion into poetry of associations from non-traditional religions is retrogressive and colonialist. May I make a counter-proposition?

The Question of Religion
That the very existence and practice of non-traditional religions be declared retrogressive and colonialist. So let us resolutely move away from the mere affects of alien religious presence and ban these religions from our continent altogether. This is a serious proposition as Chinweizu and Co. will discover when they find the energy and determination to launch a movement for the eradication of islam and christianity from the black continent. I cannot alas find the will to place myself at the forefront of such a movement but I shall readily play John the Baptist to their anti-christ. The endemic effect of great religions is incidentally neatly summarized in that last sentence – even in its declaration of anti-christian crusading intent, the metaphor of christian religious history came irresistibly to mind. Not of course that our critics object to this; it is simply that they would be better pleased if I had done a p'Bitek, written 'Joonu Bapitsisiti' as a sign of total liberation from 'positive' attitudes to christianity. No one questions the schoolboy delight to be derived from corrupting foreign names in transcription – rather like graffiti on the wall – but this of course is only a small component of what creates in the reader a rapport with p'Bitek's poetry and must of course never be used as a comparative yardstick outside its context. Okigbo's poetry is resolutely outside that context. So I must presume is Echeruo's whose own contextual bearings I confess I have never yet comprehended. That latter admission however need not provoke untenable generalities about the place of christian-religious reference in African poetry. A basic appreciation of the structuring of Echeruo's poetry – which is as far as I have ever, for lack of sustained interest, gone – provokes comparison with poets like Tchikaya u'Tamsi, not with p'Bitek. The guinea-fowl and the crow are both birds but . . .

There is a certain level of ignorance (direct or implicit) which is unpardonable in those who arrogate to themselves the task of reformulating the values of their countrymen. 'Christianity,' declare the troika, 'should be domesticated and absorbed into our existing indigenous religious systems – and it is so among the Cherubim and Seraphim sect and other such non-elite adapters of Christianity.' The immediate context of that statement – the reference is to Okigbo's use of christian terminology – implies that in these instances, the fundamentalist churches do not employ a terminology similar to Okigbo's (or Echeruo's). Earlier also, the critics had just as violently reacted to the fact that they stumble against a 'chalice, crucifix, marble sarcophagus, halo, incense, rose, passion flower'. Well, I'll concede the rose, the passion flower and the marble sarcophagus. But it is clear that these abstact purists have never stepped inside a fundamentalist christian church anywhere along the coast of West Africa or else that their experience is very strangely limited. Incense, whether in the form of joss-sticks or wafted from an incense-burner, is regularly burnt. Haloes decorate the 'naive-art' representations of angels on the walls or on crude tapestries. A chalice is always present on the altar and I hope even the troika will admit that a crucifix is indispensable. True, I have never heard Latin spoken at any of these services but I have heard Hebrew – at least the prophet assured me it was Hebrew. (I wrote *Brother Jero* from personal contact with these churches; in youth I often attended the services or watched their ecstatic dancing through the windows.) It is true that Latin (Roman Catholic liturgical Latin especially) was once more elitist than Hebrew but, since the critical methods of our troika are so geared to political fashions, how are we to know that these fundamentalist churches are not religious agents of the new Zionist-imperialist push into Africa? They might just be replacing the tired christian-colonialist axis in the new effort to subjugate Africa.

Elite, elitism ... catch-all phrases, facile cover-up expressions for the lack of a painstaking concern for truth. I recommend that the troika brush up on the subject of the Aladura churches by browsing through the numerous literature on this fascinating, schismatic outgrowth of the christian church. First, let them understand that the Aladura churches (Cherubim and Seraphim, Faith Tabernacle etc., etc.) were founded by West African elites – and this is equally true of East and Central Africa. J. D. Y. Peel (*Aladura: A Religious Movement among the Yoruba*) emphasizes, among others, this very point. He analyzes the founding membership of several sects among whom were members of the 'top Lagos elite ... their names were frequently to be found in the society columns of the Lagos Press'. Far more damaging however is the troika's astounding claim that christianity has been 'domesticated and absorbed into our existing indigenous religious system' by the Cherubim and Seraphim sect and other 'non-elite adapters'. This is a grave disservice to knowledge and truth. The Aladura sects – Cherubims and Seraphims and all – not only did nothing of the sort but entrenched in their religious doctrine a combative opposition to 'our existing indigenous religious system', to its curative techniques and social usage. They were, in addition, rabid iconoclasts, more efficient and more successful than either the Roman Catholic or Anglican churches, contrary to popular misconception on the subject. If you added together what they burnt on their own and what they had burnt in conjunction with the more orthodox christian churches upon whom they frequently descended all over the country for bonfire revivalist sessions, the Cherubs rank as the most dedicated arsonists, depleting our traditional art heritage in the name of Christ. Their power was truly enviable, their passionate rhetoric sent listeners hurrying into the recesses of their compounds to return with priceless carvings ('pagan idols') which they hurled into bonfires in an orgy of excitation.

What this means, taken together with the troika's other categorical misstatements on African traditional or neo-traditional reality is, very simply, that these would-be critics do not know what they are talking about. Incendiaries, however inspired or inspiring, can by no stretch of the imagination be conservers of tradition, and the next question is: what domesticated matrix of symbolic usages will they next recommend for religious poets? What next in the poetics of transmogrification for religious or quasi-mystical experiences? Must serious creative work really be subjected to this form of buckshot criticism, to the substitution of random pellets for an incisive attention to the written word? The serious search for a black aesthetic is a healthy move towards self-apprehension in the United States where Messrs Chinweizu & Co. have found ready audience; it is a pity that contributions towards this quest from supposedly authentic African voices should be marked by so much mis-information and irresponsible scholarship.

I have stated my preference: let us expel alien religions altogether in all forms. Until that is done, and for a century or so afterwards, it is futile to expect that a Roman Catholic, practising, believing or even merely exploring will not, because he is black, suffuse his poetry with symbols of his faith. Nor is it criminal that he finds parallels to such symbols in his own mythology and traditional religion even without consciously syncretizing them. Yoruba society is full of individuals who worship the Anglican God on Sundays, sacrifice to Sango every feastday, consult Ifa before any new project and dance with the Cherubim and Seraphims every evening. Chinweizu and Co. may be surprised to learn that they find it natural; no spiritual conflict is created within them and no guilt is experienced. Being unwesternized in religious attitudes, that is, not slavishly tied to the western concept of a single form of worship for the attainment of spiritual exaltation or divine protection, they live without any internal contradictions. The only subterfuge is committed when one or the other of the monopolistic priesthoods attempts to assert its authority. Criticism we see, aspires to the authority of the jealous priesthood; we may look to see a new poetry emasculated by conformist subterfuge, hounded by a new school of hypocritics.

The troika pronounce themselves willing to accommodate the use of English in African literature but fail to understand that language is shaped by a number of factors including the religious one. English, like other European languages, is impregnated by centuries of service as a christian vehicle. Compound that with the fact that in those African countries where English (or French, Spanish, Portuguese) is used, the christian religious fact has become an organic reality. The radio carries hours of religious instruction, services, admonitions; the newspapers answer questions in special columns for the confused faithful; each national event is celebrated by the ceremony of religious worship; the bible (and the koran) are basic equipment for the schoolboy; in times of national crisis – drought, civil conflict etc. etc. – days of national prayer are declared and all available media given over to the propulsion of indigenous anguish to alien gods. To pretend therefore that curses pronounced in the 'anathemization' idiom of Lenten service on an occasion which the troika itself declares 'this most important national occasion' is not a most effective way of transmitting, to such an audience, a direct condemnation of a national impiety – this denotes either ignorance of the social reality of that environment or a stiff-necked defence of an arbitrarily adopted position. Critics who manipulate conclusions in defiance of evidence are not worthy of the name. I do not know whether or not in two hundred years the colonial academic traditions which breed such sterile criticism will still be in vogue – if they are not however, writers will no doubt form their own conclusions about the form of criticism which actually presumes to rewrite original poetry in the critic's own design. They will be amused to read that a self-declared critic seriously proposes the legal jargon of British lower courts – 'drunken and boisterous behaviour' – as original, traditional and poetic. Two can play at the game of transposition but let us see how convincing the proffered examples are. Thus, in condemning the 'christian language and spirit' of Okigbo's opening invocation in 'Heavensgate', the critics, using a few 'minor adjustments in vocabulary' transform, to their own satisfaction, Okigbo's lines into a christian prayer. And the minor adjustments? 'Divine' for 'watery'; 'oilbean' for 'altar'; 'awe' for 'your legend'! Some profound point is supposed to be made by this gratuitous distortion. Observe how cheap it is, this facile ploy which became distinctly insulting (to the reader's intelligence) in the critics' transposition of 'Prayer to the Dead Father' into a supposed christian idiom, an exercise founded neither on logic nor on critical integrity. What link in theme, mood or sensibility does 'Prayer to the Dead Father' possess with 'Prayer to Saint Peter'? The titles and the opening lines alone preclude any belief in the honest intentions of such critics:

Prayer to the Dead Father

My father
I am giving these yams to you

becomes:

Prayer to Saint Peter

O Saint Peter, Fisher of Men,
Keeper of the Gates of heaven
I bring these biscuits to you

As these adjusters themselves point out, there is no room for the reincarnation theme in christian theology, so what is the point of this exercise? If the intention is merely to be funny, potatoes would be just as funny and a little closer to yams. Marrow would be more honest. As for the replacement of the ancestral figure by St Peter, the enigma is locked up somewhere in the critics' thinking; it is apparent to no one else. St Peter does have his own mythology; I do not recall biscuits being part of it. Loaves yes, in an effortless association with fish. But biscuits!? When critics resort to this shaky form of buttressing, they lend credence to the frequent accusation that critics are in fact failed writers. Fortunately we know that these are not. I am familiar with Chinweizu's poetry, it is highly accomplished. The little I have read of Jemie's encourages a similar response. But first they must understand that all poets will not write alike. Also that poetry is not like the day which comes to life only on the death of the last.

In Conclusion

The troika cannot however be dismissed on this note. The central issue of their contention – wilful obscurity and private esoterism – is one which does plague a good proportion of the modern poetry of Africans, and some of the examples they provide are justified. But just as critics like Anozie do not help by clogging up understanding further by undue fascination with structuralist faddism, nor a Paul Theroux by abdicating critical judgement as premature, the Simple Simons of criticism as represented by Chinweizu & Co. subvert the principle of imaginative challenge which is one of the functions of poetry. And the denigration and misunderstanding of traditional forms of African art should now stop. The sculpture of Africa alone is visual evidence of a dynamism that eschews superficial and surface meanings. Sculpture, the dance, music, the integration of various media of expression in any given public performance have all gone into the moulding of the sensibility which tries today to carve new forms out of alien words, expressing not only the itemized experience, but reflecting the unified conceptualization of the experience. And poetry, let it be remembered, is not the single work of one man but the totality and variety of this activity. Within this rich, constant expression of society, individual aberrations pale into insignificance and are deservedly ignored, their championing by masochist critics notwithstanding.

It is time also that critics and social commentators alike recognized that the more-committed-than-thou breast-thumping, in all its various forms, has become boring and suspect. Social commitment is a citizen's commitment and embraces equally the carpenter, the mason, the banker, the farmer, the customs officer etc., etc., not forgetting the critic. Yet none of these thousand and one categories of contributors to social progress spends twenty-four hours a day being 'socially committed'. That non-stop mandate is miraculously reserved for the artist alone. It does not matter that the bulk of his total work, his life is devoted to urgent social issues; every posturing critic is privileged to haul out one 'uncommitted' work, wave it aloft, mount the rostrum and bleat: 'What is this doing here? How dare this artist define one moment of private reflection?'

No, for many critics, the concept of individual experimentation – which contributes to what may be judged as a social achievement – is anathema. Some have even gone so far as to declare, solemnly and categorically, that the concept of the individual performer or creativity is alien to African tradition. This, for a culture whose poetry constantly celebrates outstanding creative talents in every art-form, whose oral history of art records most faithfully the achievements of carvers and griots, whose art criticism, alive till today, distinguishes between the technique and refinements of one smelter and another, between one father and a son in the same line of profession! The new school of art criticism will prove yet that the art of oriki-chanting (including the self-extolling interjections) by professionals is paradoxically an antithesis of that bourgeois and decadent individualism that supposedly affects modern introspective poetry by Africans. It will be asserted that while the Mbari-house sculptor who isolates himself for a period of intense self-communion, awaits divine inspiration, a visionary flash to be translated into mud figures, is working overtime at social commitment, his modern (educated) compatriot is not, even though the latter puts down his pen and ink and perishes fighting for a cause in which he passionately believes. The latter is damned because he has larded his poems with christian and private mythology though, 'luckily for him, just before his death' he was saved by events which gave him a public voice. We hope that our three-headed *Pontifex Maximus Simplicissimus* will not keep poor Christopher Okigbo burning too long in Purgatory.

The error is really a simple one: the equation of the 'immediate' with 'commitment'. The Mbari-house sculptor who shuts himself away from day-to-day contact undertakes this period of purgation and reflection on behalf of his society. The resulting mud figures are never given the same interpretation by any two individuals yet the presence of this isolated sculpting – placed usually away from the frequented parts of the village and left to crumble and decay with time – is experienced by the community as contributing to the spiritual well-being of the village in its homage to earth. The most obscure result of private reflection is a homage to life. Those to whom it communicates anything at all may be no more than the entire beneficiaries of one Mbari group of sculptures, maybe less. Both products of the spirit will perish with time, but that is no proof of their irrelevance or uselessness. I freely admit that the works of a number of African poets do absolutely nothing for me; I do not respond to them in any way. But in spite of frequent groans of irritation at the flaunting derivations of Okigbo's poetry, its frequent relapses into private biography, hagiography, geography and jokes, it performs a similar function for me as the sculptural aesthetics of several African societies. Not being possessed of that instant-tradition perceptiveness of Chinweizu and Co., I cannot claim a transparency of communication even from the sculpture, music and poetry of my own people the Yoruba, but the aesthetic matrix is the fount of my own creative inspiration; it influences my critical response to the creation of other cultures and validates selective eclecticism as the right of every productive being, scientist or artist. Sango is today's god of electricity, not of white-man magic-light. Ogun is today's god of precision technology, oil rigs and space rockets, not a benighted rustic cowering at the 'iron bird'.